BEHIND
THE LIONS

PLAYING RUGBY FOR THE
BRITISH & IRISH LIONS

BEHIND THE LIONS

PLAYING RUGBY FOR THE BRITISH & IRISH LIONS

STEPHEN JONES

TOM ENGLISH

NICK CAIN

DAVID BARNES

BIRLINN

First published in 2012 by
BIRLINN LIMITED
West Newington House
10 Newington Road
Edinburgh
EH9 1QS

in association with

POLARIS PUBLISHING LTD
c/o Turcan Connell
Princes Exchange
1 Earl Grey Street
Edinburgh
EH3 9EE

www.birlinn.co.uk
www.polarispublishing.com

ISBN: 978 1 78027 098 2
eBook ISBN: 978 0 85790 529 1
Enhanced eBook ISBN: 978 0 85790 530 7
Interactive app edition also available.
British Library Cataloguing-in-Publication Data
A catalogue record for this book is available from the British Library

Designed and typeset by Polaris Publishing, Edinburgh
Printed and bound in India at Gopsons Papers Ltd.
by arrangement with Associated Agencies, Oxford

THE BRITISH
& IRISH LIONS

AUSTRALIA 2013

would like to thank

Principal Partner

Official Kit Supplier

Global Sponsors

Official Suppliers

BIBLIOGRAPHY AND SOURCES

Beyond the original source material found in diaries, letters and articles that were used to recall the earliest tours, and the fresh interviews conducted within these pages, some accounts have been supplemented with material from the following sources:

At the Centre; Jeremy Guscott; Pavilion Books, 1996

Brian O'Driscoll: A Year in the Centre; Brian O'Driscoll; Penguin Books Ltd, 2005

The British Lions; John Griffiths; The Crowood Press Ltd, 1990

British & Irish Lions Website – www.lionsrugby.com

Fifty Rugby Stars Describe My Greatest Game; Bob Holmes and Chris Thau; Mainstream, 1994

High Balls and Happy Hours; Gavin Hasting; Mainstream, 1994

The History of the British & Irish Lions; Clem Thomas and Greg Thomas; Mainstream Publishing, 2001

It's In The Blood; Lawrence Dallaglio; Headline, 2007

John Bentley: My Story; John Bentley; Andre Deutsch Ltd, 1999

Joking Apart: My Autobiography; Donncha O'Callaghan; Transworld Ireland, 2011

The Lions Diary; Jeremy Guscott, with Nick Cain; Michael Joseph Ltd, 1997

Lion Man; Ian McGeechan, with Stephen Jones; Pocket Books, 2009

Lions of Ireland; David Walmsley; Mainstream Publishing, 2000

Looking Back... For Once; Jim Telfer; Mainstream Publishing, 2005

Martin Johnson: The Autobiography; Martin Johnson; Headline, 2004

Ronan O'Gara: My Autobiography; Ronan O'Gara; Transworld Ireland, 2009

Rugby from the Front; Peter Wheeler; Hutchinson, 1983

Size Doesn't Matter; Neil Back; Milo Books, 2000

Thanks to Rugby; Bill Beaumont; Hutchinson, 1982

Voices from the Back of the Bus; Stewart McKinney; Mainstream Publishing, 2010

Willie John: The Story of My Life; Willie John McBride; Piatkus Books, 2005

PHOTOGRAPHIC CREDITS

COLORSPORT
180, 194, 195, 196, 208, 223, 234, 242, 244, 254, 257, 260, 273, 285, 288, 290, 293, 294, 307, 315, 316, 320, 324, 329, 335, 339, 351, 356

FOTOSPORT
221, 225, 230, 233, 365, 375, 379, 381, 382, 384, 386, 388, 389, 390, 393, 397, 400, 404, 407, 408, 410, 412, 417, 418, 422, 424, 426, 429, 430, 431, 432, 433, 436, 437, 439, 441, 445, 453, 454, 456, 457, 459, 460, 462, 465, 466, 468, 472, 473, 474, 475

GETTY IMAGES
100, 117, 122, 131, 133, 136, 140, 142, 143, 144, 174, 192, 201, 204, 205, 206, 208, 265, 270, 280, 299, 311, 322, 331, 353, 358, 363, 367, 369, 387

INPHOPHOTOGRAPHY
218, 275, 422, 440, 443, 455, 461

MIRRORPIX
179, 191

THE ALEXANDER TURNBULL LIBRARY, NATIONAL LIBRARY OF NEW ZEALAND
78, 80

PRESS ASSOCIATION
103, 106, 139, 148, 150, 151, 177, 178, 197, 199, 200, 222, 336, 343, 344, 364, 394

CONTENTS

ACKNOWLEDGEMENTS

The authors would like to thank everyone who has given their time so generously to assist in the preparation of this book. Those whom we interviewed are too many to name individually but their thoughts are included in the pages which follow and we would like to thank them for giving so generously of their time and for being so honest about their great ups and downs with the Lions.

Special thanks must go to the following for their expert help in the production of this book: John Griffiths, the world of rugby's premier statistician and historian and its most meticulous recorder. No one attempting a book of this scope could hope to succeed without him; Rob Cole and his colleagues at the Westgate Sports Agency for their input with Lions history and the Welsh element of Lions touring history; Adam Hathaway of the *People*, rugby and cricket expert; and to Clem and Greg Thomas for their wonderful book, *The History of the British & Irish Lions*.

Thanks also to Peter Burns at Birlinn and Polaris for all his tireless work in bringing this project together.

Stephen Jones, Tom English, Nick Cain and David Barnes, 2012

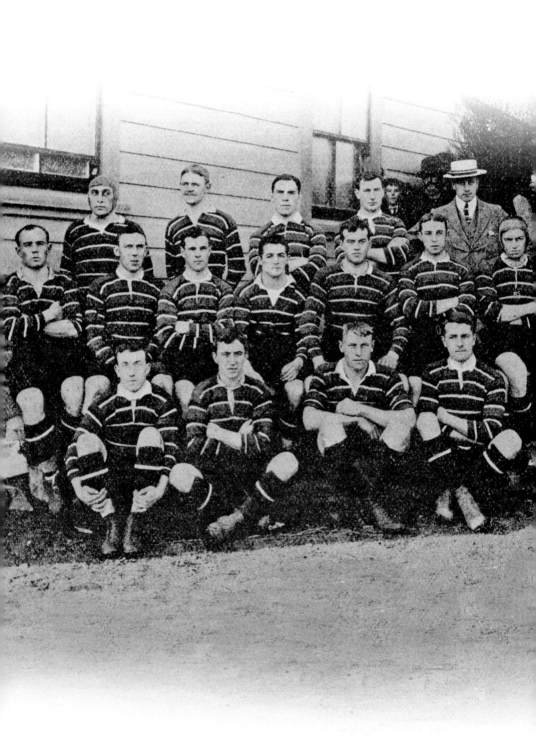

INTRODUCTION

CRUSADERS

BY STEPHEN JONES

ONE OF rugby's most important distinguishing characteristics is a wanderlust. It takes the form of a compulsion to take the sport on the road, to seek out those who play in neighbouring or distant or foreign or even alien environments, to encounter them on the field, to absorb their culture and, frankly, to have a memorable social outing away from the strains of normal life, safe in the rock-like communal solidarity of a rugby team.

And sometimes the most rewarding aspect is that once you have experienced the distant environment, perhaps even clashed harshly on the rugby field, for all the differences in culture and surroundings, you find that so much is the same. Attitudes, outlooks, affections. Experience teaches that even amongst the occasional vicissitudes of modern day professional rugby, there are still such beings as the universal rugby man and woman, with rugby's forgiving balances and love. You can travel 12,000 miles to discover an image of yourself.

And so the rugby tour was born. Tours began almost as soon as the sport had become recognisable and codified. Only rock music has anything like it. Even if the tour lasts only a night or two, even if it is just a whistle-stop trip to Cornwall or Devon or the Lake District or Cork or the Scottish Borders or West Wales at Easter, then it has traits in common with even the longest tour. The luckier schools and junior clubs these days are magnificently ambitious, and how marvellously education can be topped up, and how far eyes can be widened, by the months of fundraising leading to the trip of a young lifetime. My school tour was to Newton Abbot. Another planet.

In terms of distance and time spent, no activity on this planet has longer tours than rugby. At the highest levels, the wanderlust and all the other imperatives of rugby tours become simply the backdrop to a desire to take on the best rugby teams in the world. The challenge is implicit, it never has to be laid down. And it must always be accepted.

It is an accident of geography and of rugby's history and sociology that from the standpoint of the four home rugby union countries, England, Ireland, Scotland and Wales, the ultimate challenges are those posed by three nations up to 12,000 miles away – New Zealand, South Africa and Australia. At the top level of the game, these

Opposite: The British side for the first-ever Test against New Zealand at Athletic Park, Wellington, on 13 August 1904. Tour captain David Bedell-Sivright was injured and the Welsh wing Teddy Morgan captained the side.

were, and are, the ultimate opponents. They are the destinations, in rotating sequence, for the unique, magnificent beast called the British & Irish Lions.

The first tour down under made by a conglomerate team from the Home Unions sailed from Gravesend on 8 March 1888 – 125 years ago as I write. Seven more such tours were made in the following 12 years. The wanderlust of these heroic pioneer tourists was so powerful, that they were driven to overcome distances and tribulations long forgotten in these days of our shrunken world and flat bed air travel. One account of the 1903 tour to South Africa, led by Mark Morrison, states that often the players were hungry. And simply to leave these shores to play, was a perilous expedition.

In 1888, those pioneers – 26 young men chiefly from the North of England – departed on the RMS *Kaikoura*, a steam/sail ship with three masts, one propeller and a top speed of 15 knots. It was still largely the age of the gentleman player, so the heroes travelled in saloon class. Also available were second saloon class, and a rather grim-sounding emigrant class.

They took seven weeks to reach Australia, sailing through what were reported as 'heavy, confused seas'. The team was away from home for eight months. They played 16 matches under rugby rules and incredibly, another 19 under Australian rules – the tour had been organised by private promoters, who needed to make money, hence the Australian rules games against the top clubs of the day. The party travelled enormous distances by stagecoach, charging around the country and stopping only for fresh teams of horses.

Given the endurance, and the privations relative to the modern day, it was no doubt a relief to so many back home when they returned – and in fact, they did not all do so. The captain, Robert Seddon, a popular, principled and gentle man, was drowned during the tour while paddling a kind of canoe with which he was not familiar. Accounts of his life, and the reaction of his touring colleagues and friends to his death, suggest strongly that here was a man who typified early the essential calibre of people who were to fill the touring jersey for the following 125 years.

Tours continued regularly but it was only on the 1924 tour to South Africa, the ninth made by conglomerate parties from Britian and Ireland, that the name 'Lions' was applied to the touring team – simply because the official tie for that trip bore a lion motif. The early touring parties were invariably referred to after their captain (for example, Maclagan's team to South Africa in 1891, Bedell-Sivright's team to Australia and New Zealand in 1904).

But they were also known widely as the 'English football team', a reflection of the dominant influence of the foundation country on sport and life at the time, and disregarding the fact that those early tours usually contained at least a smattering (and often a significant representation) from Wales, Scotland and Ireland. In 1924, the team became known as the British Lions.

Perhaps remarkably, it has only been recently that the full and now accepted description of the team – the British & Irish Lions – has come into general usage. No one with a clue of the history of the Lions and the magnificent contribution made by Irishmen on the field of play and in all other aspects of the tour could ever believe that it took so long.

The early tours tended to be either unofficial (organised by commercial promoters) or semi-official (tolerated by the national unions). But it was not until 1910 when the team went to South Africa that they were first truly representative of the Four Home Unions, with each union supplying individual players. Before that, it was all done by gentlemanly invitation, with a preponderance of Oxford Blues and gentlemen of private means.

Furthermore, in those far-off days the party rarely reflected the true strength of the rugby in Britain and Ireland. There were so many reasons not to be available for tours of such length. For example, of the 28 players provisionally invited to prepare for the tour of New Zealand in 1930, only nine actually embarked for New Zealand. Wilfred Sobey was injured in the first game and never played again – a distressing tradition sadly observed on several of the later tours.

It was only for the 1950 tour of New Zealand that the Lions first appeared in their familiar red shirt; until then they had worn dark blue shirts with thin red and white stripes. This change followed the blue/black colour clash of the 1930 tour to New Zealand that resulted in the All Blacks wearing white shirts for the Test series – despite the Lions' offer to change colour. The change to red ensured that there would be no future clashes with the host nation. It was also during that tour that the Lions first played with a green flash on their socks – a recognition, at last, of their Irish contingent.

However, what does it matter? Even if every trip was not official, even if there was an *ad hoc* air around much of the operations of the pioneer tours, even if they did not wear Lion red, and even if the term 'Lions' was not used until such tours had been operating for 36 years, the early tours are so clearly and definitively the foundations of the grand tradition, the pathfinders, that they are true Lions in all but name, and absolutely must take their place in any formal retrospective.

*

The history of the Lions is a pioneer history of sporting exploration, and also a history of travel (it is not, sadly, a story of unbroken sporting success, but we will come to that shortly). The *Kaikoura*, with its largely open and windswept decks, was the original vessel for the odyssey, and its passage took seven weeks. Gradually, as the steamships became more powerful, the voyages became slightly less prolonged. Lions teams of later years travelled out on such vessels as the *Dunnottar Castle*, then on the Union steamship *Tartar*, then on the *Edinburgh Castle*; and to New Zealand in 1950, the last time the Lions did not fly, the *Stirling Castle*, with the passage reduced to a mere three weeks.

Since then, they have travelled the intercontinental legs on Lockheed Constellations, on Argonauts, on Skymasters, on Boeing 707s, on DC10s, on jumbo jets and latterly, on Boeing 777s.

They first flew on tour in 1955, on the Constellation. Clem Thomas, the magnificent flanker who became a celebrated journalist with the *Observer* and a Lions biographer, and whose hectic approach to life was tailor-made for a Lions tour, recalled that they refuelled in Zurich, Rome, Cairo, Khartoum, Nairobi, Entebbe and finally, Johannesburg. Far less convenient than the fly-by-wire, long-reach jets of today. And yet somehow, ours is a world less glamorous.

Their internal travel on tour in the late 19th and early 20th centuries was made by stagecoach – the famous coach and 10 – sweeping through the country to the next change of horses. In South Africa, they travelled miles by Cape carts, and one account mentioned 'rough unmade roads with endless corrugations.' And then later by giant steam engines hauling them through the wilderness areas of South Africa by night. It is easy to imagine the terror felt by the more reserved tourists in 1968 in South Africa, when the boisterous 'Wreckers' were heard coming compartment-by-compartment down the train in the dead of night, laying waste to the fixtures and fittings as the other faction, the 'Kippers', prepared for the worst.

It is impossible not to mention such damage was a feature of many tours, and of rugby everywhere in previous eras. John Reason, the late rugby scribe, once wrote that this was all a legacy of the public school days when people always knew that whatever their bad behaviour, 'Daddy would pay up'.

Then the internal travel took to the air – successive Lions teams travelled on Dakota DC3s, then on Fokker Friendships, then on Boeing 737s, and some on the frequently windy and bumpy flights around New Zealand must have understood just a little of the sense of unease that the pioneers experienced as they cast off into the unknown.

*

The tour of Australia by the British & Irish Lions of 2013 will be the 29th in what has become the most magnificent sequence anywhere in sport, a concept, a crusade and a brand – to use the modern term – of towering significance. There are many who note the size and prominence of the World Cup, introduced in rugby in 1987 and which now dominates the sport, but who will always see the Lions as the summit; indeed, after the much-feared transition from the amateur era to professionalism, the Lions are now healthier than ever.

But how can a tradition, and a concept, which began in 1888 possibly be still so thunderously relevant in 2012, so much so that, if anything, the Lions as a golden gladiatorial exercise and sporting brand – sorry again about the modernist tag – is actually growing?

The answer is surely that while so much has changed profoundly, so much has stayed exactly the same. It would be ridiculous to even compare tours of old with the fierce, ultra-dedicated Lions of the modern era, with all their specialist coaches, their medical teams, their analysts peering at computer screens, their mass media profile, their Facebook and Twitter networking, their commercial deals.

They do not touch their hosts and host country with such easy familiarity, or visit avidly the tourist attractions, or go anywhere much except the airport, the hotel and the training ground. It is a shame because, especially in South Africa, yet also in the slightly more reserved New Zealand and Australia, the hospitality is regularly stupendous and has often passed into legend.

In 1955 on the tour of South Africa, a rolling, glamorous epic in which the players were treated like film stars (and which really should have been turned into a film), the great Clem Thomas had been invited well in advance to stay at a farm. The farm was being bothered by a leopard, which was attacking livestock. Generously, as Thomas said, the host family held off tracking the leopard so that Thomas, their guest, could shoot it. He did not, but it was the thought that counted.

In *Lions on Trek*, an account of 1955, the prolific Lions author Bryn Thomas mentions a grand total of 71 official or semi-official functions to which members of the party were invited during the 99 days that they were away from home. Mention a cocktail party these days and the players roll their eyes in horror. It is not their fault; you can only tour in your own era.

Nowadays, Lions tours are restricted to big city stops. In previous tours they would ramble rather sedately around the country, often stopping in one-horse (or one-zebra or one-kangaroo) towns where their arrival was a seismic event, where they were treated, albeit benevolently, as beings from another planet. Before the days of mass media and blanket coverage, newsreel scraps was all either side, host or hosted, would have seen of each other. It is a shame that time can no longer be found for a stopover in Greymouth and Timaru in New Zealand, or Dubbo and Cobar in Australia, or in Oudtshoorn or Springs in South Africa.

So many differences. Yet it is amazing how many experiences the modern Lions share across the decades with the pioneers, how easily the shyness of the original gathering before the tour gives way to communal resolve in which the enmity of the home internationals are forgotten. The journalist and author John Hopkins famously described a Lions tour as 'a cross between a mediaeval crusade and a prep school outing'. Clearly, the public school element in the parties is now considerably reduced, but otherwise the description is perfect. The bond between players suffering the difficulties of travel and strange environments in the old days must have brought them together, but so too does the shared vision and the pressure of life as a modern-day Lion.

More common experiences. During the 1888 tour, Bob Seddon was quoted as expressing the view that on tour 'the umpire has strong leanings to the local man', therefore instituting a cast-iron tradition which has spanned the decades in which, rightly or wrongly, the touring team have complained in private or in public about decisions by the referee. Sometimes they changed the series. No tour has ever gone without substantial or even bitter controversy.

Every tour seems to have one game that lives in infamy, when tempers boil and thuggery breaks out. Taken together as a single history, there have been far too many instances of dirty and dangerous play, and it is a welcome aspect of the professional era that thuggery has declined substantially, with the scores of cameras, the extra match officials and the citing procedures shining a spotlight on miscreants and idiots. Long past time.

Selection, with four unions promoting their own, has often been shaky, and it would be silly to pretend that all the choices of tour captain have worked out well. Some tour leaders struggled badly with the reins of leadership and should have handed them over, while other leaders were magnificent in every respect.

Every Lions tour projects near-unknowns into the limelight, and finds that more celebrated players simply do not react to the touring environment; injuries are always a factor, with the 1980 Lions in South Africa afflicted badly, and the 2009 Lions in South Africa losing two props and two centres within minutes of one Test.

One of the grandest traditions (unless it spilled over into causing damage) is socialising, even if it is far less formal these days. In past tours it was done in evening dress and with grace. Sometimes. Even now, in this monastic era, the grand old bibulous traditions established by decades of carousing Lions are still, cautiously, observed. Perhaps Rowe Harding, a member of the 1924 party which toured South Africa under Ronald Cove-Smith, spoke for them all as he tried to account for the lack of success of that team. 'Many unkind things were said about our wining and dining,' he said.

Even Sir Ian McGeechan, arguably the greatest figure in the history of the Lions, as player and coach, sent his players away for a drink – or even more – after they had experienced the bitter defeat of the Second Test and the loss of the series in Pretoria in 2009. 'They just needed to get away and chill out,' he said. They did. They had their beers, came back and won the Third Test in Johannesburg.

Every tour seems to have its Irishman who, while he may or may not be a wonderful player, is seen as a great tourist; this is not a negligible standing when teams are away for so long, under pressure, and need to look inside for their sustenance and morale, their diversion and humour. To be a 'good tourist' is to be revered today, in any rugby community. But every tour has also heard a clash of the steel, and been an epic sporting confrontation. Nothing feels quite as massive in sport as Test rugby matches between the Lions on the one hand and the All Blacks or the Wallabies or the Springboks on the other. On these occasions, the world seems to shift on its axis.

And another 'rule' of the Lions is that no outstanding player in Britain and Ireland is allowed by perspective to sit in the panoply of all-time greats unless he has become a great Test Lion. They have to become, as Sir Ian says, 'The Test match animal.' It is possible that Will Carling, the superb England centre who was so vastly influential as player and leader in the revival of English rugby in the late 1980s and early 1990s, will never be placed in the stratosphere because he did not take part in a successful series as a key player. Furthermore, he is still the only big-name player in my memory to declare that he would not be available for a Lions tour. For the overwhelming majority of players, the Lions jersey retains mystical properties; it is the Holy Grail of the sport.

*

Another aspect binding together so many tours was their amateurism. Those new to rugby may well struggle badly to understand not only why rugby was an amateur activity for so long, but why that amateurism was policed so balefully and even ferociously. Even some people who grew up with the concept find themselves similarly confused. The idea that amateurism was at the heart of the game's unique appeal held just a little water in previous eras, but the game has discovered since that it had precious little to worry about as it stood at the barricades for 100 years.

But one defining feature of every tour until 1997 – two years after the game went open – was the tradition of painful amateurism, with players disappearing on tours lasting six months or more with a mere pittance in terms of compensation. It was not even called compensation; instead, for decades, it was called a 'communications allowance' presumably so that you could ring your family to check how much money you were losing.

Ironically, the first tour of all, in 1888, took place under a cloud because it was promoted privately and, therefore, it had to make money, with the promoters brokering deals with the host teams. The Home Unions viewed it with massive suspicion. The fact that the overwhelming majority of the team came from clubs in the North of England, where demands for 'broken-time' payments were already rising and where the grand split of 1895 between the codes was on the horizon, ruffled the feathers of the Rugby Football Union even more.

Inquests were launched, questions were asked, and at the end nothing could ever be proved; nothing concrete was ever discovered to uphold or to confound the suspicion that the first Lions of all were closet professionals. Then the unions took over the Lions, and amateurism was the enforced norm for nearly a century.

Over the years, there were some unofficial compensations. Small Welsh communities or groups of friends or local benefactors would have a collection for the local hero to make his tour. There was often a thriving trade in gifts, items of kit and match tickets, and it was never an uncommon sight in the amateur era to see the Lions duty boy anxiously shuffling tickets and notes near the main gate of grounds.

It now seems all so harmless, but in those days tour managers used to fret for hours if the scent of professionalism, even a few shillings in illegal payments, pervaded the tour. Even the smallest gift from an admiring host had to be valued to make sure that they did not consign the recipient into outer darkness. The younger rugby men and women these days may find it incredible that once, with the Lions, even to train hard was regarded as unsporting, a suspicious step towards professionalism.

Yet when the game did cross the rubicon, there were people who felt that the Lions had had their day, so inextricably linked had they always been with the concept of amateurism, of manly sacrifice, of not making sport a living.

They could not have been more wrong. The Lions were helped across the rubicon by their mighty attraction to the hosting countries. It was estimated that the 2005 Lions tour of New Zealand generated over £100 million for the host country's economy, and these days the Lions are every bit as big a commercial machine as they are a rugby operation. It was said in 2005 that in the replica jersey market, more Lions jerseys were sold than the uniforms of Manchester United, Real Madrid or the New York Yankees, traditionally the biggest players in the market.

But it is not the invitation of outsiders which has seen the Lions grow and grow. On the 2009 Lions tour, we saw at the Second Test at the gigantic Loftus Versfeld stadium in Pretoria another modern-day confirmation of everything that the Lions have ever stood for. It was a stupendous occasion and the match ended in what neutrals, and even some South Africans, saw as a victory for South Africa that had more than a few elements of the most outrageous fortune.

But in terms of underlining an enduring appeal, the most striking aspect was when the Lions ran out into the Pretoria sunlight from the darkness of the tunnel. When they looked up, their eyes were drawn across the pitch to the giant far stand at Loftus, which runs the whole length of the side of the ground. That day, the stand was an almost unbroken, boiling sea of scarlet red with tens of thousands of British and Irish rugby followers wearing their replica jerseys – on that bank alone, there must have been at least 12,000 of them.

Despite the cost of their trip and the eventual sporting trauma, they clearly felt an urge to be present at the highest altar that a secular environment has ever constructed. Amateur? Professional? Both were water off a lion's back.

*

There is another and rather unpalatable aspect of history that categorises far too many Lions tours together. Defeat. After early successes, the colonies tended to learn faster and train harder than the touring teams, taking a lead they were never to lose. The majority of tours came to grief then as they still usually do now – against host teams that were stronger, harder-headed, better coached and organised, uncompromising men who desired victory with more intensity. Teams who left less to chance, less to individual flair. A few Lions tours, if not many, have fragmented when the pressure of the trip exposed fault lines, usually when members of the party realised that their dreams of Test selection were to be dashed.

Before and after the Second World War, the process continued. Of the 17 Lions tours made since Karl Mullen's 1950 trip to New Zealand, the Lions have won the series on only four occasions – in 1971, 1974, 1989 and 1997. Otherwise, they have suffered a combination of heavy defeats, and probably even worse, narrow defeats which really should have been turned into triumphs. It would be silly to ignore the fact that wrong choices have been frequently made in terms of captains, some coaches, and many players.

Every Lions tour sets out with a pervading optimism, but it is an optimism that has rarely – except in the golden decade of the 1970s, when the Lions dominated – proved justified, and it is incumbent upon administrators in the game in the present era to study history (particularly recent history) and to conclude that in its support of the Lions, in its granting of windows for proper preparation and rest, they have hampered the team and its history. It is probably the most remarkable sign of the power of the Lions concept, that they have risen so wonderfully in stature without the precious oxygen of playing triumphs.

However, experiences cannot always be measured on a scoreboard. Surely, there are few crusaders in the past 125 years whose sporting prowess and whose lives were not enhanced profoundly by their Lions experience. The pulse quickens two years out for all those contending to play, for all those saving to support, and for all those anxious to report, in the most magnificent arena that sport has ever built.

The memories come in torrents: great matches, controversies, great men and players, great cultures and sights and sounds and tourism and travel and life force. It might be the exultation crackling over the radio into a Welsh dawn as the 1971 Lions drew the final Test and turned history on its head to win the series against the All Blacks; the odd but addictive feeling of crushing the Springboks in 1974 and 1997; the raw pain felt in the soul when the superior 2001 and 2009 Lions lost the series in a welter of ill-fortune. The glorious day, every few years, when the wraps come off the gleaming red vehicle of dreams.

And my personal first memory: sitting in the stand at Lancaster Park in Christchurch, in a kind of jetlagged awe, watching the men in red in the flesh for the first time. The next day, we drove from the city of Christchurch, over Arthur's Pass to tiny Greymouth, where we convened with the Lions in one hotel; they were objects of fascination, beings from another planet, and yet just like us. The mystique, fanned by the fact that they never play at home, has been diminished for many just a little because of mass communications, sports channels, rolling news and newspaper blanket coverage. But the awe remains.

The dedicated professional athletes boarding their plane at the end of May 2013 to begin the 29th tour by the Lions, 125 years after the first and with every bit as much a sense of occasion, become the direct descendants of the pioneer heroes boarding the RMS *Kaikoura* at the quay in Gravesend in 1888. Their tours are not so long, but still have the air of an odyssey. Lions tours were recently and accurately described as the Last Great Adventure.

Wanderlust is a powerful thing. To play rugby at home is just a sporting matter. To tour, well, that takes rugby into the realms of life experience. To become a Lion is one of life's great affirmations.

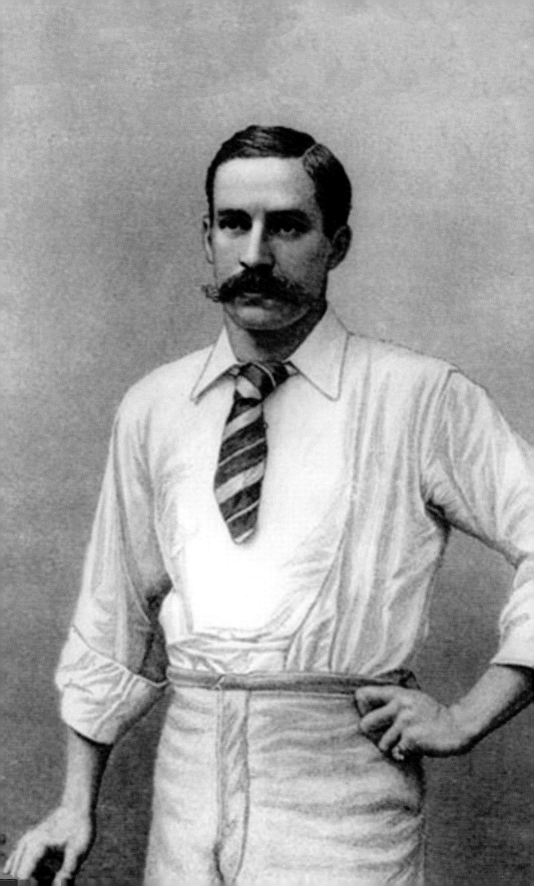

CHAPTER ONE

PATHFINDERS
1888
NEW ZEALAND AND AUSTRALIA

In 1887-88, *two teams of English cricketers toured Australia. It was before the days of proper regulation, and both teams were gathered together by private promoters. One tour party was led by the former England cricket captain James Lillywhite and organised by Arthur Shrewsbury (England's opening batsman of the day) and Alfred Shaw, the man who ten years earlier had bowled the first ball in an official England–Australia Test cricket match.*

The other touring team, competing for attention and crowds and finance, was captained by Lord Hawke. In the rather bizarre and disorganised fashion of the day, the two parties joined together for the one-off cricket Test against Australia, but otherwise remained separate entities. Debts of the Lillywhite expedition were so large that the promoters eventually defaulted and the debacle caused Wisden *to call the twin tours 'a piece of folly that will never be perpetrated again'.*

The outstanding player in Lord Hawke's team was Andrew 'Drewy' Stoddart, one of the most famous sportsmen of the era, arguably the greatest cricketer of his day (apart from WG Grace) and a man who once scored 485 in an afternoon club match, captained England at rugby and cricket, captained the first Barbarians rugby team and, according to John R. Lott, his biographer, relished top-level sport as an aspect of leisure.

The promoters decided on an even bigger gamble to try to recoup their losses. While still in Australia, they formulated the idea of arranging a rugby tour. Shaw had stayed at home in Nottingham from where he acted as the chief recruiter, mainly in the rugby centres in the North of England. Part of the plan was to sign up some of the cricketers to save costs, since they were already there. Some of them had already played soccer and the promoters believed that they would soon pick up rugby. It was an article of faith springing from the remarkable versatility of leading sportsmen of the era.

Aubrey Smith, who had played for Lillywhite's team, refused to stay for the rugby tour, departing for England and then, eventually, America, where he later played for the Hollywood cricket 11 with Boris Karloff and Errol Flynn. Stoddart, who had made his England rugby debut in 1885, agreed to jump ship from Lord Hawke to join the rugby tour.

The process never ran smoothly. The cricket promoters sent a telegram to an agent, Mr Turner, back in England. He was charged with finding players to tour, and with making arrangements to ship them out. It took him months of diligent work, all against a background of suspicion from the august and true-blue Rugby Football Union, who refused to patronise the tour, although, in the end, they did give permission for it to take place.

Most of the 22 players who formed the tour party were from clubs in the North of England. The debate regarding broken time payments had already begun in the area, and suspicions that the whole

---

Opposite: Andrew Stoddart, an all-round sporting genius.

venture was tainted by professionalism never went away. Even when the team were asked by the Rugby Football Union to sign affidavits that they were not being recompensed for the trip, suspicions remained.

What has never been in doubt, however, is the stoicism and optimism of that first party. They were led by Robert Seddon, a much-respected forward from Lancashire. There was a tiny leavening of non-English players to give the team at least a semblance of a Celtic fringe. There was Angus Stuart, the Welsh-born Scot and former Cardiff three-quarter who played for Dewsbury at the time of the tour, and there was also WH 'Fishguard' Thomas, a Welsh international, who had attended Llandovery College.

Also included were the Burnett brothers from Hawick and two Scottish doctors, Dr John Smith and Dr Herbert Brooks, of Edinburgh. Brooks was the original vice-captain but by his own testimony was preoccupied by business ventures while in Australia and had to resign the position.

Perhaps business was not his only preoccupation, either. 'Both Smith and Brooks played while intoxicated,' wrote Charlie Mathers, the Bramley forward who kept a diary of the tour. Smith, who had made the tour as part of the management team, was meant to perform medical duties and also be administrator. But such was the shortage of players that he finished off playing as a forward in several games. He had been a reserve for the Scotland rugby team several years earlier but had also played 10 times for the Scotland football team. He was the first man ever to score a hat-trick against England in a football international, and his ability to cross football codes was typical of many players at the time.

So the rugby men convened in London on 8 March 1888, and headed to Gravesend, where they boarded the RMS Kaikoura *bound for Australia via Liverpool. They reached Hobart on 14 April, when Mathers was moved to observe that: 'Hobart is the finest place in the world'.*

Five days later, they re-embarked for Dunedin and Port Chalmers, where they were met by Shrewsbury, Lillywhite and Stoddart and even though their party now seems ridiculously small for the monumental list of fixtures that they were eventually to fulfil, the party was as complete as it was going to be.

They played nine games on the New Zealand section of that tour, losing only to Taranaki and to

The Pioneer Lions.

Auckland in the second match between the two teams and then moved on to Sydney for the Australian leg of their tour. They played 16 matches between June and September, winning 14 and drawing two.

But still the books would not balance, and it was here that, famously, the team now undertook 19 games under Australian Rules, and even though these were almost all against the leading teams of the day, they still managed to win seven and draw three. They were coached by Jack Lawlor and Frederick George McShane of the famous Essenden and Fitzroy Rules clubs respectively and that part of the adventure even gave rise more than a hundred years later to a book called Football's Forgotten Tour: The Story of the British Australian Rules Venture of 1888, *written by John Williamson.*

The sports at that time were not quite so different in their play and Rules then had the kick-off from the middle rather than the bounce off by the referee. Shrewsbury, with an eye to the main financial chance, ordered a 'nice outfit for the team, something of good material that will take them by storm in Australia.'

Australian Rules was a 20-a-side game so the party was almost fully engaged and, typically, the master all-round sportsman, Stoddart, was so successful in the alien code that he was asked to remain after the tour. He did not.

Eventually, the team returned to New Zealand, played another 10 matches under rugby laws between 8 September and 3 October, winning seven and drawing three – a sequence of matches which marked the beginning and, for nearly a century, the end of any Northern hemisphere dominance over New Zealand rugby.

The day after their last game, the team re-embarked on the Kaikoura *in Wellington harbour, sailed home and arrived in England on 11 November, having been away for eight months, and remarkably, having lost only two of their 35 games.*

And if there were no Test matches on the tour, there were some sporting significances. The organisers realised that it was important to obtain official patronage and permission for future tours, because the unofficial and commercial nature of the trip had given rise to the allegations of professionalism which soured some of the proceedings.

As usual, both teams learned lessons from the rugby of the other – New Zealand and Australia were to benefit from the lessons of the passing game which the tourists played, their heeling from the scrum and their use of the dummy pass.

Andrew Stoddart was probably the outstanding player on tour although John Nolan, a prolific try scorer from Rochdale Hornets, was so impressive that he was offered a job to stay in Australia. Harry Eagles, from Swinton, played in every match – a feat of endurance which has never been repeated on a British/Irish tour of Australia and New Zealand, and a record which is safe for all time.

Robert Seddon, one of the few capped players in that tour – he had played against Wales, Ireland and Scotland in 1887 – also played in every game up until his death. He had been orphaned early in his life and when he departed on tour, he was engaged to be married. In Australia on the day after the final game of the Rules intermission, he went on a canoeing expedition on the Hunter River with three of his teammates but continued on alone in a Gladstone skiff, a type of craft with which he was unfamiliar.

He was 200 yards off the bank of the river when the craft capsized and one account held that trailing straps which should have held him in place became entangled. Two onlookers who could not swim watched his struggle. Mathers, the diarist, was not given to emphatic expressions but he reported as follows. 'We had no sooner got to the great Northern Hotel in Newcastle than a telegram comes to Mr Lillywhite, saying 'Your captain is drowned'. We were all amazed. The effect on the team when the news arrived by telegram was devastating.'

Seddon, one of the finest of men and players, was buried in Maitland where the team had played its final Australian Rules match. A procession to Campbell's Hill Cemetery was led by 180 local footballers, and then the team walked behind the Mayor and Aldermen, who were followed by hundreds of local residents. The people of Maitland have maintained the grave there ever since. There is an imposing headstone bearing the inscription: 'In memory of Robert Seddon, captain of the England football team, drowned in the Hunter River at West Maitland, August 15 1888'.

Seddon was buried 'in his flannel trousers, and his British football guernsey.' He had written home to family and friends earlier on the day of his death. In 2008, Maitland Rugby Club announced that they would be erecting a memorial to Seddon in their club, 120 years after his death.

Fifteen years after the tour, Joe Warbrick, the captain of the New Zealand Native team (known as the 'Maoris') that toured Britain and Ireland in the winter of 1888-89, and who had played for Wellington against Seddon in New Zealand, was killed when engulfed in a lava flow after an eruption of a geyser near Rotorua. Three others died after ignoring warnings from a guide that they were too close – ironically, the guide was Warbrick's brother.

Nolan, the brilliant back, was killed in a work incident in 1907 and in 1915, the remarkable Stoddart, the wonderful all-round Corinthian sportsman who had taken over as captain after Seddon's death, committed suicide, after financial problems had struck at the Stock Exchange, where he was a member.

And so the era of the great inter-hemisphere rugby tours had well and truly dawned with that eight-month odyssey. The trip launched not entirely for sport, but for solvency, set precedent and fuelled the wanderlust.

Incidentally, three months after Seddon and his men had gathered in London in preparation for this tour, the Maoris convened in Napier, North Island, for a worldwide tour. They played nine games on an internal tour of New Zealand, and left Dunedin on 1 August, bound for Australia where they played two games, and then embarked on a six-week journey to England via the Suez Canal.

On 27 September, they reached Tilbury docks in London, and on 3 October they played their first match on British soil against Surrey. All told, those magnificent warriors were to play 74 games in England, Scotland

The team in New Zealand.

and Wales, including internationals against England, Wales and Ireland – winning the latter.

They left Plymouth on 29 March, amazingly sailed to Australia for a further two-month leg of 14 rugby matches, all of which they won, plus eight more fixtures under Australian rules. A year and four days after they left New Zealand, they returned but went straight into another internal tour in which they played eight matches.

On 24 August, they played their last game, against Auckland. The whole trip had lasted one year and two months, they had played 107 games, of which they won 78. It was a staggering way to mark the era of the great tours, and surely, it remains the greatest sporting journey ever made.

ROBERT SEDDON (England)

Toured: 1888

(*Interviewed by the* Melbourne Daily Telegraph) After all the games we have played, I must confess to liking the Australian (Rules) system much better than I anticipated when we came to Victoria, but I am of the opinion now that we have finished our tour, so far as Victoria is concerned, that the rugby game is still far and away the best, and for this reason: in the game that is played here one half of the men do little or no work, and for quite half the time they are absolutely idle, so that your game is really carried on with only ten or a dozen men. In rugby such a thing as this is impossible, for out of the fifteen men engaged on each side nine are forwards – players almost the same as your followers, and the remaining six are so disposed in the field that they are continually engaged.

This is one of the objections I see, and the next in importance is the very wide power you place in the hands of the umpires. So far as we have been able to see each umpire has a reading of the rules of his own, with the result that they vary considerably in their decisions, which, as you know, are final. We who have studied the game from the rules, remark this perhaps more quickly than local men do, and often to us a gross breach of the rules is perceptible, but to our surprise the umpire passes it over or else gives a decision that astounds us. In nothing is this more perceptible than in little marking, when time after time the ball is handled and never touched with the foot. You have a rule that the player who receives a mark must be at least two yards off from the man who kicks it to him, yet I venture to say there is not one of the many thousands who witness the matches who cannot remember scores of instances when there has not been 12 inches. between men carrying on the little mark game. Either you should amend your rules to bring them in accord with the game you play, or else insist on them being properly interpreted by the umpires.

In a rugby match the ball struck a dog, and was afterwards secured by one of the sides which, out of the tussle, was enabled to claim a try. This was disputed by their opponents, who maintained that as the ball had struck the dog it was dead. The dispute was referred to the Rugby Association, who decided that the 'try' was a fair one, because the other side, owning the ground, should not have allowed a dog upon it. But here an umpire gave a decision against us through no fault of our own.

DR HERBERT BROOKS (Scotland)

Toured: 1888

(Australian Rules) is a very tricky game but as far as football goes it is a mongrel game.

It seems to me that it is more handball than football. I do not think there is one man in the team who really likes it… But I am sure that they could bring out a team that could beat the Victorians at their own game. After two or three weeks' practice.

ROBERT SEDDON

Your players are soft. That is the tendency of your game. If they get knocked down they resent it, and ask angrily whether it was done on purpose. If we get knocked down we simply get up again and go on playing, and perhaps, if we are inclined in that way, look out for a chance to treat the man who tumbled us over in the same way. Yes, of course, rugby is rougher. That is just what I say, and perhaps it requires heavier men, although I fail to see it myself, for with scarcely any exception the best players you have are the tallest and the heaviest. Before we play a match we are told to look out for certain men, they being the most dangerous, and invariably we find that they are 5ft 11in or 6ft, and weigh about 12st or 13st. I tell you what I would undertake to do. I would pick twenty men at home who would beat at your own Australian game any twenty you could bring to meet them. All they would want would be about a month's practice, and they would be stronger, faster, and quicker than any I have ever seen here. I am jealous for English footballers, and I believe I am speaking the truth when I make the assertion that they are in every way better than you could produce. The disadvantage which we have had to suffer here is that we have had to think all the time we were playing, whereas our opponents played instinctively. But reverse the positions, and let them meet us in rugby. They would not render nearly so good an account of themselves as we have done under Australian Rules. There we play by instinct, and do things naturally. It has been supposed, that it was because we are heavy that we are consequently slow, but that is not the case at all. As I say, we have to think first. I guarantee under rugby rules that people would say we are quick enough in spite of our weight. I do not know whether the chance is likely to occur or not, but I should dearly like the

The tourists before playing a match in Australia.

opportunity of picking twenty men in England just to give you an idea of what Britons are at football. I do not wish to be thought boastful, harsh, or ungrateful, but I honestly believe that the rugby game is far superior.

DR HERBERT BROOKS

We have had a grand time of it right through the colonies. The hardest game we had was with the Sydney University. They are a very good team and nine of their members are in the representatives. They were, however, very rough – in fact, they almost equalled Wellington for roughness.

You may have seen in the Sydney papers the account of the spectators. They were terrible. I never saw such conduct at any other time throughout our tour. Talk of barracking, they were all at it.

[Australians] are not nearly so good as you in New Zealand. They are a very long way behind this colony but they have some very good players.

I did not go to Queensland with the boys as business [intervened] and when the team returned they expressed themselves in high terms both of the football and their treatment. They said it was the finest outing they had had in the colonies and their reception the heartiest, if you can particularise when our reception all-round was so hearty.

CHARLIE MATHERS (England)
Toured: 1888

A telegram came saying 'your captain is drowned'. We were all amazed and decided to cancel the match with Newcastle the following day. At night everyone was very quiet.

In the morning we went from Newcastle to Maitland, 20 miles, to bury our poor, unfortunate captain, Mr Seddon. When we got there we found him laid in his coffin. They all broke down but me. We went and had a service. Church crowded. All shops closed.

Seddon had been sculling when his boat capsized. 'His feet were stuck in the straps and when he struck out, he dragged the boat after him,' said an eye-witness. 'In his death struggles he must have tried to loosen the straps under water because they were found partly unbuckled when the boat was found.'

DR HERBERT BROOKS

I and a few others left at the railway station quite jolly and when we got to Newcastle an hour and a half afterwards, we received a telegram announcing his death. It was a terrible shock to us all. I should not care to live through another day like that on which poor Bob Seddon was buried.

The sympathy extended to us was something wonderful. They had a beautiful choral service in the church at Maitland… And the procession was over three quarters of a mile long. At the front were local footballers numbering around 300, then came the hearse, the English footballers came next, and then followed some 100 carriages… On the morning of the same day a public meeting was held and £150 subscribed at once to erect a monument to Mr Seddon's memory.

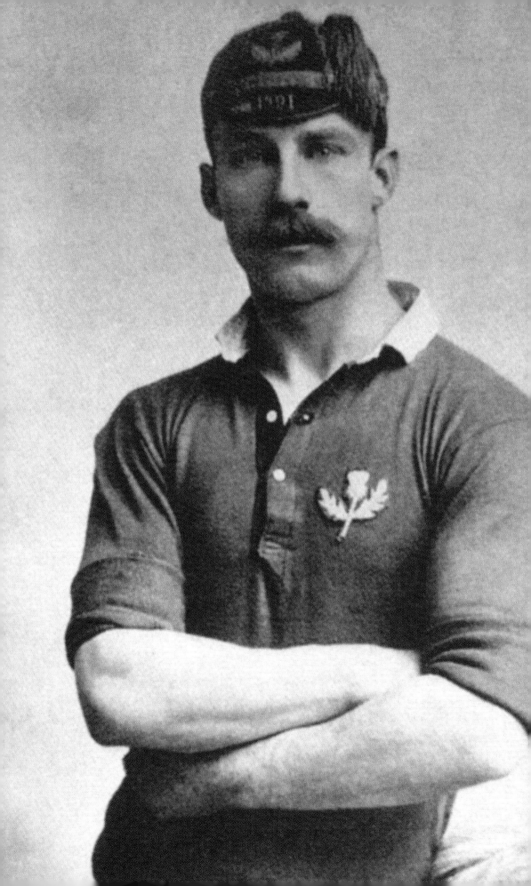

CHAPTER TWO

CHAMPAGNE AND TRAVEL
1891

SOUTH AFRICA

VARIOUS PARTIES *have been labelled the 'Greatest Lions' but the second tour of all, made to South Africa under the captaincy of W E (Bill) Maclagan, and managed by Edwin Ash, past secretary of the RFU, established an early claim, the power of which remains convincing. This time the tour was officially approved by the Rugby Football Union, who maintained the early habits which were to last a lifetime by appointing a sub-committee to pick the touring team, even though it was to be drawn from the four home countries. To be fair, they recommended that Maclagan, a Scot, be made captain.*

Amazingly, even though only 8 of the 21 tourists had been capped at the time of the tour (slightly more than half were Oxford or Cambridge Blues), Maclagan's men played 20 matches and won every one. Even more remarkably, after they had conceded a score in the opening tour match in Cape Town, they conceded no more for the rest of the tour. Whatever passed for defensive systems in 1891 worked well.

The tour, another epic odyssey, was underwritten by Cecil Rhodes, Prime Minister of the Cape Colony, and was described by one tourist as 'champagne and travel', and the trip, by all accounts, brought enormous quantities of both. The tour was a bizarre mixture of grace and good living, of dusty privation, of elevation, and endless daunting journeys.

For the first time, British players encountered the hard-baked grounds at altitude in South Africa – and in those days they were nothing more than red dust. There were also enormous journeys between playing centres, normally conducted by horse-drawn coaches. It is also true that the magnificent hospitality extended to the team may well have affected their performances. Paul Clauss, of Birkenhead Park and Scotland and one of the finest players on tour, reflected on this in an account he wrote years later: 'Had we overdone things from the social point of view? Too many dinners, dancers, smokers, etc?' Even so early in the grand tradition, it was established that most of the party tended to party as hard as they played.

The final game of the tour, played at Stellenbosch, was described by Clauss as 'a picnic match', which is not a concept that has survived the years. Most accounts do not include the picnic match in the official records of the tour.

The first Test match ever played took place at the Port Elizabeth Cricket Ground and was won by four points to nil with Randolph Aston scoring the first Test try credited to a British/Irish touring team, and the match was refereed by a former Edinburgh medical student and Welsh international, John Griffin.

Opposite: Paul Clauss of Scotland, one of the outstanding 1891 tourists.

The Second Test was played at the marvellously-named Eclectic Cricket Ground in Kimberley. The only score was a goal from a mark, kicked from near the halfway line by William Mitchell, the England fullback.

The final Test was played at Newlands in Cape Town, and the touring team completed their whitewash on their missionary tour. They were not to know that South African rugby was to prove a remarkably rapid environment for learning.

The outstanding players on tour were probably Clauss, who appeared in 12 of the games and all three Tests and scored six tries, Randolph Aston, the England centre, who played in every match and scored a remarkable 30 tries, and 'Judy' McMillan, a powerful Scotland forward, who also featured in every game.

Another point of interest surrounded Sir Donald Currie, the owner of the Castle shipping line, whose ship the Dunnottar Castle *carried the team from East India docks in London to Southampton and then to Cape Town in a record time of just over 16 days. Before the team departed, Sir Donald put his steam yacht* Iolanthe *at the disposal of the team so that they could cruise around the Isle of Wight. He also gave the captain a magnificent gold trophy, to be awarded to the team that produced the best performance against the touring team. The winner turned out to be Griqualand West, who in turn decided that they would put up the trophy for annual competition amongst the South African provincial teams; the Currie Cup became the backbone event of South African rugby, remains a powerful symbol of provincial dominance, and is a competition which is known all over the world today.*

PAUL CLAUSS (Scotland)

Toured: 1891

Mr Cecil Rhodes, then the Prime Minister of the Cape Colony, generously guaranteed to pay any loss involved in the expenses of the visit.

Our first week was spent in Cape Town, during which we played three matches, one against Cape Town, one against Western Province and the last against the Cape

The 1891 tour party. Captain Bill Maclagan holds the ball.

Colony. What seemed to strike the critics most about our play was the speed and fine dribbling of the forwards and the well-timed passing of the backs.

During the first week we were overwhelmed with social engagements, a smoking concert, and dinner given by the Western Province rugby union, Government House ball, a dance at Sea Point, a visit to the theatre, a lunch on board the MS *Penelope* lying off Simonstown, a picnic at Hout Bay. They were all a glimpse through the doors of hospitality which were flung wide open throughout the tour.

No match was played in Pretoria, the Transvaal capital, but we paid a visit there and were presented to Mr Paul Kruger, the state president. Kimberley was reached on July 16 after two nights and a day on the train. We stepped into the arena with no little anxiety as, for the first time in our lives, we were going to play on a ground that was absolutely destitute of grass. It was hard and covered with reddish dust so that with a bright sun overhead, there was a considerable glare. Frequently, too, one lost sight of the ball in the pillars of dust that rose up in the wake of the players as they ran. The hard and gritty ground somewhere dampened our ardour. It was no joke tackling or being tackled.

On August 8, we left East London in a small tug to join 'over the bar' the coasting steamer, *Melrose*, bound for Natal. As a fact, the touring at this point nearly ended, for we had a narrow escape of being drowned. It was blowing half a gale. Outside the breakwater the coaster's lights were seen through the darkness and the tug made for them; but she was badly handled and taken right across the bows of the *Melrose*, which seemed to tower miles above our heads. Luckily she struck us a little astern. Had

The first ever Test match between Great Britain and South Africa, in Port Elizabeth.

she caught the tub amidships we should have been sunk with little chance of saving ourselves. As it was we eventually made it on board and reached Durban. After a few hours' stay there we climbed, in wonderful zig-zags, by railway to Pietermaritzburg where we had an easy win.

Johannesburg, though only about five years old at the time, possessed many fine buildings... that was not to be wondered at, seeing that the wealth of the Witwatersrand had attracted some of the most adventurous spirits from all quarters of the globe.

On Sunday August 26 at 6 a.m., we left this bright spot to return to Kimberley, again travelling by coach and ten. One coach reached Klerksdorp safely but the other lost a front wheel, so we had to get what sleep we could on the floor of a hut, the only one within miles on the barren veld, while the driver rolled off to commandeer another vehicle. That arrived about 1 a.m. and two hours later brought us to Klerksdorp, our destination for the night.

Next morning we were off again at 7 a.m. and travelled almost continuously until 2 a.m. the following morning – when, stiff and hungry, we reached Bloemhof. Next day we had nine more hours coaching until we reached the railhead at Fourteen Streams. There we were thankful to board a train again and in comparative comfort arrived at Kimberley at about 11 p.m. And on the morrow, a football match! This somewhat

Tour captain, Bill Maclagan, in his Scotland livery.

detailed account of the journey from Rand to Kimberley has been given to show that the tour was not all 'beer and skittles.' One might say that apart from the football, it was all 'champagne and travel.'

During our stay we had travelled, roughly speaking, 3,263 miles by rail, 650 by coach and 260 by sea, including the voyage out and home we had covered nearly 16,000 miles.

Had the tour been a success? Judging by the scoreboard, yes. But the measure of our success was not the number of matches won, or points scored; it went further than that. Had we showed them in South Africa how to play the game in true sporting spirit? Had we taught them that self must be subordinated to side, that science and combination are better than brute strength? I feel that we did.

Playing in Cape Town, with Table Mountain dominating the backdrop.

CHAPTER THREE

GENTLEMEN IN ALL CLASSES
1896

SOUTH AFRICA

F IVE YEARS *after the invincible first tour of southern Africa came the next grand venture, with a party led by Johnny Hammond of England touring South Africa, this time for four Test matches in a rugby nation that had improved considerably in the intervening period.*

It was the first touring party to include Irish international players – previous members of the small Irish contingents had never reached that level. The Test series was won by three games to one and the only blot on the playing record was a draw against Western Province and the defeat at the hands of South Africa in the fourth and final Test. It has been something of a tradition of Lions tours throughout history that the final international of any tour, with exhaustion and injury taking its toll and with thoughts of packing and home beginning to dominate, is the most difficult to win – and has usually been lost.

There were several other significant aspects about the trip. It proved that South Africa were a coming force, having absorbed the lessons in passing and scrummaging which had been handed down to them by the touring missionaries of 1891. But this time it was the touring team that had also learned lessons. The party discovered the benefits of wheeling tactics in the scrum and what would nowadays be called the 'snap shove', to overcome the scrummaging power of the South Africans.

It was on this tour that refereeing controversies first began in earnest, after the odd reference to such matters on the two previous trips. The players were often angered by decisions made by the home referees. The tour was an official visit sanctioned by the RFU, although Cecil Rhodes agreed to underwrite all costs.

Probably the outstanding playing figure on tour was Fred Byrne, the England fullback, who scored more than a century of points on tour and played in every match, transferring successfully to centre for the Test series.

Another tradition which was to stand the test of time was that of great Irish characters forming a powerful and popular element – in 1896 Tommy Crean was such a character, he was the tour vice captain and played in every game. It was said that he could wheel a scrum on tour through his own strength and it was he who instituted guidelines for the consumption of alcohol on tour: 'No more than four glasses of champagne for lunch on match days.'

Walter Carey, a reverend who in later years became the Bishop of Bloemfontein, was a try scorer in the First Test and is the man who coined the famous Barbarian motto. A year before the tour he

---

said: 'Rugby football is a game for gentlemen in all classes but for no bad sportsman in any class.' Carey wrote a chapter on his tour memories in the book History of South African Rugby Football, *published 36 years after the tour.*

The First Test was played at the Crusader ground in Port Elizabeth and was won 8-0 by the Lions, with tries by Walter Carey and Larry Bulger, the Irish wing. The Second Test took place at the Wanderers ground in Johannesburg and was again won by the touring team, this time 17-8. Froude Hancock, the giant English forward who was a veteran of the 1891 series, gave an outstanding performance with a try in the second half. Two late tries by Theo Samuels were the first points scored by South Africa in a Test match.

The series was sealed at the Athletic Grounds in Kimberley, when the touring team came back from 3-0 down to win 9-3. Bert Mackie scored a try and Fred Byrne kicked a conversion and a drop-goal in a match which showed clearly that the gap was closing between players from Britain and Ireland and South Africa. Don't forget that in only one of their matches in 1891 had the tourists conceded a point.

It was therefore not a surprise that at Newlands, Cape Town, South Africa won the Fourth Test 5-0. It must be said that by all reports the party was incensed by the refereeing of Alf Richards, the local official, who repeatedly penalised the team for wheeling. Or perhaps the players had not stuck to their four glasses of champagne for lunch on match days.

One of the better players on tour was Alexander Todd, of Cambridge University and Blackheath who was to be capped for England in 1900. Like many leading sportsmen of the day he was an all-rounder, proficient in football and cricket. After the tour, he was to marry Alice Crean, none other than the sister of the charismatic Tommy. He had already enlisted in the army before making the rugby tour and three years after the trip he was back in South Africa – fighting in the Second Boer War. He was injured in action but recovered and entered the business world when he returned home.

On the outbreak of the First World War in 1914, he enlisted in the Norfolk Regiment, and was part of an attack on Hill 60 in Ypres. He was seriously wounded and on April 21, 1915, he died of his wounds. In its obituaries later that year, Wisden *described him as 'a capital wicket keeper'.*

One of Todd's bequests to rugby is the series of letters he wrote home to his parents from the 1896 tour – which reflect some of the peculiarly tough and yet gracious ways of the early tours, the mixing with the socialites of the booming new town of Johannesburg in the time of gold fever, and the length that players were prepared to go to to get a game of rugby.

ALEXANDER TODD (England)
Toured: 1896

[From on board the union steamship Tartar *en route to South Africa]* As we are arriving at Madeira tomorrow morning, I thought perhaps you would like to hear from me. So far everything has been first rate and the sea is somewhat like a millpond. The consequence is that everybody is extraordinarily cheerful…

I have always heard that being on shipboard for a long voyage rather tends to make one sentimental, but the steamship company did not look after us in that respect, as I don't think there are more than two unmarried ladies in our part, and they seem pretty full up with acquaintances already....

We got great cricket matches, sports, tournaments, etc on board… and cock-fighting, winning the large sum of 10 shillings in all. Concerts were in great request, but from a managerial point of view they did not go well because the second class passengers wanted to have everything in our own hands, and also do all the items of the programme, which caused unpleasantness…

On Thursday morning we got up early and saw the most magnificent sunrise on Table Mountain, the whole range going a bright terracotta. We landed on dock about eight o'clock and had a tremendous amount of speechifying at a special breakfast where all the rugby lights of South Africa were present.

On Thursday afternoon and Friday we ran about and trained on the field and finally played our first match on the Saturday. Oh goodness, it was awful!! We played 35 min each way on the ground like a brick wall, had a frightfully fast game, winning by three goals and try to a penalty goal and two tries – that is 14 points to 9. In the last 10 minutes I would gladly have changed places with a corpse. The papers rather slated us next day.

On Monday we drove out to Cecil Rhodes' place where Miss Rhodes showed us all over the house… Rhodes is not here now as he is watching the Matabele war. In the afternoon we played our second match, against the Suburban team. It was one of the hardest games I've ever played, especially as one of our men, Mackie, got his nose broken and had to go off for about 10 min. But he came back on afterwards and finished the game. The ground was even harder than before and we've lost square yards of skin between us.

Last night feeling very sore and out of sorts, I was asked around to a meeting of the Drols club… in order to meet Mark Twain, who was just completed a tour round the world. They gave him a book of photos and the old chap made an awfully good speech in reply.

In the evening one or two of us were asked to perform at a smoker. I consented along with the other songsters as we thought there would only be about 40 or 50 people present and no formality. Judge of our horror when we were taken to a place larger than the Queen's Hall in Regent Street, with the best part of 1000 people there… We were after thinking that we had been directed to the Albert Hall or a Handel Festival by mistake but in we walked… the whole place rising and cheering like mad and to think that we had to sing to them on a raised platform. I wish my boots had been sizes larger so that I could have sunk into them.

On Friday morning we came on here after a miserable railway journey from 11 a.m. to 7:30 p.m. and have got into a beastly hotel where there is no water to be had for baths…

My last letter was from Queenstown, where we had horrid weather and had nothing to do but sit in a smoky little sitting-room all day and look at one another... We started away from there on Sunday night and arrived here at Johannesburg on Tuesday morning, just about sick of the journey.

We played the Diggers on Wednesday and beat them by seven points to nil. The ground is just the road with most of the stones taken off. For the match today there are only 10 able-bodied men, four crocks and one invalid playing for us!!!

On Thursday we played South Africa and simply sponged up the non-existent puddles with them, although we won only by one goal and try. Their forwards were laid out absolutely flat several times, although they said they were heavier than we were. It was the finest forward game I've ever played.

[On returning to Cecil Rhodes' house] Miss Rhodes, his sister, presided and gave us a very good spread, with Veuve Clicquot Ponsardin 89 to drink. It was a good job that we had an hour or two to spare after lunch before playing... Against the Western Province team and after a tremendous tussle, this ended in a draw.

[On visiting Kimberley and the diamond mines] There's really very little to see in one of these diamond mines... We managed to spoil all our hands and bruise our noddles in going through the low working tunnels... Kimberley is mostly built of very rusty, discoloured corrugated iron, the land is as flat as a pancake and about 6 inches deep in

Johnnie Hammond's Lions.

dust. The football ground has absolutely not one blade of grass on or near it. Before playing they have to put a sort of harrow on it which scrapes out the hard surface to a depth of about 6 inches and then they water it.

The gloom has just fallen on us as Roger Walker, our manager and president of the English rugby union, has just had a cablegram to say that his eldest daughter is dying, so he's off home, poor chap.

[*On the end of the tour*] We are all just about played out now, having played 19 matches and travelled 10,000 miles in 10 weeks. The day I sent my last mail to you, we played against Johannesburg town and could only with the greatest difficulty manage to raise 15 men to take the field. Quite unknowingly, I did a neat bit of gallery play as I got to score a try and got winded at the same time and learned afterwards that it had happened within about 20 yards of my favourite partner at the dance the night before. I shan't forget that dance in a hurry, there were about 450 people there and I had 26 dances down on my programme.

Johannesburg people are absolutely the most untiring lot in their hospitality that I ever hope to come across. They would not allow us to pay a thing – dances, dinners, concerts, native war dances, mines, picnics, tennis parties, drives, theatres, variety entertainment, in fact absolutely everything. You will see me a week after the arrival of this letter. We sail home in the *Mexican* on September 9.

Bishop Walter Carey found his own memories vivid, even though he was writing 36 years after the momentous tour, when he was in his second year at Oxford and had played twice in the Varsity

South Africa's Second Test team.

match. He revealed that, perhaps surprisingly, the team was made up at least partly of invitees: 'Oxford was invited to send two representatives to go on the tour to South Africa. I was lucky enough to be one of the two.'

WALTER CAREY (England)
Toured: 1896

The stars of the tour were the Irish and they were brilliant in the extreme... My particular fancy was – and still is – Tommy Crean, the Irish forward. Tommy was the handsomest man I have ever seen, he weighed 210 pounds and was always the fastest man on the field. At some athletic contest he did 100 yards in 10 and two fifths seconds, and that for a 15 stone forward is phenomenal. He was the most Irish, the most inconsequent, the most gallant, the most lovable personality one could imagine. And he made the centre of the whole tour.

Tommy subsequently won the Victoria Cross at Elandslaagte [in the Boer War]. The story is that... whilst attacking the Boers something hit him and bowled him over completely. Momentarily dazed, he yelled: 'I'm kilt entoirely.' However, he got up and found he was not dead, though badly wounded. But the insult had roused his Irish blood and with a wild yell he led the bayonet charge and thus received the supreme award for bravery.

[On wheeling the scrum] We managed to carry screwing to a very high art. If you want to screw to the right, the right-hand man in the front row turns inwards and remains

immovable... And the three or four forwards in the back row and on the right of the second row carry the ball round this immovable man into the open.

In the end we played 21 matches, of which we won 19 and drew one. I am bound to say that the match we drew (against Western Province) was after a lunch... when Tommy Crean's order was that nobody should drink more than four tumblers of champagne. The only wonder is that we were not licked by 50 points. We had our revenge on this team in the return match when we didn't drink champagne and won by 32.

The last match – against South Africa – was to us very unsatisfactory as the referee kept stopping our screwing in the scrum, telling us we were offside.

Alex Todd.

The enemy who worried us most was a chap called Alf Larard – a red-headed, hard-bitten sort of fighter.... And there were hard-bitten fellows from the mines at Kimberley and Johannesburg. At Johannesburg we were told that the great Jack Orr, supposed (I am sure it was libel) to be a regular man-killer, was waiting to put us all in the hospital. He did seem very formidable at first but luckily for us, broke or hurt his ankle in the first 10 minutes, so we survived.

There were the long treks across the country, such as from Grahamstown to King William's Town. We travelled by Cape carts and took two days jolting over sluits, trying to catch monkeys, and sleeping five in a bed at the inn on the way, as accommodation was limited.

I hope and pray that South African teams will always play like gentlemen… It is so easy to cheat at it (rugby) and so destructive of this wonderful game. If a man wants to do dirty tricks let him cheat at ninepins in his own backyard, but let him keep clear of rugby football. There have been many tours since ours, better football perhaps, but I do not think there's ever been a tour with more fun and more sporting play in it than our long-ago tour of 1896.

Tommy Crean.

CHAPTER FOUR

MANLY PLAY
1899
AUSTRALIA

THIS WAS *the first tour made exclusively to Australia, with no New Zealand leg. It was to be 90 years until the Lions next made a tour to Australia alone; all the intervening tours until 1989 would see Australia as a short lead-in or as an epitaph to more extensive visits to New Zealand. This time, the tour was an official visit and unlike the pathfinders of 1888, there was no need for extra Australian Rules games.*

It was a feature of the early tours that the party included not only men of the cloth but those who were to win medals for gallantry. Matthew Mullineux was both, because he was to win the Military Cross in the First World War. He became a regimental chaplain, but before the outbreak of war he studied medicine. He was at a field hospital in France, which came under attack from the Germans, and the chief medical officer of the post was incapacitated by his injuries. Mullineux took command, continuing to treat the injured and evacuate the worst cases even though the post was continually shelled by high explosive and gas for 12 hours.

Back in 1899 in Australia he had at his disposal a party which included for the first time players representing each of the Four Home Unions, including the great Gwyn Nicholls, the Prince of Welsh three-quarters who went on to become the first Welshman to appear in a Lions Test, eventually featuring in all four in this series.

As usual, the party did not reflect the true strength of rugby in Britain and Ireland at the time because less than half the players had been capped. Nicholls was the only representative from a Welsh club and with the split, which formed the rugby league code now four years in the past, the old preponderance of representatives from the North of England had diminished so that only three players came from clubs in the North. However, even though all Four Home Unions contributed players, the party was always referred to as 'the English football team'.

Arguably the most colourful player was the roughhouse Northampton and England forward, Blair Swannell. So many legends and myths surrounded Swannell, both for his exploits as a player and away from the rugby field; many of these were not substantiated, although it is said to be true that he wore the same pair of breaches for every game, and that they remained unwashed for most of his career. At a time when good manners on the field were still deemed essential, Swannell's over-vigorous playing style stood out.

He was to make the next tour, to Australia and New Zealand in 1904, and after settling in Australia was later capped by them. He fought in the Second Boer War, which began later in 1899,

---

Opposite: Alf Bucher.

and he was killed in the Second World War at Anzac Cove, Gallipoli, in 1915, when serving in the Australian army.

The tour party triumphed by 3-1 in the Test series, although they did lose three of the twenty-one games – they lost the First Test against Australia and also the provincial matches against Queensland and Metropolitan Districts.

The poor performance in the First Test led to Mullineux making a brave and selfless decision. He was an accomplished half-back, and had been to South Africa with Johnny Hammond's team in 1896, where he played in one of the Tests, but after the First Test defeat in Sydney in 1899, he stood down for the remaining three Tests of the series, with Charlie Adamson taking over at half-back and Frank Stout, a Gloucester boy who would later play for Richmond, leading the Lions in the last three Tests, all of which were won.

The First Test was played on the famous Sydney Cricket Ground, and Australia snatched the game with two converted tries in the last 10 minutes. The hosts were bolstered by two New Zealand players and there was also a New Zealand referee. However, it would be many decades until neutral referees became the norm in international rugby.

But the tourists revived. With Stout now at the helm, the Second Test was won 11-0, at the Exhibition Ground in Brisbane, where a crowd of 15,000 was a new record for any sporting occasion in Queensland.

Back at the Sydney Cricket Ground for the Third Test, Alf Bucher, the Scotland wing, scored two tries in a very tight game, although Australia would have won had they landed a late penalty kick. For the Fourth Test, also played at the Sydney Cricket Ground, Australia called on five New Zealanders in a desperate bid to square the series and in a gesture which would now be seen as entirely bizarre. But last game of the tour or not, the gallant British and Irish forwards relished the wet and heavy conditions and the victory was convincing.

At the time, the British devotion to open play was notable and almost unique and it captured the

The 1899 Lions.

imagination of the Australian public. In later decades, the roles would reverse, with Australian rugby
players seen to put attacking rugby first while the British would often resort to stodgy forward power as
their default tactic.

There was also controversy, never far from the scene on such tours. Sharp Australian practises such
as pushing at the lineout and obstruction in open play were criticised by Mullineux in his end of
tour speech, words which the supporters of the touring party deemed brave and apposite and which
Australian rugby men deemed to be rather patronising.

Adamson and Nicholls were seen to be the outstanding players on tour. Adamson, the half-back from
Durham, scored more than a century of points on tour and the legendary Nicholls was described by an
Australian sporting newspaper as 'possessing intuitively quick judgement'.

First-hand accounts of the tour are very scarce, although the slightly more sophisticated state of
Australia ensured that communications and travel were marginally more comfortable for the touring
team than in, say, South Africa. Seven of the twenty-one games took place at the Sydney Cricket
Ground, and there were heavy victories along the way against teams such as Mount Morgan, Bundaberg
and Victoria. The series had been close, but no-one in the southern hemisphere had managed to take the
Test series from the marauding visitors from far-off Europe.

REVEREND MATTHEW MULLINEUX (England)

Toured: 1899

[A report from the post-match dinner after the Fourth Test] The guests were toasted with
Royal Maximum Champagne and after the Australian captain had made some remarks
with some possibly light-hearted excuses as to why the Australians have lost, the Rev
Mullineux responded:

'I am here as a representative of English rugby football, and feel it is my duty to speak
against anything that was not conducive to the game being played in a sportsmanlike
way.' He pointed out that he was a clergyman of the Church of England and 'therefore
he should denounce anything in the game that was unmanly.'

Whatever he had pointed out he wished those present to understand that it was simply
for the 'purpose of affording them information and would improve the game and that it
was not done in any carping spirit.'

He referred in particular to various examples of cheating he had encountered from
the Australians, 'the trick of holding players back when coming away from the scrum;
at the lineout, pushing a man who has not got the ball, as, for instance, A and B are
Australians, they push an opponent away while another Australian comes along and
secures the ball.

'And finally, placing the elbow in an opponent's face in the scrum; and shouting to an
opponent for a pass, this being the lowest thing that he had heard of, and was taking a
mean advantage. Please block these things from your football for instead of developing
all that is manly they bring forth always what is unmanly.' Mullineux added that the tour
had been 'one of joy and delight, in which both teams have learnt a lot from the other's
play.'

CHAPTER FIVE

HERALD OF DARK DECADES
1903

SOUTH AFRICA

A ND SO *the masters became pupils. The British & Irish team were beaten in a Test series for the first time, and a mini-era of success had ended. The defeat of the 1903 team heralded some dark decades because it would not be until 1974 under Willie-John McBride that the British & Irish Lions would win again in what, rugby-wise, had become a dark continent.*

It is also remarkable to realise the historical context of the tour and, perhaps, rugby's ability to cross political boundaries. It was less than a year since the end of the Second Boer War, and yet the welcome for the tourists was as warm as ever. The party visited sites where battles had taken place only a few months earlier, and scrabbled around for souvenirs such as empty shell cases.

By 1903, and by way of contrast from previous tours, most of the tourists were established internationals instead of the invited former Blues and public schoolboys who had made up the majority of the earlier sides. However, the move towards some kind of merit selection was not a success because, particularly in the forwards, and even though two of the three Tests were drawn, the team were often second-best and in fact won only 50% of the matches on tour. The manager was Johnny Hammond, who had captained the party in 1896, and the captain was Mark Morrison, a powerful forward from Royal High School FP in Edinburgh who was eventually to win 23 Scotland caps. Amongst those who had also toured in Australia in 1899 were Frank Stout, who had led the previous party in the latter Tests of that series.

There were some notable players. Reg Skrimshire, the Newport and Wales centre, played in all 22 of the tour matches and was the leading try and points scorer. Alfred Tedford was singled out by the South African captain as the best of the forwards, 'the finished article in every department of the game'. Tedford is still regarded as one of the best forwards in Irish history. In opposition, Japie Krige, the brilliant South African centre, is equally still regarded as one of his country's best.

The tour began in melancholy fashion. The team played all three of their opening games at Newlands, against Western Province Country, Western Province town and the Western Province provincial team – and lost all three. Soon afterwards they lost twice in succession to Griqualand West, although they did gain a revenge victory later in the tour over the same opposition in Kimberley – one of the grounds where the hard-baked and concrete-like surface, the glare from the sun and the rising dust always presented alien conditions to any visiting player.

The First Test was played at the Wanderers ground in Johannesburg and ended in a 10-10 draw,

Opposite: Captain Mark Morrison casts a relaxed but focused figure among his teammates.

and this after the British team trailed by 10-0, which in that era was not an insignificant margin. But Skrimshire scored a spectacular try at the posts just before half-time and the team drew level in the second half. Among the notable aspects of this match were that Alex Frew, a former Scotland international, captained South Africa and Bill Donaldson, another Scottish international, refereed the game.

The Second Test also ended in a draw, in one of those 0-0 matches so incredibly rare in the current era, but which were by no means unknown at the time. Patrick Hancock, the English half-back, was outstanding in defence and attack and the touring team came closest to scoring a try when Skrimshire went over, only to be recalled for a forward pass.

In the Third Test, played at Newlands in Cape Town, South Africa wore green jerseys in a Test match for the first time, and even though there was no score in the first half, South Africa won the match in the second half and the series belonged to them. The try scorers were Joel Barry and Alan Reid, and there were excited home celebrations in a crowd of 6,000.

ALFRED TEDFORD (Ireland)
Toured: 1903

The British touring side of 1903, which comprised eight Englishmen, seven Scots, five Irishmen and one Welshman, were the happiest crowd that ever left the mother country.

Arriving at Newlands. The first thing that struck us was the keenness of the Malay and coloured population. As Hind and I were walking onto the ground together, we overheard the following conversation between two Malays: 'The tall one is fine – a triple Blue at Cambridge, and the other is Tedford, who played in the last six matches for Ireland.' As neither of us had been in the country before, it was obvious that their

The 1903 tour party before the Third Test in Cape Town.

knowledge had been gained from the press and showed how closely they kept in touch with the game overseas.

After our first two matches we came to the conclusion that we were rather a poor side and that our forwards and half-backs alone counted... Outside we were going to get all (the trouble) we wanted with men of the class of Carolin, Hobson, Barry, Loubser and Krige opposed to us.

Next, long journey to Kimberley... as we passed through country where much fighting (in the Boer War) had occurred a few years previously. We saw many block-houses and barbed wire and we had lunch at Stormberg Junction (site of a reverse at the hands of the Boers in what was known as 'Black Week' in the Boer War), and were lucky in having as travelling companions two ex-soldiers who had fought on that famous battlefield.

Our first Test match was played on the Wanderers ground, it was about the best match of the tour so far and we were rather unlucky in only making a draw of it. Our farewell to Johannesburg was a real event, practically the whole town turning out to speed us on our way.

Later came our second Test match and how we managed it to hold South Africa to a draw, I do not know how, as our three-quarters were dreadful. Frank Stout played his best game of the tour and Skrimshire got what we and some of the crowd thought was a try, but it was judged not. There was no score.

We were also taken to the Magersfontein battlefield, where the Highland Brigade was so badly cut up during the Anglo Boer War. We managed to collect a number of shells and other fragments of war, all of which are still treasured in many of our homes.

We had great hopes of the final Test match as quite a lot of rain had fallen in Cape Town, and we were to play our first match of the tour on a wet ground. But our hopes were dashed... As South Africa won a good match and with it the rubber. Joe Barry scored early in the second half, and Reid scored the second try near the end and Heatlie converted.

I must put in a word of praise for the referees who controlled our games on the tour. We were more than fortunate to have such men...

Another thing that is against a team visiting South Africa is that all the players chosen cannot obtain the leave for such a long tour. All said and done, however, we had a glorious time. And the friendships made so long ago still prevail, it has been the greatest pleasure to us all to meet in after years at international matches and have 'a good old craic' about the happy time we spent together in sunny South Africa.

I must pay tribute to our captain, old Mark Morrison. He was always the life and soul of the team... no keener man ever played football, and in my opinion he was one of the great forwards of all time.

3 p.m.: "See the Conquering Hero Comes!"

Duncan McGregor shows a clean pair of heels to the Britishers — no "cold feet" on this occasion.

Bedell-Sivright's neck.

Nicholson in his Champion sky-scraping act on the line out.

GATE MONEY £2114.

Jimmy Duncan to Secretary Norris: "Alone I did it!"

Wallace with steam up.

N.Z.

RUGBY CHAMPION BELT

Let 'em all come!

The World.

Harding's great feet. This is the foot that kicked the goal that made up John Bull's score.

The New Zealand Forward Rush! Earthquakes not in it!

Bushed!

4.45 p.m. The Kiwi has developed into a moa.

Types of British Beauty.

The Lion is not so chirpy now.

J.C.B.

CHAPTER SIX

THE KIWI ROVER
1904

AUSTRALIA AND NEW ZEALAND

THE APPETITE *for these lengthy rugby tours was such that the next trip in the formative years of the Lions tradition departed for New Zealand and Australia only one year after Morrison's men. The captain, David (Darkie) Bedell-Sivright, had toured in South Africa with the unsuccessful party in 1903. He was described by Clem Thomas, the great 1955 Lion, as: 'a man after my own heart, being a rough handful as a player. He was one of the first in a long line of Scottish forwards to master the art of wing-forward play.' And he led a successful and attractive touring team, with household names of the game.*

Bedell-Sivright played in 22 internationals for Scotland, and was clearly one of the best forwards to tour in those early trips. Like the formidable Blair Swannell, his colleague in the party in 1904 and who had also toured in 1899, Bedell-Sivright was to die at Gallipoli.

There were only four capped forwards in the 1904 party, but outstanding talent in the backs, with what might be termed the first generation of Welsh superstars. For the first time, Wales were to make a really significant contribution to a 'Lions' tour in terms of class and numbers as the first Wales golden era was now in full swing – the year after the tour, Wales were to triumph over New Zealand by 3-0 in Cardiff in one of the most famous games ever played.

Four of their outstanding backs, Percy Bush, Willie Llewellyn, Rhys Gabe and Teddy Morgan, featured on the 1904 tour with the outstanding Bush reaching a century of points on tour, including 11 tries. Llewellyn, Gabe and Morgan scored 19 tries between them. Tommy Vile of Newport, also on tour but then uncapped, would enjoy an international career that spanned 17 years, ending his Wales career as captain against Scotland at Swansea in 1921, before becoming a famous and dapper international referee. The little man's aura and influence was so significant that a book appeared on his life as recently as 2011.

Arthur 'Boxer' Harding, the forward from London Welsh, was another who made the tour and who would feature in the Wales win of 1905. He was later to captain the 1908 tourists to New Zealand and Australia. Yet not even he could forge an inexperienced set of forwards into a formidable pack.

The party was the only one from Britain and Ireland to win all its matches in Australia, with the Test series ending in a 3-0 whitewash in favour of the tourists. In the other tour matches in Australia, the team were rarely seriously challenged, sweeping through the country and playing exciting attacking football – and only in the final tour match against New South Wales did the team fail to win by a substantial margin.

Opposite: 'The Triumph of John Bull, Junior' – a depiction of the Lions tour of New Zealand, 1904, from *The Free Lance.*

In the First Test, played at the Sydney Cricket Ground, Australia held the tourists scoreless until half-time, but two tries by Willie Llewellyn and a drop-goal by Percy Bush set the visitors on the way to a 17-0 victory. In the Second Test, played at the Exhibition Ground in Brisbane, tries by Llewellyn and Bush were the highlights in a match in which, again, the tourists dominated the second half.

Back at the Sydney Cricket Ground for the Third Test, Teddy Morgan scored the only points of the first half with a try, and in the second half, Llewellyn and the formidable Swannell also scored, to complete the dominance of the series with a 16-0 win.

Another feature of the tour was that Denys Dobson became the first British & Irish tourist to be sent off, receiving marching orders in the game against Northern Districts at Newcastle.

In New Zealand, where Bedell-Sivright broke his leg in the first game in Canterbury, and where only five matches were played, the Test match was played at Athletic Park in Wellington; it was 3-3 at half-time but New Zealand wing Duncan McGregor scored two tries after the interval. The match was described by Mr Rand, a member of the New South Wales Rugby Football Union, as: 'The greatest ever played in the southern hemisphere.'

The tourists struggled with the forward power of the home teams on the New Zealand leg of the tour and failed to cope with what was called the loose-wing-forward, or 'rover'. Dave Gallaher, the celebrated All Black, was the rover in the Test and caused chaos to the tourists. The rover was a concept, originated in New Zealand, in which one of the forwards stood off the scrum, which packed down in a two-three-two formation, and was deemed by many as illegal. It was not until 1930 that the tactic was outlawed, and three players were required by law to form the front-row.

During the Test, one of the British backs – most likely Bush, who was renowned for his quick wit – is reported as saying to Gallaher: 'You should be wearing a red, white and blue jersey. You are always on this side.' Bush regularly wrote columns on the tour for the Cardiff newspapers. Bush was

an indomitable tour character, brilliant on the field and a magnificent personality off it. In Australia, he built up a collection of pipes, walking sticks and umbrellas which he won as a result of wagers. The pattern of play in that Test match, which drew a crowd of over 20,000, with New Zealand's forward power successfully attempting to stifle the brilliance of the touring backs, was to be repeated frequently down the decades, and it was to be only in 1971 that the British & Irish Lions won a Test series in New Zealand, and only then that the team with the outstanding backs came through.

PERCY BUSH (Wales)
Toured: 1904

Reggie Edwards, the Irish forward, bet that I would not drop-goal in our game against New South Wales in Sydney. 'You Welsh terrier, I'll

Tour captain, David 'Darkie' Bedell-Sivright.

wager you a new pipe that you can't drop-goal today, if you are game enough to take me.'

Thus compelled I accepted the gauntlet. When we had been playing about five minutes Frank Hulme, who was working the scrum, sent me a lovely pass. There were about 60 Australian forwards bearing down on me and only about six inches away, so I decided that I had better get rid of the spheroid. I kicked frantically at it and to my surprise and delight, the ball soared up and up and finally crossed the bar, and won me a pipe.

RHYS GABE (Wales)
Toured: 1904

[Speaking after the Test in New Zealand] (I object) to the putting down of men after the ball left them… Your men are clever enough to win without indulging in these tactics… it would be a healthier game and the public would enjoy it better. Conditions also helped to beat us.

DAVID BEDELL-SIVRIGHT (Scotland)
Toured: 1903 & 1904

[In an interview after the Test in New Zealand] The better team won… but I think that the British scrum formation is better than the New Zealand 'two-three-two' and New Zealand would be able to feed the backs better, and to score more, if the British style was adopted.

(I have) no fault to find with the British backs, whose attack was rendered very difficult because they were playing behind beaten forwards, and the defence was as good as could be expected in the circumstances.

The 1904 tour party.

CHAPTER SEVEN

TEMPERANCE NATION
1908
NEW ZEALAND

Eⁿᵍˡᵃⁿᵈ'ˢ ᵘⁿˢᵘᶜᶜᵉˢˢᶠᵘˡ *campaign in the 2011 Rugby World Cup in New Zealand was marked by some rather lurid events off the field. The players were criticised for their behaviour, and for incidents involving excessive drinking, and then one of the party – Manu Tuilagi – hit the headlines near the end of the visit for diving from a ferry into the waters of Auckland harbour.*

The history of Lions tours from the early years proves that there is very little new under the sun. The party which toured Australia and New Zealand in 1908 had drinking and fraternising with the opposite sex firmly on the agenda and there was also an Auckland harbour incident which might have ended in tragedy.

When the team was preparing to depart the harbour on the steamer Victoria for a trip to Australia on the way home to the United Kingdom at the end of the tour, Percy Down, a forward from the Bristol club, leaning over the rail of the steamer to bid farewell to a lady acquaintance on the dock, turned a somersault over the rail and fell into the water below.

One account says that 'Jackett the British fullback and Francis, of the New Zealand team (some home players had gathered to see off the tourists) jumped in the water to give assistance to the Britisher, who was loudly appealing for help.' Apparently, Down was 'handicapped by his heavy overcoat and crying loudly for help'. The danger of the steamer crushing the swimmers against the wharf was always present. The boat had to swing away from the wharf to facilitate the rescue and eventually, with ropes, Down was brought safely to the dockside. The farewells then continued and the commotion caused by the incident died down – though it was the subject for cartoonists in the New Zealand papers next day.

At the time, a clear difference had already grown up between the approaches to rugby of New Zealand and of British players. The All Blacks had not long returned from their epic 1905 tour to the United Kingdom, Ireland and France and despite their defeat against Wales in Cardiff, they had set high standards in their strict training regimes and their play, as well as with their behaviour off the field. In their post-tour comments, Arthur 'Boxer' Harding, the Welsh forward who captained the 1908 party, left no-one in any doubt that he regarded the practice of training hard as unsporting, and unbalancing for the ethos of the sport as British people then understood it.

In many senses, this was a difference which was to mark – in perception at least – much of the time between the start of the 20th century and the passage of rugby from the amateur to the

Opposite: Captain Arthur 'Boxer' Harding sits with the ball beside tour manager George Harnett and the rest of the 1908 tourists.

professional era. The post-tour comments of George Harnett, the 1908 manager, complained of the number of hotels on tour which did not serve alcohol. Temperance appeared to play little part in tour proceedings.

One of the New Zealand writers who covered the tour, R A Barr, expanded on the difference in dedication and focus, and probably spoke, even if he did not know it at the time, for the ages of clashes between the two countries. He wrote of the touring team: 'There was a casualness about the whole proceeding which struck the serious-minded New Zealander as being quite foreign to the subject. 'You take your rugby as a religion,' remarked a Welsh international to me one day… 'While we in England look back upon it as a pastime. With you New Zealanders, it is business; with us a pleasure.' From the cradle, a young New Zealander learns the art of kicking a rugby ball, and he goes to his grave jibbering of the grand old game. The average British footballer, on the other hand, takes his rugby as he takes his bath – with a great deal of pleasure – and while he plays earnestly he leaves the theories and tricks of the game on the touchline.'

Barr also observed that the majority of the tour players, 'Landed in New Zealand pounds overweight, ill-fitting to battle up against the highly-trained New Zealand provincial sides, and with only an outside chance against the flower of the Dominion.'

The class consciousness of rugby was illuminated when some members of the Welsh Rugby Union decided that the selection of Welsh players had not been based on egalitarian principles but on social class. They later stated when the 1910 tour of South Africa was being arranged, that 'players should be chosen… irrespective of the social position of the players.'

Class was also something of an issue with New Zealanders at that time. The 1908 touring team, which actually comprised players only from England and Wales as the Scotland and Ireland unions had declined to participate, probably set new standards in terms of off-the-field shenanigans and celebrations. It is clear from reading between the lines of much that appeared in print at the time that the antics of the tourists came as a surprise to the New Zealand rugby public, who viewed some of the team as Edwardian snobs and upper-class twits. That is not to say that the party was not much loved, because they played some attractive rugby and were socially charismatic. But their playing results were disastrous, and more than one of the touring party called into question in later years their true commitment to rugby excellence.

Certainly, many visitors appeared to find the New Zealand public alluring. Henry Vassall, the Oxford University centre, fell in love with a New Zealand girl and contrived to miss the boat back to England. The couple were married back in London two years later.

Two other members of this party married New Zealand girls and settled out there – one was 'Boxer' Harding, the tour skipper, the other Fred Jackson, a big Cornish forward who married a Maori girl and whose son, Everard Jackson, played in six Tests for the All Blacks between 1936 and 1938.

New Zealand won two of the Tests easily and drew a third, utterly outclassing the Anglo-Welsh team. Bertie Laxon, the former Cambridge Blue half-back (though not an international) commented after the final Test drubbing: 'Why we lost, was because the All Blacks were too good for us. They beat us at all points of the game. They are the best players in the world. The Welshmen can think what they like, but in my opinion New Zealand would beat Wales three times out of five.'

The background to the tour was unusual. As mentioned, this side was called the Anglo-Welsh team because the Scots and Irish, though invited, refused to participate. Tours were beginning to raise the spectre of tour allowances – however small they were even by standards of the day, and even though they were meant to cover a few incidental expenses rather than be compensation for money lost. Such allowances had worried the ultra-conservatives of the Scottish Rugby Union so profoundly that they entered into dispute with the RFU that, at one stage, threatened to derail the 1909 Calcutta Cup match.

As well as declining to take part in the tour, the SRU and IRFU also declined fixtures against Australia, who came to Britain in the winter of 1908-9; incidentally, the 1908 Anglo-Welsh party played no Tests in Australia because the top Australian players had already sailed for Britain.

This was to be the last tour to Australasia for 22 years, at first because the First World War intervened. Nine games were played in Australia, of which the Anglo-Welsh team won seven, and seventeen games were played in New Zealand, of which only nine were won. There were three Test matches, and while the team managed to draw the second in Wellington, they were comprehensively defeated in the other two.

Yet again, the team was not remotely representative of the true strength of rugby even in the two unions who were represented, and at the time that the tour took place, only 11 of the 28 tourists had played international rugby. A further point of interest is that six of the party were former pupils of Christ's College, Brecon. As usual, injuries bit deep into the party strength as the tour progressed.

The tour brought an early outbreak of crowd trouble. The interest in rugby in New Zealand had grown even higher after the exploits of the All Blacks team which toured in Britain in 1905 and the local population had been infuriated when tickets for the First Test in Dunedin had gone on sale at the exorbitant price of two shillings each. Fences at the ground were torn down and several hundred entered the ground for free, boosting the attendance to over 23,000.

The 1908 Anglo-Welsh tour party.

Very few Lions tours in history have ever taken place without some kind of dispute between tourists and hosts on the philosophy or application of the laws and bylaws of rugby, and the 1908 visit was no exception. If a team lost a player to injury, it was a common occurrence at the time in Australia and New Zealand for the opposing captain to offer to allow a replacement. It was strictly against the laws of the game but it was frequently done and when Jackett, the fullback from Falmouth, left the field in the match against Wellington, the Wellington captain offered the touring team the facility to bring on a substitute. The offer, sporting though it was, was declined because it was against the laws of rugby at the time. In several parts of the world, and especially France, the replacement of players was condoned decades before replacements became officially allowed in the 1960s.

The Dunedin Test was lost 32-5, an enormous score in those days. The Anglo-Welsh forwards were overwhelmed in the lineout and hardly won a scrum against the New Zealand two-man front-row. The All Blacks were still employing the rover, as they had done on the previous tour in 1904, and the tactic was still causing mighty controversy.

The Second Test was played at Athletic Park, Wellington, and the conditions were wet and muddy – hardly a rare situation in that historic but windswept ground over the years. New Zealand took the lead with a penalty before Jack Jones, the centre from Pontypool, scored an excellent try. The final score was 3-3, giving the touring team some hope of rescuing the series.

This hope was shattered when, at Potter's Park, Auckland, the team were overwhelmed 29-0 in the Third Test and their strict adherence to the laws cost them yet again when Boxer Harding, the captain, suffered a serious injury as early as the third minute and the team had to play with only 14 men.

Over the tour as a whole, and while the party could not call on anything like the glorious back division talent of the 1904 party, there were two outstanding players in Jack and Tuan Jones, brothers from Pontypool. Fred Jackson, the giant West Country forward, was ranked as high as Harding, but

A souvenir programme from the 1908 tour.

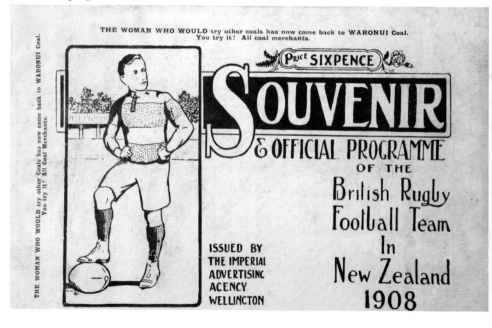

the team was short of depth and quality and duly subsided, and already the triumphs of the pioneer tours were becoming something of a distant memory. Life experiences were plentiful, but sporting glories were becoming thin on the ground.

ARTHUR 'BOXER' HARDING (Wales)
Toured: 1904 & 1908

The first point that struck me on landing at Wellington was the intense interest taken in rugby football by the men, women and children of the Dominion. In Wales we are sometimes accused of giving too much attention to the game, but the Welsh people cannot for one instant be compared to New Zealand where enthusiasm is concerned.

This indicates a keenness of the public which to us appears to be practically approaching a religion, whether this is beneficial to the sport or not is open to doubt. Personally I think that it tends to make the game far too keen... it seemed to us quite a common thing for a considerable amount of money to be exchanged over here in the way of wagers, which is decidedly of no advantage to the sport.

Coming to the players themselves, we could not help noticing the fine state of fitness in which every man appeared to take the field. Teams in New Zealand are in much better training than at home... where a man practises twice a week only... and such thing as getting a side to live together for a week prior to a match – no matter of what importance – is absolutely out of the question and unheard of, and would not be tolerated by the governing bodies.

Forward play in New Zealand in the loose is very good, dribbling rushes being a strong feature of many of the best packs. Lineout work is also in high order throughout, however, in scrummaging, I think I can claim without any self-conceit, that we are superior to them....

The team line-ups for the West Coast and Buller match.

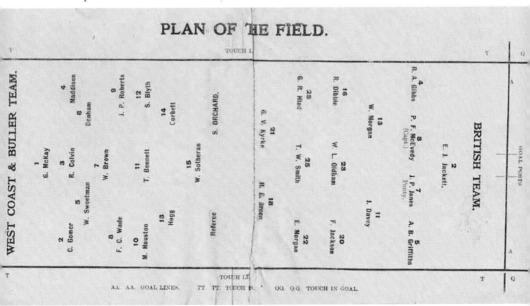

Unfortunately, with regard to the New Zealand backs, in many instances our players have been prevented from receiving the ball by opponents standing over him and in some cases tackling him. At times when we have been in our opponents' territory, their backs are lined up actually on our side of the scrummage ready to bring down our men before the ball has left the forwards' feet.

We have also repeatedly had our attack nipped in the bud by the wing-forward getting on our scrum-half before he received the ball, and have been astonished by the latitude allowed to this player in almost every game… he is responsible for spoiling much open play after possession has been fairly gained by his opposing forwards and when defending he is breaking the rule governing obstruction on the field by deliberately preventing the opposing half getting round the scrummage.

Every important rugby man here seems to be anxious to make the wing-forward position a thing of the past, admitting that it is harmful for the game. Yet funnily enough, they look to the English Union to take action when at the same time they know that the position only exists in New Zealand.

GEORGE HARNETT (Manager)
Toured: 1908

Well… I have been very much impressed with the prosperity of New Zealand; with the beauty of its country, hospitality of the people and the enthusiasm displayed for

sport, particularly in the direction of rugby football.

Generally speaking, the hotels were very comfortable. There was one thing, however, that struck us very much, and that was the difference between the hotels in the prohibited districts and those where licence rules. The comparison is all in favour of the licensed places, notably this was the case in Invercargill, where we were surprised to find that no licensed houses existed – they were all temperance boarding houses.

I have also been very impressed with the loyalty of the New Zealanders to the sovereign, and this also applies equally to the Maori people.

To start with, (rugby) it is your religion… For so it has struck me after

A cartoon depicting Percy Down falling into Auckland harbour.

touring the colony. The whole soul of New Zealand, young and old, seems centred around that bit of inflated leather when it gets going... There is a tendency to roughness but this should be dealt with by the strong hand... And certainly, that wing-forward (rover) is nothing but an obstruction in some districts, and is always off-side.

I do not consider that the practice of teams leaving the field at half-time is a good one. At home, this being quite unknown, both sides merely taking a breather at 'lemon-time'.

Crowds at the Auckland match.

CHAPTER EIGHT

PUPIL TURNED MASTER
1910
SOUTH AFRICA

Clem Thomas, *the great Lion of 1955 in South Africa who became an outstanding rugby journalist, wrote of the growing dominance of the southern hemisphere teams over the Lions: 'No longer was it a question of missionary work, and spreading the message that rugby was the best character building game of all, with its huge demand on physical and mental bravery. These, together with its more intellectually stimulating requirements, were all qualities which saw the colonials, tempered in hard and tough environments, taking to the game like ducks to water. It has often occurred to me that rugby always seems to find its spiritual home where life is at its toughest and most unsophisticated, as in those southern hemisphere places.'*

By 1910 as the Lions prepared to travel on another heroic South African odyssey, they knew they were no longer travelling as favourites and teachers. This brought about a few improvements in emphasis. The team, captained by Dr Tom Smyth and managed by Walter Cail and Walter Rees, was the first fully representative British/Irish side to tour and the first under the official auspices of the Four Home Unions.

The team wore a distinctive blue jersey with the Home Unions quartered crest. A concession was also made to the severity of the fixtures because Test weeks became largely fallow, with no midweek game to sap the touring party. However, even though it was an official party in every respect, it did not mean that the finest players could all take a leave of absence from their working lives and their families.

The party that eventually mustered was 26-strong and was reinforced by official replacements when injuries struck; but of the original party, less than half were international players and, indeed, arguably one of the most talented tourists turned out to be Jack Spoors, the Bristol centre or fly-half who scored a try in each of the three Tests, but who was uncapped.

But the dominant figure of the tour, in the eyes of both teams, was C H 'Cherry' Pillman, who was a back-row forward with Blackheath and England. It is recorded that the South African captain, Billy Millar, considered Pillman to be the greatest back-row forward of all time and Clem Thomas wrote that Pillman 'revolutionised the South African concept of forward play.' Thomas also suggests that Pillman was the template for brilliant back-row forwards of the Springbok future in Hennie Muller, Doug Hopwood, Jan Ellis and others.

Remarkably, with injuries decimating the squad towards the end of the tour, the redoubtable Pillman was pressed into service at fly-half, from where he played a wonderful role in a famous win in the Second Test.

Opposite: The 1910 tourists before departure.

Perhaps the other remarkable aspect of the party was that there were seven players from the Newport club, which was to become one of the finest nurseries for the Lions throughout history. The tour was typically gruelling in terms of travel and opposition strength, with three Test matches against South Africa and most of the most powerful provincial teams were played twice – notably Transvaal, Western Province, Border, Natal and Griqualand West.

The trips to Kimberley to play the Griquas were always an experience for the touring team. By 1910 the hysteria of the diamond era in the town was lessening, but the alien conditions, the dust swirling thickly over the bare pitch, never failed to cause a sense of wonder in the visitors, whatever the tour.

There was a very fine early win on tour against a Western Province team that had been practically invincible for several years and this hinted that had the team managed to stay intact and more rested, then they could have been competitive. But those injuries took their toll, the team declined and of the 16 games they played before the First Test match, they lost five and drew one.

The First Test took place at the Wanderers ground in Johannesburg and the touring team gave a monumentally brave performance. They played in the absence of the great Pillman, who was injured. They trailed by 11-3 at one stage but Spoors scored a try and Jack Jones, who had made the previous Lions tour, dropped the goal and this rally left the match balanced there at 11-10. But then a late Springbok rush brought a try for Carl 'Cocky' Hahn. It came after a clever kick ahead from Douglas Morkel, who was from one of South African sport's most famous families – ten of the clan won South African caps between 1903 and 1928.

The Second Test match took place at the Crusader ground, Port Elizabeth, and ended in a memorable victory, inspired by the restored Pillman playing at fly-half. South Africa led 3-0 at

The 1910 tour party.

half-time but then tries by Spoors and Maurice Neale, both inspired by Pillman, and a conversion by Pillman, gave them victory, one of the finest in Lions history.

Millar, the South African captain, paid an amazing tribute to his illustrious opponent. 'My memories of this game are all dwarfed by Pillman's brilliance. I confidently assert that, if ever a man can be said to have won an international match through his own unorthodox and lone-handed efforts, it can be said of the inspired, black-haired Pillman I played against on the Crusader ground on August 27, 1910.'

The deciding Test of the series took place at Newlands in Cape Town, and yet again the luck of the touring party was almost brutal. They lost Stanley Williams, the fullback from Newport, who was later to be capped by England, to a serious injury early on in the game and had to play the rest of the Test with 14 men. It may seem odd to the younger rugby follower, to whom the system and concept of replacements are a given, that the aspirations of a team could so easily be ruined.

South Africa took full advantage and even though Spoors maintained his record of a try per Test, it was not nearly enough. South Africa scored tries through Gideon Roos, Percy Allport, Freddie Luyt and 'Koot' Reyneke, while Dougie Morkel converted three of these and landed a penalty goal for a convincing 21-5 victory that secured the series.

The Lions' failure had been, in many respects, gallant, but the suspicion through history's perspective is that the sheer length and severity of the tours had begun to mitigate against victory for the Home Unions' teams; but also that the discipline and dedication of the players from the hosting countries exposed the cavalier and socialite approach of those who travelled so far south to play their rugby.

It was to be 14 years until the Lions toured again. Eleven young men who had taken part in the pioneer years were killed in the First World War, and from the 1910 party, three players were to be lost in battle within a few years of returning home from their South African sporting adventure.

Noel Humphreys, who played five matches on tour, was born in Bridgend and became a captain in the tank corps and won a Military Cross, before dying of wounds in 1918. Eric Milroy, nicknamed 'Puss', played four games on tour as a replacement. He was a lieutenant in the Black Watch and was killed during the Battle of the Somme in 1916. The third was Phillip Waller, who played no fewer than 23 games on tour. He was born in Bath, stayed in South Africa after the 1910 tour and served in the South African Heavy Artillery. He was killed in action at Arras in 1917.

One of the other fine forwards in the 1910 party was also to die soon afterwards. Harry Jarman, one of the Newport seven, threw himself

Charles Henry 'Cherry' Pillman.

into the path of a runaway coal wagon at a South Wales colliery as it rattled towards some children playing in its path. He was badly wounded, and contemporary accounts hold that he saved lives. He died shortly afterwards from his injuries.

It had been a long time since one of the touring teams had been successful on the sporting field. But it is no exaggeration to say that the early tours were full of the finest of men.

ALEX FOSTER (Ireland)
Toured: 1910

We boarded the *Edinburgh Castle* at Southampton, all full of *joie de vivre* and eager to see the world...

My impressions tend to be blurred but much still remains perfectly distinct – the glorious sweep of Table Bay and the lift of Table Mountain, a star throwing a path of light across the bay to the liner at 4 a.m.; the brown, rolling veldt; the Buffalo River; sea bathing at Durban; Groot Constantia wine farm; the South West Cape ostrich farms; the valleys and heights of the Tugela; the mines at Kimberley and Johannesburg; Sunday mornings in the kaffir compounds with tom toms booming and war paint ablaze; the dust storms that plagued us in training as we worked our way up country; the grand line of the Drakensberg; the battlefield at Magersfontein strewn, after all those years, with cartridge cases and scraps of shell; and last and chiefly the stupendous sight of the Victoria Falls and the boiling gorge below.

The first match was played at Mossel Bay and we then had to face the opposition of four first class sides in Cape Town. The famous Western Province team had not... been beaten for 13 years. Excitement ran high in Cape Town that fortnight as we won the first two matches, drew against Cape Town and won the last and toughest, against the Western Province itself. That was a glorious game – I think I have never played in a keener one – and we just managed to win by the narrow margin of a goal to a try... We left Cape Town in high feather.

The hopes were soon to be dashed. At Kimberley against Griqualand West, we were astonished to see the field there devoid of grass and still more astonished to find that for the first 15 minutes of the game we were completely puffed and could not raise a gallop. We had reckoned without the altitude and lost by eight points to nil. Another effect of the altitude which we found disconcerting was a great length of the kicks. I well remember dropping a goal in practice at Kimberley, from over the halfway line. I can hardly do it in Ireland from 40 yards out. Douglas Morkel had all our hearts in our mouths in any match he played against us for a penalty might produce the uncanny spectacle of Douglas sniping at our posts from his own 25 yard line.

Conditions under which a South African team (plays) in the British Isles are... easier than those which a British team in South Africa has to face. First, many South African grounds were so hard that our list of casualties was always heavy. Elbows and knees were skinned in spite of elbow guards and reinforced kneecaps; you were lucky if the wounds did not fester... Eric Milroy, who joined us late... contracted dangerous poisoning from gravel rash. I would strongly urge all touring teams to travel accompanied by a medical man...

The First Test was as fine a spectacle as anyone could wish to see, a bright sky with play surging from end to end and each side scoring in turn, more than once. My chief recollection of that afternoon is the superb play of C H Hahn on the left wing (for South Africa). He ran like a buck.

In the Second Test on the grassy ground in Port Elizabeth, we were back in our element and won a fine game by eight points to three. But in the final Test at Cape Town, we suffered a heavy reverse by 21 points to 5.

Charles Pillman and Tom Smyth were wing-forwards as good as any who have since appeared and the wing-forward has not been born who could stop J. Ponty Jones from darting through the opposition when things were looking black...

In 1910, the standard of South African football was high. The players were almost all fast and the game was fast. The forwards attempted little or no dribbling but they were formidable in the scrum and at the lineout. We, on the other hand, played a mixed game, combining forward rushes with back play.

I cannot conclude without a word of grateful appreciation not only for the kindness which South Africans conspired to show us, but the high sportsmanship we found during the game in every district of the Union. I would not have missed the tour of 1910 for a fortune.

Tour captain, Tom Smyth.

CHAPTER NINE

BENNIE'S BOOT
1924

SOUTH AFRICA

THERE HAD *been seven tours in the 22 years since the first in 1888, but after the 1910 party returned home, there were to be only three more tours in the next 40 years. The privations in Britain after the end of the First World War, not to mention the enormous number of casualties who were rugby men of all levels, may for a time have depressed the appetite, and at times of economic hardship it was even more difficult than it had been before for the team to be representative of the strength of rugby at home.*

Indeed, the fact that the 1924 team was missing such a large number of top players, that they lost heavily and that one of the players (Rowe Harding) doubted the value of such tours unless a full side could be chosen, may also have contributed to longer gaps between tours and the general loss of confidence. Defeats were now commonplace, attitudes of hosts and visitors vastly different.

But the 1924 team at least continued the Lions heritage under the captaincy of Dr Ronald Cove-Smith, a noted physician, and an England lock first capped in 1921. Cove-Smith, a character and a grand forward, was on the winning side in 22 of his 25 appearances for England.

However, it was not an era of any great strength in the Home Unions and the 1924 tour was immersed in mediocrity, with only nine wins from the 21 games, and with a defeat in the Test series by three matches to nil, with one draw – although it must be said that the tourists put up a terrific fight in the series, which is reckoned in South African rugby history to be one of the most attractive to have been played on their shores.

The list of the players who were not available to make the tour was lengthy, and probably doomed Cove-Smith's men from the start. Wavell Wakefield, the great and influential English forward and later Lord Wakefield, was among those who could not spare the time and it is a telling fact that Wakefield was never to make a Lions tour. George Stephenson, of Ireland, and Leslie Gracie of Scotland were among the other giants of the day who could not travel. The older days of the gentleman adventurer tourist were receding.

The other problem was that because of the gap between tours, none of the players had any experience of South African conditions and so were, like the pioneer tourists, taken aback by such aspects as the dust of Kimberley, the length of journeys in between matches and the sheer size of the country.

Opposite: Lions captain, Dr Ronald Cove-Smith, with the captain of the *Edinburgh Castle* en route to South Africa.

There were several significant aspects to the visit and the first was that the team were called, officially, Lions. They still played in blue jerseys, but the fact that the tour tie bore the crest of a lion gave them the name that was to resonate through history. They were called the British Lions, even though there was a strong Irish element in the team led by James Daniel (Jammie) Clinch, then in his early twenties but to go down in history as one of rugby's most vivid characters and hardest forwards – though the injury problems of the tour party were such that he also played in the backs. Tom Voyce, the versatile England wing forward also turned out at fullback and on the wing, was the top scorer on tour, embellishing his reputation as one of the finest players in the game.

Lions tours had now been going on for long enough for the sons of earlier Lions to make tours – Jammie Clinch was the son of Andrew Clinch, who toured with the 1896 team.

The tour was not the birth of the Lions, as we have seen that took place in 1888, whatever that party was called. But now it was official. The new status, however, did not improve their fortune. 29 players set out but the team was cruelly afflicted by injury throughout, and at last the authorities realised that more cover should be taken on tour, especially in the specialist positions of hooker and scrum-half.

The itinerary was heavy and onerous, with 21 games in all, with midweek games in the week of Test matches. With all the travelling involved, it left the Lions on a hiding to nothing and underpowered yet again.

And yet gain, the question arose as to whether the Lions had really come to dedicate themselves absolutely to victory in the Test series or whether they had come in part for a social event. Most of them clearly played their hearts out on the field but famously, Rowe Harding, the Swansea and Wales three-quarter who was later to become a judge, did point out that 'many unkind things were said about our wining and dining.'

It was Harding who wondered if the tours were all they should be at the time. He said that attitudes had to change, and that 'poor performances damage the respect you receive from the country you are visiting.' He added: 'There has always been too much condescension by the British rugby authorities about our attitudes, both to our continental neighbours and to the colonies.'

Harding's main reservation was the weakness of the tour party relative to the strengths of rugby at home, but he was raising an important point in the difference in perception in the attitudes of the visitor and the visited which, if he only knew, remained a salient observation of practically every tour until the advent of professionalism. In one sense, it was gentlemen versus players.

The South African teams they met had few such problems. The Lions began in defeat against the Western Province town and country team and although they won their next four games on the trot their weaknesses were found out. In a melancholy period in the middle of the tour, they played eight games, including the First Test match in Johannesburg, without winning one of them.

The Lions also met a man who was to become a legend in South African history – Bennie Osler, one of the greatest kickers that the game has seen. He had the ability to kick penalties and drop-goals from vast distances, and he probably began the lineage of great Springbok kickers to break the hearts of so many opposition teams over the years, right to the present day. And, as ever, there is a resonance in history. Through the decades South Africa's great kickers have always been controversial, with many questioning whether their emphasis on kicking denied opportunities for their backs. Cove-Smith brought up this very question in his published thoughts after the tour.

Also in the South African team for the 1924 series was Pierre Albertyn, one of the greatest attacking centres of the era, and another man who gave the Lions more trouble then they could handle.

But it was Osler who dictated the tactical course of the First Test, played at Kingsmead in Durban. His early drop-goal gave his team a lead that they never relinquished. Even though Arthur Blakiston, a forward from Blackheath, scored a try for the Lions, and although they attacked for long periods, the Springboks held out.

The Second Test of the series in Johannesburg was remarkable for the interest it stirred after so long without a Lions visit. As had happened on a couple of occasions on the past tours, the crowd broke down one of the surrounding fences and poured through, taking the stadium well beyond its advertised capacity of 15,000, and it was to be the home spectators who left happier. South Africa won by a thumping 17-0 and, with what was to become a familiar combination of Osler's tactical kicking and the power of the home pack, the Springboks demolished the touring team.

The best performance by the Lions came in the Third Test at the Crusader ground, Port Elizabeth, which was drawn 3-3. The match demonstrated some of the realities of touring life with the Lions and their ill luck with injury because the try scorer in the match was Bill Cunningham, a former Irish fly-half. He had emigrated to South Africa but was called up when a rash of injuries cost the Lions some leading backs.

The Fourth Test, played at Newlands in Cape Town, was won by the Springboks but the game went down as one of the most exciting seen on South African soil. The great England forward, Voyce, scored a try, as did Stanley Harris. The Lions tried to take on the Springboks' power with their own pace and deftness and it was only when Jack Slater scored on the final whistle for South Africa that the victory was guaranteed.

The 1924 tour party gathers at Waterloo before departure.

Statistically, the Lions had the worst record of all touring parties and scored the fewest points. After so long without a tour, the tradition had revived strongly but on the field, the defeats had become worrying.

DR RONALD COVE-SMITH (England)
Toured: 1924

On June 30, 1924, the first British rugby touring team to leave the British Isles after the Great War set sail from Southampton to visit South Africa. There was considerable difficulty in selecting the representative side but in the end 29 players were selected, and the forwards formed a formidable array. Behind the scrum, there was less experience, but it was hoped that the useful blend of youth and enthusiasm would soon settle down into a prolific scoring machine.

Unfortunately, none of the players, nor even the manager, Harry Packer, had any knowledge of the climatic conditions that have to be faced and before long our store of stalwarts was considerably depleted....

With the exception of Griqualand West, who were surprisingly weak, close games were played in all the first seven matches and we returned from the dusty track into Rhodesia to draw with Transvaal. It was here that the staleness of the overplaying of such stalwarts as (Herbert) Waddell and (Dan) Drysdale became apparent but without adequate reserves little else could be done. Against Natal on the eve of the First Test match, only seven forwards were available so Vincent Griffiths was deputed to act as a rover and a draw was eventually forced.

In a grand game in Durban that was in doubt right to the end, the robust (Wally) Clarkson scored a very fine try... Here again, ill luck told as (Reg) Maxwell dislocated

The tourists gather for a photograph before training.

his shoulder and left us with only two centres and two fly-halves for the remainder of our visit.

Had it not been for the graciousness of the SA board in allowing us to bring out Harold Davies and also to include Bill Cunningham, who we met in Johannesburg, the tour might well have come to a sudden stop through lack of personnel... Looking back, one cannot help but laugh at the subterfuges to which we were forced to resort in order to place 15 fit men in the field.

Tours such as this, where everything is new and fresh, live long in the memory. The veritable kaleidoscope of ever-changing impressions would be liable to produce mental indigestion, even though the high standards of South African hospitality strain the most robust gastric organs. The hospitality extended to us throughout was extraordinary – in fact, almost excessive.

Some incidents stand out sufficiently strongly to dwarf the others... Perhaps the most noticeable of these was the quietly efficient captaincy of Pierre Albertyn in the Test matches. He always seemed to have his players well in hand and able to produce the requisite thrust at the right moment.

Bennie Osler was just making a name for himself but even then tended to kick more than was warranted... I was astounded to see (in later years) to what extent these kicking propensities had stultified South African three-quarter play... The main glory of the team lay in its pack.

The inherent weakness of our team could not be covered up for long and manfully though the fellows tried, they were no real match for South Africa in the Test games, where superior speed and experience outside the scrum eventually took its toll. The impossibility of coping with such a heavy programme... travelling upcountry, sleeping on trains and too little exercise are enervating and soon sap the strength of an athlete.

ROWE HARDING (Wales)
Toured: 1924

The long train journeys (often of 48 hours' duration), the hard ground and a heavy casualty list had taken a heavy toll of players unaccustomed to such conditions.

It is not difficult to analyse the reasons for our failure. Dissipation had nothing to do with it. I will not deny there was occasionally what was termed a 'blind' when we were thoughtless and careless of what other people said or thought of us and that contributed to our unpopularity. The real reason for our failure was that we were not good enough to go abroad as the representatives of the playing strength of these islands. It is not sufficient to send abroad some players of international standard and others who were only second class. Every member of the team must be absolutely first class or disaster is bound to overtake it.

CHAPTER TEN

PLAYING TO THE LAWS
1930
NEW ZEALAND AND AUSTRALIA

B Y NOW *it was firmly established that the Lions tradition gave the journey and the experience of a lifetime to those taking part. But some of the other realities of life as a Lion were underlined again on this tour where, once again, too many of the Test and other major matches were lost for the venture to be termed anything other than a sporting failure. This after a win in the First Test against New Zealand, which had briefly raised hopes.*

One recurring difficulty was the fact that the touring teams in this era between the wars were often effectively reduced to their second or even third best team by the end of the tour and, in fact, sometimes even at the start. In 1929, 28 players were provisionally invited to make the tour, carefully chosen from the best of the home nations. Of those 28, only nine actually embarked for New Zealand. When they got there, they lost Wilfred Sobey, the outstanding scrum-half and the tour vice-captain, in the first game. He never played again on tour. Sobey's partnership with Roger Spong, the superb fly-half, was meant to be the driving force of the party.

Wavell Wakefield, one of the great men of England rugby history, had not played for England since 1927. But such was his enormous status in the game that he was invited to captain the tour party. George Stephenson, the Irish captain, was also earmarked as a leading player. But both Wakefield and Stephenson had to withdraw from consideration as they could not spare the time and, as mentioned previously, Wakefield was never to make a Lions tour.

So Doug Prentice, the forward of Leicester and England, a future secretary of the Rugby Football Union, was chosen to lead the party in their absence. His philosophy is enshrined in an article he wrote after the tour, which would hardly resonate with the driven and dedicated young men of the modern day. Touring sides, he said: 'Do not make the journey with the sole object of winning all its matches, or setting up new scoring records. The principles and ideals which guided the founders of the Rugby Union cannot be stressed too forcibly. Rugby should and must be played for the love of the game.'

Perhaps oddly (or perhaps not), it was to be another 50 years before the next Englishman was chosen as Lions captain – Bill Beaumont in South Africa in 1980. At least Big Bill had more notice than Prentice. He was told that he was to captain the tour in the lounge of the Hotel Metropole in London on the night before the party sailed to New Zealand. 'Look here Doug,' one of the officials said. 'We think you'd better skipper this side.'

Opposite: Lord Bledisloe shakes hands with Jack Bassett during a pre-match line-up, 1930.

Of the 29 players, all but six had been capped before departure, so there was at least a leavening of experience, but class was lacking, and especially power and organisation up front. A familiar refrain. The tour was also famous, as were many other tours, for strident disagreement and controversy surrounding the laws of the game – especially a tendency for New Zealand and Australia to tinker with international rugby law to suit their own particular environment or preference. Not unknown in the 21st century.

Some examples: it was at the time not permissible for teams to leave the field at half-time and replacements were categorically not allowed – if they had been, then the course of several Lions tours may well have been different. Yet both the half-time practice and the use of replacements were commonplace throughout the tour and they infuriated the Lions and especially the hawkish James 'Bim' Baxter, the manager, who conducted a campaign of rectitude against the New Zealand authorities throughout the tour.

And as on the previous Lions' visit, the antics of the New Zealand wing-forward/ rover and their two-three-two scrum were bitterly contentious. In 1930, the home team used Cliff Porter, the back-row forward, as a disruptive rover.

Famously, Baxter, a stickler for the law, enlisted the support of the RFU on returning home and succeeded in forcing through the International Rugby Board a scrummaging law which made it compulsory to have three men in the front-row, forced New Zealand rugby to abandon their old diamond-shaped scrum and returned the rover to his position in the scrum where he belonged.

On tour, the height of the dispute was reached when Baxter accused Porter of being 'a cheat'. Ted McKenzie, a selector of the New Zealand team, was to strike back later in the tour at a post-match function in which he accused the Lions of illegalities. Carl Aarvold tried to interrupt the speech and

The 1930 tour party.

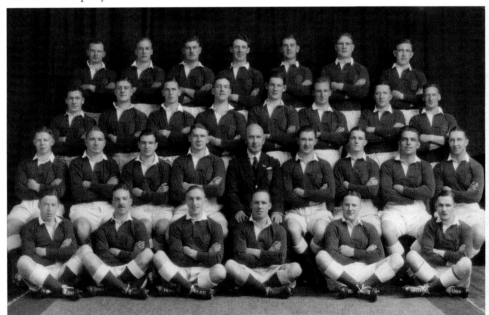

McKenzie angrily remonstrated. Some historians have seen the laws disputes of the era as akin to the Bodyline controversy in cricket.

There were successes on the field. The party raised those high hopes by winning a thrilling First Test against New Zealand in Dunedin, and in general the team were popular in the two hosting countries for the brand of exciting rugby they played and for the thrilling individual bursts that roused the home crowds.

Clem Thomas wrote that the tour was still essentially a middle-class escapade, and that each tourist had to take a dinner jacket, chiefly to wear on a six-week boat journey to New Zealand when players were required to dress for dinner on board. Tourists also had to take £80 spending money, so the tiny working-class Welsh element on tour were effectively sponsored by their clubs, who in that era would have an informal (and top-secret) collection to ensure that their local heroes could tour.

There is no doubt that socialising was again a high priority, forcing some players to defend some of the behaviour on tour in later years. Clem Thomas wrote that they were 'a team popular with the opposite sex due to the number of very good-looking men in the party.'

The trip out was made via the Panama Canal and, as Thomas pointed out, there was no coach, no doctor, no physiotherapist, no back-up of any kind. Prentice was expected to act as coach.

As often happens on Lions tours, the captain was not one of the outstanding players and indeed, Prentice played in only one of the four Test matches against New Zealand plus the one Test in Australia. The tour allowance was three shillings a day and this was not doled out in cash, but in the

The 1930 Lions meet at Waterloo Station before departure.

form of vouchers that could be exchanged for goods and services in the team hotels. Professionalism was still 65 years in the future.

The party was the first to be known as 'the Lions' from the very start – the 1924 tour had been christened 'Lions' during the trip. The 1930 party wore a badge bearing three Lions on their blue shirts and they carried Lion brooches to present as gifts to well-wishers.

Even though at the time it tended to be the host nations who took the lead in new tactics, the Lions at least unveiled one new ploy on tour – they used the blindside wing in attack, running off an inside pass from the fly-half after the set piece. The move became known as 'The Morley' after Jack Morley, the Newport and Wales wing who played in three of the Tests against New Zealand on the tour.

The outstanding players on tour were Roger Spong, the England fly-half and the mainspring of a strong attacking back division, and Ivor Jones, the great Welsh back-row forward who had a rare turn of speed, who could fill in at scrum-half and who was also a useful place-kicker. Harry Bowcott, a back from Cambridge University, went on to become a distinguished administrator in Welsh rugby and the chairman of selectors for his country. Bowcott had led Wales at the age of 22. Carl Aarvold, the England wing who was at Cambridge University, had a distinguished legal career and went on to become Recorder of London and the president of the Lawn Tennis Association.

The First Test, which was played in Carisbrook, Dunedin, had been eagerly awaited as it was the first time the Lions had been seen since before the First World War, and although New Zealand seemed likely winners before the game, the Lions played with great resolve and courage – against an All Black team playing in white, because of a clash between the dark blue jerseys of the touring team.

Carl Aarvold (left) and Jack Bassett (right).

The great George Nepia, the remarkable Maori fullback, took part in the match, although he missed the conversion of a try by George Hart, and since James Reeve had scored a first half try for the Lions from a diagonal kick from Spong, it was still level in the dying seconds.

Then the remarkable Jones made one of the most dramatic individual runs in the history of the Lions, bursting from near his own line through the defence, running up to draw Nepia and passing to Jack Morley, who raced on to score the winning try. It was a dramatic moment, one of the finest in Lions history, and it saved the team from being whitewashed.

The Second Test was played in front of a huge crowd at Lancaster Park, Christchurch and although the Lions lost only by 13-10, over the course of the match it was not quite as close as the score suggests. Jones had made another late break leading to a try by Carl Aarvold which Prentice converted and the Lions were pressing at the end. But the series was levelled.

And yet could it have been different? Yet again, the Lions were to rue their misfortune with injury – or perhaps their wish to stick to the rules regarding replacements. Paul Murray, their scrum-half, left the field with a serious shoulder injury in the first half, leaving the Lions to play the rest of the Test with 14 men. Ivor Jones had to move to scrum-half and senior members of the touring party always believed that they could have won had they remained at full strength.

The Lions took the lead in the Third Test when Bowcott's clever approach work led to a try by Jones, but New Zealand pulled clear at 15-5 and eventually went on to win 15-10. As was to happen often, New Zealand won the final Test by a convincing margin, 22-8, scoring four tries in the second half in Wellington and six tries in all.

By now, the Australian leg of the tour was not seen to have quite the status of the former days, which was rather odd since interest amongst Australians still seemed to be high and over 30,000 attended the only Test in Australia, played at the Sydney Cricket Ground. Disappointingly, the Test was won 6-5 by Australia, with Tom Lawton masterminding the victory. Tony Novis scored a try for the Lions, which Prentice converted and in the dying seconds Jones was tackled just a metre short of the try line by Cyril Towers of Australia. Close. But yet again, not close enough.

Jack Bassett looks to evade New Zealand's Don Oliver during the First Test in Dunedin.

Major provincial games were also lost – to Wellington, Canterbury and Auckland, and to New South Wales in Australia. Another chance had slipped by, another team with a certain creativity, a certain style, and a certain attitude to their sport at odds with that of the more stern and dedicated home teams, had been out muscled and beaten.

HARRY BOWCOTT (Wales)
Toured: 1930

At the time of the party announcement I was considered the one certainty to go but when the selection was announced my name wasn't there. I was so fed up that I went with the Cambridge team to France a few weeks before the Lions were due to leave. Then an Irish chap dropped out of the original party. Lo and behold, I was chosen. I'd have been quite happy to have said no. I asked my father, 'Should I go?' He said: 'Of course, you must go.'

I got back from France on the Monday, my father gave me the £80 we all had to pay before departure because I didn't have a penny and I was off to London to join the Lions the following morning for a farewell dinner attended by the Duke of York. Excellent meal, as you can imagine, with more courses and more wine than you get nowadays, and we all shook hands with the future King.

There were no journalists. There would be no urgent messages flashing back to London saying that we'd been naughty boys. We had the place to ourselves.

Nobody had any idea of flying around the world at that time because flying was still a thing of the future. We travelled first class and every player had his own berth for a voyage that lasted five weeks. We had the usual sports on deck. There was the mock court run by the players, but I suppose eating took up most of our time...

DOUG PRENTICE (England)
Toured: 1930

I suppose most people think that a rugby football tour in New Zealand is just a lovely six months holiday. It is, but at the same time there is a great deal of really hard work confronting one. Furthermore, let us remember that a British tour does not make the journey with the sole object of winning all these matches, or setting up new scoring records.

The principles and ideals which guided the founders of the rugby union cannot be stressed too forcibly. Rugby should and must be played for the love of the game. Some are likely to think that this is an unattainable ideal, but I believe that it is a wonderful ideal. Well worth the striving for.

On our first day out we felt a happy little family, and as the tour progressed, so our friendship was cemented. A happy team in which all the men are friends is generally a good one, for each man likes and trusts his fellows and knows they will not let the side down.

When we had rested for a few days (on the voyage to New Zealand) and found our sea legs, arrangements were made to commence training... Physical training classes were organised... and we were pretty thoroughly put through our paces by Lt Tony Novis and

Flight Lt George Beamish, who acted as instructors. At 11 a.m. we had scrum practice, where many knees and elbows were grazed through falling on the hard decks.

HARRY BOWCOTT

For a team of young men, there were times when it was a fairly dismal journey. There weren't many other passengers on ship and the youngest woman on board must have been about 50. I would have to say that it wasn't terribly exciting.

Jack Bassett (the Penarth and Wales fullback, who was to play outstandingly on the tour) was seasick as soon as he got on board. He didn't get out of his sick bed for 10 days. It was entirely mental, if you ask me. No one else suffered.

DOUG PRENTICE

When we finally arrived in New Zealand, we listened to speeches of welcome from various members of the New Zealand Rugby Union at the harbour and later that night we broadcasted to the country. This was easy for me, as I had taken Jimmy Farrell to give them a few Irish-isms, I had Ivor Jones to talk to them in Welsh and Jock Welsh to bring in a few 'Och-Ayes' from Scotland.

The first match was at Wanganui... and proved the most unlucky one for us. Our vice-captain and a very fine scrum-half – Wilfred Sobey – damaged his knee so badly that he did not play a game all throughout the rest of the tour. This was indeed a terrible blow.

I suppose the most exciting game of the tour was the First Test, played in appalling weather at Dunedin; Great Britain scored a try early on from a well-placed cross kick by Spong, taken by Reeve, who after beating Hart, crossed in the corner. Black missed the kick. New Zealand scored soon after, Hart getting a lovely try in the corner after skilfully eluding Reeve and (Jack) Bassett en route. Nepia's attempt at a conversion struck the upright.

Amid tense excitement, a ding-dong struggle was fought right to the last minute, and just when everyone was resigned to the draw with Great Britain defending her line like grim death, Ivor Jones suddenly burst from the scrum with the ball in his hands. He ran like a deer, very cleverly into George Nepia's arms, and just at the right moment passed to Morley, who anticipated the move and was perfectly placed. Then off went Morley on a run of 80 yards, with (Bert) Cooke of Wellington coming across like an express train. It was a thrilling race, with a huge crowd on its feet, and with barely a yard to spare, Morley touched down amidst terrific applause!!! Great Britain had defeated New Zealand.

We had many more exciting and thrilling games, and all were played in the hardest and best spirit.

HARRY BOWCOTT

It was a very cold day for the First Test. There were snow showers before the game and a blizzard during it. We trained at the hotel and it was entirely due to Ivor Jones, the king of the tour, that we got off to a winning start. He broke clear and went all the way down the field so that there was only George Nepia left to stop him. He drew Nepia and slipped the ball to Jack Morley for him to get over in the corner. We had beaten this wonderful team called the All Blacks, much to their disgust. We were delighted. We lost the next three Tests, the third when we were down to 14 men, but if it had not been for poor Sobey, I think we'd have seen them off over the four matches.

DOUG PRENTICE

Golf was played by most of the team and a very fine side we were! I'm not quite sure whether we were not a better golf side than football team. Tommy Knowles had not brought any clubs with him and being left-handed, he had difficulty sometimes in borrowing some. So he bought a set in Dunedin, and one day, when the whole team were on the links, he started off, very proud of his new clubs. On the first short hole, he did a hole in one, amid loud cheers on all sides.

Shooting, too, we found time for. At the dinner after our first game I was asked if I was fond of shooting. I replied that I had shot a rabbit or two in England and loved it. My friend then said: 'Well, come out tomorrow to my place and we'll shoot a few deer.' In a very short time, we had shot a deer each. Deer are vermin in New Zealand and one is paid for shooting them. Very different from deer stalking in Scotland. Wild-pig hunting is also grand sport. George Beamish and I used to get as much of it as we could.

We arrived in Sydney in glorious sunshine and were met by Gordon Shaw, the manager of the Waratahs (party which had toured) in Great Britain in 1927-28, and Ted Thorne, one of that team. I had played against Thorne at Leicester and in that particular game we had 'looked after' one another in the lineout. We had a battle royal that afternoon and the same night, over a friendly pot or two of beer, we discussed the charm of our delightful feud.

I saw him off from the station at Leicester. The following morning as we said goodbye, and the train was steaming out, he shouted: 'We'll meet again some day and when we do we'll have a beer together!' He was as good as his word. Four years later, and 12,000 miles away! These rugger friendships are things which make not only tours worthwhile, but life itself.

HARRY BOWCOTT

We were no better and no worse than the young men of today in our behaviour. We drank a bit and enjoyed female company but we tended to carouse only after matches. Wives would be chasing us and their husbands would be pleased if we looked after them. There was one woman who followed me all over both islands with the permission of her old man. He thought it was an honour, and I never abused it. All the fun of the fair.

The New Zealand public worshipped us. Entertainment and hospitality were laid on for us and I can't ever remember having to buy a drink. After every match we had a dance. There were no bars in the dance halls and no bars outside because they were all shut so we'd go to the tables, which were heavily laden, knowing that a lot more liquor would be stored underneath.

We enjoyed ourselves at the right time. We were never denied alcohol but I don't recall any wild boozing. We had just one law before every game: in bed by 10.

DOUG PRENTICE

Everyone enjoyed every minute of the tour and I believe that the people of New Zealand, and indeed everywhere we went, also enjoyed having us with them. The hospitality shown to us was wonderful in the extreme and I am quite sure that every member of the team has nothing but the happiest possible memories of the tour of 1930.

Ivor Jones.

CHAPTER ELEVEN

TWILIGHT OF THE SPORTING GODS
1938

SOUTH AFRICA

THE 1938 *tour to South Africa took place in the shadow of rising tensions in Europe and elsewhere, with the Nazi party in power in Germany and with the air of menace afflicting international relations. On the sporting front, it was a tour which brought yet another defeat of the Lions in a Test series, on what was their last tour for 12 years, and the last time that they would be decked in blue, before the transition to the fiery red jersey for which they are now famed throughout the world.*

But if it was ultimately a failure, it was also an epic tour, and the Test series against the Springboks restored credibility to rugby in the Four Home Unions and to the whole concept of Lions tours. It was a tour with extraordinary characters on both sides, with magnificent Test matches and great courage in the play of the British and Irish players as they tilted at a magnificent Springbok team while contending with all the usual alien conditions and dusty privations of life on tour in that country.

Incidentally, some of the travel was almost as onerous as it had been for the pioneers in the previous century. As the great Vivian Jenkins wrote: 'More often than not we found ourselves (travelling) on rough, unmade roads with endless corrugations over which the cars had to "skate" at top speed to avoid the occupants being shaken to pieces... I recall spending no fewer than seven nights out of eleven on trains during the Rhodesian part of the tour.'

The Test series was lost by two games to one, with all three matches remarkable in one way or another. There was no shame to lose to the South African team of that era, because they were a team regarded as one of the greatest in South African history, and had just returned from a long tour to Australia and New Zealand with victory in both Test series, having suffered defeat in only one provincial game (against New South Wales) and one international (the First Test against New Zealand). There were no World Cups in that era, of course, but clearly South Africa were world champions.

The South Africans were captained by Danie Craven, who was already seen as a brilliant rugby thinker and tactician, and who in New Zealand had become famous for the development of his dive pass at scrum-half. Craven remains after his death both a celebrated and controversial figure in South African history and society. He was to go on to become vastly influential as a South African coach, as

---

Opposite: The 1938 Lions – the last to play in blue.

a lecturer and a professor of the laws, and to be arguably the most famous rugby administrator the game has seen, especially as the man at the forefront in the years when South Africa were barred from international rugby, and in the years when they returned to the fold.

Also in the team met by the Lions was the great Gerry Brand, the fullback and a monstrous kicker who had scored 209 points in Australia and New Zealand and who, even with the relatively basic rugby balls of the era, could regularly put over kicks from 60 yards or more. There was also 'Boy' Louw, the great South African forward who, like Craven, is still regarded as one of the all-time greats. Brand and Louw were in their twilight career years, but still outstanding players.

Against this array of formidable talent, the young touring team – selectors at the time still retained the nonsensical notion that players who had reached 30 were probably over the hill – was led by Sammy Walker, the Irish forward (who played both prop and second-row for Ireland and the Lions). It almost goes without saying that many leading players were unavailable to tour – among them were Wilf Wooller and Cliff Jones, two outstanding backs from Wales; Ray Longland and Fred Huskisson, grand England forwards, plus the celebrated Wilson Shaw of Scotland.

Yet the Lions could also field all-time greats of the game. Among their own celebrated contingent were Vivian Jenkins, then a young fullback from London Welsh, who was in the class of Brand as a goalkicker, and who was later to become one of the most respected writers and commentators in the history of the game. There was also Bill Travers, the hooker from Newport and Wales, whose father, George, had hooked for Wales in their famous win over New Zealand in 1905. Travers established a friendship with the giant and vivid Irish forward, Blair Mayne, who was later to become a war hero, winning the Distinguished Service Order and three bars – each bar awarded for separate acts of heroism. He was also awarded the Legion d'Honneur and the Croix de Guerre by the French Government for his work in the liberation of France. He is seen now as one of the founding troops of the Special Air Service and is the subject of a campaign to posthumously upgrade his DSO to a Victoria Cross for an action after which his citation was signed by Field Marshal Montgomery. He remains one of the most decorated soldiers of the Second World War.

The 1938 tour party.

By all accounts, the combination of the two forwards set new standards in rumbustious behaviour on the field. However, both Jenkins and Mayne were to suffer injury, with Jenkins missing the Second and Third Tests.

The Lions also had in Haydn Tanner at scrum-half a player with claims to be one of the finest in his position in Welsh history. Yet Tanner did suffer injury on tour and the contribution of Jimmy Giles, the Coventry and England scrum-half, was essential to tour momentum. His versatility saw him play at centre in a Test, and also at fly-half in the provincial games.

And, perhaps oddly, there were three players who were to go on to have distinguished careers in rugby administration – Bill Clement of Wales, became a powerful secretary of the Welsh Rugby Union; Stan Couchman, became a president of the Rugby Football Union in the 1970s; and Harry McKibbin, from a famous Irish rugby family, was also to serve the game in several top administrative posts.

Most Lions tours tended to bring some kind of technical advancement to the game and the gift from 1938 was South Africa's development of the 3-4-1 scrum formation instead of the 3-2-3 formation. They found that to move the flankers up to pack on the props, and developing the role of the Eighthman, or No 8, made the pack far stronger.

As far as the Lions were concerned, one of the lessons they learned yet again was that injury will always be a problem on the hard and fast grounds of South Africa and that cover for the specialist positions of hooker and scrum-half was absolutely essential. It was still the era when the team travelled by ship. No rapid replacements were available.

The touring team played 24 matches in all, losing two Tests and four other games in their provincial programme. They played two brutal games against Transvaal, one of which they won; but even to this day it still seems staggering that they would undertake a tour of such severity with only 29 players. In other words, they did not even have cover for every position, nor did they have any prospect of rapid reinforcement from the old country.

Aboard the *Stirling Castle*, en route for South Africa.

The Lions were kept in the hunt in the First Test in Johannesburg with three fine penalties from Jenkins. It was a tremendous game, played in front of a crowd of 36,000, and South Africa eventually ran out winners by 26-12. They scored four excellent tries, two from Dai Williams on the wing and one each from Fanie Louw and Tony Harris.

The ball soared through the thin air of the high veldt. One of the penalties by Jenkins came from eight yards inside his only half and one of the constituent parts of the 14 points scored by the prodigious Brand was a drop-goal kicked from way out on the touchline. The absence of Travers, who had been concussed in the previous match against Transvaal, may just have been the decisive factor.

The Second Test, played in Port Elizabeth, was easily won by South Africa by 19-3 although arguably the most memorable aspect was the ferocious heat. Jenkins always asserted that the temperature was well into the 90s, somewhat freakish even for the resort city of Port Elizabeth.

South Africa's juggernaut pack dominated proceedings in the furnace-like conditions and the series was lost, but considerable consolation came at Newlands in Cape Town when the Third Test was won 21-16 by the Lions in a match still regarded as one of the greatest in the histories of both South Africa and the Lions.

At half-time, the Lions trailed by 13-3, in those days a considerable margin. Yet gradually, they began to make inroads up front, and a converted try by Gerald 'Beef' Dancer followed by a penalty by McKibbin brought them to within two points. Bob Alexander scored another try for the Lions to put them ahead, Freddy Turner of South Africa regained the lead with a penalty but then Charlie Grieve, the fullback from Oxford University and Scotland deputising for the injured Jenkins, dropped a goal – in those years worth four points.

The Lions scored again in their wonderful second half revival when forward Laurie Duff, of Glasgow Academicals and Scotland, forced his way over the line. In a dramatic finale, a South African try by Williams was ruled out for a forward pass and the Lions held on for a magnificent victory.

Vivian Jenkins kicks a penalty to touch against Transvaal.

In the final analysis, with key players left at home and others injured, they had fought a magnificent battle against the best team in the world, they provided wonderfully attractive play and were highly popular around the country. Lions tours and most forms of top sport now went into cold storage for the duration of the Second World War and its aftermath.

But there were enough warm memories in the hearts of touring teams and hosting nations alike, to ensure the resumption of the grand traditions was to be a formality.

VIVIAN JENKINS (Wales)
Toured: 1938

The team travelled to and from South Africa by sea and internally in the Union almost solely by rail. I recall spending no fewer than seven nights out of 11 on trains during the Rhodesian part of the tour.

Our shorts were so long – they reached almost down to the knee – that they caused a certain amusement and were given a rude nickname by the South African public.

At Cape Town, a well-known Springbok forward appeared (by invitation of the Lions management) to take charge of a scrummaging practice. Eventually Bill Travers would have none of it. 'What I learned from my father is good enough for me,' he said. Travers had always packed down with his arms over those of the men outside him. The Springbok was advising that he should use the arms-under method. Anyhow, Travers did not change his methods, and proved to be one of the most successful hookers ever to visit the Union.

HARRY BOWCOTT (1930 Lion, recalling the 1938 tour)

Blair Mayne and old Bill Travers, the Welsh hooker who was a very tough boy too, would put on seamen's jerseys, go down to the docks in Cape Town, wait until someone would say something rude about them and then demolish them! That was their idea of a night out. Blair was the heavyweight champion of the Irish universities. Magnificent physique, and a very quiet fellow you thought wouldn't hurt a fly – until you saw him roused. Mad as a hatter.

Vivian Jenkins.

VIVIAN JENKINS

Both games against Transvaal were tremendously hard and in the first the British team ended the match with only 12 men. Fly-half Jeff Reynolds, left-wing Bill Clement and centre Basil Nicholson were all injured. Thus hooker Travers had only five forwards with him at one time but miraculously still managed to hook the ball. In the second match, which was equally fierce, Travers himself was badly concussed. As a result he had to miss the First Test which we lost 12-26. There is no knowing what a difference the presence of Travers might have made.

Gerry Brand played opposite me in the First Test. He was the most accurate goalkicker I have ever known, and admits that his longest of all was the one he put over in the First Test at Ellis Park against the 1938 Lions. It was a penalty kick on the halfway line and on the edge of the touchline. 'I wanted to kick for touch,' Gerry told me, 'but Danie Craven said: "Have a shot at goal. You can do it all right." So I took a belt at it, and over it went.' I know, for I was under the crossbar when it did so.

At half-time in the Third Test, the Springboks were leading 13-3 but the British team scored 18 points in the second half with only three against. That was memorable rugby, if you like. How Dai Williams (the South African wing), still the greatest wing I have seen, failed to score for the Springboks in the closing minutes is something I shall not forget. He ran 45 yards to touch down under the posts, only to be recalled for a forward pass! It was bound to have been a goal and anything could then happen. A wonderful game of rugby, by any standards, and at the end of the match the defeated Springboks carried Sam Walker shoulder high from the field. That was the most pleasant memory of all.

Boy and Fanie Louw.

The crowd at the Transvaal game.

The 1938 Springboks.

CHAPTER TWELVE

12

THE FLYING LION
1950

NEW ZEALAND, AUSTRALIA & CEYLON

LEWIS JONES, *aged 19 and a young naval rating, won his first cap for Wales against England in 1950. He had just been on the point of departure for Hong Kong on an aircraft carrier when news of his selection came through and he was released to play. He went on to appear 10 times for Wales and then switched codes to rugby league, launching a magnificent career with Leeds and Great Britain which was to make him arguably the most brilliant convert ever to move from union to league, and the loss of his glorious running and kicking talents was keenly felt in the union game at the time.*

But he made history of a different kind later in 1950. Lewis Jones became the first man ever to fly to a Lions tour. The 1950 Lions, under Karl Mullen, had departed at the end of March via the usual means of transport used by Lions parties since 1888 – ship. The party had sailed from Liverpool on the Shaw Savill line flagship, TSS Ceramic. *One of the tourists was to observe that the ship normally carried livestock.*

The precocious Jones had not made the original selection for the party, who had fine fullbacks in George Norton of Ireland and Billy Cleaver of Wales, and Jones was preparing for a season of top level cricket. However, Norton, from Bective Rangers, was injured in an early tour match. Jones was called up, rushed back to his native Wales from a cricket match to pack his bags, and then rushed back to London. There, heady with excitement, he boarded a BOAC Stratocruiser. Effectively, in one take-off run, Lions tours of the future were transformed. Even though the Ceramic *was a vastly more advanced ship than the RMS* Kaikoura, *which conveyed the heroic 1888 touring team, it still took Mullen and his men 32 days to reach New Zealand and roughly the same on the return voyage.*

Admittedly, the flight option to New Zealand involved an enormous number of hops which, as Jones was later to testify, took him through a kaleidoscope of exotic locations. But in the future around nine weeks could now be lopped off a Lions tour to the Antipodes and around five weeks off a South African trip, and it meant the parties would be stronger. No Lions party before the Second World War ever toured in the southern hemisphere without missing a considerable number of elite players because of the sheer time involved.

The 1950 team also made history by wearing red jerseys, now inextricably linked with the Lions tradition and mystique. Even though the tour still involved two long sea journeys, the party had fewer absentees than most – John Gwilliam, who had captained Wales to a Grand Slam, was unavailable, but for the first time in Lions history every one of the touring team was an international player for

---

Opposite: Bleddyn Williams hacks the balls through as he attempts to evade a tackle.

one of the four home countries – good news considering that they faced a fierce 30-match playing itinerary, with four Test matches in New Zealand, two more in Australia and even a fleeting visit on the way home to play in Ceylon (now called Sri Lanka).

The party boasted class in several positions. The great Jackie Kyle was at fly-half, and for his performances on tour he was to go down in history as one of the finest and best-loved players that New Zealand had seen. On the wing, they had Ken Jones, the international sprinter and a sensational attacking runner, who until he was overtaken by Gareth Edwards in the 1970s was the most-capped Welsh international – the excellent Ken Jones: Boots and Spikes *by Steve Lewis, reveals a sporting character of ability and richness. On tour, Jones was to score 16 tries in 16 games.*

And in the centre, a complementary partnership was forged between Dr Jack Matthews and Bleddyn Williams, two great friends from Cardiff – who remained almost inseparable friends throughout their lives – with the pugnacious Matthews providing the defensive hammer and the incisive Williams the kind of attacking brilliance which was to see him dubbed the 'Prince of Centres'. He created countless tries for the touring team backs with his sidestepping and also led the Lions in Mullen's absence in three of the six tour Tests.

The glorious Tom Clifford, a prop from Munster, was clearly the core character of the tour, with Jim McCarthy of the Dolphin club and Jimmy Nelson from Malone running him close. The top points scorer was the young Welsh three-quarter Malcolm Thomas, who scored 96 points and who was to return to New Zealand with the 1959 party.

Tour preparation once again came into sharp focus after one Lions prop used to living on rations in the austerity of post-war Britain, ballooned by two stone after tucking into the first-class travel fare on the outward sea journey. However, the team took fitness more seriously than some of their predecessors, with many other players recounting weeks of hard work, even scrummaging, aboard ship.

One of the features of the tour was the use of the ruck as an offensive weapon in New Zealand, and particularly in the Otago province, which became known as the home of the ruck. The Lions found that rucks were deliberately set up by the home teams as a means of winning quick second phase possession with a tackler buried at the bottom. The tactic was exceedingly difficult to combat, as was proved when Otago heavily defeated the Lions at Carisbrook, 23-9.

And in the final analysis, despite the strength of the Lions and despite the excellence of their crop of world-class players, they still lost the series – they were beaten by 3-0 in New Zealand, with one draw, though they did do well to recover to gain convincing wins in the two Tests in Australia. Yet at no time did they appear likely to end their melancholy run against the All Blacks.

It was a feat in an itinerary of such intensity, that they only lost two provincial games – against Otago and Southland, both deep in the south of the South Island; and in Australia, they lost only to a New South Wales XV. The 32-9 win over Auckland, with Lewis Jones in wonderful form with his kicking and dazzling running, was a high point, and it showed what could be done when the forwards stood their ground and allowed their backs to play. The match was a Lions classic.

The failure in the Test series can be put into stark perspective because the New Zealand team which romped to victory had been whitewashed by South Africa the previous year. Ultimately, the level of fitness and organisation amongst New Zealand forwards was too much. They were more aggressive than the Lions, the new rucking tactics were irresistible in some games and, in the end, the Lions were left licking their wounds.

However, the Lions party was one of the most popular of all time, because they were the first British team to visit New Zealand since 1930 and the two countries had been brought together by their common cause and losses in the Second World War. It was to become known as 'the friendly tour'.

Mullen was a quiet leader; one of his own Irish colleagues was mildly critical in later years of the tactics that were employed, particularly with the feeling that the Lions concentrated on their backs at the expense of their forward play.

The manager, Ginger Osborne, was not a disciplinarian, and in an austere period may have made himself unpopular if he tried to be one. One of his tour party offered the opinion that he knew 'bugger all' about rugby but, for many managers, being liked and respected by his players was a start.

One of the most unfortunate players on tour was Doug Smith, the Scotland wing, who was recovering from a broken arm and did not play until the 18th game of the tour. However, Smith put his down-time to good use, and when he returned to New Zealand in 1971 as the manager of the celebrated party, he had learned many lessons about the difficulties of life as a Lion in the country.

Remarkably, there were only three English players in the party, and this after decades when the tours had been dominated by the English. Perhaps this was an indication that strict merit selection was now in place, because England had finished bottom of the International Championship in 1950. Wales provided the bulk of the touring party, with 14 in all.

Scotland's representation was led by Gus Black, a clever and articulate scrum-half who was expected to strike up a fine partnership with Jackie Kyle. He did play in the first two Tests, though first Gordon Rimmer and then Rex Willis took over the berth.

The Test series was competitive at the start, with the Lions drawing the First Test in Dunedin, 9-9. Indeed, late in the second half, the Lions were leading 9-3 after John Robins kicked a penalty and

The 1950 tour party.

Kyle scored a memorable individual try. Ken Jones also scored after chasing a kick by Kyle, but with six minutes left, Bob Scott, the great fullback, came into the line for New Zealand and kicked ahead; from the resulting ruck, Ron Elvidge, the New Zealand captain, forced his way over for the draw.

The Lions were never to get so close again, and their forwards were second best in the series from then on. As Bleddyn Williams once told Clem Thomas, 'It was as if they had burnt themselves out in that one game!'

New Zealand won the Second Test at Lancaster Park, Christchurch, by 8-0 with their forwards well on top, and only courageous defence by the Lions kept the score down. New Zealand scraped home 6-3 in the Third Test at Athletic Park, Wellington, with John Robins putting the Lions in front with a first-half penalty before Elvidge scored a try and Bob Scott a penalty, giving New Zealand the match and the series.

The final Test in Auckland was won 11-8 by New Zealand, and again the Lions showed courage to the very end, with Bleddyn Williams launching two attacks which came so close to a try. It was during this match that Lewis Jones and Ken Jones conspired to create what the well-known New Zealand rugby critic Terry McLean was later to describe as 'the greatest try of all'.

By now the New Zealand section of the Australasian tour was seen as the more significant but that should not detract from the achievement of the Lions of beating Australia in Test matches in both Brisbane and Sydney, and by thumping margins. This achievement by a tired team was memorable.

By this time, Lewis Jones was established as a tour star and in the First Test in Australia at the Exhibition Ground, Brisbane, he went through the card of scoring actions to collect 16 points – try, two conversions, two penalties, and a drop-goal from 50 yards. The 16 points was a new record for a Lion.

Roy John, Rees Stephens and Billy Cleaver disembark the *Ceramic* upon arrival in New Zealand.

And this time, their grievous ill luck with injury did not cost them too badly – Malcolm Thomas broke a collarbone early on, yet the touring team still came home 19-6 with 14 men. Bleddyn Williams scored a captain's try and Doug Smith, belatedly coming up to speed after his injury, played his first Test match.

Jimmy Nelson, the Ireland lock, scored two of the Lions' five tries in a record win against Australia in Sydney. There were 25,000 at the match, although by this time rugby league was making greater inroads and it is said that a bigger crowd watched a rugby league match played at the same time at a nearby stadium.

On their passage home, which took them through the Suez Canal, the Lions played an unofficial game against Ceylon which they won 44-6, and yet another tour had ended with fine memories but, in the end, disappointing results.

Yet the friendly tour had enraptured New Zealand crowds with the creativity and pace of the tourists' play. In his description of the 'greatest try' scored in the Fourth Test, McLean said that when the ball reached Lewis Jones, 'rugby lore commanded that Jones should kick for touch. A whimsical rugby genius commanded that he should feint and dummy and start to run…' McLean described the passage of the young genius through defenders, until he was in the clear. 'What lay in front of Lewis Jones was not a tangled mass of All Black jerseys, but a green field and faraway, Scott, the lone sentinel. Lewis Jones ran, Lord how he ran!'

McLean goes on to describe the process and the ingenious way in which Jones drew Bob Scott, the final defender, altering the height of his pass to Ken Jones so that it would not be intercepted. 'The ball reached Kenneth at chest height. He ran at all times with the sinuous grace of a greyhound and now his long legs stretched forth, flashing over the green and driving onward toward the goal.…

'What a sight! Modest maidens, stout matrons, gawking schoolboys, the long and the short and the tall, were jumping, throwing paper and hats and bags, waving scarves and programs and yelling, bellowing, making any kind of noise that seemed proper as an expression of total joy.'

BLEDDYN WILLIAMS (Wales)

Toured: 1950

It was the first tour since the war and a great honour to be selected in the first place. They hadn't had a Lions side travel to New Zealand and Australia since 1930 so there was a lot of interest. I didn't know I was going to go because I was injured. I didn't play in a Wales game in 1950 – I missed all four internationals – so it was a great surprise.

I had to prove my fitness before I went, though. I had to play for Cardiff against Bath on the day that Wales were playing at the Arms Park against France. I was only out of plaster the week before I played the game. Can you imagine what my muscles were like? I just went through the motions but, thanks to Cliff Morgan, I scored a try in the last few minutes of the game. I think the media were fooled by that because they thought 'Williams is fit'. There were five weeks aboard ship, though, so I did a lot of exercise and I was alright for the tour.

JACK KYLE (Ireland)
Toured: 1950

It was all so different, life in those days. The furthest I had ever been from my home in Northern Ireland was Paris, for a Five Nations international against France, and that journey took 24 hours via Liverpool, London, Dover and then the English Channel. When we got to Paris, I stood in awe at sights like the Champs Elysees, the Eiffel Tower and the Louvre. People didn't travel.

There had been a war, times were still tough and for the lucky ones where I lived who could afford a holiday, it was maybe a week on the sands at Portrush, on the County Antrim coast. Suddenly, we were presented with what was an unbelievable concept. We were being offered the chance to go to the other side of the world to play one of the best teams in the world.

GUS BLACK (Scotland)
Toured: 1950

I was a student so I took a year off and didn't have to worry about lost wages. The only problem I had was that I was fairly recently married and had a young child, who was only 18 months old, and I wasn't very sure whether it was going to do damage being away for that period of time.

But my wife said I should go. And later on she met another wife at a dinner down in London, whose husband had been selected for the Lions tour of 1936 to Argentina and she'd objected to him going so he hadn't gone, and she regretted it for the rest of her life. So I think that reassured her – but it wasn't just a matter of packing a bag and going. There were a lot of things to be thought about.

The team arrives in New Zealand.

ACK KYLE

Ve sailed on the *Ceramic* from Liverpool. I think normally it carried sheep and lambs. took us about 31 days to get to Wellington. We had three in one cabin. I was with ill McKay and Jim McCarthy. I being the youngest had to take the upper bunk.

We were the first Lions touring team in New Zealand for 20 years and the reception e received everywhere we went, even the brass band at 5.30am in the morning, left n indelible impression on every member of the party. We set sail from Liverpool on April, voyaged across the Atlantic and Pacific Oceans before arriving in Wellington Iarbour on 2 May. Only hours after we left Liverpool we hit rough seas and we turned nto a pretty miserable group. Our only Naval man was Malcolm Thomas, but he was truck by seas sickness more than anyone. Dr Jack Matthews, my Cardiff and Wales entre partner, worked wonders with some inoculations at sea that stopped us from eeling ill, but he was dealt with by the ship's doctor and carried on feeling unwell.

IM McCARTHY (Ireland)
oured: 1950

ommy Clifford (Munster and Ireland prop) was undoubtedly the character of the our. He was from Limerick. A magic man.

ACK MATTHEWS (Wales)
oured: 1950

he tour cost me a lot of money! As a doctor I had to pay a locum doctor over £5,000 nd we were given seven shillings a day expenses by the International Board. It wasn't ery easy but my wife said, 'Yes, you can go.' I enjoyed the rugby and that was the main ning. I think it is the ultimate for any rugby player, whatever nationality, English, Irish, Velsh or Scottish. There was lots of training on board the ship on the way over as two f the players, John Robins and Ken Jones, were Physical Training officers. We also ad lots of meetings together daily so the bond was good.

;US BLACK

Ve got £12 a week, which was to return hospitality we got from New Zealanders. ut each of us had to find £100, I think, before we went on the tour. That was our nancial contribution to the whole thing. In some cases, such as with Cliff Davies, the eople of Kenfig Hill raised the money.

I think the blazer was provided, but we all had to have a dinner jacket, and in some istances that was again funded through local donations. So apart from the £12 a reek to repay local hospitality, which I'm not sure was properly within the rules, it was rictly amateur.

LEDDYN WILLIAMS

Ve got to know each other on ship as we knew we were going to be away for a long time. There were only 72 of us aboard ship in total. There was lots of training on board – we were exercising and we even had scrummaging on ship. We didn't lose any balls overboard, though, as our passes were accurate!

GUS BLACK

The leader of the choir was Cliff Davies. He was an extraordinary chap. He was a miner, and after a couple of pints he could sing all night in Italian, or perhaps it was Welsh, I don't know, maybe they are similar. But it certainly wasn't English.

Quite apart from his dedication to rugby, as a human being he was a truly democratic sort of person. It didn't matter who we were meeting – whether it was a governor or a local man from the pits – he treated them exactly the same way. Whether this was particularly a Welsh trait, I don't know.

We had a very good manager – Ginger Osborne – who used a very loose rein. He wanted each country to represent their heritage, so the Scots did their dancing, the Welsh did their singing, there wasn't enough English to make a noise and I don't recall what the Irish did – stood around being amusing, I suppose.

I had a photograph at one time of us doing an eightsome reel on the deck of the boat going through the Panama Canal.

JACK KYLE

The Welsh formed us into a choir. Tom Clifford's song was 'O'Reilly's Daughter'. '*As I was walking down the street, who should I meet but the one-eyed Reilly, with two pistols in hand,*

Hine Awatere and Karl Mullen share a traditional Maori welcome.

ooking for the man who married his daughter, yiddy aye oh, yiddy aye eh.' I stayed clear from the inging. Couldn't sing at all.

BILLY CLEAVER (Wales)
Toured: 1950

We discussed back play in attack – variations on the plan – and forward play around he scrummage. These topics caused infinite arguments and never seemed likely to top until the meeting was adjourned for the laying of tea.

GUS BLACK

There was a daily training routine on the journey out which consisted of running ound the deck, doing press-ups, playing violent games and that sort of thing – but othing like the sort of effort you made at home and some of the forwards may have ut on a bit of weight.

JIMMY NELSON

Tom Clifford arrived on the boat with three trunks when most of us had two suit-ases. One night, about midnight, when we had a drink or two, Tom says: 'Would nyone like something to eat?' When we got down to his cabin he opened up one of he trunks and it was stuffed with fruitcake and biscuits.

TOM CLIFFORD (Ireland)
Toured: 1950

My mother said, 'You're not going to be going short of food. I'll give you this to tide ou over.'

JIM McCARTHY

When Tommy got on the ship he saw the menu and there was about 12 items on it. We were going through the Bay of Biscay and the ship was very up and down. Well, 'om ate every item on the menu. Three types of dessert, three starters, three main ourses. He shovelled the whole lot in.

JACK KYLE

Bill McKay was a runner-up, six courses behind.

When we got on board I think it was George Norton who suggested to us, 'Lads his is an opportunity we'll never get again, we're a month or more on this ship nd I'm told if you get your hair all shaved off right down to your skull with only a uarter of an inch left, by the time we get to New Zealand your hair will be thick and uxurious.' We said to George: 'You go and try it out.' George came back with a quarter f an inch of his hair left. By the time we got to New Zealand, George's hair had only rown about another eighth of an inch. I don't think his hair ever recovered from the hock.

GUS BLACK

I think the success of the 1950 Lions tour – and it was a success – was the impact we had socially. Not as a whole group but as 30 individuals who went out there and got to know the people. We met a lot of New Zealanders and I think a big part of the reason why the Lions has evolved into this hugely popular phenomenon had a lot to do with the good impression we made in 1950.

We landed in Wellington then sailed from there to Nelson on the South Island – which was really a shack town with a main street in those days – for our first game. It was quite markedly Scottish, and I met a family called the Campbells, with whom I became quite friendly and they introduced me to a lot of locals.

After playing there we headed down the West Coast through places like Westport and Greymouth, which were predominantly mining towns. Now, I come from west Fife which is a big mining area, and the number of people who had emigrated there from my neck of the woods was astonishing.

I remember speaking to the barman in one pub and asking if there was anyone from Dunfermline in the house, and he opened the door to the back parlour and shouted the question. Well, the next minute there was this line of people coming through to greet me. It made the world seem an awful small place, for a wee while at least.

It's funny the things that stick in your memory: there was a strong Catholic presence and as we went from place to place the first person to greet us was the president of the local rugby club – but not two paces behind him was the local priest, as often as not. It didn't interfere in any way, or cause any tension – it was just one of those peculiar little things you notice.

BLEDDYN WILLIAMS

We couldn't have had a better captain or nicer man than Karl Mullen to lead us. He was a fine player and he was marvellous off the field. He was not a tub-thumping type of skipper. He knew his game and he was a very positive sort of guy. We were all coaches on that tour and he leaned on me pretty heavily as his vice-captain because we had so many Welshmen in the squad.

He took care of the forwards and I looked after the backs. He was very good to me and it was a very good and happy tour.

KARL MULLEN (Ireland)
Toured: 1950

We had a good out-half in Jack Kyle, and Jack Matthews and Bleddyn Williams, the two famous Welsh guys were in the middle of the field. We had Ken Jones on one wing and we had Lewis Jones on the other. We had a magical backline. I'd say it was the best backline ever to play for the Lions. Before we went to New Zealand I met the Rugby Union at Twickenham and I was told specifically that we had to play open football.

JACK MATTHEWS

We had a great post-war side with Cardiff. Our home gate was 35,000, that was the average. Cardiff soccer were in the first division then and we were getting more than them. Bleddyn and I had been playing together since 1938 and we've been friends ever since. It was such a pleasure playing with him for the Lions as well because we knew each other's play so well.

GUS BLACK

I spent rather longer going through medical school than I should have done and that meant I had eight years playing for Edinburgh University, which was great rugby. And for most of that time I played with the same outside-half, a chap called Ranald Macdonald, who was on the tour as well.

In Edinburgh we didn't have a coach as such, but the director of physical education was Charlie Usher, who captained Scotland back in the 1920s, and he trained us to be physically fit. And he also introduced a lot of ideas about how we should be playing rugby with the natural advantages we had.

He used to get Ranald and myself to train together blindfolded, passing the ball. So we'd get in position, then blindfold ourselves and he'd shout, 'ready – go'. Then Ranald would start running while I reached down for the ball, and nine times out of ten I would smack it into his chest. You don't have to see the outside-half. In fact, if you can see him it's a slow pass. You pass it into space and it's his job to run onto it.

So, Ranald and I were a great half-back pair. We knew each other inside out, by instinct by the time we were thoroughly bedded in. But the Scotland selectors never picked us together. He was capped on the wing, and played on the wing for the Lions as well – and for the life of me, I can't understand the sheer stupidity of not playing an established pair of half-backs. Ranald playing at outside-half in New Zealand would have been a great advantage.

Now, I was suddenly being paired up with Jack Kyle, who didn't play the same way. He stood absolutely stock still until he saw the ball coming to him, but he had the agility to get up to speed very quickly whilst also avoiding the onslaught from any forwards who had the nerve to go for him. I don't think I could really come to terms with that – it was a waste.

I don't think the Scottish members of the Lions selection team chose me. I think it was the Irish selectors who turned it in my favour, in the belief that I would team up with Jack Kyle to form a very good half-back partnership. I had a longish pass and Jack Kyle, who was at the top of his form at that time, was pretty mobile. But it didn't work out – at least not as it should have done.

KARL MULLEN

We travelled by train through the South Island and every station we stopped at we had a full band to meet us and we all marched up to the hotel. Tom Clifford always said the band was especially for him. On the way home I wrote to the Lord Mayor of Limerick saying how proud they should be of Tom Clifford and mentioned the band. So when he got home and got off the train from Dublin, the Lord Mayor had arranged a different band on every street and he was chaired to the town hall and made a freeman of Limerick.

JACK KYLE

We had one journalist with us, a lovely man, Dai Gent, who wrote for the *Sunday Times*. A wonderful, delightful little man. The only reporter on the trip. I can remember him reading us poetry on a train. Dai wasn't a man who enjoyed going out with the boys, so you can imagine after he'd written his piece he'd go back to his hotel on his own. Dai played scrum-half for England but he had Welsh connections. You remember that controversial 1905 try in the Wales versus All Blacks game? (The Kiwis played 35 games on tour in 1905, won 34 and had a try disallowed in their one defeat, to the Welsh). Well, everywhere Dai went he got attacked because of the try. I have a notion he got a bit tired listening to the locals going on about the try. I think he got homesick. He went home after about five weeks.

JIMMY NELSON

We had a very good manager, Ginger Osborne, who knew bugger all about rugby. He was a charming man but that was a real problem because we didn't have a coach. It was impossible for Karl to coach 30 people and be a captain at the same time. We trained hard, but it was basic stuff. We should have had a lot more technical training.

GUS BLACK

If we'd had a pack that could give us the ball at the right time in the right way, we

The First Test team before kick-off in Dunedin.

would have had a tremendous advantage. With Bleddyn Williams, Jack Matthews and plenty of pace on the wings – it should have been good, shouldn't it?

Of course, all the teams we came up against were liable to be playing well above themselves – so it wasn't easy. The Test matches were fairly stodgy affairs. There wasn't much running rugby, they were battles for possession and territory.

Some of the rugby was pretty good, but I don't think I'll be the only one who thinks the weakness was in the forwards. They just weren't up to it. And there had, of course, been many New Zealanders across during the war, playing Services rugby for the country where they were stationed, so they had knowledge of how the game was played in Britain, and I wouldn't doubt for a minute that they transferred that knowledge back home.

There was training every day, but Ginger Osborne gave us a long lead, which meant that if I didn't turn up he wouldn't bother me. I think he realised that there were psychological circumstances that contributed to me behaving not quite as well as I should have. So I missed training quite a lot – I'd lost interest.

The Lions team hadn't played much rugby before the war, and I think wartime rugby didn't have this vigorous physicality that everyone talks about now. It was more gentlemanly. So our forwards hadn't been tried and tested, while the New Zealanders had looked a bit further ahead, and dominating in the forwards was already a big part of their philosophy. They introduced us to a new way of playing rugby.

The dominant team in New Zealand at the time was Otago and we played them in Dunedin the week before the First Test. They had discovered that if you heeled the

Scrum-half Gus Black makes a break during the First Test.

ball quickly and passed it wide quickly with everyone running full speed when they got the ball, then the winger would be going at full speed and when he was eventually tackled the forwards would find it easier to get up to the ball and heel it again, and the whole process could then be repeated coming the other way. The idea was that you would eventually get an overlap.

It's almost childish – when you think about it now. But it was very effective and we weren't quite into that level of fitness and coordination. We tended to rely more on individual skills and the combined skills of a handful of players linking together – but not a whole team working in unison.

Unfortunately, I don't think we learned any instant lessons from being beaten by Otago to take into the First Test.

JIM McCARTHY
Karl was a quiet captain. You probably wouldn't know he was captain unless you were told. He had a quiet authority.

JIMMY NELSON
It must be very hard for a captain to monitor all these players especially if you're the hooker in the middle of it. That's where we missed a coach and a manager. Somebody from the outside looking in and saying, 'This is where things are going wrong.'

KARL MULLEN
I could see where it was going wrong. We weren't jumping at the lineout or marking the fellas who were jumping, so we got very little ball at the lineout.

The Lions defence pushes up quickly to smother the All Black attack.

JIMMY NELSON

As much as I liked Karl, he was a boy among men, if you know what I mean. He wasn't hardened. He was a very good man to get you going, to get your enthusiasm up but in the Irish team at that time the tactical chap was Des O'Brien. One person who should have been in that Lions team was Des. To me, he was the one forward in the Irish team I looked up to.

KARL MULLEN

The physicality was a big shock, I can tell you. I went on the ball in one match in Whangarei, I think, and I got a kick and if it didn't break all my ribs I was lucky. They were letting us know, 'Get off the ball otherwise we'll kick you off!' So we got off it pretty quick the next time.

LEWIS JONES (Wales)
Toured: 1950

Looking back on my career, I cannot recall that things ever went better or more effortlessly for me than on Eden Park when we played Auckland. When the end came we had piled up 32 points to Auckland's nine, my own personal tally was 17 (four conversions and three penalty goals).

Even so, the day belonged to Jackie Kyle. The great little Irish stand-off played one of the most wonderful matches I have ever seen even him play and that despite being

Bleddyn Williams leads the Lions out for the Third Test after Karl Mullen withdrew.

kicked about at the feet of the Auckland forwards. I've seen some dirty play in my time but nothing so ruthless and deliberate as the kicking of Jackie on the ground right in front of the grandstand at Eden Park that afternoon.

JIM McCARTHY

Every Welshman was born with a side-step. I don't think there was anybody in Ireland who could do a side-step, not even Jack Kyle. Jack was not a side-stepper. Bursts of speed and swerves, but Jack was such a pure player, and a pure person, that he'd think selling a dummy was a mortal sin and he'd have to go to confession.

LEWIS JONES

I was able to sit in the stand at the famous Athletic ground in Wellington and enjoy the spectacle of Bleddyn Williams at his peerless best. What a spectacle it was, for the famous jink flashed in and out like a neon sign to elude Wellington players with its brilliance.

JACK KYLE

Before the First Test I think people had written us off. They were thinking, 'Well, Otago have beaten them and they were beaten by Southland in Invercargill.' We pulled the stops out and drew it. I scored a try and it was one of those where you never know how you scored it. Subconsciously something happens. I think I got a stray ball from somewhere and started running and managed to get round a few guys. I would say that was one of the most important tries I ever scored because we really were up against it and it was nice to do something to put the tour on a sound footing. But then we lost the next three Tests. There was so little in it. But that's the way sport goes. Small things.

GUS BLACK

We would have won that First Test if I had only looked to my right. Oh dear, oh dear, oh dear. Ken Jones was right there ready to take the ball, and he was yelling his head off, but I wasn't looking and didn't hear him. All I had to do was make a simple pass and he would have been in under the posts. There are a few things I really regret in life – and that is one of them.

I played in the first two Tests, and I think the New Zealand chaps were being kind in the first one – but not in the second one when I spent more time in the bloody air than I did on the ground. Pat Crowley was in the back-row for New Zealand that day, and he attended to me quite admirably.

New Zealand had re-evaluated the way they were going to play the game – and a virile defence was going to be a part of it. The physicality they talk about now I think maybe started with them, and the South Africans didn't need a second invitation to adopt the same approach.

JIMMY NELSON

New Zealand had a certain amount of ruthlessness and that really was the problem with our team. We weren't ruthless enough. That team should have been much better. When it came to tactics they were all 'get the ball to the centre' and in my opinion that was all very well but I thought our forwards were very quick and we should have used the forwards around the field a lot more.

We had a tremendous backline and that was the problem. That was the only tactic. I'm still angry about it. We should have used the forwards more because the forwards were very quick. Even until the day he died I argued with Karl about that. If anybody would agree with me it would be Bill McKay. He'd have agreed with me.

JACK KYLE

He was a boxer, Bill. A very hard man. McKay had been in the army in the war and fought in the Burmese jungle along with the Gurkhas. There was a man in New Zealand called Charles Upham who had won two Victoria Crosses and McKay knew roughly where he was and asked the management if Upham could come and have lunch with us, which he did. We met this very quiet sheep farmer, this man with two VCs. McKay sat beside him. I think Bleddyn Williams had been in the air force during the war and then we all went over and shook hands with him. He didn't look like he wanted the limelight, a guy who said he only did what was necessary. You remember the rugby but you remember all the other things as well.

BLEDDYN WILLIAMS

I came into the side for the Second Test as one of two changes, but we were undone by the Auckland breakaway Pat Crowley. He turned into a scrum-half killer as he tormented Angus Black and stopped him producing his normal service. In one strategic blow the All Blacks had thrown a spanner into our attacking machinery. In the end, everything in the series boiled down to the fact that New Zealand had a better pack of forwards than the Lions, won continual possession and so smashed our more polished attacking back division before it could even purr into action. We lost the Second Test 8-0 after losing Bill McKay with a broken nose just before the interval.

I was captain for the Third Test, when Mullen was injured, and the All Black pack hit us with sledge-hammer force. At one stage they played with only six forwards through injury yet were still winning the ball against the Lions' eight! It was our chance, and we should have taken it, but New Zealand took the glory against all the odds with a 6-3 victory.

GUS BLACK

We lost Bill McKay during the Second Test, and that was quite a loss because he was a really rangy sort of forward who was a real pest amongst the opposition three-quarters – so that maybe contributed to what happened.

I was replaced by the Englishman Gordon Rimmer for the Third Test. He was significantly bigger and probably more robust than me. I was 5ft 10in and lucky if I was pushing 10st 10lbs, which would be a laugh today. So I think it was an attempt to beef the team up. But he had only one Test, and in the Fourth Test they brought in Rex Willis, who was the Welsh scrum-half at that time, and he didn't have a particularly happy time either – so I'm inclined to believe it wasn't a remotely sympathetic environment for a scrum-half. The ball was coming back slowly and the half-backs were minced meat, really. In a nutshell, the forwards were taken by surprise and they never recovered. They weren't fit enough, they weren't hard enough and in some instances they weren't big enough.

KARL MULLEN
I was advised that I should move sideways and give the other hooker a game, so I feigned injury. I wasn't injured at all. I gave the other hooker, Dai Davies, three of the six Test matches. I wouldn't do it again.

JACK KYLE
The last Test was a regret. We were so near. Ken Jones' try was one of the highlights of the tour. From a long lineout, I got it, Lewis Jones burst through the middle and ran to the halfway line and gave it to Ken who had wonderful anticipation. He got the ball and went charging, chased by the wing three-quarter, but Ken having won a silver medal in the Olympics was not going to be caught. I can still see it and feel it and remember thinking, 'We have a chance here.' He was a wonderful player, Ken.

BLEDDYN WILLIAMS
The Fourth Test was notable for Ken Jones' unforgettable try. Rex Willis to sent out a cannon-ball pass to Jackie Kyle. He was preparing to pass to me when Lewis Jones sliced between us and took the pass intended for me. We were as flabbergasted as the All Blacks and Lewis freed Ken to side-step Bob Scott and race three-quarters the length of Eden Park to score. What a try!

We ran the All Blacks off their feet in the last 20 minutes and twice I got within inches of scoring. We took every risk and tried every ruse but still they won 11-8.

LEWIS JONES
We failed in the final Test, but gloriously and the crowd knew it. How they cheered as we made for the dressing room and how sweet and plaintively the strains of 'Now is the Hour' sounded across that vast stadium. It was almost like being back again on the Arms Park and for us Welshmen especially it was a link with far-off home.

GUS BLACK
The last game we played in New Zealand was against the Maoris and, you wouldn't believe it, I was winding down in somebody's house, it was well after midnight and we were all well and truly *relaxed*, when somebody appeared at the door to say I was playing the next day. Rex Willis was injured and Gordon Rimmer was ill so neither

of them was available – and that was the longest game of rugby on the tour as I was concerned. I was a bit hungover, I must confess. But we won.

BLEDDYN WILLIAMS

Wherever we went we were treated royally and, at Ashburton, I had never before seen so much food on one table in my life. Eventually the hospitality we were getting became so lavish that our manager, Ginger Osborne, requested that after games other than Test matches there should be no official dinners.

Of the things I would never forget were seeing a sheep with five legs in Gisborne and the scene at the end of our final game against a Maori XV. The whole crowd seemed to pour onto the field at the end of a game we won 14-9 in typical 'windy Wellington' conditions and sealed off our path to the dressing rooms. They clutched our arms and sang 'Now is the Hour' and 'Auld Lang Syne', many of them with tears in their eyes. 'If rugby football could do this,' I thought, 'it must be the greatest of all games.'

MICK LANE (Ireland)
Toured: 1950

I remember the send-off from New Zealand. It was tremendous. Goodbye on the quayside. Thousands there singing.

JACK KYLE

Leaving Wellington to cross to Sydney, we had these big long paper ribbons. People on the shore held one end and we held the other and as the ship pulled away people were singing *'Now is the hour when we must say goodbye.'* I think a few tears were dropping. After about 60 or 70 yards the ribbons broke and we waved farewell.

Ken Jones breaks away to score a spectacular try at Eden Park during the Fourth Test.

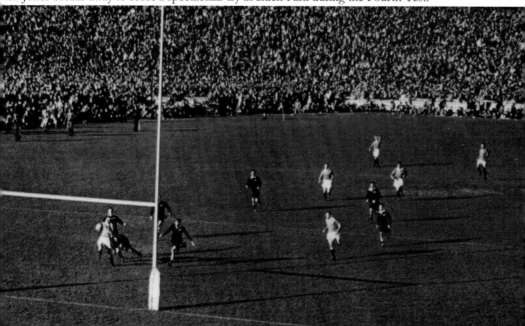

KARL MULLEN

Australia was a big contrast. The Australians were a bit brash like the Americans. It wasn't a country village place like New Zealand, it was a brash place. We had upped our game physically. We were tougher. They might have been a bit surprised. We had no trouble in Australia.

GUS BLACK

Australian rugby wasn't much cop. I only played once there, against Newcastle on the hardest surface I ever played on – I think it was just sand. It was a bit of an afterthought. We were already winding down, and the Wednesday team briefly became the Saturday team.

   We had one particularly unpleasant match against a Metropolitan XV, the captain of which was a chap called 'Jika' Travers, who had been a troublesome bugger at Oxford and had played for England during his university days; he was determined that whatever else happened he was going to slaughter us, and he did quite a good job of it as I recall.

JIMMY NELSON

I scored two tries in the Second Test in Sydney. It should have been three in actual fact, because I fell over the Australia fullback going for a third. I'm the only second-row to score two tries in a Test, I think. I have to admit, it was a moment in time when I was the fittest I'd ever been. In the second half of the tour I played nearly every match so when I got to Australia I was absolutely fighting fit. I'm 90 years old and you're asking me questions about things that happened more than 60 years ago. But one abiding memory of 1950 is that the team didn't live up to its reputation. That's true.

GUS BLACK

On the way home we played in Ceylon, on the racecourse. And the crowd all seemed to have been to Aberdeen Grammar School. After the game we were divided up into three groups to go to three different clubhouses – one was all British, one was all Ceylonese, and one was mixed – and I was in the group that went to the all-Ceylonese clubhouse.

   Well, they were interested in only two things: dirty songs and beer. And I had never seen such a mess of beer in my life.

Lewis Jones kicks for goal, Fourth Test.

For some reason they didn't hold their glass by the handle, they had a thumb inside the lip, which meant it was getting spilled everywhere.

So we were all enjoying the beer, and suddenly this gecko fell off the roof and onto the counter in front of me – which was, of course, covered in beer. I remember thinking: 'Good God, it's finally happened – I've got the DTs [delirium].' Then the gecko got up and ran out the room – and as I looked round I noticed that there were geckos all over the place, climbing the walls and crawling across the roof.

Looking back, I don't think I was 100 per cent enthusiastic about the tour. It began to be traumatic about halfway through… living out of a suitcase, travelling by bus, getting roughed up by the All Blacks at regular intervals. It was six months of new experiences every single day – and I suppose in a way we began to draw the curtains on what was going on around us unless it was quite dramatic. I can remember a bus trip through some beautiful countryside, and we were playing cards and what was going on outside didn't seem to matter very much anymore.

Six months is quite a long time and certainly during the second half of it I wasn't feeling the same enthusiasm as I was at the beginning. I can't remember feeling like I was riding on the crest of a wave or anything like that.

In retrospect, I wouldn't have missed it – but at the time I was glad and relieved to get back. Was it a life defining-experience? I don't think so. I am just glad I was chosen, glad I decided to go – and like most people I am not loath to the idea of leaving my own small mark on history. We left at the end of April from Liverpool and it took about three weeks to get there by sea. We went via the Panama Canal and home via the Suez Canal, so we went right round the world and were away for six months altogether, which I think would break a lot of today's young men in two.

BLEDDYN WILLIAMS

I've still got vivid memories, even after all these years. It was a marvellous tour and a great side to play with. It had to be, though, as there were 14 Welshmen on tour! There was a Welsh society in New Zealand, as there was in Australia, so we had a great following. When I was over in New Zealand three years ago, I was told that the 1950 side would have given the 1971 team a good run for their money.

We weren't quite strong enough up front but we had a great back division and we played some lovely rugby. The idea was to entertain. It was instilled in us that we must play entertaining rugby and we were very successful at that.

CHAPTER THIRTEEN

LORDS OF AFRICA
1955
SOUTH AFRICA

IN MANY *ways, this was the ultimate Lions tour. It was not so much in the results that the significance springs, even though by coming away with a drawn series in an epic quartet of matches, the Lions avoided defeat for the first time in decades of touring; it was not even the class shown by both sides in the matches or the sheer style of open rugby played by the Lions, and it was more than the enormous crowds at the four stadiums. It was the sheer glamour, and from the moment that the party hopped their way down from London as the first Lions to fly, South Africa welcomed them with a reverence, entertaining them at every turn and treating them like film stars.*

The tour was ferocious in the sense that it included 25 matches against aggressive home teams, including the four Tests, but it was also played in a wonderful spirit, with so little of the rancour which tended to mark Lions' visits to New Zealand. Catapulted into the limelight were the extraordinary 19-year-old Irish prodigy, Tony O'Reilly, later to become a stratospheric businessman, and Cliff Morgan, the mesmeric Wales fly-half, small in stature but who towered over events on tour both on and off the field.

There were many other great players in the Lions team, and a torrent of great play and memorable stories surrounding the team's frantic social life of the trip. In his book On Trek, *the late author, Bryn Thomas, unveils a panoply of cocktail parties, home visits, official receptions, dances, parties, game drives and a general social whirl.*

South Africa hadn't lost a Test series for nearly 60 years when the Lions arrived at Jan Smuts airport, late on the evening of 11 June. The side, led by Irish forward Robin Thompson, went on to thrill South Africans and followers back home with their adventurous running rugby in the Test series and came away in a blaze of glory by sharing the four-Test rubber. It was the best British & Irish performance in South Africa since Johnny Hammond's side of 1896.

Thompson was barely 24 and had captained Ireland only three times – all defeats – in the Five Nations, so was regarded as a surprise choice. His big presence belied his quiet bearing. He became a popular leader and won many plaudits for the manner in which he fulfilled his duties as skipper, though there are some who believe that he lacked the extra edge of the true Test forward.

As soon as the side stepped off the plane in Johannesburg they entertained the large welcoming party which had endured a five-hour wait with an impromptu concert. The irrepressible Cliff Morgan was choirmaster and launched the Lions into a repertoire of hymns and arias that had been practised at Eastbourne during the tour party's preparations. The Rand Daily Mail *next day greeted*

Opposite: Cliff Morgan looks to break through the South African defence.

them with the banner headline: 'This is the greatest team ever to visit South Africa.' As Morgan pointed out, this was before they had played a game.

As on previous tours, the selectors had, bizarrely, put a strict age restriction on players with the result that no one the wrong side of 30 was considered for the tour. Many aspects of the old tours baffle us today, but quite why the Lions would deny themselves their most experienced players in a ferocious environment like South Africa is astonishing.

This ruled out former Lions Ken Jones and Jack Kyle, though Wales and Ireland still exercised a strong influence on the team. Behind the scrum Cliff Morgan was the tactical spearhead of the side with the teenaged Tony O'Reilly a strapping presence on the wing to score the tries.

For the first time in the modern era the Lions possessed a pack capable of holding its own against the Springbok juggernaut. An all-Welsh front-row of Billy Williams, Bryn Meredith and Courtenay Meredith (no relation) provided a strong platform for Thompson and Rhys Williams to flourish in the Test second-row. Scotland's Jim Greenwood was the brains of a back-row that had a good balance of speed and skill in Reg Higgins of England, Tom Reid of Ireland and Russell Robins and Clem Thomas of Wales. Hugh McLeod and Ernie Michie led the Scotland forward contingent.

England's Jeff Butterfield, a former Loughborough PE student, took charge of the squad's fitness and prepared the side to a very high standard. The late Tom Reid always reckoned he was never as fit in his life as on that tour. Butterfield formed with Phil Davies, his England colleague, a creative midfield partnership that helped O'Reilly finish the tour with a record 16 tries.

The Lions lost their tour opener against West Transvaal and were trounced 20-0 by Eastern Province their only reverses in the dozen provincial matches before the First Test. Cliff Morgan suffered an ankle injury early in the tour and was on the sidelines for the provincial setback in Port Elizabeth. Following their dominating performance, the Eastern Province front-row was selected for the First Test.

More than 95,000, then a world record for a rugby union international, arrived at Ellis Park to witness one of the most exciting Tests ever staged in South Africa. Morgan, Butterfield, Davies, Cecil Pedlow and O'Reilly were outstanding on the hard ground. Bryn Meredith, well supported by his tight five, gave a masterly hooking display and the back-row of Higgins, Robins and Greenwood did their bit in the loose.

The match turned out to be a cliff-hanger. The Lions trailed 11-8 at half-time and soon after lost Reg Higgins through injury. Yet again, they were forced to play a major match with a denuded team. Playing with 14 men they reacted positively to adversity and Cliff Morgan, with a lightning break, swerved past flanker Basie van Wyk to inspire the Lions with a try. Next, O'Reilly ran hard to create the opening for Greenwood to score and the big red-headed Irishman's speed to a lucky bounce brought him the Lions' fifth try of the match.

Scotland's Angus Cameron, the tour vice-captain, converted four of the tries to give the Lions a 23-11 lead, but back came the Springboks. Eleven points from a penalty, a converted try and a late try brought the score to 23-22 with the conversion attempt to come. Then came one of the most famous kicks, or more precisely, famous misses, in rugby history.

Up stepped fullback Jack van der Schyff who, to the joy of the Lions and despair of South Africans sent his kick wide and the Lions were one up with three to play. The Springboks had been considered invincible. The result sent out shock waves around the rugby world.

Speaking at the post-match dinner skipper Robin Thompson summed up the Lions' feelings at beating South Africa: 'To win a rugby international is fine, but to beat the Springboks is really something.'

The tourists were well-beaten 25-9 in the Second Test and were plagued by injuries in the run-up to the Third Test in Pretoria, where they were without their captain and vice-captain. Cliff Morgan took over as leader. His team talk, by all accounts, was stirring and his masterful tactical control on the day guided the tourists to a 9-6 win. It was a test of their character which they passed with flying colours.

The Lions showed they could tough it out against the 'Boks and win ugly, abandoning the flowing rugby that had characterised their earlier tour games and First Test win. Doug Baker, a fly-half for England, who had the unenviable job of understudying Morgan, which he did with dignity and team spirit, filled in for Angus Cameron at fullback and kicked the penalty that put the tourists 6-0 up early in the second half. Butterfield was the Lions' other scorer. He contributed a left-footed drop-goal in the first half – the only one he ever kicked in his entire career he always claimed – and he crossed for the try that put the Lions a score clear. The end came with the Lions 9-6 ahead and thus 2-1 up with one to play.

The traditional forward strength of South African rugby was evident in the last Test at Port Elizabeth where the Lions were worn down, conceding seven tries in a 25-9 defeat. There were no excuses from the party. Manager Jack Siggins, disappointed with a tied rubber, conceded: 'On the day's play we were thoroughly beaten by an extremely good side.'

However, in later years some players were to express the opinion that the post-match schedule counted against them. The Lions had to pack before the game and departed very soon after the post-match festivities. Some players believe that the organisers should have elongated the tour just a little so that they could have given total concentration to what was, after all, arguably the game of their lifetimes.

One of the Lions' unsung heroes on this tour was the English scrum-half Dickie Jeeps from Northampton. There were no uncapped players on the 1950 tour to New Zealand and Australia. Jeeps had been a surprise choice when the tourists for South Africa were named, for he had never

The 1955 tour party.

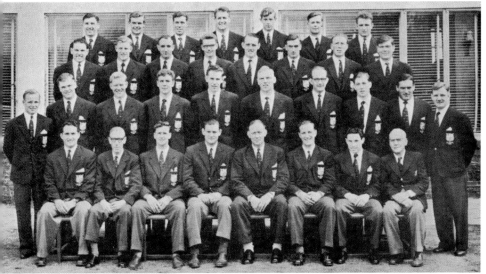

played international rugby. It was expected that he would be the third scrum-half behind Wales's Trevor Lloyd and the England team incumbent, Johnny Williams.

But Jeeps hit it off perfectly with Cliff Morgan from an early stage in the tour and the tough little Englishman was named as the Welshman's partner for all four Tests. He was a brave defender in the face of oncoming forwards, had a fast, accurate service and kicked well in defence. He would go on two more Lions tours and when he finished his career, back in South Africa in 1962, he would have 13 Lions Test caps to his name, a record that only Willie-John McBride has overtaken.

The 1955 tour engaged the wider sporting public's interest back home. Short agency reports had been the only source of first-hand Lions details on previous tours, though Dai Gent (off his own bat) had covered part of the 1950 visit to New Zealand as a freelancer. For the first time British newspapers sent their own correspondents to cover an entire tour, Vivian Jenkins of the Sunday Times *and JBG 'Bryn' Thomas of the Cardiff* Western Mail *sending back evocative reports of the Lions' progress through South Africa.*

The great media tradition of a large press corps following the tour was therefore instituting, although those few pathfinding journalists of the 1950s would be absolutely staggered by the size of the media party following the modern tours. Modern journalists would be similarly amazed to read in On Trek *that Jenkins and Thomas, the two writers, clearly had an influential say in some aspects of Lions selections as the tour progressed, with the ear of manager Jack Siggins.*

The 1955 Lions were the first required to sign a form of tour contract. Benefits covering injury were among the clauses favourable to the players though there was a restriction on writing books or giving press interviews until two years after the end of the tour. Despite that, Viv Jenkins and Bryn Thomas were fully embraced by the tour party, often travelling with the team on non-match days and becoming akin to father figures to many of the players.

Gerald Davies, a later Lions legend, remembered his imagination being captured by Jenkins's post-tour book, Lions Rampant. *It was the first time a British journalist had distilled the excitement and events and the essential rhythm of a full-blown overseas tour into book form. It was instrumental, Davies said, in converting him to rugby. It was clearly a landmark tour, one that heralded the beginning of the modern Lions era.*

PHIL DAVIES (England)
Toured: 1955

The Lions as an experience was second only to getting married to my wife, Nancy, and having our son, Simon, and our daughter, Judy. But it was still a hard situation for us both. Nancy and I were married in 1954 and lost our first child on the Thursday before the Calcutta Cup match in 1955, with the Lions team selection announced on the Monday.

Nancy insisted that I played (and we won), and then I went on tour for four months.

My headmaster at Christ's Hospital, where I was teaching, wrote that the Council Of Almoners had approved my absence for four months and that the replacement costs (£50) had been donated by one of the governors. So I was very grateful, but at the same time naively unaware of what was involved and what was to come. I knew little of South African rugby.

My salary was maintained by the school, the £28 a month still came in. Nancy went back to work as a nurse, so we had no worries. Other teachers were only given unpaid leave. I took £25 of my own money and we were allowed 7/6d. (37.5p) a day to be able to return hospitality. This was impossible such was the generosity, so it came as pocket money (the same daily wage that I had earned in the RAF) – so, no hardship in those non-inflationary days. I saved and bought a camera for Kodak colour slides, which was the latest thing. My best investment was a £3 nylon shirt, which I washed each night and sold the following year in Romania.

We had left practically unnoticed with two travelling journalists, Vivian Jenkins (a 1938 Lion) and JBG Thomas. The media pack gradually strengthened as we were surprisingly successful.

ERNIE MICHIE (Scotland)
Toured: 1955

The decision was made to only take players under 30 and there were some very good players at that time who didn't qualify, like Jackie Kyle, Bleddyn Williams and Ken Jones. They were really top class players, so I suppose I was lucky to get on the tour in that sense. It was a complete surprise to me when I was selected. I didn't know a thing about it. I wasn't asked if I was available or anything like that – I don't know, I think I may have been a late selection.

I was actually on a bus travelling down to London with the Aberdeen University rugby side for our Easter Tour to play four games in the capital. There was no Forth Road Bridge and no motorways in those days so it was a long, long trip. It must have taken 15 hours to get down.

We had stopped on the outskirts of London and I was half asleep at the back of the bus when one of the chaps, Dr Doug Robbie, came in and said: 'You're in the Lions side.' He had a newspaper and it said that I was in the squad. I didn't believe it. I thought it must have been a mistake and I think I went off to sleep again.

CLIFF MORGAN (Wales)
Toured: 1955

I never really thought twice about accepting Jack Siggins' invitation to join the Lions tour of South Africa in 1955. It was an offer you couldn't refuse, a chance and a challenge to play the best rugby in your life. I felt that once I had been a Lion I would have done everything I could in the game. I looked at the company I would be keeping. The other nine Welshmen I knew well, of course, but the buzz I got was from the thought of playing with Jeff Butterfield in the centre and Tony O'Reilly on the wing.

HUGH McLEOD (Scotland)
Toured: 1955 & 1959

Billy Williams told me that before the tour that the Welsh Rugby Union had a special dinner for the nine players they had going on the trip and after the dinner they all got an envelope with £100 in it. We got bugger all. They suggested you have £40 in your pocket before you went away. Now, I got out the army five weeks before my time was up to go on the tour and I had nothing saved, so £40 was a lot of money for my family to come up with.

We got blazers, towels and socks – but you had to have your own flannels, your own shoes, your own boots (although we got a free pair from a company called Elmer Cotton when we got down there), your own shirts, your own shorts and plenty more. All of that cost money – so even after you were selected you had plenty to think about before getting on the tour. When you were out there, you got £3 10s a week and three badges.

DICKIE JEEPS (England)
Toured: 1955, 1959 & 1962

I was selected for the 1955 tour before being considered for England, so I was an uncapped tourist. I understand that Haydn Tanner, the great Welsh scrum-half, had recommended me to the Lions selectors in a railway carriage. Northampton had played Cardiff pre-Christmas and we had won, 22-9, against a wonderful side that included

The party gathers in front of their tour bus.

Cliff Morgan, Bleddyn Williams and Jack Matthews. And if I tell you that the ball went into touch just four times in that match it is no word of a lie. It was a brilliant game of rugby. I was lucky because I had a good game and Cliff was playing, so he saw me at first hand. I think Cliff got me on to the party because he liked my service – they said I could always make something out of bad ball. That was the reason I was asked to play in an invitation match with him in Cornwall a few weeks before the Lions tour. It got me on the ladder, and although I'd had trials for England, I didn't get in – but I got picked for the Lions instead. Brilliant!

ERNIE MICHIE

We flew out by one of these big Lockheed Constellation aeroplanes and we literally hopped all the way out. Our first stop was in Rome, then Cairo, and then Khartoum at two in the morning, and because these planes didn't have the air conditioning and so on that they have now, we were all very hot and bothered in the plane, so we were desperate to get off and get some fresh air. And we stepped out and it was like stepping into an oven. So we literally ran to the airport lounge where they had these big fans going and we stood under them to try and cool down. Then it was through Nairobi and I think we might have had a quick stop to refuel in Entebbe and onto Johannesburg.

I was meeting a lot of these chaps for the first time, the likes of Cliff Morgan, who was a tremendous little personality. Because he was Welsh he loved to sing, so on the way out he taught us songs to sing to our hosts. So we practised and practised, and when we arrived we sang 'Sarie Marais', which was an Afrikaans song, to the welcoming party – which seemed to go down well.

CLIFF MORGAN

We came to the decision that we were going to be a singing team. I was appointed choirmaster, with first call on the hotel piano, and every day for a week we practised, English, Scottish and Irish songs in English, Welsh songs in Welsh and, in a four-part harmony, 'Sarie Marais' in Afrikaans, which we thought would go down well with the people over there. We learned this parrot-fashion, and the words of the Welsh songs I wrote on a blackboard.

It paid off eventually because, although there are always some hurt feelings when players are competing for a place, we were an extremely happy side.

Coming down the steps of the plane, we were amazed at the crowds who had waited so long to greet us. I turned round and said, 'OK lads, look at the people.' So we all came to a stop and sang practically our full repertoire from 'Sospan Fach' to 'Sarie Marais', cheered on by the crowd. And that was the spirit of that trip, everybody together.

Later that week the *Rand Daily Mail* carried a front page headline: 'This is the greatest team ever to visit South Africa'. And we hadn't even played a match!

CLEM THOMAS (Wales)
Toured: 1955

The South Africans were kindness personified to us… They were always in my view aware of the flaws in their politics with their appalling policy of apartheid. They wanted us to ignore the bad elements and love them for themselves, their country and their great hospitality… It was not surprising, therefore, that some rugby people were beguiled by it and became so ambivalent over their racial politics.

It was to have a profound effect on many of us and the first time that I really began to think about apartheid and worry about our role in it was when female members of the United Party organised themselves into an anti-apartheid organisation called the Black Sash Women, and picketed our hotel in Port Elizabeth. I also observed at the games how the black people were segregated behind the goal posts, and I saw how they were treated in so many other aspects of normal life.

DOUGLAS BAKER (England)
Toured: 1955

Regarding political issues, the place was very strongly policed. Black people were very much subservient and in the background, and we were sheltered from the differences between blacks and whites.

The First Test team at Ellis Park.

HUGH McLEOD

We had a good manager in Jack Siggins. He was a major in the army and he spoke about us being on parade. He wouldn't put up with any nonsense – we weren't even allowed to sunbathe because Jack didn't like you taking your shirt off.

The pitches were that hard out there that we were all getting grass wounds, and Jack Siggins would insist on putting this pink iodine disinfectant on the cuts. I'd never seen anything like it before, and I haven't seen anything like it since. He'd dab it on with cotton wool and you'd be about hitting the roof because it stung so much. It got to a point that the boys would rush out the showers and put their flannels on as quickly as they could so that he couldn't get at them – but he'd come in and demand to see our cuts.

ERNIE MICHIE

We had a fortnight before our first game, which was against Eastern Province – and we were beaten. We just didn't gel. I didn't play until the third game. I maybe shouldn't say it, but there seemed to be a little bias against the Scots. We didn't seem to get the benefit of the doubt that the English and Welsh got. But as far as I was concerned I was young and I was light for a second-row. Robin Thomson was the captain and Rhys Williams from Wales was about 16 stone, so they were paired up right away because of their weight, to counter the heavy South African pack.

PHIL DAVIES

The tour character was Tony O'Reilly, a 19-year-old with a very bright mind and

Action from the Western Province match at Newlands, Cape Town.

tremendous speed and elusiveness on the wing, allied to an Irish sense of humour. Over the years he has so eloquently teased and properly caricatured my forthright approach and last-second off-loads in the centre, with accompanying public school/ BBC speech. But it was the wings that scored the tries, as they continued to do in New Zealand in 1959, so I've always felt that he could say what he liked.

Jeff Butterfield, my great centre partner for England and the Lions, a Loughborough PE teacher working at Worksop, the great Midland rival of Denstone (my old school), ran the training. This was a mixture of warm-up exercises for muscle groups and intense, stamina-testing repeated sprints. This I had been used to at Cambridge, where the Austrian coach, Franz Stampl, had introduced 'fartleks', or repeated sprints with jogs in between. The athletics scene at Cambridge included Chris Brasher (steeplechase gold medal) and Angus Scott (half mile), who were later Olympians with Roger Bannister. Although winning my event (440 yards) in the University sports selection procedure, I did not win a half Blue.

DICKIE JEEPS
Tony O'Reilly was a great player – he was so young, but the quickest winger any of us had ever seen.

DOUGLAS BAKER
Cliff Morgan was a wonderful character who skylarked a lot, and could play the piano perfectly by ear. He had never learned the piano, yet could just pick up a tune and play it. I remember we went to an ostrich farm and Cliff got on the back of one of them and rode it, then we went to a corn farm where he put a cob between his legs and stood behind the farmer. Tony O'Reilly was a young god, very handsome, and the girls swooned over him, so he enjoyed himself thoroughly.

HUGH McLEOD
When the boys went out on a Saturday, some of them would find a girl, and sometimes another one of the boys would whisk her away. Well, Trevor Lloyd, the Welsh scrum-half, objected to this – so he brought it up at a Sunday meeting and from then on we called that Lloyd's Law (a term still used decades later).

CECIL PEDLOW (Ireland)
Toured: 1955

Tony O'Reilly and I would be lent a car and we'd cruise around the best areas of Johannesburg on a Saturday night after a match. When we saw a lot of cars, we'd stop, knock on the door and ask if that was where the party was. If it wasn't a party then, it was once the people had seen Tony standing at the front door.

CLIFF MORGAN
All the girls used to come up and say, 'Oh, I touched Tony O'Reilly!' because they adored him. Tom Reid used to joke and say, 'It's all immoral. It's like Our Lord, oh, I touched his feet!'

CLEM THOMAS

The hospitality was overwhelming. One farmer, whose wife was the daughter of my tutor at St John's College, Cambridge, actually kept a leopard – which had been decimating his cattle – alive for a couple of weeks so that I could shoot it. Jack Siggins heard about it and decided to ban my involvement but the farmer shot it anyway and gave me the cured skin. It was not so politically incorrect in those days... On another occasion, a farmer came to our hotel in the centre of Johannesburg, and presented me with a lion cub. Siggins insisted on my donating it to a local zoo, which I did with some relief.

DOUGLAS BAKER

Socially it was magnificent, and we were feted wherever we went. We got on very well, there were no schisms between English, Welsh, Irish or Scots, and although it was three months long, it was a very happy tour. The Welsh contingent were really social, had good voices, and always organised the choirs. We visited Table Mountain, the vineyards, and the old Dutch settlement in the Cape.

HUGH McLEOD

Phil Davies only had one shirt with him. He washed it in the sink every night and hung it up in the room to dry. At the end of the tour we all chipped in and bought him a new one. Phil objected to having to wear an overcoat or a pullover at night, so the manager told him he could be exempt from that rule, but if he got a cold and couldn't play then he would be on the first plane home.

The South Africans used to ask us how we liked their country and Billy Williams would say: 'Bloody awful, I wish I was home for a fish supper in a paper poke.' He was that sick of eating steak and lamb and chicken. You'd be sitting having a meal and the waiter would come up and ask: 'Is everything alright, boss? Is everything good, master?' And Robin Roe, who was a church minister, objected to this. 'I'm not your master,' he'd say.

But Courtenay Meredith, the Welsh tight-head prop, quite liked being called boss and master, so they disagreed on this and I thought there was going to be fisticuffs. So there was friction there.

I was very friendly with Dickie Jeeps. We trained together and we talked about rugby a lot, but Dickie was a fearless bugger when he got the worse with drink. We were at the dinner after the First Test in 1959, and were served oysters, and Dickie started throwing them about, and he hit the president at the top table with one. I thought there was going to be big trouble then. There was plenty of drinking and I was teetotal, but that didn't bother me. As a matter of fact, I quite enjoyed watching them play their drinking games.

Felt boots were the fashion of the time, and I remember Angus Cameron threw one into the pool, and it happened to belong to Dickie. So he grabbed Angus and dragged him into the pool fully clothed. That served him right.

Tom Elliot was a hell of a man. I didn't go to bed early but I didn't last as long as Tom, who would find some locals to go drinking with until all hours. He'd come in at two or three in the morning and lift my whole bed up, so that I would come out like a bundle of tatties. I'd climb back into bed and go to sleep, and in the morning I'd be up, fresh and ready to go out, while Tom was still passed out. So I'd get my own back. I'd lift the bed up and bundle him out, and when I came back in for lunch he'd still be passed out on the floor. He'd never moved.

Whenever you went out for a meal with the Welsh, you could tell when they'd had enough. You'd hear them jabbering a bit of Welsh and that meant they were ready to go home.

DOUGLAS BAKER

Cliff Morgan's speed off the mark was electric, and he was often past his marker before they could move. He was an incredible dynamo, and had a very good rugby brain, linking well with his centres and putting them away. The only downside was that he wasn't a great tackler – it was not his forté – but his wing-forwards looked after him. For the South Africans it was Tom van Vollenhoven. He was not the biggest wing, but he ran very hard, and in the last Test he went through me to score when

Bryn Meredith throws out a protective screen as Dickie Jeeps gets the ball from a lineout in the Third Test in Pretoria.

thought I could put him into touch. Dickie Jeeps partnered Cliff in all the Tests, although he didn't have the flair of Johnny Williams, who was brilliant at times, but erratic. Jeeps would be the feeder, and absolutely reliable – he rarely made a break himself, but he fed Cliff very well, and that's why he outdid Johnny.

CLEM THOMAS

It was a magnificent experience, I always saw it as the peak of my rugby career, even though because of appendicitis, I missed the first 10 games of the tour. South Africa could still be a rough place in those years, you still came across dirt roads quite near the middle of the big cities. But it was also fine and glamorous, and it felt like a crusade. Decades later, whenever I met fellow tourists, the stories would flow and the years would fall away.

PHIL DAVIES

I became very friendly with my final room-mate Jim Greenwood, then teaching at Glenalmond in the wilds of central Scotland. To train he would sprint alternate telegraph poles down the glen and back. We would talk about literature and music as well as the poetry book, *Comic and Curious Verse*, that kept me more or less sane. Once we watched opera in Afrikaans. He spoke English in a soft Scottish accent with fervour and enthusiasm, though on the pitch without his teeth he was incoherent. No mouth guards then.

He later, after teaching at Cheltenham and Tiffins, became Professor of English at Loughborough University, and, with John Robins, transformed attitudes to attacking rugby. He was also very instrumental in putting the women's game on the map. He would have enjoyed seeing how far it has come these days.

Defence was not coached on the tour, and this was usual for the day. We did practise a few attacking moves – the wings and the fullback joining in as an extra man, scissors, and long lineout throws, but there was little co-ordination with the pack. Jim Greenwood, captain of Scotland, and a back-row forward, said, 'It was the only team I played for in which you broke going forward,' rather than covering to the far post. He later changed attitudes with his seminal coaching book, *Total Rugby*, which so influenced Clive Woodward.

The truly great player for the Lions was Cliff Morgan at fly-half. So quick off the mark and so elusive, leaving Basie van Wyk (his great rival and the South African flanker) for dead in the First Test. For South Africa, it was Karel (Tom) van Vollenhoven, a policeman and ruthless side-stepping wing or centre who went on to play for St. Helens in Rugby League with great success. I still carry a split-cheek scar from his elbow when we beat Northern Transvaal, with 14 men again, and value my picture of him sprawled on the ground as I went in under the posts. There is no love lost there.

The great social experience was the food – for breakfast, they would ask: 'One or two steaks, eh man?' Rationing had only just ended in the United Kingdom. We were generously entertained, often privately on farms where the hosts were delightful. More formal occasions were more stilted, and occasionally unpleasant as political issues emerged. This was hard dutiful work, and often dull. The visit to the Kruger Park and Victoria Falls were memorable scenic high points which much appealed to my biology background. Generally, I was, I suspect, rather aloof and withdrawn – hardly surprising as a newly-wed.

GARETH GRIFFITHS (Wales)
Toured: 1955

I wasn't in the original tour selection but, happily, they sent for me within about three weeks.

In many ways, the ball bounced at the right time then. They'd had a number of injuries and I seem to remember playing a lot of games on the trot, Wednesday, Saturday, Wednesday, Saturday. I played close to three games a week for four weeks.

I was a sprinter so I could play wing, centre or full back because I could run and catch a ball, and I wasn't a bad kicker either. The rugby was great. I think it was the toughest rugby I'd ever played.

A lot of those South Africans were farmers and were very tall and strong. Their forwards were better than our forwards, I think, because of their background. I think we had the better three-quarter line because we could all sprint a bit and we played fairly regularly.

It was 2-2 at the end – but it was like a dream in many ways.

Phil Davies leaves Tom van Vollenhoven in his wake as he sprints in to score.

DOUGLAS BAKER

had great admiration for Cliff Morgan, my rival for the stand-off position, who was
 great player, and a great person. He was mercurial, really quicksilver, and you could
 arely get your hands on him, whereas I was cumbersome, a couple of stone heavier,
 nd much more solid. So, I had no thought of usurping his position, and was delighted
 o play in two Tests. I had been selected for the Lions because I covered inside-centre,
 ly-half and fullback.

   I played in the Third and Fourth Tests, both times at fullback. I had played four
 ames at fly-half for England in the 1955 (Five Nations) Championship, but I could
 ever possibly outdo Cliff Morgan. So, I was lucky enough to play fullback, where
  had played quite a lot for East Midlands and Middlesex – while poor old Angus
 Cameron (vice-captain and fullback), who was injured after the first two Tests, had a
 reat tour in terms of enjoying it, and put on a bit of weight.

ERNIE MICHIE

 or the First Test, all I did was play the bagpipes and lead the team onto the pitch. When I
 vas sent all the details of the tour I asked if I could take my pipes with me, and they were

 Gareth Griffiths is caught by Roy Dryburgh inches from the line early in the Third Test.

quite happy with that. The only problem was that it was so dry and hot that it was difficult keeping them blowing properly. We had some good fun when we were letting our hair down, and I'd get the pipes out and the chaps would prance around and try to dance.

HUGH McLEOD
The Welsh front-row (Courtenay Meredith, Bryn Meredith and Billy Williams) had been successful so I couldn't see myself getting in. They were good players and they were older than me – so I was happy playing in 13 of the 25 games – and I would have played in 14 but I got dysentery and couldn't play the last match, against East Africa in Nairobi.

We won the First Test, and we had the backs to win the series – Tony O'Reilly, Jeff Butterfield, Phil Davies, Cliff Morgan and Dickie Jeeps could have held their own in any company – but our forwards couldn't match the Springboks. They had bigger and better-equipped guys

CLIFF MORGAN
The South African Rugby Union took us to see one of their own games and put us in seats on the touchline which were below ground level. We were looking up at the players, who all seemed 15 feet tall, and they frightened us to death. We looked at each other and, in comparison, we were all little fellows: how could we compete?

Yet on the field in the months to come, the Lions team proved that size and weight weren't all-important, particularly in winning a reasonable share of the ball against the odds

Probably the most glorious sight in rugby was to see O'Reilly in full flight. Like the rest of Tony's life, not one of his tries he scored was ordinary. Everything was slightly

The Lions offer up a brick wall of defence during the Fourth Test.

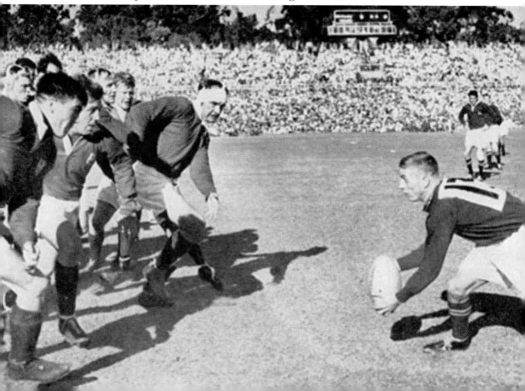

ectacular. He was only 19, but he had the wit and wisdom of someone 20 years der. He gave the tour a touch of class. It made you feel slightly inadequate that you eren't in the same mental bracket. He towered over you in every sense.

ONY O'REILLY

he First Test in Johannesburg was the most striking Test of its time. It was the ggest attendance ever seen at a rugby match. South Africa led 11-3 and we lost our nker Reg Higgins with a broken leg. There were no replacements, of course, so e had to play with 14 men, three scores down at 6,000ft up in front of more than 0,000 Afrikaners baying for our blood.

Then Morgan scored one of the great tries of his life, Jeff Butterfield made a autiful break and Cecil Pedlow shot away to score, and then I scored and we had got to -11 from 11-3 down. But suddenly we ran out of puff and they came back at us. And the very last minute Chris Koch crashed over and they had a very easy kick to win.

VIAN JENKINS

(riting in the *Sunday Times*)

ck van der Schyff to take the kick at goal. Van der Schyff, the automaton, the robot, e kicker fantastic, who earlier in the game had put over two penalty goals and two onversions from all angles like a mathematician going about his work with a set-uare. Although the kick was out towards the touchline, it seemed inconceivable that could fail. As he placed the ball and walked back for those few deliberate paces of s, the visiting heart stood still.

ONY O'REILLY

om Reid, the big second-row from Limerick, said: 'Jesus, if he kicks this I'm turning rotestant.' So that was the magnitude of what he felt about the kick. There was dible silence, van der Schyff came up and just pushed it to the left of the post. It as amazing, but we had won.

VIAN JENKINS

he gods were on the Lions' side and the ball hooked, by a surely trembling foot, went iling far away to the left of the uprights and the spoils were ours. The groan rising om over 95,000 throats had to be heard to be believed.

LIFF MORGAN

aying in the First Test would have been an extraordinary experience whatever had hap-ned on the field. It drew the biggest crowd ever to watch a rugby international – of-ially 96,000. But thousands more got in without paying, since tickets were pushed back er fences to people waiting outside to re-use them. There was a grandstand on only e side of Ellis Park at that time, so the rest were crammed into standing areas. Their pact was almost overpowering as you came down the flight of steps on to the field.

And another thing that staggered us was that, on the touchline 20 yards out from the front of the grandstand, the Springbok selectors sat in a row of chairs on their own. Everybody knew who they were, and so they were there to be booed, cheered, heckled or whatever took the fancy of the crowd.

DOUGLAS BAKER

I had a pair of plastic lenses which I bought in Germany playing against the British Army. An officer suggested I buy some – you bought them off the shelf in Hamburg. Contact lenses were not really known in the UK, but I couldn't read a blackboard at school in the back row, and it made all the difference when I played rugby being able to see the ball coming out of the scrum, or a high ball, a split-second earlier. Unfortunatel prior to the Third Test in Pretoria, a cleaner knocked them off my bedside table and trod on one, shattering it. Jack Siggins, our manager, got hold of the British High Commissioner and said, 'See what you can do for this man.' I was told that an optician i Johannesburg could make me a pair, so I went down to see him on three successive day – they fitted my eyes perfectly, and I wore them for the Third Test. They fitted under the eyelid with lubricant fluid, and were not especially comfortable, but they made a big difference. The South African Rugby Board very kindly paid for them.

The first time I used my instep to goal-kick was against Western Province in Cape Town, and it was a fairly new approach to kicking. It was a spur of the moment decisio – I had an intuition that if I used my instep I could hook the conversion over, and it worked. However, I didn't use it for the penalty in Pretoria in the Third Test, which was pressure kick about midway from the centre to the touchline, 30 yards out.

PHIL DAVIES

We were to draw the series 2-2 with two good wins at high altitude. The First Test, dubbed 'the Greatest Test ever', played with the Lions reduced to 14 players, was on my 27th birthday. It was the tenth anniversary of the dropping of the first atomic bomb on Japan. The lovely Welsh forwards and Cliff Morgan agreed, 'It was just as well we went to chapel last Sunday.'

In Durban and a wet Cape Town we seemed stolid. Hard grounds and grazed knee suited our running, which completely tore apart the all-conquering Orange Free State something not before witnessed.

Gradually defences were tightened and studied. Defence analysis had begun – how unfair to use cine cameras! I injured an ankle and lost form just before the last Test, playing in a dismal game against Border. We did everything but score. What would have been a winning try in the last few minutes was knocked out of my hands over the line. 'The tackle of the tour' it was said. I was not amused, and very downcast. Correctly, I was not selected for the last Test. I would not have made a difference.

DOUGLAS BAKER

I don't think we should have won the series, and part of the problem with the Fourth

est was that we were due to fly out on the Sunday immediately after playing on
he Saturday. We had to get packed up beforehand and were a bit brow-beaten, so
e didn't have our minds focused on the game as much as we should. In terms of
ganisation, the Home Unions should have given us a bit of leeway, and time to relax
ter the final Test.

LIFF MORGAN

he Lions party had such a strong family spirit that the friendship within it survived even
e strain of arguable team selections and inevitably unfair shares of the limelight.

What you realise now is that bonds are created and people stick together when
ey haven't got too much to spend. In our case, the bond held too, as our reunions
terwards proved.

I find it sad to contemplate a rugby world with no more Lions tours, and none of
e opportunity they provide to play alongside former and future opponents, sharing
eir lives and their views on life.

That tour to South Africa did a great deal to teach me that you had to have confidence
your fellow man and faith that he wasn't going to let you down. Your life was enriched
a feeling that everybody wanted everybody else to do well, which is what made the
hole experience for me. I hope that the Lions continue to tour for ever more.

HIL DAVIES

here are not too many of us left, and we have not had a reunion for some while.
e last met in Ireland staying with Tony O'Reilly, watching his wife's racehorses and
s pedigree herd of Belted Galloway, which, as we sipped wine on the terrace in the
ening, slowly meandered across the lime tree avenue down to the Liffey river for a
ink. As it got dark we withdrew to the two drawing rooms to admire the Picasso and
e Monet of Rouen Cathedral. Wonderfully civilised.

We were a very civilised and friendly bunch of lads back in 1955, many abroad for
e first time. We learned rapidly and became very good lifelong friends, sadly now
ry reduced in number.

UGH McLEOD

2007, Tony O'Reilly organised for a group of us to go to the World Cup Final in
ris, and we stayed in Le Bristol Hotel, which was about £600 a night. Because we
ere both by ourselves, I was put in a room with Courtenay Meredith and I wasn't that
eased about it.

So when I went in the room I said: 'Right, Courtenay, I'm going to tell you from the
art, I've not shared a room with a man for fifty years.'

And Courtenay said: 'Well, you're alright with me, Hugh, because I'm in the same boat.'

And you know it was the funniest thing, you would have thought we had never
en away. Straight away, it was like we were back on tour. We were in and out of the
ower, and just got on with it – just like we would have back in 1955.

CHAPTER FOURTEEN

KINGS OF RUGBY
1959

AUSTRALIA, NEW ZEALAND AND CANADA

ONE MAN *dominated the press coverage of the 1959 Lions tour of Australia and New Zealand, another tour when the Lions played magnificent rugby that thrilled even home supporters, and another when, agonisingly, they fell short. His name was Don Clarke of New Zealand. The All Blacks' fullback was a hefty figure, and far from the fastest mover with the ball in hand. But he was a match-winner with the ability to land goals from anywhere in an opponent's half and, sometimes, even from inside his own. His feats in the Test series and the dominance of the penalty goal led to an outcry for a change in the laws. At the time, every penalty could give rise to a kick at goal, even those awarded for relatively piffling offences. Furthermore, the try in 1959 was still worth only three points.*

Eventually, the International Rugby Board introduced the concept of the differential penalty, rugby's indirect free kick, into the game. They have never been famous for rapid decisions and the move came 18 years after the tour. Gradually, the value of the try was also increased – first, three points to four then upwards to five. Both moves can be traced, indirectly, to one day in Dunedin in 1959.

Clarke's kicking broke the tourists' hearts in the First Test. New Zealand's hero was the Lions' villain, landing a then world record six penalty goals. The Lions, living up to their tradition for running rugby, scored four tries. But with tries and penalty goals valued at three points each at the time, the All Blacks ran out 18-17 winners. As the Lions licked their wounds, the world's rugby columns were filled with calls for rule changes. The debate over what many felt was a travesty expanded to include questions as to the nature of rugby itself, and what kind of sport it was supposed to be. Terry McLean, the leading New Zealand rugby writer, called it 'a day of shame'.

If there was not enough controversy surrounding the day, the Lions were also privately incensed at the refereeing of the New Zealand official, Allan Fleury, refereeing not only in his home nation but in his home province. Fleury was never to take charge of an international match again and his performance gave fuel to a debate in the game as to whether neutral referees should be introduced. Eventually, they were – but not until the late 1970s.

At Athletic Park, Wellington, the tourists were 8-6 ahead with barely two minutes of the Second Test remaining. The All Blacks launched a last-minute attack, Clarke moved up to join the three-quarters to add an extra man and, sensing an overlap, cut in, surprised the defence and crossed near the posts. It was the first time a New Zealand fullback had scored a try in a Test and his conversion put the All Blacks 11-8 in front. Victory had been prised from the Lions' jaws.

Opposite: Ronnie Dawson leads his team out for the First Test in Dunedin.

The Lions could not quibble at Christchurch where they were crushed 22-8 in the Third Test. Clarke kicked four goals but the All Blacks scored four tries to one and the tourists were overwhelmed in both the forwards and backs.

The usual round of injuries and tiredness had taken its toll on the tourists so it was a wonderful surprise when the Lions finally played to their full potential at Eden Park in the final Test and secured a 9-6 win, with three tries to two Clarke penalties. There the running of Tony O'Reilly, the brilliant Irishman who had come sensationally to the fore in South Africa in 1955, Peter Jackson, the mesmeric England wing, and Bev Risman, later to enjoy a stellar career in rugby league, thrilled the huge crowd with their pace and power, and when the final whistle brought down the curtain on the tour the visitors were given a standing ovation.

Don Clarke had missed a late penalty that would have equalised the score, but the relief among New Zealanders at that miss summed up the feelings about the series. Jack Griffiths, a noted All Black of the 1930s and later a respected NZRFU council member, spoke for many of his compatriots when he wrote two days later: 'It has amazed me to hear so many voice the opinion, genuinely, of how pleased they were that the last kick did not go over. I don't think we could have lived it down.' The Lions were left to reflect on what might have been had it not been for that man Clarke and his devastating accuracy with the boot.

The 1959 tourists were managed by former Scotland internationalist Alf 'The Manager' Wilson and captained by the young Irish hooker, Ronnie Dawson. They included the usual mix of youth and experience. Malcolm Thomas, who had been to Australia and New Zealand with the 1950 party, became the first Lion to make a return visit there since 'Boxer' Harding in 1908, and although England's Peter Robbins, an original choice, had to withdraw after breaking his leg against Newport on the Barbarians' traditional Easter tour of South Wales, every member of the original tour party was an established international.

The Scottish prop Hugh McLeod had been a dirt-tracker in South Africa in 1955, while Rhys Williams, Bryn Meredith, Tony O'Reilly, Jeff Butterfield (nearing the end of his career) and Dickie Jeeps (who had actually been dropped by England for the winter's Five Nations) survived from the Test side that had shared the spoils with the Springboks. O'Reilly, as in 1955, finished as top try-scorer with a remarkable 22 in 23 appearances and captured the imagination of the hosts with his strong running and searing pace. Indeed, it was always said of the future business tycoon that the best was seen of him in a Lions jersey: somehow he never quite matched his tour form wearing the green of Ireland.

That the Lions came anywhere near competing with the All Blacks in 1959, was arguably a miracle. So too was the fact that they played with such rare style. The Five Nations had been dominated by France who won the title outright for the first time. It's true that the laws of the game at the time were heavily stacked in favour of defensive tactics, but in the six games played among the Four Home Unions that year only 50 points, including just seven tries, were scored. Two of the matches yielded no tries and England had been try-less in five international matches dating back to March 1958.

So it was a pleasant surprise to see the Lions hit the ground running (literally) when they arrived in Australia for the opening leg of the tour. They won five of their six matches – losing 18-14 when playing with only 14 men for 77 minutes against New South Wales – but were convincing winners of the two Tests. O'Reilly scored a classic try in the Brisbane Test, leaving several defenders trailing in his wake as the Lions powered to a 17-6 win. A week later they won the Sydney Test 24-3, O'Reilly crossing again, and the party set off in high spirits for New Zealand.

The only setback up to this point was a serious injury sustained by Niall Brophy. The Irish wing had had the uncomfortable experience of having to take his accountancy examinations as soon as he stepped off the plane when the Lions arrived in Melbourne for the start of the tour. Then, in the third minute of the game against New South Wales, he turned on his heel gathering a loose ball, fell to the ground and took no further part in the tour. What at first was diagnosed as a badly twisted ankle showed up on X-ray to be a broken instep bone.

Life on the field was much tougher in New Zealand, where the Lions were invariably held or bettered by the provincial packs. The 'long ruck' had become part and parcel of the New Zealand game by now but was a mystery to the Lions. Neither the ruck nor maul were then defined in the laws of the game and there was a tendency among European referees to blow up for a scrum almost immediately play broke down in the loose. Not so in New Zealand. Forwards arrived in force, often all eight together to pack in a scrum formation around the ball where they would heel it back on the floor (ruck) or wrest it free from a man holding it (maul).

Yet despite their forwards' unfamiliarity with this aspect of loose play, the Lions resolved to use such morsels of possession that came their way for attack. In O'Reilly and Jackson they had wings who were electric opportunists. Jackson in particular went down well with the locals for his mazy running. One commentator said that when play swept away from Jackson's wing he should be given a unicycle to amuse spectators. Crowds had come specifically to see him perform and expected to be continuously entertained by the Coventry man his teammates had nicknamed 'Nikolai'.

Big Rhys Williams' lionhearted performances at lock, particularly in the Tests, won him immortality. He so impressed the All Blacks that they called him 'one of us' and New Zealand's rugby Wisden, its Rugby Almanack, named him one of the five outstanding players of the year. In fact four of the five so honoured were Lions, testament indeed to the impression they made. Williams' Llanelli and Wales team-mate Terry Davies, the Lions' fullback, Ken Scotland (also a fullback who

The 1959 tour party.

*appeared at centre, fly-half and scrum-half during the visit) and England's fly-half Bev Risman were
the others recognised for the star quality they brought to the tourists' back-play. Davies and Scotland
provided rare quality for the Lions, with Davies more of an old school fullback of substance, and
Scotland a regal footballer.*

*The Lions were a lively and personable party off the field and made many friends in Australia
and New Zealand where hospitality was once again unbelievable. Viv Jenkins, who made eight
Lions visits as player or journalist, maintained that the class of '59 were the most gifted and talented
– academically, socially and in business – that he toured with. The tour also gave Jenkins grist
to his mill; he espoused the cause of the indirect penalty and neutral referees in columns in many
publications until both measures were brought in.*

*There was a great camaraderie among the party. Ray Prosser, the famous Pontypool bulldozer
driver and later coach and mentor of ferocious Pontypool club teams, and Alan 'Neddy' Ashcroft, were
natural comedians. O'Reilly and Andy Mulligan, a scrum-half replacement, provided amusing Irish
banter while Cambridge Blue-turned-City-gent, David Marques, was the friendly butt of some of the
party's humour.*

*Marques, the Harlequins and England second-row, stood 6ft 5in – the tallest man ever to have
played international rugby up to then – and took everything in his stride with a whimsical sense
of humour. He was such a gentleman that even when he was duffed up in the shocking roughhouse
match against Auckland before the First Test he stood up, dusted himself down and simply smiled
at his assailant. Asked by a puzzled team-mate why he hadn't retaliated, Marques is said to have
replied: 'I wanted to make him feel a cad.'*

*Rough play was often an issue in New Zealand. Obstruction, late tackling, what would today be
called lazy running and sheer brutality were rife. There was a vicious match in Auckland near the*

Peter Jackson scores the Lions' second try against Auckland at Eden Park.

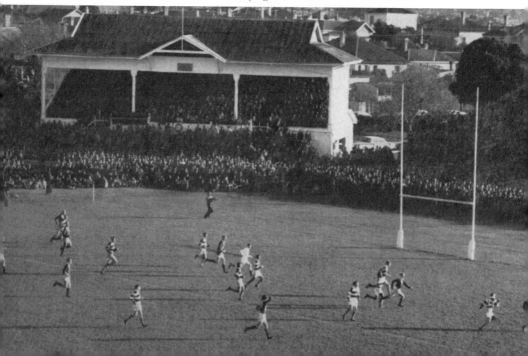

end of the tour against the Maori and Terry McLean of the New Zealand Herald *pulled no punches in his post-tour summary: 'It is of the highest importance to the future of New Zealand rugby and its reputation in world affairs that there should be a disinterested and objective inquiry into the incidents of rough and obstructive play in matches of the Lions' tour.'*

One internal issue caused the tourists angst. Manager Wilson had to enforce the strict ruling that injured players be sent home. Brophy and the Irish fly-half Mick English were early casualties and though invited to stay for part of the tour as guests of the NZRFU, both were eventually requested to depart for home. The team felt aggrieved at this and there was even talk of a mutiny. At length the issue was resolved, the two Irishmen departed but still managed to get the last laugh. English, a great wit and engaging story-teller to his dying day, used to tell with relish how he and Brophy left mid-tour, travelled halfway around the world on the Four Home Unions' expenses and contrived to get home after the main Lions tour party had returned.

All three of the Lions tour parties which toured in the 1950s were referred to by the great Clem Thomas as 'Buccaneers'. There was something thrilling and fine about all three teams. However, yet again, and after months of entertainment provided to the New Zealand public, they had come up short, feeling the rough edges – or more precisely, the toe – of Don Clarke's boot. Pausing to play two games in Canada, the Lions nursed their memories and their regrets on their way home.

One of the younger tourists was with the Lions for the first time. He propped in the Second Test against New Zealand, missed the other three but played in both the Tests in Australia. He was from Ballymena, in Northern Ireland. His name was Syd Millar, and the name would resonate in Lions stories of the future.

SYD MILLAR (Ireland)

Toured: 1959, 1962 & 1968. Coach: 1974. Manager: 1980

I played for Ballymena for a year and then I went to sea. I was a cadet and in 1955 I was in the Indian Ocean in a tanker delivering fuel in Beira, in what was then Portuguese East Africa. The only entertainment we had on board was the radio and

Andrew Mulligan spins the ball away from the scrum to launch an attack against Auckland.

when we went off the coast of Africa there'd be commentaries of the 1955 Lions and that was really the first interest I ever had in Lions rugby.

RONNIE DAWSON (Ireland)
Toured: 1959. Assistant Manager/Coach: 1968

I got a letter from Mr Bradforth, honorary secretary of the Home Unions Tour Committee and it was just a brief letter. It started with your surname. 'Dear Dawson…' It went on to say, 'You are invited to join the tour… blah, blah, blah… of Australia, New Zealand and Canada,' and when I got it I was absolutely delighted and didn't really finish the letter, I just put it down with a big 'Yippee!' The last few words when I went back to look at it again said '…and to be its captain.'

KEN SCOTLAND (Scotland)
Toured: 1959

It was very much a player-driven tour. There was a manager, a secretary and a guy looking after the bags – but on the field it was Ronnie Dawson and the senior players who decided our tactics. The management had a say in selection, but they never appeared on the practice ground or anything like that.

DICKIE JEEPS

I've never written a book about it, but, if I did, I'd tell you about the bad management on Lions tours. We didn't have a coach, we largely trained ourselves – Jeff Butterfield being a good fitness 'coach', he worked on us in that department and got us fit. We had to work everything out for ourselves, because the management wasn't capable of working it out.

The players inspect the pitch before the First Test in Dunedin.

SYD MILLAR

Ronnie was captain and had to play, coach, make speeches, be the bag manager, the lot. He was very focused. A clear thinker. He was a very good captain and deserved better. He was a very good analyst of the game. He had the respect of the boys.

BILLY MULCAHY (Ireland)
Toured: 1959 & 1962

He was ahead of his time in that he'd done a lot of research on the opposition.

KEN SCOTLAND

We had three particularly experienced players with us. Bryn Meredith had been the hooker in South Africa in 1955, Jeff Butterfield had been one of the stars in 1955, and Malcolm Thomas had been in New Zealand in 1950, so he was able to tell us a little bit about what to expect. Sadly, neither Bryn nor Jeff had any luck with injuries or selection.

Bryn Meredith must have known when he went that he was going to struggle to get games given that his rival hooker, Ronnie Dawson, was the captain, but he couldn't have been more supportive. Jeff Butterfield had a lot of niggly injuries and he had also started to lose his pace. So, although he was still a lovely rugby player, he had virtually no impact on the field. Where he was of great value to the tour, however, was in taking the training sessions. He was fantastic socially, was the life and soul of the party in a sensible way, and never complained about his rotten luck.

MALCOLM THOMAS (Wales)
Toured: 1950 & 1959

Each team member had his part to play in the way of personality, character and ability, in making the party vitally alive. It has always been very difficult for me to imagine a bad rugby tour, such has been my good fortune in my playing career.

ALAN ASHCROFT (England)
Toured: 1959

I was made up about being selected for the tour, but there was a lot of competition. It was a hell of an experience touring Australia and New Zealand, and people there were very welcoming. It's bound to be one of your most cherished memories because you cannot have a better one in rugby – you met so many good people, no baddies. It was great.

I was a teacher on unpaid leave, and the tour allowance didn't cover you. It was about 50p a day, enough for an odd beer, but fortunately my wife worked, and we lived in the flat that came with my job.

STAN COUGHTRIE (Scotland)
Toured: 1959

It was a great cross section of people, from David Marques, who came off the plane in the full attire of a city gent – white shirt and military tie, dark suit, bowler hat and rolled umbrella – and his great pal Ray Prosser, this gnarled Welsh prop, who Rhys Williams said had to be coaxed out of Pontypool to go on the tour because every time he crossed the bridge to leave town he felt he couldn't cope.

Haydn Morgan was a mechanic, and Tony O'Reilly swore that when they were sharing a room he woke up one night to find Haydn under his bed fiddling with the springs – dreaming that he was back in the garage fixing cars.

SYD MILLAR

It took us three days to get there. We went from London-Zurich, Zurich-Beirut, Beirut-Bombay, Bombay-Calcutta, Calcutta-Singapore, Singapore-Darwin, Darwin-Sydney and Sydney-Melbourne. Ray Prosser didn't like one bit of it. He hated flying. When people went walking around the plane he used to get nervous.

STAN COUGHTRIE

Our first game (in Australia) was in Melbourne and they still had the six o'clock swill there in those days. If you went into a bar just before 5 p.m. they would have these little glasses, they called them ponies, lined up along the bar, and a guy with a hose would go from one end to the other filling them up with beer. Then all of a sudden the locals would appear and go: wallop, wallop, wallop, wallop; because they only had an hour to drink before the bars closed at 6 p.m.

When we stayed in Melbourne, which was serious Australian Rules territory, it was like we were on a missionary quest to spread the rugby union gospel. And I remember we had this meeting in the hotel to discuss all these important issues crucial to the tour, and at

Ronnie Dawson and Wilson Whineray lead out their teams before the First Test.

one point Alf Wilson, the manager, asked if anyone else had any serious points to raise, expecting important issues like tour discipline and team selection to be on the agenda.

There was silence, then Noel Murphy, who had this wonderful Cork accent, piped up, 'Alf,' he said. 'In the morning, can we have a pot of tea and not a cup of tea?'

It was hilarious. The rest of the squad fell about laughing – but I'm not sure Noel could quite understand what was so funny.

TERRY DAVIES (Wales)
Toured: 1959

That 1959 tour was huge for me. I got injured early on and then had to climb back into the team again. It was magnificent playing for the Lions. It meant you'd reached the top of the ladder. It was a very long tour, six months practically. I had to give up my business to go on the tour and very few people had any wages out of it. We lived on 10 shillings a day, which is 50p in modern money, but we managed and we had an absolutely magnificent tour.

The welcome that we had when we arrived in Auckland is the abiding moment that I feel when I look back at the tour. There must have been 40,000 people in the airport waiting for us – we were the second Lions party to fly. We were then transported by these antique, open-top cars to our hotel and we passed through streets laden with people. It seemed that the whole of New Zealand had come out to meet us. New Zealand was definitely one of the places I would have emigrated to if I was that way inclined.

BILLY MULCAHY

I had to put off my final medical examinations to go on the tour much to the distress of my mother, who was widowed. She wanted me to get my exams and get the hell out. I had an elderly uncle who was a parish priest in Kilmallock, County Limerick, and he was a sort of father figure because my old man had passed on and he said I should go, so she pulled back her objections and I travelled. He was 89 at the time and wrote her a nice letter. The finals were put off but I had a big medical book with me on the tour.

RONNIE DAWSON

I think everything about New Zealand was about a decade behind what we had to come to know. The housing was all single-storey buildings with corrugated iron roofs. Very pleasant, though. The geography was the thing that interested me most. The Bay of Islands up in the north and the volcanic agricultural lands and then the southern Alps and the Canterbury plain – and in the southern Alps you had Queenstown, a beautiful part of the world – and then down to Invercargill, next stop the South Pole. I learned a lot about Maori culture and their people and their meeting houses and their wonderful wood carvings and schoolgirl choirs and of course the Haka. The big thing was the 12,000 mile difference. You had to book a telephone call about a week ahead or otherwise we sent postcards – and we arrived home before they did.

KEN SCOTLAND

We had a week in Eastbourne before we went, where we looked at an overall strategic plan, based on the fact that we knew we had a very quick set of backs. Dave Hewitt was only 19 years old and was the quickest thing on two legs I'd seen, John Young was a sprinter, Niall Brophy sadly didn't play very much because of injury but he was another really quick player.

So with these guys we wanted to move the ball as much as we could. Of course, you are always limited by how much possession you get and the weather conditions that you play in, and we were lucky on both those counts in 1959.

SYD MILLAR

Tony O'Reilly had looks, intelligence, was very articulate, could play rugby, could sing, could play the piano, and was a good cricketer. We were at a reception and the prime minister of New Zealand was there and they'd just announced the budget, so O'Reilly had him in the corner and after a while we saw the PM nodding. O'Reilly was telling him where he'd gone wrong in the budget. The ladies loved him. He'd turn up in his short shorts. He and Mulligan were a pair.

ALAN ASHCROFT

Our outstanding players were Tony O'Reilly and Peter Jackson who could score tries and create total havoc among the opposition. I had to do all the tackling, covering behind them in defence, but that was no problem. The New Zealanders were all good basic players, and their fullback Don Clarke kicked the goals, although a few of the penalties in the Tests were a bit dubious.

KEN SCOTLAND

Apart from that week in Eastbourne, we did very little serious training while we were away. We played virtually every Wednesday and Saturday, and travelled Thursday and Sunday, so you had a run-out the day before a game and that was about it. I kicked a ball about a lot with Terry Davies.

The New Zealanders were, as always, extremely focused and really hard to beat, but they played to a pretty limited game-plan. It was nine and ten man rugby. But, although they didn't do very much, what they did, they did with conviction and pace – so even if

Roddy Evans takes a lineout against Waikato.

you knew what was coming, it was very hard to cope with. Apart from the performance of their pack during the Third Test, I wouldn't say that they were anywhere near the best side I played against – they had some good players but their tactics were limited.

ALAN ASHCROFT

Basically, we tried to play open rugby, which was stupid, really, against the All Blacks. They just knocked down our backs and then played it through the pack, and went for a kicking game. We were told to play 'open attacking rugby' by Alf 'The Manager'. He didn't know much about rugby... and one of the problems was that he wouldn't let us get stuck in up front. Open rugby is all right, but if you're getting knocked down in the backs, you need to find other ways of going about it.

NOEL MURPHY (Ireland)
Toured: 1959 & 1966

It was tough, hard and brutal rugby.

RONNIE DAWSON

Very, very tough. No quarter asked or given. It was quite strange, one of the basic skills we learned was getting off the ball fast because if you stayed on it your back was in tatters. It was just the hard way the New Zealand forwards won possession from the ruck. It was most impressive. There were a few nasty incidents. We had a ferocious match with King Country. That was a tough one. I remember somebody dragged O'Reilly about a metre by his hair, which wasn't accepted. There were some punch-ups, but they were inevitable.

BILLY MULCAHY

Some matches were very tough and of their time. I think it was my first game back after a long period out injured. Wanganui – a game we were expected to waltz through. We won 9-6 and I scored a try. I remember being the recipient of a lot of hospitality on the ground in that match. We had a situation where they awarded us a penalty and Bev Risman was lining it up when a policeman, who was walking up and down, tapped the ref on the shoulder to point out to him that the touch judge on the far side had his flag up. The ref told Risman to go ahead. He kicked the goal, then the ref went over and discussed it with the touch judge and they gave New Zealand a lineout instead.

RONNIE DAWSON

We played Hawke's Bay and they kicked off with us in the normal formation to take the kick. The three of us in the front-row turned round as the ball flew over our heads to go and get in the ensuing maul and as we did I remember being hit flat on my face by the following-up New Zealand forwards. I looked round and there was Hughie McLeod flat on his face as well. Neither of us were anywhere near the ball but that didn't matter. They just stormed through, took the ball and within a relatively quick succession of maul and ruck they scored a try within the first two minutes. I remember thinking, 'Bloody hell, what's this about?' We went on and won the match well, 52-12, but clearly we had a lot of work to do.

SYD MILLAR

Some of the matches could be hard. Most were okay. We had not a very good game with the Maoris. A bit nasty. We were a bit naive in many ways. They had their coaches, we didn't. Ronnie did a superb job but you can't expect one man to be captain, coach, after-dinner speaker, man-manager, press officer. We weren't allowed to talk to the press, you know.

HUGH McLEOD

We used to train at the universities, and Dickie Jeeps and myself were desperate to do our own thing – we didn't have time for the students who came out and wanted to run around with us. I was young and it was all about rugby for me. But Peter Jackson had time for everybody. You'd see 20 students around him, or running up and down with him passing the ball.

Looking back, that is what I really admired about the great Peter Jackson: he had time for everybody.

Years later, when Colin Deans was going on tour in 1983, I went up and saw him before he left. I said: 'I'm not going to tell you how to play rugby, but take this advice: have a bit of time for the boys that come out and all they want to do is run with a Lion.' My one regret was that I grudged them that.

MALCOLM THOMAS

There was one aspect of the tour, which was given little publicity but which was of immense value. The management insisting at the outset that as many schools as possible should be visited in all the countries that we played. In all, over 1,000 schools or institutions were visited by members of the team.

Caulton scores in the Second Test.

Don Clarke dives over to score in the Second Test.

STAN COUGHTRIE

Peter Jackson was amazing. I remember him receiving the ball on the left wing in the first game in New Zealand against Hawke's Bay and coming inside with a sidestep, and he then sidestepped past six or seven more players before scoring in the opposite corner of the pitch. It was absolutely magical.

HUGH McLEOD

What a player Peter Jackson was. He'd get the ball on the touchline and take off with it, and everyone would be having heart attacks but he'd keep going and keep going. He could beat a man on a sixpence. He was big and elusive and had good players inside him.

After the first game of the tour, I came off exhausted. And I said to Peter, 'The hardest job I had today was keeping out your road.' He'd be going back and forward, beating a man and beating him again. His only weakness was his kicking, but when you can run like that then what do you need to kick for?

The boys used to say he slept with one eye open in case he missed something, so they christened him 'Nikolai the Russian Spy'.

TERRY DAVIES

I recall one game when we came on the field first and received a good cheer. The home team came on and they had an even bigger cheer. But then the referee ran on and got the biggest cheer of the lot. We scored a couple of tries and were refused two more. Then there was a long drop-out and it went to Tony O'Reilly. He'd been practising his sidestep all tour so, with 50 yards to go, off he went. He sidestepped all the way across the field until he reached the other touch line, beating about four men.

Then he found he was boxed in and so he started coming back again. He reached the other side and then had to change tack.

He shot up the edge of the field, handed off a few players, and then went in between the posts and put the ball down. The poor referee who had chased him all over the place arrived and Tony turned to him and said: 'Jesus ref, I nearly scored that time.'

After the game Ray Prosser said to me: 'Ter, did you see that O'Reilly? He passed me twice. He sidestepped me once, and then he gave me a dummy.' They were two great characters and players.

NOEL MURPHY

Ray Prosser was one of the great characters of all, some of his sayings were wonderful and he'd slag anybody. He was great. Tony O'Reilly and Andy Mulligan as well. Andy had a guitar and he'd entertain us on trains, planes and on the bus. They were a double act. If they went into the opera house in Auckland they'd have filled the place.

ALAN ASHCROFT

Off the field Ray Prosser and I would do a double act, taking the mick out of each other. He was my closest mate, and we were known as 'Ned and Ray – The Immortals'. Ray was a bulldozer driver by profession, Welsh as you like, and very basic but when spirits were low we would make the boys laugh. One of the social highlights was when I trained the lads to do a Maori dance and sing one of their songs, 'Epo-

An aerial view of the Third Test at Lancaster Park, Christchurch.

e-tai-tai-e', in Maori – and because we had taken the trouble to learn the song it went down a storm. We were very popular, and would sing it on request.

HUGH McLEOD

I roomed with big Roddy Evans from Wales. I had him for about 18 rooms. He was allowed a phone call every week because he'd just got married before he came away and he was hellish homesick. I think he was going to bail out if he didn't get his call.

One night at dinner the receptionist came and said he had this phone call, so off he went. And when I got back to my room he was writing her a letter. So I dragged him out to the pictures – because he would just have sat there feeling sorry for himself.

SYD MILLAR

We were playing a Wednesday match and I left my overcoat in the hotel room, a new overcoat that my mother insisted I buy before I went and I left what few quid I had and I came back and it was gone. Burgled. This was headlines in the paper. A few days later our manager, Alf Wilson, called me down and there was a pile of letters. He said, 'Those are for you and I've opened them.' I said, 'What do you mean you've opened my letters?' He said, 'They're all addressed from New Zealand and they're all full of cheques and money for you. You'll write a letter to every one of them and send the money back.' I said, 'Oh, all right Alf.'

We called Alf 'Magoo' after the little cartoon character. He was hard but fair and he was obsessed about things like that. I had to write the letters and send the money back. One of the guys who had sent me a cheque came to the hotel and brought me a

Ken Scotland (left) and Peter Jackson (right).

transistor radio which was very, very expensive at that time. So I did rather better out of it. There was also a case of whisky stolen. Alf had whisky sent at regular intervals from Scotland. As the boys said, there was a bigger investigation into who stole the whisky than there was into why we lost the series.

NOEL MURPHY

I remember the First Test and the man I was marking was a fisherman who came in from the sea, tied up his boat on the Thursday, played his rugby on the Saturday and went back out to sea. A fella called Peter Jones. He was 17st 2lbs and about 6ft 3in or 6ft 4in. I remember being at a lineout and I couldn't see the scrum-half. He was huge and an incredible All Black. They had a great pack.

RONNIE DAWSON

They had a wonderful back-row; 'Bunny' Tremain was terrific but there was a smaller guy and an immense player called Red Conway, who had an absolutely extraordinary game that day.

SYD MILLAR

The First Test was the one that got away. We lost it 18-17, scored four tries and had a fifth disallowed. Don Clarke kicked six penalties. In the last quarter of the game, the crowd usually shouts, 'Black, Black, Black!', but they were actually shouting, 'Red, Red, Red!' There were headlines about the unfairness of it.

RONNIE DAWSON

In those times the refs were always from the country you were in and we had a few problems, but the most painful of all was in the First Test. You could say, 'We wuz robbed'; 18-17. I feel it badly. We should have drawn that series instead of losing it 3-1.

NOEL MURPHY

You never talked about a referee as a player, but the New Zealand public and the press

The Junior All Blacks and the Lions march out before their match at Athletic Park.

talked about it. We were looking like we were going to win the First Test and it was taken away from us and whether the penalties were right or wrong, we still were beaten by six penalty goals.

SYD MILLAR

I have never forgotten his name!

BILLY MULCAHY

Fleury from Otago. Lovely man, God bless him.

SYD MILLAR

I was chairman of the Northern Ireland sports council and I was in New Zealand for the Commonwealth Games in 1990; I was walking down the street in Auckland and there was a big crowd outside a bookshop. There was a man with a microphone and he was asking sports questions.

He said, 'The 1959 Lions versus New Zealand, score 18-17, who was the referee?'
And I piped up: 'Fleury.'
He said, 'By the name of God, how did you know that?'
I didn't tell him. I just said, 'I'll remember that name until the day I die.'

Ken Scotland crosses the line against the Maoris, but his try is disallowed.

BILLY MULCAHY

In that First Test every time they got in our half it seemed like a penalty would result. Even when we went 18-17 behind we scored another try and he found reason to disallow it, whereupon Roddy Evans threw the ball at him with a few expletives.

KEN SCOTLAND

Every referee we had out there was a New Zealander and they were all okay. I didn't think any of them were biased, particularly. But these little niggly things were frustrating. I don't think Fleury refereed again on the tour, which was a bit unfortunate because I'm not sure that any of us, at the end of the day, blamed the referee totally. We only converted one of the four tries we scored, and we had been sufficiently on top to win the game – even with these marginal calls going against us.

HUGH McLEOD

The referee was bent. Colin Meads once said that 'referees decide who is going to win a match' and he was right. That day proved it. We should definitely have won that game. It was robbery. During the game I knew he had it in for us. Any chance he got he gave them a penalty, and Don Clarke just booted them over. It was hard to take – but there was nothing we could do.

KEN SCOTLAND

We were hugely disappointed, and there were tears shed in the dressing room, which was very rare, and we weren't terribly well behaved at the dinner afterwards. That was the only bad publicity we got on the whole tour. We had one notorious roll thrower amongst us, who will remain nameless, but in Dunedin we were fed oysters and oyster throwing is a bit more dangerous than roll throwing – so the New Zealand hierarchy weren't too chuffed about that.

RONNIE DAWSON

We should have won the First Test and we threw away the Second by our own stupidity. There was a touch kick missed and we were leading 8-3.

SYD MILLAR

I was standing beside Dawson when he said to Terry Davies, 'Terry, put it in touch,' and we would have stayed up in their corner and that would have been it. Terry said, 'No, I want to kick at goal.' And Ronnie said, 'Put it in touch,' and Ronnie was absolutely right. Maybe he wasn't concentrating as well as he might, but Terry missed touch, the ball came upfield, Clarke came on the blindside, scored the try, kicked the goal and New Zealand won.

KEN SCOTLAND

I think Don Clarke was underrated as a fullback. He had a reputation as a kicker, and as a lumbering player – but he tackled well, his positioning was excellent, and had much more all-round ability than he was given credit for.

Bev Risman dives over the line to score the decisive try in the Fourth Test.

RONNIE DAWSON

We were hammered in the Third Test. Absolutely hammered. That was when we really, really felt the power and the excellence of the New Zealand forward play. We were leading and we had a brilliant piece of back play on a lovely hard ground in Christchurch, David Hewitt made a marvellous break. He was a marvellous player on that tour, so fast – the fastest we had over the first 20 yards. He made a break and only had Clarke to beat with O'Reilly outside him on the left wing, and David was sort of caught by the collar when passing the ball and it went forward. That was going to be a try and we'd have been further ahead. You could feel the pin going into the balloon. New Zealand went on and hammered us. It was the worst forward beating I ever experienced.

PETER JACKSON (England)
Toured: 1959

By the time the final Test had come along Gordon Waddell had gone home for a knee operation and Roddy Evans had gone home injured as well. In terms of team spirit and commitment, winning the Fourth Test was by far and away the most uplifting experience I ever had in rugby. It would have been so easy to be down – it was game 31 on tour and we had already lost the series – but there was this collective will to win.

KEN SCOTLAND

The week before we had played Auckland, and they had a huge side who were pretty physical, nasty and cheap – but we beat them quite comfortably. So we were in reasonably good shape, but psychologically we had been through the wringer. The weather couldn't have been worse, there had been thunderstorms and rain all night, and they had played a couple of warm-up games on the pitch so it was a bit of a quagmire. Despite this, we played really well and scored three very good tries, to their two penalties, so for everyone playing and in the stand as well, we took a lot out of that. It was the first time we had won a Test in New Zealand since 1930.

And with that, Hugh McLeod and I became the first Scots ever to win a Test match against the All Blacks. Not many Scots have added to that number since: Ian McLauchlan, Gordon Brown, Andy Irvine, Ian McGeechan and Gavin Hastings.

TERRY DAVIES

We scored three tries in the final Test and they didn't score any; it was a great way for us to finish and we felt we deserved something out of the series.

KEN SCOTLAND

I went as number two fullback and five months later I came back still as number two fullback – but I'd had the most fantastic time in between. Everything went right for me. Terry Davies started off with an injury and that allowed me to stake a claim, and we were playing on hard grounds with a lot of quick three-quarters moving the ball around all the time, and that was my game, not Terry's.

He was a traditional fullback. Very good under the high ball, kicked well, tackled well, was brave with the ball on the ground – and that was really what the fullback should be doing. I learned a lot from watching him play, and we had a reunion after nearly 50 years and he was kind enough to say that he learned some things from watching me play as well, which I took as a great compliment.

By the time we got to the end of the tour we were playing on heavier grounds and I had been playing in different positions – and I'm sure he was selected for that final Test on merit, and I'm quite happy with that.

MALCOLM THOMAS

It said much for the team spirit that after a severe hammering in the Third Test, the team could summon a series of such great displays. It must also be remembered that the team was beset by a crop of injuries which severely upset planning in the crucial stages of the tour.

KEN SCOTLAND

Hugh McLeod was a fantastic tourist. He had been to South Africa in 1955 and hadn't made the Test team, but in 1959 he was one of our anchor men. He didn't drink, he was first up for breakfast, he was first on the bus, he was first to every scrum and every lineout, and did everything he was ever asked to do. He was just a perfect guy to have on tour – I have always had a huge regard for him. He was an incredibly strong and clever rugby player.

He was pretty popular in a dour sort of way. He was called 'the Abbot', of course, referring to his monastic lifestyle. But he was by no means unique as a teetotaller – I would think six or seven of the guys in the squad were non-drinkers. It wasn't a hugely boozy tour at all.

TONY O'REILLY

It was a very exciting experience trying to beat Ken Jones's try-scoring record; I equalled him four matches from the end and then had to try to find a way to beat his record. I finally got the try to do it in about the last minute of the final Test, which was the great game of the tour for me. First of all we beat them fair and square and we beat them in Auckland, which was really their home ground, and I got that vital 18th try that I had been trying to get for the previous four matches. I can still feel the heavy ball and the mud on my face as I went through the last tackle of Don Clarke.

RONNIE DAWSON

I would like to think that there were a lot of stars in that side but because of his record Tony shone brighter than the rest.

TERRY DAVIES

I'm still a big fan of the Lions. I think there should always be a British & Irish Lions team. The tradition has to go on because it brings together all the countries. That's what the spirit of rugby is about.

KEN SCOTLAND

Principally, it was the fun we had and the friends that we made for the rest of our lives. That was the big thing about touring, everybody became a personal friend. To meet some of those guys almost 50 years later might seem strange to outsiders but for us it is like we have never been away.

SYD MILLAR

Something the New Zealanders told us at the end of the tour. They said, 'If you guys were organised we would never have got near you.' They were right. We were the better team in three of the four Tests, but they were more worldly-wise and had Don Clarke as a kicker. That was the difference. That was the best rugby-playing side I ever played on. Ken Scotland was the first attacking fullback; Jackson and O'Reilly on the wings; Hewitt and Malcolm Price in the centre. You had Jeff Butterfield. A very attacking side. A bit naive at times, but I think that side had the capacity to beat any Lions side if they were as organised as the great Lions sides we saw years later. Terry McLean called us the Kings of Rugby.

CHAPTER FIFTEEN

DECLINING FORTUNES
1962

SOUTH AFRICA

THE MIX *of six Scots, seven Irishmen, eight Englishmen and nine Welshmen originally selected to visit South Africa in 1962 – all of them international players – stands to this day as the most uniform Home Unions distribution for any Lions tour. The balance was fine on paper, but no Test wins resulted, and the optimism generated by the heady tours of the 1950s evaporated. In no sense did the 1962 tour live up to the sensational 1955 trip in either glamour or results. The players seemed to enjoy the tour, but as a rugby exercise, it was a disappointment.*

They were always likely to be up against it. In the previous year, a South African team led by Avril Malan had cut a swathe through British and Irish rugby, losing only to the Barbarians in Cardiff in their last game.

For the first time the Lions management was entrusted to a pair of well-known and highly respected former international players. The side was managed by Brian Vaughan – Commander DB Vaughan R.N. to give him his full title – a former England forward who had been a Lions contender in 1950. Harry McKibbin, a popular Irish rugby administrator who had played centre for his country between the wars and toured South Africa with the 1938 Lions, was his assistant manager.

In his professional life Vaughan was involved with the commissioning of the early nuclear submarines. On tour he led from the front. Jeff Butterfield had been responsible for team preparation and fitness on the two previous Lions tours. This time it was the manager who saw his role also include head coach, and he made a stab at drilling his forwards and conceiving match-plans. His approach paved the way for specialist coaches to assist future British & Irish tours. Whether this was effectively by default is hard to say.

Arthur Smith, the Scotland wing, skippered the side, breaking an Ireland monopoly of the Lions captaincy that stretched back to Sammy Walker and the 1938 tour. Off the field he was an academic high-flyer with a first in mathematics from Glasgow University before studying for a PhD at Cambridge. As a player he was a powerful runner with a deceptive change of pace. Smith was injured in South Africa in 1955 but turned his down time to good use, spending hours learning to place-kick on the hard, dusty grounds. It gave him an extra string to his bow and he went on to kick many goals, often as the long distance option, in a distinguished career during which he won 33 caps for Scotland.

He had returned to South Africa in 1960 as a member of the Scotland side that created a small piece of history by becoming the first individual home union ever to undertake an overseas Test tour. On the field he had an ice-cool rugby brain and with his unparalleled knowledge of South African

---

Opposite: Alun Pask scores against Western Province at Newlands.

conditions he was the ideal choice to captain the Lions. Bryn Meredith and Dickie Jeeps, the Welsh and English captains, were the only other survivors from the previous Lions visit to South Africa.

Among the other notable tourists were Mike Weston, the accomplished back from Durham City, Derek 'Budge' Rogers, the flanker from Bedford, who for many years held the record as the most-capped England player and who was later to be chairman of selectors for England; there was also David Rollo, who for Scotland held the record as the most-capped player for an equally long period of time. Also on tour, frustrated and storing away the hurt, were the Northern Ireland pair of Willie-John McBride and Syd Millar.

Yet a shadow was cast over the tour in the opening match. Stan Hodgson, the Durham City and England hooker, broke his leg 15 minutes from the end of the game against Rhodesia in Bulawayo. This immediately put pressure on Bryn Meredith, the only other specialist hooker in the party, who had to play in three of the next four matches before Coventry's Bert Godwin arrived as a replacement.

Even Meredith, however, needed some rest, so prop Syd Millar was press-ganged into the middle of the front-row for the narrow win against the Western Province Universities in the fourth match.

Disappointingly, dirty play was a feature of many of the provincial and Test matches. Richard Sharp was the outstanding back in the 1962 Five Nations, viewed by many as the paragon of attacking fly-halves. The Lions' hopes for a successful Test series rested heavily on his shoulders. But in the last match before the First Test he suffered a broken cheek bone when crash-tackled by 'Mannetjies' Roux, the well-known Springbok three-quarter. The pack was rearranged to cover a gap in the back division and the Lions, with only 14 men for 75 minutes, fell to their first defeat.

The tackle by Roux was criticised then and since, and was seen by some, perhaps wrongly, as a typical home team gesture in targeting the key touring players before the Test series. It was also very far from the only nasty incident in which Roux had been involved in his career.

Sharp was out for five weeks, missing the opening two Tests of a series that was lost 3-0. The Lions showed character to draw the First Test at Ellis Park. John Gainsford's first-half try for the Springboks was cancelled out ten minutes from time. For the Lions, centre Ken Jones made a lung-bursting 55 metre run, sidestepping and changing direction before scoring a spectacular try in the corner. The visitors had held their own with the much-vaunted Springbok pack and the press view was that the result was a moral victory for the Lions. Yet another.

There was nearly a month between the first and second internationals. The Lions were unbeaten during this spell and went into the Test at King's Park, Durban, with high hopes of scoring a win and going one up. The main action was distilled into the last two minutes. Keith Oxlee kicked a penalty goal from the touchline but from the restart the Lions threw everything into attack. Welsh lock Keith Rowlands appeared to touch down in a pushover, but the referee was apparently unsighted and immediately blew the whistle for full time. It was one of the most controversial officiating incidents on any Lions tour, which is saying something.

Beaten by the referee again – that was the view of many of the Lions' camp followers – but the series was still alive as the tourists, with Sharp restored, headed for Cape Town and the Third Test a fortnight later. Sharp had proved his fitness by finding his best form in the 24-3 win against a Transvaal side that included four Springboks and three Junior 'Boks. He scored 15 points as the Lions prospered in ideal conditions.

The week after at Newlands, Sharp opened the Lions' account in the deciding Test with a neat drop-goal after 25 minutes but the celebrated Keith Oxlee, his Springbok counterpart, levelled with a penalty before half-time. Oxlee had been the tactical brain behind the Springboks' heavyweight pack during a Grand Slam tour of the Home Unions two winters earlier, and now he was to be the British and Irish nemesis again, scoring the winning try eight minutes from time.

Deep in his own half Bryn Meredith won a strike against the head and Dickie Jeeps served Sharp. People will argue for the rest of their lives about whether he should have sought the safety of the touchline. But the blond Cornishman decided to open up in a last-gasp bid to break the deadlock. The ball went across the three-quarter line. Sharp to Weston, Weston to Jones, but then Melville Wyness, the Springbok centre, caught the Welshman with a big tackle. The ball spilled loose, Oxlee gathered and inked his way to the line for the winning try and with it a 2-0 series lead with one to play.

On tour the Lions management adopted a policy of packing their back-row with heavy forwards - second-rows were used at No 8 and No 8s as flankers. Budge Rogers of England and Haydn Morgan of Wales, a Lion in 1959, were chosen as specialist opensides for the tour, but no out-and-out blindside had been selected.

Mike Campbell-Lamerton played all his rugby for Scotland as a second-row but he was used at No 8 for the Tests. Alun Pask, arguably the first of the modern breed of No 8 in British rugby, was used on the flank. The idea was to bring ballast to the Lions scrum and match the South Africans pound for pound. This was all very well, but it was too much. It compromised severely the pack's overall mobility.

Even so, apart from the 14-6 loss to Northern Transvaal on the eve of the Test series, the tourists came a cropper only once more against provincial sides. Eastern Province beat them 19-16 in the

Mike Weston and Arthur Smith.

penultimate match in South Africa, winning with a converted try from the last move of the match.

Pask was one of the finds of the tour. He was such an intelligent all-round rugby player that he adapted easily to blindside duties and played the game of his life in the victory over Transvaal. For a man who had a passion for running rugby he put paid to the criticisms that he shunned the donkey-work. He showed that he could perform defensively in a match that was approached as a full dress rehearsal for the Third Test. Alas, he cracked a rib at Newlands and never again played on tour.

His absence was sorely felt at Bloemfontein for the Fourth and final Test where Dickie Jeeps, making a then-record 13th Test appearance for the Lions, was captain for the day, Arthur Smith standing down the day before with a pulled muscle. The Springboks were a developing side with the series in their pocket and in the finest match of the series they gave a superb exhibition of fast, open rugby. Their forwards ran and handled like backs and all told the side scored six tries to three, exploiting some sloppy Lions tackling to crush the visitors 34-14.

By 1962 the British travelling press party had grown to eight, Pat Marshall (Daily Express), *Terry O'Connor* (Daily Mail), *Uel Titley (*The Times*), Tony Goodridge* (Daily Telegraph), *John Reed* (Sunday Express) *and Ian Todd* (Daily Herald) *joining Viv Jenkins and JBG Thomas, who were making their third Lions tours. Unlike in the modern era, press and players frequently mingled and one fascinating joint-interlude took place at the Kruger National Park game reserve. A round trip of some 500 miles by road from Springs via the Park and on to Bloemfontein before the final Test proved to be one of the most memorable experiences of the tour for many.*

The 1962 tour also marked the Lions debut of Willie-John McBride. He appeared in ten of the matches including the last two Tests. He faced tough competition for the Test spot from Keith

Dickie Jeeps clears the ball upfield against Griqualand West.

Rowlands and Bill Mulcahy (who had to play blindside in Bloemfontein) but the young Ulsterman showed good technique and with his big hands and huge upper-body strength was already a redoubtable mauler.

South African and Lions rugby would see and hear a lot more about him in the years to follow.

MIKE WESTON (England)
Toured: 1962 & 1966

The Lions were the peak of my career. I played in six Tests overall on two tours and only won one and drew one, but it was a fantastic experience. I was only 22 when I went to South Africa in 1962, and the highlight for me was getting in the Test team and experiencing the huge crowds and the excitement that surrounded those games.

BUDGE ROGERS (England)
Toured: 1962

It was something I would not have missed out on for anything. To play alongside players you have only ever played against before was something really special, in particular to see the friendships coming together with people from different backgrounds and countries. It meant a huge amount, and was a wonderful experience, just marred by a couple of injuries that probably kept me out of two Tests. And of course, the series defeat.

We may have lost the series but we weren't hammered, although we lost heavily in the last Test when I was really our only true back-row forward. However, it was a very good South African side at that time, and we also had significant early injuries losing David Nash, the Welsh No 8, with a neck injury, Richard Sharp, our fly-half, with a broken cheekbone, and Stan Hodgson, who was a bloody good hooker, with a broken leg against Rhodesia in the first game.

But winning and losing was not quite as dramatic as it is today because there was not the same media coverage, and if you lost, you lost. It wasn't a great success in terms of results, but it didn't ruin the tour.

WILLIE-JOHN McBRIDE (Ireland)
Toured: 1962, 1966, 1968, 1971 & 1974. Manager: 1983

It was the national game in South Africa and we went there and we had nice people, we had a nice manager who was ex-navy, and we had a nice captain, Arthur Smith. A nice man, a quiet man. Nice men don't survive in South Africa. Or New Zealand for that matter. There was no such thing as a coach. I used to joke and say, a coach is a thing that brings us to the match. We did it all ourselves. It was the captain and the senior players who put the tour together.

We had good players but we weren't organised. Not only that, there was a lot of snobbery and I'm not scared to say that. A lot of snobbery in the game in those days

– in England. It's not the winning and losing it's the taking part and all of that rubbish. There was snobbery from the point of view that we were sending out, in some cases, ambassadors. When you go to do a job, you pick the men to do the job. And if there's a discipline problem you deal with it. There were guys you felt that should have gone who weren't picked.

BILLY MULCAHY

We had some sort of briefing from an embassy individual before we left London about the situation in South Africa. Some of us threw a couple of awkward questions at him which he batted away. I asked him about some South African fella who'd written a book about his mixed-race marriage and how he had to leave the country. I asked him what he thought of the book. He wasn't too pleased with the question.

DAVID ROLLO (Scotland)
Toured: 1962

We'd all been asked whether we were available for the tour and on 26 March 1962 (which was nine days after Scotland had drawn 3-3 in our last game of the International Championship against England at Murrayfield), this letter appeared addressed to myself stating that the Lions committee 'have the pleasure of inviting you to take part in the above tour which assembles at Eastbourne on 13th May 1962.' I was a farmer and I

Northern Transvaal lock forward Stompie van der Merwe and British Lions' Bryn Meredith leap high during a lineout.

asn't sure I would be able to get away, but I discussed it with my brother – who I was in usiness with – and we decided that it was an opportunity of a lifetime.

We had to take our own flannels and shoes with us, but the rest of the kit was upplied, including a dress blazer and an everyday blazer. We went down to London, let up at the Wellington Hotel in the West End for two nights, then went down to astbourne for a week's training – which was pretty tough going.

Instead of getting an orange slice when we took a break we got a lemon slice – and think that was to try and help us get used to the dry conditions we were going to ncounter out in Africa. There were no water jugs or anything like that.

YD MILLAR

changed in 1962 in terms of the press coverage. In New Zealand we had people like 'erry McLean, JBG Thomas, Viv Jenkins and a few others and they actually travelled the team bus. Imagine that now! There was about six or seven of them and nothing ame out. They heard many things they could have printed but they didn't print them, ther than the rugby. It changed in '62. We had a fairly large number of press.

UDGE ROGERS

/e didn't have a coach, just the manager, Brian Vaughan, and our captain, Arthur mith. Arthur was a wonderful man and he and Dickie Jeeps, the England scrum-half, n the playing side. It was the first time you could give as much to the game as you

ritish Lions captain Arthur Smith steps around two Northern Transvaal defenders.

wanted to because you weren't having to work. So, if you loved training like I did, it was great – and I was always checking to see if I beat Haydn Morgan, my fellow flanker, in the sprints.

As for the journey out – I hadn't been on a long haul flight before, and, as I was interested in planes, it was pretty amazing to be in a Comet. We stopped in Khartoum and walked into a wall of heat, and then later the pilot let me and Richard Sharp into the cockpit for the landing at Salisbury. We were still in the cockpit when we hit the runway, which was a completely new experience.

WILLIE-JOHN McBRIDE
I had broken a bone in my leg in the French game in the Five Nations and it was in a cast and I only got it off a couple of weeks before we went, so I had a lot of work to do. Keith Rowlands, he was the big man in the second-row at the time. I remember having a bit of a barney with him. It was my first tour. He threw this at me at the start: 'Why did you come on this tour, you're not fit.' I thought, 'I'll target you and I'll put you out of the team,' which I did

MIKE WESTON
There weren't any great players in 1962, but there were some very good ones. Dickie Jeeps was always in the Test team, and had a good tour. Also, Willie-John McBride was making his first tour, and before we left I had a dodgy ankle, and the two of us were

Bryn Meredith watched by David Rollo attempts to get the ball away from scrum half Popeye Strydom during the game against Eastern Province at the Boet Erasmus Stadium in Port Elizabeth.

aving to see the medics. I asked him what was wrong with him and he replied, 'I've got broken leg.' He had a broken fibula, but it was not long before he was playing. The nkle bothered me throughout the tour, but before going I had trained with Sunderland 'C, where they taught me how to strap my ankle. I got through the tour thanks to that.

BUDGE ROGERS

rthur Smith was already a great wing, and Alun Pask and Richard Sharp could be rilliant. But, for me, Dickie Jeeps stood out. He was a fantastic player. He wasn't that uick, and he didn't have a long pass, but he always gave his fly-half good ball and took hammering if he needed to. I will always remember his tigerishness and ebullience – as got off a scrum or lineout I'd hear him shout, 'Tackle! Tackle!' And he was still doing it ears later when we were watching England play from the stands at Twickenham. Jeeps ad tremendous guts, and every bit of the scrum-half game he did right. He would never natch Gareth Edwards for innate ability, but he was a huge competitor.

BILLY MULCAHY

Ve played Northern Transvaal the week before the First Test and there was some debate bout whether Richard Sharp should be played or not because he was the golden boy at y-half; a lot of the South Africans who were well disposed to us and looked after us said, Don't play Sharp in this match, don't play him.' We played him. What we said to him was, Don't attempt anything for the first 15-20 minutes, just move it on.' We thought their fellas ould want to put a stamp on him and, usually, if that kind of thing doesn't get done early probably doesn't get done at all. The game settled down, but then, unfortunately, Sharp as going openside and then changed his mind and came on the short side and he met Iannetjies Roux who hit him high and caused a depressed fracture to his jaw. That was our olden boy gone for quite a while.

MIKE WESTON

harp was a marked man, and before the game against Northern Transvaal I said to im, 'Just move it.' So, instead, the first time he got it he dummied and went for the ap, and the second was the Mannetjies Roux tackle. The South Africans were not irty, but they were bloody hard, and the grounds were rock solid.

YD MILLAR

Iannetjies Roux was a fighter pilot who literally dived on Sharp and smacked him and own he went. He wasn't fit again until the Third Test. Roux was a madman. I suppose ghter pilots are. You don't tackle like that. You'd be off the field now if you did it.

WILLIE-JOHN McBRIDE

always admired Roux as a player. He wasn't a big man but he was a committed player. remendous. He was on the verge of danger all the time, but he was damned good. nd I know he hit Sharp and maybe hit him illegally but he was a very good player.

The South African game was based entirely on the scrummage. In one way I enjoyed that because I loved scrummaging and I loved the physical part of it.

BILLY MULCAHY

We had an infamous match in Potchefstroom against the Combined Services and it was like another Test match. It was very nasty. I think Roux played in that one as well. Lots of fisticuffs on either side. The guy coaching them was the same guy who coached Northern Transvaal. He seemed to have a certain ethos about how the opposition should be treated. Mayhem. Fists flying, boots flying. It was dangerous. The crowd were baying for blood.

SYD MILLAR

'The Battle of Potchefstroom' they called it. They had everybody in a uniform – postmen, army, air force – they took them into a camp about two weeks before the game and one of them told me they started off saying, 'These people (the Lions), their great-great-grandfathers put your people into concentration camps in the Boer War.' So they came on the field and Keith Rowlands, who was our biggest forward, got the ball from the kick-off and his feet didn't touch the bloody ground until he was about 10 metres from our line. Mad. This went on the whole bloody game and the referee let them get on with it. It was an all-Afrikaans crowd. My opposite number was pulling me down in the scrum, so I smacked him. The referee said to me, 'Millar, you do that again, you're off.' I said, 'Well, if you don't look after me, I'm going to look after me.' I said to Wigs (Billy Mulcahy), 'Next scrum, you smack him.' I went up and Wigs put his fist through. Bang! Hit me right on the bloody nose. And the referee said, 'Penalty to the Lions!'

There was digging, raking, late tackling. It was an horrendous scene. We never played them again. Our press were terribly critical and the South African press were critical, saying, 'This can't happen again.' But at the end of the day, their objective was to win the Test series and they would do these things.

BILLY MULCAHY

Rugby football is a game, not organised warfare.

BUDGE ROGERS

The Springboks had some really good players, and the one who always comes to mind is Frik du Preez. He ran 40 yards in the last Test in Bloemfontein, and bumped off about six tacklers. He was not especially tall, about 6ft 2in, but was very thickset, quite similar in build to Colin Meads – however, he was a huge athlete, more athletic than Meads. Avril Malan, Keith Oxlee and John Gainsford were also very good players.

MIKE WESTON

In the First Test I missed a fairly easy penalty, and then I hit the post with a drop-goal from just inside our own half which would have won the match. In the Second Test we had a try awarded to Keith Rowlands, but then the referee was besieged by South Africa players – on the grounds that we had handled the ball at the scrum – just as John Willcox was about to take the conversion. He then awarded a penalty to South Africa, which was one of three that they were given in succession, including the winner in injury time. We never got the rub of the green with the referees, and we could have been 2-0 up. In the Third Test we paid for trying to run the ball from our own line, and in the Fourth Test they overwhelmed us physically – we were out on our feet.

SYD MILLAR

In the Second Test we were being penalised so often for Bryn Meredith allegedly having his foot up early in the scrum that we just tried to hold and push. We lost a few as a result but we were being penalised so often that we just couldn't afford to strike. We drew the First Test and went to Durban for the Second Test and put the Springboks over the line from a scrum, there is no question in my mind that the ball was over the line and that Keith Rowlands scored. The Springboks actually turned to go under the posts and the referee called them back and said, 'I was unsighted.' Danie Craven said afterwards that everybody in the ground except the referee saw the try. It was hard going.

BILLY MULCAHY

We had a big heavy pack and, remarkably it might seem to a lot of people, we hooshed them over their own try line. The press photographers with their zoom lenses had the clearest picture of the pack and the ball over the white line and then the ref found a reason not to give it.

WILLIE-JOHN McBRIDE

The Third Test, we lost it in the last bloody minute. There was a little guy called Keith Oxlee, an outside-half, somebody missed a tackle and he scored. They beat us 8-3. It was the biggest day of my life at that stage and one I'll never forget because it was such a huge occasion.

DAVID ROLLO

There was no scrummage machine so we did a lot of live scrummaging in training – and I felt I had established myself as the Saturday tight-head prop by the start of the tour. I played the first two Saturday games and then I injured my back. We had very little medical back-up – we had someone to call upon if you wanted a massage but that was it – and I didn't discover until I got home that this floating rib in my back was cracked and that was where all this pain was coming from when I bent down to scrummage.

I struggled on with it for six weeks, during which time I was constantly getting massaged on this sore bit, and I soon found out that that was the worst thing I could have done. What I should have done was put a strap around it and rested, and it would have been fine within a fortnight. Looking back, it is frustrating that we didn't have the wherewithal to treat these things properly. To young ones playing now, it must seem like complete madness.

BILLY MULCAHY

We didn't have the same depth of talent in the back division that we had three years previously. We had a big heavy pack in 1962 but not the talent of 1959. I ended up on the blindside flank in the last Test because we were running out of players through injury.

DICKIE JEEPS

To answer why we won, lost or drew is too complicated to answer simply, other than the losses were against better sides on the day… Although the loss of final Test against South Africa in 1962 was a fixture too far on a very hard tour.

BUDGE ROGERS

The tour was four months long, and when we weren't playing or travelling we spent a lot of time at parties in people's houses. There were so many wealthy South Africans, with servants and swimming pools, who were happy to entertain us. As a tour it was remarkably well disciplined, and I can't think of any inappropriate behaviour. It was just good fun.

I remember one trip when three of us were invited to go shooting guinea fowl with a couple of Afrikaners, and we sat in the back of the car and they hardly spoke. We

Mike Campbell-Lamerton, right, tries to stop Springbok Fanie Kuhn as he blasts his way through with the ball in the Second Test.

thought they were pretty dour people, but they turned out to be extremely hospitable – after we had done a bit of shooting it broke the ice, and we had a wonderful braai with them afterwards.

Later in the tour we had a trip to the Kariba Dam and Victoria Falls in two Dakotas, and we were terrified when the pilot zoomed towards the ground – but he was just doing it to give us a better look at a herd of elephants! Victoria Falls was out in the wild and uncommercialised at that time, and the only hotel was shut. Overall, we were well looked after, staying at the Arthur's Seat hotel in Cape Town, and playing the wonderful golf course at the Durban Country Club, where I've still got a picture of me chasing a monkey that picked up my ball on a fairway.

DAVID ROLLO

We got 70 shillings a week, which was quite a lot of money – especially as you didn't need to spend a penny while you were there. We all had an official fixture card, which was a pretty basic little piece of folded card with the Lions logo and a diary of the matches in the middle, and that would get you anything you wanted: a round of drinks, a crate of whisky, you name it. Everything was available to us. The South Africans really looked after us well. If your case began to look a bit worn out they would take you away and get you a brand new one, without a word being spoken.

Any gifts you got were collected by the South African Rugby Union, and once you had a trunkful they would send it home by sea and it would be delivered to your door. I had quite a lot of stuff and it arrived about three months after we got home – so that was a nice belated surprise.

BUDGE ROGERS

I was training as an engineer in Bedford and it was unpaid leave for me, but we hardly needed the 70 shillings a week allowance we were given. There were a few characters who stood out: Jeepsy was an engine on the field, and never stopped shouting or talking to you, and then there was the wonderful friendship between Bill 'Wigs' Mulcahy, our Irish lock, and Dave Rollo, our Scottish prop. After a few drinks Rollo, who never wore a jock strap when he played, and Mulcahy would both be talking simultaneously in their broad accents, with neither able to understand the other.

DAVID ROLLO

Ronnie Cowan always seemed to have money to spend, he had a camera then bought a second one, and they were a real luxury in those days. And when we got back to London, the Monday morning papers had this headline: 'Lion goes north.' And it turned out Ronnie had signed to play rugby league for Whitehaven. He must have signed up before he went away, and they had given him a wee bit extra pocket money.

I don't think any of us knew about it. All I knew was that he was a good player. He didn't get in the team for the first three Tests because he played the same position as

Arthur Smith, who was captain. Then, in the final Test, Arthur stood down and let Ronnie get a Test place – and I'm sure he did that out the goodness of his heart.

BUDGE ROGERS

I pulled stomach muscles playing a game of football at the end of training and had to miss the Second Test. Thankfully, I was fit again by the Fourth Test, when, despite the result, I played out of my skin. It's something I'd never have missed.

WILLIE-JOHN McBRIDE

I can remember setting out for the tour in 1962 and having no idea what to expect. What I discovered very quickly, as we all did, was that rugby in South Africa was superior to ours in just about every way. They were fitter, better organised and more committed; they had a pride and a will to win that totally outstripped us.

BUDGE ROGERS

We never had a reunion until we got together in 2002 – a 40th reunion – and almost everyone that was alive came. We held it at the East India Club in London, and I had a client who made lovely enamel boxes. So I asked him to make everyone a two and

Dickie Jeeps lets go of the ball as he is brought down in a flying tackle by Springbok Hannes Botha, during the Second Test.

a half inch square red enamel box with the Lions badge on it, and the names of the team engraved on the inside of the lid.

SYD MILLAR

My first boy was born while I was away and he was three months old before I saw him. Peter. Because we moved from Joburg down to Windhoek our mail was held in Cape Town and I was down there four or five days before I knew. I think my wife felt I'd deserted her.

DICKIE JEEPS

The Lions was the pinnacle of my career achievements, particularly the opportunity to play with and against the best players in the world at that time. It was also a chance to see parts of the world I would never have experienced, and to meet sportsmen from the southern hemisphere, particularly Don Bradman in 1959. It was an immense privilege to be involved.

Arthur Smith, Syd Millar, Bryn Meredith, Dickie Jeeps, Mike Campbell-Lamerton and Ken Jones celebrate scoring during the Second Test – but the try was disallowed.

CHAPTER SIXTEEN

LAND OF THE LONG DARK CLOUD
1966
NEW ZEALAND

NOT EVEN *the most fervent Lions supporter could deny the gulf in class between Kiwi and Lion down the years, since they first met at Test level in 1904. With the sole exception of 1971, the Lions have finished on the losing side in every series played.*

Never, however, was that gulf as wide as in 1966 when the tourists were whitewashed in a four-Test series for the first time. It is a series which continues to be discussed, a tour which in many ways repeated and illuminated the essential failings of Lions tours in terms of a lack of organisation, realism and of hard-headed sporting judgment, which often seemed to revert too readily to old-fashioned norms.

The tour was doomed from the outset. The selectors convened to name the party on the weekend of the Calcutta Cup match in March 1966 and dropped several bombshells. First and foremost, Mike Campbell-Lamerton, an Army captain and 1962 tourist in South Africa, would be captain. Second, Brian Thomas, the fierce Welsh lock, the toughest forward in the Home Unions at the time, was considered unsuitable for a tour to New Zealand, as was his uncompromising Welsh team-mate at hooker, Norman Gale. Finally, no genuine openside flanker was chosen.

Controversy reigned during the tour after many incidents of foul play and also the suspicion that the Lions in general were not tough enough to absorb the onslaught of the home teams.

Eyebrows were raised because Campbell-Lamerton was not seen as a certainty for a position in the Test second-row. The argument was that the tour skipper should be a player who was an automatic Test choice in his position. The outcry was loudest in Wales for apart from the omission of Thomas, Campbell-Lamerton's appointment robbed the Welsh skipper, Alun Pask, of the honour.

Pask, a classic No 8, was too good to leave out of the party, but many felt he had been cruelly slighted over the captaincy. He had been an integral member as pack leader of the 1965 Welsh side that won the Triple Crown and led Wales to the Five Nations title in the year of the tour. It's true that Wales lost narrowly (9-6) to Ireland in Dublin the week before the tour party was announced, but it was felt that his credentials for the job were impeccable.

The omission of out-and-out opensides such as Budge Rogers and Haydn Morgan, both experienced internationals and past Lions, deprived the Lions of speed to the ball in the loose.

The original party comprised 11 Welshmen, eight from Ireland, six from Scotland and five Englishmen. Another curiosity was that Delme Thomas, an uncapped Llanelli lock on the verge of

---

Opposite: Sandy Hinshelwood dives over for a dramatic score in the Fourth Test, 1966.

the Welsh team, was surprisingly selected ahead of Brian Thomas. Delme was to be a great servant of Wales and the Lions in later years, but the fact that the management turned him into a prop for one of the New Zealand Tests added further grist to the critics' mills.

For the first time the Lions' assistant manager was a designated coach. Previously the assistant had been merely to preside over administrative matters and any 'coaching' was done by a manager, often with no deep grasp of the game, or the players themselves.

The coach was John Robins, a Lion in 1950, who won 11 caps for Wales in the early 1950s before embarking on a distinguished physical education career and was lecturing the subject at Loughborough Colleges at the time of his appointment. Loughborough was an institute of excellence that was to give the lead to elite coaching in many sports and disciplines throughout the years.

However, at the time, the pre-eminence of the captain remained paramount; coaching was a concept new to rugby and Campbell-Lamerton clearly believed that the technical guidance of the team was his responsibility, in addition to that of leading the team and performing a whole raft of onerous ceremonial duties. Robins was sidelined and it is said that he became ever more frustrated as the weeks in New Zealand went by.

The tour opened in Australia where the Lions emulated the 1888 and 1904 pioneers by winning every game, including two Tests. The first international, at the Sydney Cricket Ground, was a fast, open affair. The Lions came from 0-8 down early in the second half to win 11-8 thanks to tries from Irish front-rowers Ray McLoughlin and Ken Kennedy, and two successful goal kicks by fullback Don Rutherford.

A week later at Lang Park in Brisbane, the famous rugby league stadium better known today as the Suncorp Stadium, the Test side had its best day. The floodgates opened in the second half with the Lions scoring 28 points, including five tries, to rack up their highest score and biggest-ever win in a Test. Stewart Wilson kicked 13 points from a first-minute penalty goal and five second-half conversions as the Lions handed out what was then the fourth biggest hiding ever suffered by a team in a Test between the major rugby-playing nations.

Then the Lions came down to earth with a heavy thud in New Zealand, losing their first three Saturday games. They lost 14-8 in their opener against Southland, not one of the country's strongest provinces, but who have always given touring teams a harsh welcome at their Invercargill base – and there was a 17-9 defeat to Otago a week later.

The Lions forwards were unable to sustain any control in the set piece and brittle tackling among the backs gifted away soft tries at critical times. It was the same story at Wellington where, for the third Saturday in a row, the Lions were comprehensively beaten up front; they lost 20-6 and prospects for the Tests looked grim.

There were flashes of brilliance as the side improved in the matches leading up to the First Test. David Watkins and Mike Gibson, the fly-halves, and Allan Lewis and Roger Young, the scrum-halves, featured prominently as the Lions backs began to fire in the matches against Taranaki, Bay of Plenty and North Auckland. But at Carisbrook, Dunedin, one of the best sides to represent New Zealand dominated the opening international from the start. The only Lions score was a first half penalty kicked by Stewart Wilson and the final scoreline of 20-3, was then the biggest margin the All Blacks had ever achieved against the tourists.

Overwhelmed in the rucks and on the back foot for most of the game the folly of omitting Brian Thomas was becoming apparent. The Lions' lineout hopes rested with Brian Price, the Newport and

Wales giant who had formed such a successful second-row partnership with Thomas in three successive Welsh Five Nations-winning sides. Price was easily the most productive lineout ace of his day in Europe. His two-handed catching and timing were phenomenal at home. In New Zealand, where the lineout was a jungle of barging and obstruction, he looked uncomfortable against the Meads brothers, Stan and Colin, in the All Blacks' second-row.

As usual, home refereeing didn't help. Lineout interpretations differed and barging, blocking and petty indiscretions were condoned. The sorry fact was that the Lions' skipper and team did not think to employ a 'When in Rome' strategy to exploit the refereeing until too late in the tour.

Rough play was frequent and led to some famous outbursts. The Lions manager, Des O'Brien, was a former Irish No 8 who had missed out on selection for the 1950 tour. He hit out after the England centre Colin McFadyean had his nose broken during the Lions' 8-6 win in a brutal match against Canterbury. Neither the first nor the last such game against that province.

After a game which had included a scene of open warfare in which 15 or 16 players engaged in a sustained slugging contest a frustrated O'Brien delivered his invective: 'We have found obstruction, stiff-arm tackling and other illegal tactics. We are sick of it. We have enjoyed the hospitality of New Zealand, but the most unenjoyable part of it is the 90 minutes on the field – I add ten minutes for the usual injuries.'

Scotland's Jim Telfer was the captain on that occasion and he was characteristically direct in his post-match comments. 'I am not going to say today's game was dirty, because every game we have played in New Zealand has been dirty.' Duggie Harrison, the incoming president of the RFU was out there at the time and he expressed his disgust at the spectacle, saying, 'I never thought I should feel physically sick watching a game of rugby.' It was an irony that Brian Thomas had been left at home as he was considered 'too rough' for New Zealand rugby.

Fighting again broke out in the early stages of the match against Auckland where David Watkins was captain. He showed the New Zealand public what his back division could achieve and steered his side to a 12-6 triumph, dictating the game tactically and contributing two drop-goals.

David Watkins deputised when skipper Mike Campbell-Lamerton finally dropped himself for the Second Test in Wellington the following weekend. The Lions lost 16-12 but Watkins led the side admirably, his drop-goal and three Stewart Wilson penalties keeping the tourists in the hunt after they had surrendered their one-point half-time lead. Delme Thomas was called up to play in the second-row alongside Willie-John McBride for this match. Delme's jumping and the play of Ireland's Ron Lamont in the loose inspired the Lions to their best performance of the series. The teak-tough Lamont was consistently the best of a strong back-row. Despite carrying an arm injury for much of the tour the Irishman's dogged defence and speed to the breakdown made him the unsung hero of the Test series.

The Lions' midweek game after this Test was against Wanganui-King Country and they were defeated by a side led by Colin 'Pinetree' Meads. It was the first time that a combined provincial team had won a match against a major touring side and Meads took 15 minutes to reach the dressing room after the final whistle. The great man signed hundreds of autographs for delighted fans before leaving the scene of what he later described as one of his fondest moments in the game.

Delme Thomas moved up a row to prop to allow Campbell-Lamerton to return to the second-row for the Third Test in Christchurch. But the Lions were deprived of possession, Watkins was suffocated *by tight New Zealand marking and the series slipped away with a 19-6 defeat. Watkins was captain again for the final international at Auckland, but was ruthlessly tackled out of the game by an outstanding All Black back-row. The Lions lost 24-11 but in mitigation had to play for nearly an hour with only 14 men after Alun Pask was upended at a lineout. The Welshman fell awkwardly and broke his collar-bone, prompting calls for substitutes to be allowed for injured players.*

It was evident on this visit that the warm relationship that had existed between the Lions and the British press on the three previous tours was beginning to cool. A more formal separation between the management, team and journalists was clear. This was probably as a result of the Lions' poor showing in New Zealand, particularly the ensuing welter of criticism thrown at the management over selection.

By the end of the tour, the early promise of the eight unbeaten matches in Australia was a distant memory, and the first whitewash of a Lions team in the Test series had become a fact. The battered party even managed to lose against British Columbia on one of those old clock-in visits, which some Lions parties undertook.

Perhaps strangely, the Lions remained a huge draw, with nearly 60,000 attending the final Test in Auckland. New Zealand were certainly an excellent team, with the traditional combination of tough forwards and solid and powerful backs, augmented by an excellent kicker in Mick Williment at fullback. But the tour remains something of a low point in the proud history, marking the transition to a new era when British and Irish rugby finally became serious on the field – but painful at the time.

COLIN McFADYEAN (England)
Toured: 1966

The travel logistics were amazing. On the flight out we stopped in Germany, the

Middle East, India, Singapore, Fiji and then Perth, which was about 36 hours. On the way back four months later we flew to Hawaii, where the sun was out. We hadn't seen it for a few months, and we all got sunburned – Dai Watkins' skin peeled off – and none of us wanted to tackle. Which is why we lost to British Columbia, although there were only 12 fit players left in the tour party by then.

JIM TELFER (Scotland)
Toured: 1966 & 1968. Head coach 1983. Assistant coach 1997

Only three players who went were not paid,

Mike Campbell-Lamerton addresses the welcoming party at Christchurch airport.

and that was the three teachers – Alun Pask, who sadly died in a fire in 1995, Brian Price and myself. The rest were paid for by their employers or by their community, which happens a lot in Wales. I remember Gary Prothero coming into the room in the London hotel we were staying in with his pockets stuffed with pound notes and fivers, which he had received walking through the streets of Bridgend before he left.

MIKE WESTON

I was a student in '62, penniless really, and we got about 10 shillings a day tour allowance. By my second tour in '66 my estate agent business was beginning to flourish, and, although we were away for six months, I had a partner who looked after things while I was gone.

COLIN McFADYEAN

Playing for the Lions was something I had dreamed about. I had first read about the Lions in a mobile library in Saltford – it was a book on the 1959 tour and I was inspired by Bev Risman's try-scoring feats. I had been playing at Loughborough, and was part of the same team as Gerald Davies and John Taylor there, and getting in the England team was more predictable because I had played in the trials. But it was my first season of international rugby, so it was a big surprise to be in. I didn't think it would be possible. When I got a phone call from a friend telling me I'd been selected by the Lions my first feeling was elation, and my second was fear – was I good enough? I was aghast, but the concerns didn't last long.

It was the highest accolade as a rugby player, and it is my greatest rugby achievement – and I was helped because I had a good tour. I was the fourth choice centre, and started as a second team player behind Mike Weston, DK Jones and Jerry Walsh. However, when we got on the heavy grounds in New Zealand my tackling got me into the Test team. Mike Gibson came out late on and we played together in the last three Tests, with him at inside centre and me outside, which was rare in those days because centres tended to play left and right.

DON RUTHERFORD (England)
Toured: 1966

Looking back, I was never convinced that the manager, coach, and captain ever sorted out a clear command structure. Who was to do what, and why, was never worked out. I had the strong impression that the captain thought he was running the playing side; I don't think the relationship between John Robins and Mike Campbell-Lamerton was ever acrimonious. I just don't think they communicated much.

Meanwhile, Des O'Brien, who was a delightful bloke, was on a trip of his own. For instance, Des had a bike lined up in every town we went to, and went off for a spin by himself. Then he disappeared mid-tour for a trip to Fiji. It really was amateursville, but for all of us it was a great experience. It was also a watershed, because the lessons we learned were all filtered through to the 1971 Lions at a meeting I attended the year before they left.

WILLIE-JOHN McBRIDE

It was all total nonsense. Total nonsense. The two guys in the running for the captaincy were Ray McLoughlin and Alun Pask and the committee said, 'No, we'll pick Mike Campbell-Lamerton, he's a leader in the British Army.' It was total nonsense and bullshit. 1966 was a sad scene. A good bunch of boys, and it was never the players' fault, it was the selection. The manager and the coach were divorced from the game, they weren't part of the game here, not part of the living game day-to-day, they'd lost touch with it. They didn't realise what was required.

NOEL MURPHY

Lovely captain, Mike. He was a surprise choice. He was picked and did his best. He did his best.

DAVID WATKINS (Wales)
Toured: 1966

We were forever torn between wanting to be a true running Lions side, and one which could take on all-comers up front. Our inability to decide on our tactical strategy led to chopping-and-changing in selection and it undermined us.

Colin McFadyean scores against South Canterbury-Mid Canterbury-North Otago Combined.

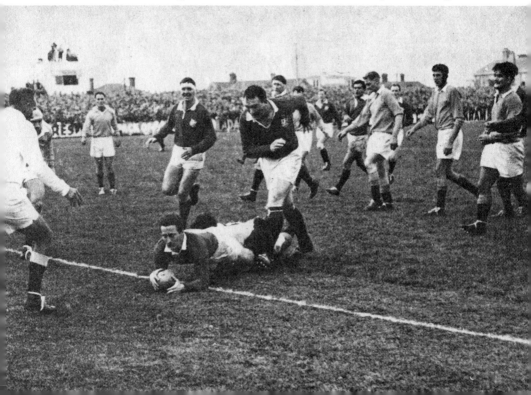

BRIAN PRICE (Wales)
Toured: 1966

Mike Campbell-Lamerton was a decent man and much maligned. We knew how hard he was working, and it was because we respected his efforts that we stuck together. Despite the defeats it was never a downcast tour.

COLIN McFADYEAN

John Robins could have done a terrific job, but he was usurped. Robins was a PE lecturer at Loughborough, and was our coach, so I knew him well. But, great coach that he was, he didn't have a free hand. He was the assistant to the assistant, with Des O'Brien the manager number one, and Mike Campbell-Lamerton the captain number two. Robins, at number three, was not able to pick the team and, I gleaned from him later, he felt like a man without a role. At the time I was unaware of the politics, and, as a 23-year-old who was a junior member of the tour party, I concentrated on the rugby and the social side of things.

WILLIE-JOHN McBRIDE

There's a certain amount of bitterness in me about all those years. There was no medical attention, there was nothing. I have friends in terrible agony with new hips and knees and so on and rugby has done nothing for them. We were just inadequate. We picked the wrong people, we had the wrong leader.

DES O'BRIEN (Manager)
Toured: 1966

Ray McLoughlin should have been captain of that side. He would have made a hell of a difference. The captaincy was a problem. Mike Campbell-Lamerton was a delightful character and a really good man but his playing days were nearly over – in fact, I don't think he captained Scotland that year – and the one thing I said to the selection committee was that they were electing a captain who wouldn't play in the Tests, and they said that they accepted that.

KEN KENNEDY (Ireland)
Toured: 1966 & 1974

Ray McLoughlin was a thoughtful tactician who brought a radical change into the way Irish teams prepared for games and this discipline brought very tangible rewards. Until then, preparation had been a little haphazard. Unfortunately, he put a few noses out of joint at committee level and because of this they fired him from the Ireland captaincy just before the Lions were picked and that effectively ruled him out of captaining the 1966 Lions.

RAY McLOUGHLIN (Ireland)
Toured: 1966 & 1971

Des had a philosophical approach to management and in my view did the job well.

One of the difficulties about that tour was that it was the first occasion that there was a coach. Previously the captain was everything – captain and coach. But on this occasion there was a complete vagueness over what the coach's role was and who was the boss. In the eyes of some officials back in England the coach would have been seen as just a trainer, a physical fitness man. John Robins saw himself as more than that. He was a good rugby technician and thought he should run the show. Mike Campbell-Lamerton thought differently because no one had told him otherwise.

WILLIE-JOHN McBRIDE
We got a hell of a thrashing, losing every one of the four Test matches to suffer the ignominy of a whitewash, but it was no surprise because in my view the whole composition of the touring party, and also the attitude, was wrong. Des O'Brien had been a wonderful back-row forward for Ireland at the end of the 1940s and was one

Brian Lochore and Mike Campbell-Lamerton lead out their sides ahead of the First Test.

of the nicest men you could ever meet in your life. He was courteous, charming and delightful company and hardly ever uttered a cross word in anyone's direction. Once again, the Lions selectors could not have chosen a better diplomat to represent the public face of the Lions, but if you wanted a man who was a winner, who would crack the whip and make sure every player in the squad was determined never to take a backward step then O'Brien was never going to be your man.

COLIN McFADYEAN

The last thing I want to do is run it down, but some crazy things happened. It was so amateur it was unbelievable, and, when I look back, I wonder sometimes how we managed to be competitive at all. For instance, when Terry Price came out to replace Don Rutherford he was not fit, and came down the steps of the plane limping with a leg injury. That's why on a couple of occasions in the Maori game when there was a high ball he called out, 'Your ball!' because he couldn't run freely. With regards to Des O'Brien's mid-tour trip to Fiji, to be quite honest I'm not sure I knew he had gone. That's what the tour was like – you didn't necessarily know who was missing.

RAY McLOUGHLIN

On the tour there were no rows or politics but there was a lack of focus as far as leadership was concerned with each man not wanting to step on the other's toes. It would have been better if any one of them had had total control and run it with an iron fist. But there was nothing the manager could do about it because he didn't have a mandate from home.

I loved the tour. Despite the defeats it was a happy occasion. Undoubtedly the team had a lot of potential, undoubtedly we could have done better in New Zealand if we'd been more focused and, undoubtedly, the lack of focus and clarity at the top had a lot to do with that, but I would regard that as a fault of the system and organisation rather than of any of the individuals involved.

JIM TELFER

If you were going to the other side of the world in 1966 then you might as well go for a while. So we went to Australia first, then New Zealand and stopped off in Canada on the way home, playing 35 games altogether.

We left on Jedforest Sportsnight, which was 21 April. I went down to watch the tournament, came home to Newtown St Boswells where I was living at the time, to pick up my bags and get on the train. Frank Laidlaw had already got on at Melrose, Derrick Grant got on at Hawick and together we went down to London. We were away all May, June and July before coming home on 20 August – and straight back to work.

NOEL MURPHY

We won all our six matches in Australia and they were talking about us being one of the great Lions sides. The New Zealanders sent us down to Invercargill for our first match and it was very cold down there. We never thawed out.

DAVID WATKINS

In scheduling terms we were pulled from pillar to post. Imagine the culture shock of swimming in the warm waters of subtropical Queensland one minute and being in Invercargill in the cold, wet and windy south of New Zealand the next.

WILLIE-JOHN McBRIDE

Des O'Brien was the manager. A very nice man. Full stop. Had no connection with rugby at that time. John Robins was very quiet and introverted. His Achilles tendon snapped and he ended up in hospital and all sorts of things. He was assistant to the manager and tried to do a bit of coaching but it went out the window because he was in hospital.

MIKE WESTON

I speak very highly of Mike Campbell-Lamerton. However, he didn't come over well to the New Zealanders, mainly because he had theatrical movements on the field, and their press got stuck into him. In terms of organisation there were mistakes. We went

Bruce McLeod scores the All Blacks' first try, with Brian Lochore and Kel Tremain in support.

to Queenstown, which was snowy and icy, and then when we tried to train the ground wouldn't take a stud. Campbell-Lamerton would take us for a run through the trees every morning – but it was a place we should have avoided. Things like that were very wrong.

MIKE CAMPBELL-LAMERTON (Scotland)
Toured: 1962 & 1966

I haven't read the books on the tour because one got so hurt. But what I regret most is that because of the criticism my children got hurt at school, and now my grandchildren have to hear about it. It doesn't give them a fair break. One didn't ask to be captain. There was strong feeling among the Welsh for Alun Pask, and maybe they were right. There was no one more surprised than myself when two press men phoned to inform me of my appointment.

Although I'd captained Scotland, it had never entered into my head that I would captain the Lions, and my first response was tentative. If you look at the wood for the trees, I was probably the compromise choice when the selectors couldn't agree on either Pask, Mike Weston or Ray McLoughlin.

The criticism is not very flattering, and some of it nasty, but obviously you have to take it if you lose a Test series. However, it's off the mark in many areas, and it

Jack Hazlett grounds the ball, but his try is disallowed.

was not balanced because we never got credit for winning the two Tests in Australia, where some of the running lines by our backs were brilliant. We won the Second Test by a record 31-0 against a side that had beaten South Africa and New Zealand in the previous two seasons. Nobody had gone through Australia unbeaten, and we remain the only Lions to have done so.

In New Zealand there were mistakes made, certainly, and the rucking took us all by surprise. Some of us sustained welts on our backs which came out as bruises on the chest weeks later. The All Blacks were formidable, but even so our pack was never juggernauted and the Second Test could easily have gone our way.

Selection was often difficult because of injuries, and many of us played injured because there was no option. We didn't have a medical officer with us. As far as dropping myself for the Second and Fourth Tests is concerned, it doesn't take courage to do that if you loved your team, and you knew someone else could do a better job.

Des O'Brien and John Robins were charming men. I don't know where the story about strife with John Robins has come from, although a lot of senior players did come to me with concerns about the lack of game plans and the PT style of training, rather than skills. So as captain you are the go-between, and it seems to me that Joe Soap here carried the can. All I can tell you is that I ended up doing a lot of administration, because it was not in my nature, or in my training as a soldier, not to help out when help was needed.

MIKE WESTON

I thought David Watkins was great in difficult circumstances. Piggy Powell stood out too, not because of the quality of his play, but because he was a character. He went down well in New Zealand because he could talk to all the school kids about his farm. It was also unwise to play cards with Ray McLoughlin – he was a mathematical genius who could remember all the cards.

The irony for me was that on the 1963 England tour of NZ we were stuffed by JP Murphy – and guess who was refereeing in 1966? You should not criticise refs, but they are so important to the outcome. John Willcox was at my house recently, and it was still a talking point for us.

DAVID WATKINS

Pat Murphy, the New Zealand ref who had charge of the last three Tests, whistled to stop the game when we would almost certainly have scored a try in the Second Test in Wellington after Colin McFadyean had broken clear. He then awarded us a penalty 65 yards back! We were trailing 8-6 in the mud with 20 minutes left, and a try then would have put us in a very strong position.

We complained bitterly afterwards to the New Zealand Board and asked them to replace Murphy, but they refused. Before the Third Test began at Lancaster Park he came into our changing room and assured us that he was a fair ref. Then, at the first scrum two minutes into the game, Allan Lewis, our scrum-half, asked him whose put-in it was. His response was, 'Ours – whose do you think it is?'

WILLIE-JOHN McBRIDE

I remember one match and they scored and the referee jumped up in the air with delight. The bastard's name was Murphy. That was the sort of stuff that was going on. We were totally lost, there was no organisation. Campbell-Lamerton was what they called a devout Catholic. He came from church and said that he had lit a candle for the Lions and I said, 'Mike, there's only one thing that works with these bastards and that's going out on the field and kicking the shit out of them. It's nothing to do with lighting candles.' And then Terry McLean wrote something about McBride not believing in God!

COLIN McFADYEAN

We had a culture of never blaming the referee at home, but we were naive. We didn't respond to the punching and holding down after the tackle, and lived in a fantasyland of 'God would look after us' and make sure the refs did too.

JIM TELFER

The background to my speech after the Canterbury game was that we were sick of being intimidated in provincial games where we were constantly coming up against dirty teams. They made me captain for that game and we played well and won 8-6

Dewi Bebb speeds around Ron Rangi in the Second Test.

in front of 50,000 wild Canterbury fans. But it was a dour match with several nasty skirmishes from the first scrum onwards.

Des O'Brien came out to me and said, 'Look Jim, I'm going to lambast them today. You behave yourself and be nice about them.'

But I couldn't and I said at the post-match function that, 'I wouldn't say today's game was dirty because every match we have played on this tour has been dirty.' I started on about the referee. Derrick Grant was urging me to sit down before I caused any more trouble, but I felt that was what I had to say. I never regretted it, because I am one of those fellows who has to say what they believe. I had played in some of the midweek games and because I was the kind of player who ended up at the bottom of rucks, I had been kicked to death…

It certainly didn't change the way they approached their provincial games against us, as Auckland proved the following week in a game of absolute thuggery on the same day as England were winning the football World Cup at Wembley.

What really annoys me was that a number of New Zealand reporters came up to me after the speech, shook my hand and told me that was exactly the right thing to say, that the rugby there was filthy. But when I read their report the next day they gave me dogs' abuse.

JBG THOMAS (writing about Jim Telfer's comments post-Canterbury, in *Lions at Bay*)

Mr Blazey (president of the New Zealand Rugby Union) called Telfer's outburst

Frank Laidlaw is caught in possession by Ken Gray in the Second Test.

'peevish and ill-mannered' and perhaps it was not in keeping with the right diplomatic approach, but the men from the Scottish Borders are inclined to say what they think and apologise afterwards. The strange thing is that many a New Zealander said to me later that there was much truth in what Telfer said, but the furore that followed in the 'Readers' Letters' columns of all the papers was quite amazing. Most of the letters, strange as it may appear, said that New Zealand rugby was over-vigorous and they consequently disapproved.

MIKE WESTON

Jim Telfer was not right to launch into his tirade against the New Zealanders in 1966, but it did highlight the problem, because their main plan was to intimidate. The Canterbury game turned into a fight, and beforehand the call was, 'If they fight, we all fight.' I was playing against a guy called Bruce Watt, and we both stood off and watched. After the First Test defeat Kenny Jones and I were left out, and it was quite right because the rest of the series was played in mud and was very physical. It was not my strength, and I had no complaints about being dropped.

BRIAN PRICE

There was a definite attempt to intimidate. Against Canterbury I have a picture that shows me fighting Alex Wyllie, and that's all I remember of the match. You can forget running, jumping, and pushing.

COLIN McFADYEAN

I had my nose broken twice in the Canterbury game. There was a little red-headed guy called Derek Arnold playing opposite me for Canterbury who I knew already from 1963 when the South West Counties played the All Blacks, and he had taken me out by obstructing me time after time. So, I went on the pitch determined to fight fire with fire, and after I'd barged into him he elbowed me and broke my nose. Ken Kennedy came over and straightened it up, but then later in the game I was on the ground in open field after a tackle and Fergie McCormick came past and kicked me in the face, breaking my nose again and knocking me out.

RAY McLOUGHLIN

New Zealand played with great drive and determination and had the philosophy that a guy who lies on the ball and prevents good second-phase ball is a criminal of the worst kind – and if the referee can't get him out of there then the thing to do is walk on him and there's a fine line between walking and kicking.

WILLIE-JOHN McBRIDE

I got a thoroughly unpleasant reminder of what it was like for a visiting rugby player in New Zealand on the tour in the provincial match against Canterbury. The local team kicked off and I caught the ball. Suddenly, I was surrounded by the physical hurricane of their pack, which started punching, kicking and assaulting me because I'd had the temerity to hang on to the ball. They got hold of me and took me thirty or forty yards downfield towards my own line, the blows raining down upon me as we went. What maddened me was that not one of my fellow Lions players came to my aid to help me hold on to the ball and give the New Zealanders some of their own treatment back. When the referee eventually blew the whistle to end this spell of physical torment I was bloodied and bruised and bloody angry, but when I looked up the nearest Lions forward was about twenty yards away. 'Where the hell were you bastards when I needed you?' I shouted at them. And their reaction? Well, they laughed and one of them said, 'Why the hell didn't you let go of the ball you bloody fool?' I knew then that we had no hope of winning the series.

RONNIE LAMONT (Ireland)
Toured: 1966

In the Auckland match, one of their flankers kicked Noel Murphy, right across the kneecap.

NOEL MURPHY
Yeah, I had a few words with the fellow – Keith Nelson – when he did that.

RONNIE LAMONT
Now the thing I liked about Murphy was that he was keen to share his problems. Once

the obvious and immediate pain had left him he took me aside and muttered, 'We're going to get him.' And we did. That was the start of the inglorious battle of Auckland... Which we managed to win 12-6.

The final whistle was relief all round, and as we trooped off the field a spectator suddenly assaulted me. She was at least 5ft nothing and 80 years old. While she berated me with violent swipes of her umbrella, she used a lot of expletives that grannies would not be expected to use. Directly behind me, bloodied but unbowed, was McBride. 'Do you always need to be looked after?' he growled, snatching the umbrella

Jim Telfer closes in B Milner of Poverty Bay.

from supergran before breaking it in two and handing it back to her, then shoving me through the crowd to safety.

WILLIE-JOHN McBRIDE

The training programme before the First Test was conducted on a grass runway at Queenstown airport. I remember someone suddenly shouted, 'Plane! Plane!' and we all ran off the runway and rushed to the hangar until the plane taxied in. We had to run into the hangar three or four times and in the end I thought, bugger this, and I went in and had a smoke with my pipe beside the hangar.

DAVID WATKINS

In one of the Tests, Ken Jones got the treatment at the bottom of a ruck. It looked like a red shirt going round and round in a spin dryer.

COLIN McFADYEAN

The All Blacks were a good side. They demolished us in the First Test, and they had a good goalkicker in Mick Williment, who was a very accurate torpedo-style kicker. But we contested two Tests very closely and there was mitigation for us losing all four. In the Second Test in Christchurch I was running from half-way with two men in support, including Dewi Bebb, our top scorer, and only one man to beat... only to be called back for a penalty to us with an almost certain try on.

JIM TELFER

We got New Zealand at the wrong time. They had Waka Nathan, Brian Lochore, Kel Tremain, Stan Meads, Colin Meads, Bruce McLeod and Jack Hazlett. The only one there who would not be regarded as an all-time great is Hazlett.

COLIN McFADYEAN

Colin Meads was a great player, but also a filthy player. There was one incident where Waka Nathan tried to tackle Dai Watkins, who side-stepped and put a kick into touch, only for Meads to pile in and punch him on the chin, knocking him to the floor. Mike Gibson and myself were standing next to Dai, who was only 5ft 7in tall, and stood there open-mouthed as Meads told the ref, 'He hit me first,' and got off scot-free.

Ray McLoughlin.

JIM TELFER

We had some good players. Ronnie Lamont of Ireland must have been the bravest I ever saw. He had an injury that affected a nerve in his arm, he couldn't lift it properly. He took cortisone injections and used a leather harness so he could play openside flanker and he was out of this world. He became the hero in New Zealand because they realised how tough he really was.

COLIN McFADYEAN

The big characters? Willie-John McBride was all-round popular. A laid-back Ulsterman with a lovely accent who could sing – his party piece was 'Scarlet Ribbons'. Noel Murphy was so cheerful all the time I thought he was an alcoholic, but he was tee total instead.

Dai Watkins stood out on the field for the Lions because he would always do something. So often he beat two men off bad ball, but then was forced to kick. He was very nimble, and the fastest man in the tour party over 25, 50 and 75 yards – only Dewi Bebb could just beat him over the 100 yards. Alun Pask had fantastic hands, and was a great player. He seemed to care about everyone, and was generous in helping other players, myself included. The outstanding New Zealander was Waka Nathan, another great All Black open-side. He was everywhere, all the time, and I've got a photo of him getting out to me on the wing off set-piece play.

JIM TELFER

Every player was adopted by a school during the trip, and my school was Papakuhu High School in Auckland. They produced this wonderful scrapbook of my tour and the lad who presented it to me near the end of the tour was called Bob Lendrum, who went on to play for the All Blacks in 1973 against England. I've still got the scrapbook.

MIKE WESTON

We had flights mostly – and a very bumpy one coming into Wellington one time which was frightening – but we did also travel by train. My memory was of school pitches on the outskirts of each town with hundreds of kids out there practising their goal-kicking because they wanted to become the next Don Clarke or Mick Williment.

Mike Campbell-Lamerton in a happier moment with Peter Stagg.

JIM TELFER

As we went around the country, we realised that out there, rugby was much better organised than back home. They had fully established provincial championships, whereas our district structures were very much in their infancy.

Every time you went to a new town it was a huge festival, with street parades and all that stuff. It is a shame that places like Gisborne and Napier are no longer on the schedule anymore. Those places took the Lions to their hearts and really treated us well.

COLIN McFADYEAN

I found special friends in Australia, with (Australian flanker) Jules Guerassimoff, and in our own tour party, with Derrick Grant. Sometimes you just hit it off with someone. In New Zealand it was Ron Rangi. He was my opposite number in the Tests and took me to one of the All Black drinking sessions where I remember Meads talking about rugby, and what was wrong with the Lions mid-tour. When Fred Allen found out that Rangi had been socialising with us he rewarded him by putting him opposite Meads at the next training session.

NOEL MURPHY

We were trying and trying and trying to get ourselves into a winning formula. The enthusiasm was great going out onto the field. Young lads who went on tour for the first time would say it was one of the greatest experiences of their lives.

COLIN McFADYEAN

The phrase we found most annoying was, 'When are you Lions going to come good?',

because most New Zealanders wanted it to be competitive. We got a ticket allocation of two for each game, but someone sold a ticket, which was splashed all over the local newspapers because, as amateurs, it was a big deal. The UK press men on the tour, Vivian Jenkins and JBG Thomas, were part of the team, but the reporting of the tour back home was minimal. A one-inch by one-inch cutting was all I saw. I listened in bed to the 1966 World Cup final on the radio at three in the morning. I think we were in Wellington, and the reception always seemed to fade just when a goal was scored!

Brian Lochore.

WILLIE-JOHN McBRIDE

We went to the west coast, Greymouth. Unbelievable place. They couldn't put us all up in the one hotel. The hotels in those days were dreadful. We were in a doss house and the other half were in another one at the bottom of the street. There was only one street in the place. And there was nothing to do. Literally nothing to do. I said, 'Why did those buggers get into the good hotel and we're in this dump?' And somebody said, 'We'll go down and rough it up.' There was a bicycle and I took the bike and Ronnie Lamont was on a horse. There was a horse grazing in the green and we went down and roughed this place up, threw stuff out the window, coz they were sitting in the bar. The next day there was murder because they thought bandits had come in and wrecked the Lions hotel.

NOEL MURPHY

An abiding memory: I was in bed on tour when a telegram came to say that my son, Ken Murphy, had been born. It was August 1966. I spoke to my wife that night and sent flowers and everything was grand. I came home and I had a strapping young lad.

Roger Young attempts to clear the ball against the Junior All Blacks in Wellington.

't wouldn't happen now. You wouldn't be allowed to go on that tour, it wouldn't be the thing to do. Imagine your mother-in-law!

JIM TELFER

Having been kicked and stood on by folk the three months, I came back like a caged animal. In my first game back for Melrose, I charged into this ruck, drove into somebody and knocked the living daylights out of them. Barry Laidlaw, the referee, blew his whistle and shouted: 'Penalty, you can't do that.'

I said, 'I've been doing that three months in New Zealand.'

MIKE CAMPBELL-LAMERTON

Funnily enough, it was a very happy tour. It was an incredible journey, and when we had our 25th anniversary dinner, unsponsored, at The Savoy, only five couldn't come. That was the *esprit de corps* of the 1966 Lions. But really, we weren't quite strong enough.

Allan Lewis shows audacious skill to send out a reverse dive-pass as (from left to right) Chris Laidlaw, Stan Meads (both NZ) and Ronnie Lamont and Alun Pask (Lions) look on.

CHAPTER SEVENTEEN

LEARNING THE LESSONS
1968

SOUTH AFRICA

THE MOST *positive aspect of the Lions' very disappointing results in the sixties was the soul-searching it provoked among the Four Home Unions; so at least there was eventually a positive outcome, for in overall results, the 1968 team were as poor as their predecessors of 1962 and 1966, who had been so badly beaten.*

The team were captained by Tom Kiernan, the Irish fullback, and coached by Ronnie Dawson, and after the unhappy events of 1966 when the coach was not allowed to coach, and the chain of command became hopelessly tangled, Dawson at least took charge of the playing side as befitting a man who had captained the 1959 side in Australia and New Zealand.

Yet the Lions were beaten 3-0 by the Springboks in the Test series, managing a draw in Port Elizabeth in the Second Test. They also lost 14-6 to Transvaal in the midweek match before that Test, their only setback outside the series. But in the record books the reading is stark: the Lions sides of the 1960s failed to win a single Test against the superpowers of New Zealand and South Africa. British and Irish rugby had let the rest of the major unions pass them by – France had dominated the Five Nations for most of the seasons between 1959 and 1968. It was long past time for action.

The analysis that followed was more by accident than by design, each of the Home Unions planning their own approaches to the changing demands of the game more or less in isolation. There was broad agreement that a more focused approach to coaching was needed. England, Scotland, Ireland and Wales embraced the national squad concept and each ended the decade with its own coach taking charge of team preparations.

The upshot was fitter players with sharpened basic skills at international level. Coaching was becoming rugby's fastest growing industry – although even as late as 1971, a leading official of British rugby said in a Lions meeting, 'Of course, I don't believe in all this coaching nonsense.'

Dawson, who had led the 1959 Lions, was among the most respected of this breed in the Home Unions and in 1968 he was appointed assistant to manager David Brooks, a former Harlequins forward, for the visit to South Africa. Dawson thus became the first Lion to make tours as a skipper and as a coach. The captaincy also returned to Ireland, where it has always enjoyed mixed success, with Kiernan, their popular fullback who had visited the Republic with the 1962 team, leading the side.

In some ways, Brooks was the most remarkable figure of all. The fun-loving Harlequin was as far removed from the normal style of disciplinarian as it is possible to imagine, so much so that he was a willing participant in many of the legendary nights out enjoyed on tour – and it is said that he even

---

Opposite: Tour captain, Tom Kiernan.

*took part on the side of the 'Wreckers', those tourists who caused damage late at night, against the
'Kippers', who simply wanted to go to bed and sleep undisturbed.*

*It was a tour that yet again exposed British and Irish forward weaknesses. Giving away
considerable weight and power to the South African scrum containing such great forwards as Frik du
Preez, Tiny Naude, Tommy Bedford and Jan Ellis, the Lions found themselves living off morsels in
the Test series.*

*They were only really outplayed in the final Test, but without attacking ball they failed to score
tries. Indeed, 35 of the Lions' 38 points in the series came from the boot of their skipper, Kiernan,
a sad commentary. Their only try was a forward breakaway by Willie-John McBride at Pretoria –
ironically, the Lions' opening score of the rubber.*

*A contributing factor to the try-drought was that the tourists' strike runners were cut down
by a dispiriting run of injuries. Hamstrings seemed particularly vulnerable to the South African
conditions. When the side was originally named it was expected that the natural runners like Gerald
Davies, Billy Raybould, Keith Jarrett and Keri Jones among the three-quarters would flourish on the
hard, fast South African surfaces. Yet all were sidelined and none of them reached double figures on
the appearance list.*

*Barry John and Gareth Edwards were also invalided out. The pairing, who were to ascend to
rugby immortality, carried huge responsibilities on their young shoulders; but John was injured early
on in the First Test when he was tackled by Jan Ellis and broke his collarbone, and Edwards had to
miss the last two Tests.*

*Thereafter, the Lions were unable to find an attacker capable of regularly breaking the strong
defensive formation deployed by the Springboks. Until his injury in the 15th match of the tour,
Edwards had been a star attraction. It was on this visit that he refined his passing technique,
developed the confidence in his ability to beat opponents with his explosive strength and mastered a
strong kicking game.*

*Bob Hiller – 'Boss' to his colleagues – was the England fullback who understudied Kiernan. The
unsung hero of the adventure, he was the model tourist. He was a positive and lively influence behind
the scenes and notched up 39 goals (and two tries) in the midweek matches. He only played eight*

The 1968 Lions party.

imes but with 104 points he was the tour's top scorer. With the skipper in the form of his life, Hiller had no chance of making the Test XV, but he accepted his fate as second-mate with dignity. Arguably ever was a Lions tour party so strongly covered by its fullbacks. Hiller, loyal as ever, performed the ame key role in 1971 in New Zealand as understudy to JPR Williams.

The British & Irish forwards did improve as the tour progressed. The great Lion Jim Telfer led by xample. He was the fittest member of the pack and enjoyed unswerving support from his back-row ompatriot, Rodger Arneil, who had joined the Lions at the last minute when England's Bryan West, n original selection, had had to drop out on the eve of the visit. Arneil was the find of the tour, but he forward who really made his presence felt was Willie-John McBride. It was his third Lions trip nd though held back by minor niggles he was the outstanding performer among the tight forwards. On the hoof with ball in hand he was as threatening a sight as Colin Meads or Frik du Preez. His nauling was renowned and his lineout presence – standing at three or five – was a thorn in the side f opponents. If only the Lions had had two or three more forwards of the same calibre as these three, he series result could easily have been overturned.

The rubber opened with a 25-20 Springbok win in Pretoria. The IRB at its meeting the previous March had finally caved in to pressure to allow replacements in international matches for injured layers and Mike Gibson guaranteed himself a footnote in the game's history by becoming the first sub o appear in a Lions Test when he replaced Barry John. How many more Test results might have been ifferent over the decades had replacements always been allowed?

Kiernan kept his side in touch with five penalty goals and the conversion of Willie-John McBride's torming try. For South Africa, Frik du Preez matched McBride, scoring a try in the second half ohich momentarily put clear water between the sides.

In the Second Test, Kiernan landed two penalties from two attempts for the Lions but the ipringboks landed two from eight in a 6-6 draw at Boet Erasmus Stadium in Port Elizabeth.

Bob Hiller (left) and Syd Millar (right).

Scottish winger Sandy Hinshelwood pulled off a match-saving tackle on Corra Dirksen in the second half to save the Lions from another agonising defeat.

Kiernan was his side's only scorer again in the third international at Newlands, Cape Town. The penalty-goal deadlock was broken after half-time when Thys Lourens, the flanker, scored the only try of the match and Piet Visagie converted on the way to an 11-6 Springbok win.

But at Ellis Park in the final Test the Springboks broke free to win 19-6, scoring four tries and underlining their forward power and the effective finishing of their backs.

The dominance of the penalty goal, unusual law interpretations that yet again confused the tourists and objections to the referee nominated for the Second Test led to renewed calls for the introduction of the differential penalty and neutral referees. The tour also sparked a debate about raising the value of the try to four points (finally introduced in 1971).

Politics were never far behind the rugby on this tour. Back home the Lions' controversial decision to undertake a visit to Rhodesia after that country's Unilateral Declaration of Independence was a talking point, while for many of the players making their first visits to South Africa, especially the cohort of fresh-faced students in the party, the first-hand experience of the country's apartheid laws caused revulsion.

John Taylor, the young flanker from Loughborough, was so perturbed by the situation that he was eventually to turn down the chance to play for Wales against South Africa two seasons after the tour, before declining his invitation to return to South Africa with the Lions in 1974. The issue of sporting contacts with South Africa gradually caused greater debate and, eventually, the severing of connections for a time.

For the first time the Lions were subjected to disagreeable media coverage back at home. The nature of the relationship between press and players was beginning to change, with some journalists intent on describing the high jinx off the field as well as reporting the events on it. It's true that the

Gareth Edwards and Billy Raybould practise their dive passes.

Lions divided into Kippers and Wreckers but most of the high jinks were good-humoured – though they did cause damage, and eventually the tourists who wanted to take their rugby far more seriously began to tire of the endless partying. One wrecking party caused a very irate hotel manager to accost the tourists' manager in no uncertain terms the next morning, with accusations that fire hoses had been unlashed in the middle of the night and non-rugby guests soaked.

Brooks, blithely unconcerned, asked the hotel manager how much the damage cost. On being told he flourished his pen, wrote out a personal cheque and handed it over with the riposte: 'Couldn't have been much of a party.'

Mock courts are a feature of Lions tours. The players appoint a judge who each week imposes a series of fines on players for petty misdemeanours. John O'Shea, the Cardiff and Wales prop, was judge in 1968 – and had to rule punishment against himself after he was sent off by referee Bert Woolley against Eastern Transvaal at Springs. (O'Shea was actually assaulted by a spectator as he marched off and was absolved after the post-match enquiry.)

*Also on the lighter side, John Reason (*Daily Telegraph*) solved once and for all one of the game's greatest contemporary mysteries. Peter Stagg of Scotland was one of the locks on this tour. He was the first international player to scale over 6ft 6in but was very guarded about divulging his true height (which was a few inches more). Reason found him asleep on the beach during the side's stay in Cape Town and later revealed all to his readers. 'Carefully marking the points [in the sand] at each end of him I sneaked out later and measured them. They were 6ft 9in apart.'*

The decade was over. Three tours and three defeats, and victory in the Test series – any Test series – seemed as far away as ever, even though in the background, key technical experts in some of the Home Unions were plotting a future with less damage to the fixtures and fittings of the hosting nations, and more damage on the field of play.

The tourists prepare for departure.

BOB TAYLOR (England)
Toured: 1968

When I was picked for the Lions I had to go to the school (Wellingborough Grammar) to get permission for time off. I went to see the headmaster, Harry Wrenn, and I told him I'd been asked. He said straight away: 'You tell 'em you're available. I plan to bask in your reflective glory.' At the next governors' meeting he stood up and said, 'Mr Taylor will be away for a while, he's been selected for the British Lions. He'll be on full pay.' There were other schoolmasters who came with us on that tour, but some of those were released without any pay. Most of us were very lucky that we could wrangle it.

We were a motley crew when we turned up. We all had different shirts and shorts on and we all wore different tracksuits. There were no Lions tracksuits back then. We were genuine amateurs. We were asked to buy two pairs of shorts, a pair of boots and a Lions shirt – which I actually swapped for a South African one so I don't even have one of those anymore. And you had to provide receipts for everything if you wanted the money back.

Bryan West turned up in Eastbourne with a broken ankle. We knew straight away he wouldn't be able to play until late on in the tour, but he gave it a go anyway.

JIM TELFER

I'd been to South Africa before in 1967 with the Borders so I knew about apartheid. I knew that black people walked along the road and had to cross over if they saw a white person coming. I knew they were treated like slaves. But I wasn't politically

Jim Telfer feels the impact of his pack of forwards in training.

motivated enough to make a song and dance about it. I was never not going to go. But there were two kinds of apartheid: white against black, and also Dutch white against English white.

SYD MILLAR

Players are very apolitical and we never thought much about that; 1968 was when the first pressure started to come, but it wasn't too bad. Of course we were aware of the problems but people just wanted to play rugby against the best. I wasn't thinking much about politics. Sometimes I look back and say, 'Were we right or were we wrong?' You'll never know.

BOB TAYLOR

To be quite honest we were young rugby players and we weren't particularly interested in the political scene back then. We had a presentation from the South Africa embassy where we were told not to associate with women of a dark skin. And we were told quite clearly there were areas that were white only and areas that were black only. One or two of the players had a hang-up about going, but I had no hang-ups at all.

BOB HILLER (England)
Toured: 1968 & 1971

I enjoyed South Africa, but we were aware of Apartheid. It was much more obvious on the high veld than in the Cape Town area. You accepted it was the status quo, but also knew that it wasn't right and that it probably would not last. All the blacks and coloureds wanted us to win – and at fullback I was always very close to them because they were in the cheap seats at the end of the grounds. That's where my nickname 'Boss' Hiller came from, because they would shout out to me, 'Boss!', and I would give them a few waves or a clenched fist salute. I think we were popular because we treated the non-white staff in our hotels well, and always had a laugh and a joke with them.

GERALD DAVIES (Wales)
Toured: 1968 & 1971. Manager 2009

The Welsh team had recently toured South Africa and apparently, so we were told, they had been rather homesick and cliquish, so in 1968 we all had to share rooms with somebody from another nation, the English could not share with the English and so on. That was the factor that brought us all together.

BOB TAYLOR

No supporters travelled to watch in those days. We had a press pack of about 15, and four or five from BBC2, who were providing the first ever live television coverage of the Lions. The only support we had were representatives from the Four Home Unions, who came out because it was a duty. We didn't suffer, because we weren't expecting it. It was low profile back then.

GERALD DAVIES

It was a mind-blowing experience to be out there. I grew up with the 1955 Lions in South Africa. I used to read *Lions Rampant* by Vivian Jenkins. If you wanted to see the Lions play or follow the tour, there was nothing on television and nothing on the radio so I had to go to the Regal Cinema in Llanelli and watch it on the Pathé News. Sometimes, you would only get about a minute of it.

What appealed to me, even though it was in black-and-white, was that they were playing in sunshine; in black-and-white the pitches looked white with the kikuyu grass. I saw pictures of matches with palm trees in the background, and I found that exotic. My rugby was Welsh rugby – cold nights, cloudy and sometimes dark and gloomy. That glimpse of the Lions in 1955 had something exotic about it. I always wanted to be a Lion, where palm trees grew.

When I went to South Africa in 1968, it was the culmination of a dream I had ever since seeing the pictures at the cinema. That's the way it was for me. I wanted to be a Lion and even then there was a magic attached to it. It was wonderful, you experienced the four nations knitting together very well.

SYD MILLAR

We didn't have a particularly strong team in '68. Ronnie Dawson was the first coach and he did a very good job. The coach before was John Robins in '66 and he was not allowed to do his job because Campbell-Lamerton didn't like the idea of a coach.

RONNIE DAWSON

I had done a lot of reading, spoken to a lot of people in South Africa whose opinions I respected and produced an overall concept of what South African rugby was.

BOB TAYLOR

It was always fierce in the pack, no matter who we played. And it was all pretty ruthless. If you did something that was gaining you an advantage the opposition would take measures to stop you. The fist was commonplace. And they had a lot of good footballers too. But we actually did well in the forwards, we got quite a lot of ball. If anything our backs lacked an extra bit of pace. We had the players, but I'm not sure the backs were as well organised as they should have been.

SYD MILLAR

The Second Test was a draw and we had problems with the referee in the scrum. JP Schoeman was the ref. I said to John Pullin, 'Stop striking, John,' because every time he was penalising us. The games were close, up to a point. The referee was a significant factor at times. You can't dispute that; that's life.

RONNIE DAWSON

There was the same old syndrome of home referees, and there were a few dreadful decisions. After the match you had an opportunity to talk to the ref but there wasn't any mileage in slagging him.

JIM TELFER

The refereeing of the lineouts and scrums was what really affected our play right from the outset of the tour. The South Africans played with all sorts of different interpretations to us, from hooking early and the scrum-half feed in the scrum, to putting a forward outside the lineout to receive a tap-down, which was illegal in Britain and Ireland at the time.

As a result, we gave away umpteen penalties a game and struggled to create any sort of platform. In almost every scrum our hookers, John Pullin and Jeff Young, would be penalised. Our scrum-half, Roger Young, was penalised so often for his scrum put-ins that he didn't know what to do.

It emerged later that Dr Danie Craven had used his influence to tell the referees to keep us in check in these areas.

SYD MILLAR

I used to say to Doc Craven, 'People have come here under great pressure and we don't expect to be treated like this.' The referee was biased and prejudiced and they picked the referees. It was very difficult. We expected that we weren't going to get a fair deal and we knew that we had to be better than them. You went and said we hope we'll get a fair deal and we hope the ref will be fair but we always knew there was a fair chance that when things got tight the decisions would tend to go the other way. You had that feeling about it. Schoeman was penalising us for feet up in the scrums or collapsing the scrums. It was always our fault in his opinion, which it wasn't. I said to John, 'Just scrum, don't put your foot up, so they can't penalise us.'

There were two hard places in South Africa – Port Elizabeth, against Eastern Province, and Springs, against Eastern Transvaal. 'Tess' O'Shea was having a go at some player and then he hit him and got sent off. Then a spectator had a go at Tess. I was sitting in the stand. What could we do about it? Willie-John McBride jumped over the fence.

JBG THOMAS (Writing in *On Trek Again*)

As O'Shea and friendly escorts reached the mouth of the tunnel, *bang*, a spectator leapt to the gate and punched O'Shea full on the side of the face! This was the spark that set the situation alight. In a split second, several spectators from both camps were in action. Willie-John McBride was first there and a right-cross virtually stopped the spectator in his tracks; the police managed to stop McBride applying the KO, although he did well to follow up with his left!

RONNIE DAWSON

It was entirely wrong that John O'Shea was sent-off. He threw a punch but there was a hell of a lot of punches that had been thrown beforehand, most of them by their guys. There was a sort of acceptance of foul play and misconduct that was allowed to take place in the game. It's terribly, terribly tough now and hard and vicious at times but there was a lot more nasty play back then, no doubt about it. Punches would come through a front-row from a second-row in the set-scrum, players would be hit off the ball, and there was always a vicious use of the boot on players lying on the ground.

JIM TELFER

I remember going to see O'Shea in the dressing-room afterwards and he was crying because he felt he had let everyone down. He apologised to the powers that be and he was let off with a reprimand. Bert Woolley, the referee, later wrote to Tess saying that he regretted sending him off – and Tess gave him two tickets for the Third Test.

WILLIE JOHN McBRIDE

It was a piece of nonsense that O'Shea was sent off. There was lots of niggly stuff and they had set out to annoy and niggle and it was successful because O'Shea belted somebody. It was a disgrace that he was sent off because this nonsense had been going on for ages and he had to walk all the way around the pitch to the tunnel and the South Africans were throwing oranges and beer cans at him. Then this bugger ran out and belted him and I had taken enough at that stage. I jumped in and hit the guy. I'm not that sort of person but I couldn't take any more. Poor O'Shea was left on his own with nobody looking after him and it was wrong. I hit the spectator and he had glasses and the glasses

John O'Shea is sent off by Bert Woolley against Eastern Transvaal.

went flying. The police got me and took me away. I had a laugh because they tore my Lions sweater and I said I was putting in a claim for a new Lions sweater. I said, 'It's your responsibility, you didn't look after that player.' Och, we had a bit of fun. It was all right.

GERALD DAVIES

I'm not sure whether the 1968 tour was the birth of the Tour Court, perhaps we inherited it, but it was certainly the tour when court became more defined and regular. We used to have every Sunday off and the court would sit. The judge was John 'Tess' O'Shea from Cardiff, who now lives in Australia. The charges would only be daft things – not wearing the right blazer, etc – but it was always a great day off and great relaxation.

For some reason I was asked to be the prosecuting counsel, so I would draw up a list of eight or nine cases and compose the list of charges in legal jargon. Tess was a Harry Secombe figure, with a high-pitched laugh and a high-pitched voice, and was very, very funny. It was great fun, one of the bonding things which happen.

BOB TAYLOR

The drinking on that tour was fantastic, absolutely fantastic. But it wasn't terribly sociable with the opposition. We'd meet for the reception and obviously we'd chat. But you could sense their focus was more on the game and how they were going to win it. We'd often be kept separate too, staying in different parts of the city.

RONNIE DAWSON

The legend of the Wreckers and the Kippers has obviously gone down in history, but it wasn't as bad as it has been recorded; having said that, there were occasions when

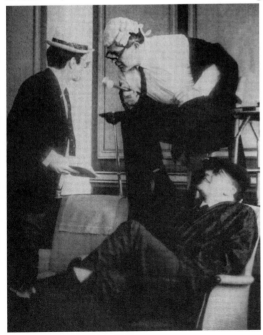

things happened that shouldn't have happened. We had a marvellous character as manager called David Brooks who was the proverbial guy who never grew up. He was a brilliant character, a pilot in the Second World War. We had great fun with him. But there were one or two occasions when things got right offside. There was a problem in a hotel and it became legend.

JBG THOMAS

After an early breakfast there was a rush to the news stall at the railway station to obtain copies of the *Jo'Burg*

The players' court session. John O'Shea as judge, with Gerald Davies and Syd Millar.

Sunday Times. Even VIPs on holidays were in the hunt for the sensational news. When we got the paper, there it was, across the top of the front page in a banner headline – 'Lions Behaviour Shocks City'… 'Hotel man tells of "unmitigated drunken revelry". The opening paragraph read, 'The touring Lions rugby party have left a trail of havoc and stunned incredulity after three days in East London marked by severe drinking bouts and riotous behaviour at hotels and night clubs. They left broken hotel doors, broken glasses by the dozen, unpaid liquor debts and girls in tears because of outright rudeness'. After a lifetime of travel, and of meeting players in all countries, I was amazed at this attack. This front page story almost made them appear to be international criminals. It was a most controversial form of journalism. I am most ready to admit that such stories on sport sometimes appear in the British press, but I felt the *Sunday Times* lost prestige in the eyes of many of its readers after this sensational story.

SYD MILLAR

There was an awful lot of exaggeration about the Wreckers and the Kippers. Some of the team were quieter than others. You had a few party boys in there but the ones who were quieter were called the Kippers – they went to bed early. And the guys who partied a bit were called the Wreckers. In any tour there's a bit of nonsense goes on.

JIM TELFER

It was quite an unhappy tour in many ways. Quite quickly we were split into factions with the Kippers and the Wreckers. I was in the Kippers, naturally.

Gareth Edwards receives attention during the Test at Loftus Versfeld.

It started off when we were on our way to a short break at Kruger National Park, when we were on a long train journey from Johannesburg to Nelspruit, and you'd be sitting in your carriage and you'd hear the song roaring down the corridor shouting: 'The Wreckers are coming, hurrah, hurrah; The Wreckers are coming, hurrah, hurrah!' And your heart sank.

JOHN TAYLOR (Wales)
Toured: 1968 & 1971

The Wreckers and the Kippers sounds like a bit of horseplay but as a Kipper myself it can still bring back rather anxious memories. Imagine going through South Africa behind a steam locomotive in the middle of the night, locking yourself in your compartment and hearing the Wreckers coming closer and closer, door by door!

JIM TELFER

It was originally a small group of about eight or so enthusiastic Wreckers, led by the captain and manager, and more than 20 Kippers, but people started realising that resistance was futile and swapped sides.

There was little you could do about it and you just accepted that you'd be woken up if you tried to sleep – but I think overall it actually helped team spirit.

WILLIE JOHN McBRIDE

Some parties got out of hand. The most famous occasion was on the night sleeper train to the Kruger Park. The tour itinerary permitted a few days' break which was a splendid idea, but I'm not sure the Lions' behaviour on the journey was so commendable. A lot of drink had been spilled and eventually Syd Millar and I said, 'Let's get out of here,' and rushed down the train to our cabins. The next thing we heard was the beat of war drums, crying, 'The Wreckers are coming, the Wreckers are coming!' Syd and I were hiding in the corner of our compartment and somehow they missed us. Inadvertently, they launched a raid on the next-door compartment, which was occupied by an old lady and gentleman. Both were turned out into the corridor by the mob before the blunder was realised. The commotion during the night had caused such a fuss that the train authorities had unhooked our two carriages and dumped them into a siding while the rest of the train proceeded on its way. There was one hell of a mess in those carriages.

JIM TELFER

Dare I say it, but it was the worst kind of public schoolboy behaviour. No regard for other people's property. They would say: easy come and easy go – but that's not good enough.

I remember David Brooks coming up to me during a night out early in the tour and saying, 'I knew when we picked this squad that there would be three of four guys who would be different and not approve of this sort of thing, and I knew, Jim, that you would be one of them.' But he had got me wrong. I don't mind people letting their hair down and enjoying themselves. I'm not a monk. I enjoyed going out for a drink and occasionally got drunk, but it shouldn't affect your performance on the pitch – and it doesn't need to be ignorant towards other people. So I said that I understood what he was trying to do and it was fine by me so long as the focus was on winning the tour.

It wasn't malicious – it was just stupidity. You've got to remember that in those days there was a lot of drinking that went on, but they weren't getting drunk every night or anything like that. The manager was a bit if a drinker and he maybe led on some of the youngsters at times.

But sometimes it did go too far. I remember sitting after a function in Cape Town, and two Lions were picking up glasses and throwing them into the fire, one after the other, dozens and dozens of them. I remember looking at them and thinking: 'What are you doing? Is this really entertaining you?'

The Lions management were given a bill for damages – which was reported to have been half of the true cost, and then halved again, before a bill for £900 was handed over. David Brooks wasn't too concerned by it all – apparently he looked at it and said, 'Is that all? It couldn't have been a very good party!'

WILLIE JOHN McBRIDE

Och, if you had seen the places we were put in… It was frustration. The hotels we were in were rubbish. Terrible places we were in. There was just a crowd of guys who had a bit more fun than others. When I say we had fun, we always knew when to have a bit of fun. It wasn't that we were out every night on the rampage. If you were playing you stayed in and you were ready for the game. When you had a couple of days off you had a bit of fun. There was nothing that was all that serious. I slipped on a floor and there was a broken bottle and I went down on the piece of glass and cut my knee and got stitches. It was all stupid, innocent stuff. David Brooks was probably the

An aerial shot of the First Test in Pretoria.

leader of it all. I remember one Sunday coming back from somewhere and he'd fallen into the fish pond outside the hotel. He was a good manager.

SYD MILLAR

Yeah, there was one incident on a train when there was a bit of damage done and occasionally things got broken. Of course they did. But there was a lot made out of it. The press, you see, get hold of this stuff. Always when we went to East London, whoever the press guy was there he used to write rubbish. He was talking about naked scrummaging in 1974.

BOB HILLER

When you look back at the Kippers and Wreckers it was a bit childish, but it was also great fun. It started on the train to Kruger Park, which was a bit like something out of an old Western. It took forever to get to Nelspruit, which was not that far from Johannesburg, and we had a few beers. There was a bit of a rumpus during the night when a couple of blokes started raiding the carriages chanting, 'The Wreckers are coming, hurrah, hurrah!', but when we got up in the morning it was rather quiet. It soon became apparent that there was no train and that the carriages we were on had been unhooked and left out on the veldt. We thought we had been abandoned – but then some vehicles arrived to collect us and we were taken to Skukuza game park where we had a marvellous three days with beers and barbecues.

I was the 'King of the Kippers', and always trying to get some sleep, and by the end I was almost left on my own. We were split about 50-50 to start off with but then there were a lot of defections, mainly to the Wreckers. All our games of touch in training were Kippers v Wreckers, and it was the same when we played golf. I knew David Brooks very well, and he was a great character. Brooksy was always loads of

Gerald Davies in full flight as he races in to score a sensational try against Boland.

fun, and all the high jinks were done with great humour and no malice at all – and the press travelled as part of our party, and joined in.

WILLIE JOHN McBRIDE

It was my third tour and I had more hope that we might win than on the previous two because Ronnie Dawson was involved, but we still weren't good enough. Ah, I was disappointed. That's why I more or less made up my mind about 1971. You reach a stage in life when you get sick of losing. The reason the Lions lost the Test series 3-0 with one match drawn was because of us forwards. We were inferior to the hard-grafting South African packs that dominated possession and played a tough, physical game. We were not good enough. I was probably not the lineout forward that some of the guys I played against were. Our players started questioning themselves when things started going wrong, which is why the mind is so important in rugby football. We crumbled. We had this feeling of being inferior. Physically we could prepare, but mentally we were not strong enough. Mankind discovers the power of his mental faculties in adversity. Ours were insufficient to handle the task before us.

JIM TELFER

All that Wreckers and Kippers stuff took away some of the lustre of the Lions ethos, I think, and the incident certainly seemed to affect our display in the Third Test at the end of the week. To be honest, we should still have won that Test match.

I knew Danie Craven very well, and got on well with him because he looked after us when we toured South Africa with the Borders in 1967. But he was ruthless, absolutely ruthless. He would do anything to win a Test match. He made sure we had this crazy itinerary where we were up into the high veldt for one match, then down to sea-level for the next, then across to the other side of the country, and back up into the high veldt. In those days, the Home Unions would just accept what the South Africans scheduled – they wouldn't want to argue about something like that.

The thing I remember most about South Africa was that the landscape was so different to anything else I had experienced before; the pitches were also as hard as rock and we played on cricket wickets, so injuries mounted up fairly easily.

BOB TAYLOR

Loftus Versfeld was an incredible ground to play rugby. The whole place was open. The stands went up into the sky. They just went up and up and up. As a player the best thing you could do was to get somewhere near the middle of the field and orientate yourself, because you could lose track of where the game was taking place if you weren't careful. They were hostile crowds in South Africa. They'd throw things at you.

JIM TELFER

The Springboks team was full of great players, guys like Jannie Engelbrecht, Dawie de Villiers and Frik du Preez. I remember du Preez catching a kick-off and going on a run that took him all the way down the pitch to score. But they were so forward-dominant, and so reliant on kicking most of the time. They could have done so much more, have been so much more, if they had broadened their thinking and opened their minds a bit more.

GARETH EDWARDS (Wales)
Toured: 1968, 1971 & 1974

That was my first Lions tour. You look back on the Test records and see that we drew one Test and lost the others, but with some better finishing, we could certainly have won the Third Test in Cape Town. But the big thing about that tour was that we went unbeaten in the provincial games, and that certainly takes a bit of doing in South Africa.

Matches against the likes of Northern Transvaal, Transvaal and Western Province are not far off Test status and I guess we built on the respect and enjoyment that the 1955 Lions established through players like Cliff Morgan, Tony O'Reilly and Jeff Butterfield – something that was still talked about as fervently then as it is today. South Africans don't forget the great players.

Despite the Wreckers and Kippers fiasco, which spoiled the way the tour is remembered by some, a lot was put in place under David Brooks and Ronnie Dawson that has perhaps not been fully recognised or appreciated in the histories of the Lions. You could see the beginnings of a more professional approach in preparation and training – and although, when compared with later tours, it was still pretty naive in its overall approach, you could definitely begin to see the genesis of a change of attitudes.

John Taylor shows off his souvenirs upon the Lions' return home.

CHAPTER EIGHTEEN

THE HISTORY BOYS
1971

AUSTRALIA AND NEW ZEALAND

THE WAIT had been interminable, and there had been very little evidence on the most recent Lions tours that British and Irish rugby was about to turn history on its head. Yet suddenly, it happened. The remarkable 1971 group, beautifully managed and beautifully coached (such a contrast with history on both counts), with an inner core of players who will go down amongst the all-time greats, and a squad which had depth in terms of ability and self belief, downed the All Blacks on their own paddocks.

They gave rugby itself a magnificent boost and as a result of some thrilling and tense months in New Zealand, catapulted rugby into the affections of a whole new audience and gave rugby in the four home countries an unfamiliar swagger. There are the people of a certain age who will never forget the excitement of following the momentous matches over the radio in a British dawn.

In the first part of the 1970s, and for the first time in the 20th century, British and Irish rugby ruled the world. The Lions won the series in New Zealand in 1971 and then, spectacularly, in South Africa in 1974, and England, the only home union to tour overseas in between, stunned rugby followers by winning one-off Tests against South Africa in Johannesburg in 1972 and New Zealand in Auckland in 1973.

At home, moreover, spectators saw a Barbarians team – a Lions XV in all but name – carry off a sensational 23-11 victory over the All Blacks at Cardiff in January 1973. These were heady days.

The coaching revolution in the Home Unions reaped dividends, with the likes of Ray Williams at the Welsh Rugby Union revolutionising the way the sport was played and organised at the top level. Forward play improved beyond recognition and, in New Zealand in 1971, the Lions pack won sufficient possession for a talented back division to run riot. The forwards had mastered the art of efficient rucking and applied the theories of good body position to hold their own in mauls and scrums. They also realised, from the sorry example of past tours, that they could not afford to be intimidated.

Careful planning was the secret to the success of the tour. Everything was precise. Dr Doug Smith, an Essex GP who had played for Scotland and toured with the 1950 Lions, was their charismatic manager. He smoothed the path for the players and coach. Carwyn James, an erudite, cerebral West Walian, was able to concentrate on the playing side.

Smith forged good relations with the media and New Zealand administrators, was firm yet understanding with his players, and turned out to be a remarkable sage – he predicted that the side would win the rubber 2-1 with one Test drawn. And they did.

Opposite: Gerald Davies contests for the ball with Bryan Williams during the Fourth Test.

Where Smith was big and outward-going, James was scholarly and thoughtful. Yet he commanded unwavering respect among his squad. His rugby philosophy was simple: he saw himself as the players' guide, not their commander; players should take responsibility for their actions on the field and adapt tactics to the situations presented. His technical approach was equally straightforward. Rugby was a handling game. The basic skills of passing and running were the tools for success.

As a schoolmaster at Llandovery in the sixties he had applied these tenets to make the college's 1st XV the most exciting school team in Britain. He copied the template successfully as Llanelli's coach and extended it triumphantly to the 1971 Lions. Yet for all his encouragement of freedom of expression on the field, he still spent hours in garnering the thoughts of his senior players before carefully preparing his match plans. It is said that he chose the first five Lions teams of the tour before he left London.

In John Dawes, the first Welshman to lead a fully representative British and Irish tour, James had a like-minded skipper. Dawes believed in the unpredictability of counter-attack as a powerful tactic and at London Welsh had been among the first to appreciate the potential of the attacking fullback in the wake of the law change that, since September 1968, had restricted direct kicking to touch when outside the 25-yard line. By a happy coincidence, he had found in the young St Mary's Hospital medical student, JPR Williams, the perfect prototype for the counter-attacking game.

JPR was at the height of his powers in New Zealand, as were the entire back division. Dawes was an unobtrusive centre who perfectly complemented the penetrating attacking potential of his co-centre, Mike Gibson, not the first Irishman to reach a career peak wearing red rather than green, and whose midfield performances caused New Zealanders to regard him as among the greats. As a pair they exercised perfect judgement to bring the best out of outstanding wings Gerald Davies, John Bevan and David Duckham, who replaced Bevan in the Test side after the first international.

Then there were the Welsh half-backs, Gareth Edwards and Barry John – John was christened 'The King' by admiring team-mates. He broke records by scoring 188 points, but it was his tactical acuteness allied to an astonishing self-confidence that was the real key to the Lions' success. His line-kicking and tactical punting reminded critics of a chess-master moving his pieces into checkmate positions around the board. At Dunedin in the First Test, he tormented the New Zealand fullback

The 1971 Lions party.

Fergie McCormick so cruelly, pushing him from one touchline to the other, that the famous All Black never again played for his country.

The outstanding forward was Willie-John McBride, the Irish lock whose ability to impose himself physically and mentally on the opposition challenged the aura of invincibility surrounding All Black forwards. McBride, who had endured three grim and losing Lions tours, at first intended to make himself unavailable for the tour.

Carwyn James was the first to admit that tight forward play was not his strong suit, but he made good use of the knowledge he had at his disposal. Prop Ray McLoughlin, mathematician and pack professor, had such a depth of knowledge about scrummaging that James handed early responsibility for the planning of the tight aspects of the game to him.

The Lions lost only twice. There was a stopover in Australia – matches against Queensland and New South Wales with no Tests – before the side moved on to New Zealand. The Lions were beaten in Brisbane in their first game. The refereeing was questionable but in the post-match conference Dr Smith was in great form. The side had arrived only two days earlier long haul from Hong Kong and when put on the spot by the press, Smith was brilliant. There was no whingeing about officials, the team was suffering 'circadian dysrhythmia', he said. The press fell silent as they wondered what he was talking about (jet lag, apparently). Smith was on the front foot and remained so for the rest of the trip.

Incredibly, in the cauldron of New Zealand provincial rugby, the Lions were to win every provincial game. The thrashing of Wellington early in the tour by an incredible 47-9, arguably the greatest non-Test performance in Lions history, set the tone.

Carwyn James.

Another keynote performance in the provincial games came at Napier against Hawke's Bay, when the local team tried to strong-arm the Lions out of contention. The response of the touring team was a brilliant display of attacking rugby in which Gerald Davies scored four glorious tries.

It almost goes without saying that the tour was not marked by the same excesses of drunkenness and high spirits associated with the 1968 tour, and with many of the previous excursions. The tour did a service of sorts to the Beach Boys by making their 'Sloop John B' the regular tour song, and soon it was being sung by rugby touring teams the length and breadth of Britain and Ireland – and it was even played at the end-of-year sports awards programmes when the Lions, fittingly, were named the sports team of the year. They also popularised the term LGT (large gin and tonic), as it was the drink of choice for many of the players.

Another point worth mentioning is that Bob Hiller, the Harlequins fullback, passed into Lions folklore not only with his humour off the field and his expert kicking at goal in the midweek games, but with the selfless manner in which he backed up JPR Williams, even though he realised that his chances of appearing in the Test series were slim.

One other pleasant surprise was that the refereeing during the tour was at least adequate in most of the games, with one man, John Pring, taking charge of all four Test matches, the first time this had happened on the Lions tour.

The tourists swept through New Zealand, racking up the points before the First Test in Dunedin. The week before the Test they played Canterbury, fierce and controversial opponents for Lions teams down the decades. It was a game that became notorious. The Lions won 14-3. If the 1966 Lions match there had been dubbed 'World War One', the 1971 return might easily have been 'World War Two'.

The home side carried on matters where they had left off five years earlier, and the Lions lost both their front-line props as a result of calculated thuggery. Sandy Carmichael was punched out of the tour, suffering a multiple fracture of the left cheekbone, and Ray McLoughlin broke his thumb in an altercation with Alex Wyllie. Carwyn James described his team's dressing room after the match as resembling a 'casualty clearing station'.

And so the Lions suddenly faced the All Blacks in the First Test with two new props, Ian 'Mighty Mouse' McLauchlan on the loose-head (for McLoughlin) and the Dublin vintner, Sean Lynch, on the other side for Carmichael. Remarkably, it was McLauchlan who crossed for the only try of the match to open the scoring in the first half. Fergie McCormick equalised before half-time but two Barry John penalties sealed a 9-3 victory for the Lions. They had to defend with mighty courage as the All Blacks, led by Colin Meads, tried desperately to recover.

Colin Meads.

The tackling of Peter Dixon, Mervyn Davies and John Taylor in the back-row was extraordinary. So too the play of Ray 'Chico' Hopkins, who arrived as replacement for Edwards early in the second half.

The only defeat the side suffered in New Zealand was in the Second Test in Christchurch. Syd Going and the New Zealand pack dominated to such an extent that the All Blacks had a commanding 22-6 lead in the second half. The Lions were badly missing McLoughlin, who had returned home, but a late try by Gerald Davies and drop-goal by John gave Carwyn James the optimism to predict that the Lions would bounce back. Dawes always claimed that the late Lions rally convinced him that they could win the series.

In the Home Unions there had been a move to abandon the old blind- and openside flanker style of back-row play when the law restricting touch-finding was introduced in the late sixties. Many sides switched to using left and right flankers and the Lions had adopted that system for the early part of the tour. It had let them down in Christchurch, and for the all-important Third Test in Wellington, the blindside/openside convention was restored. Derek Quinnell, who was an uncapped player at the time, came in on the blind with Fergus Slattery chosen to play open.

On the eve of the Test Slattery, who had been suffering with a cold, was struggling with his breathing so John Taylor was recalled. The London Welshman had the game of his life and the threat of Syd Going was effectively strangled by an effective pincer movement from the flankers.

James's legendary attention to detail was evident. Shortly before the toss he phoned the local met office to check the windy Wellington conditions. Assured that the wind would not increase as the afternoon progressed, he passed a message to John Dawes and, on winning the toss (for the third time in the series) the skipper chose to play with the wind (whereas they had opted for the kick-off in Dunedin and Christchurch).

It was one of the games of Lions history. Gordon Brown had been called in to beef up the Lions pack and the tourists started with a blitz, scoring 13 points without reply in the first 18 minutes. Edwards, playing one of his great games, made a try for John with a charge, and then another for Gerald Davies. Their forwards took charge and John kicked with precision to exercise a tactical stranglehold as the wind steadied in the second half. The Lions won 13-3 and could not now lose the series.

Vivian Jenkins waxed lyrical in his cable for the Sunday Times. *'Glory Be! The day – the unforgettable, almost unbelievable day – has dawned at last. Mark well the date. It marks a turning point in Britain's rugby story.' After so many long years covering the Lions in New Zealand he could be forgiven, perhaps, for rejoicing. His longstanding colleague JBG Thomas was even quicker into print, the* Western Mail *match report appearing on the Cardiff streets by 6am that morning – barely an hour after the end of the match.*

The Lions only had to draw in Auckland to fulfil Dr Smith's prophecy and become the first British & Irish side to win a series Down Under. The All Blacks established an 8-0 lead in a rough opening quarter before the Lions bounced back to equalise with a John penalty and a try by Peter Dixon just before half-time, converted by John. Near the end JPR Williams dropped a goal from 40 metres (winning a bet he had made with Bob Hiller) to put the Lions 14-11 ahead and all the New Zealanders could muster was a late penalty goal by fullback Laurie Mains to draw the match. Some of the Lions looked back in later years with a sense of frustration, because they felt that they could have signed off in style with a convincing win. But in the end, they had made history and had secured their legend.

The live middle-of-the-night radio commentaries of the earlier Tests had been followed closely by millions of enthusiasts at home. Satellite arrangements were relatively primitive at the time, but through special efforts the second half of that final Test was broadcast live on television. The thrill of seeing the grainy black and-white pictures of that historic rugby match unfold from the other side of the world will remain in the memories of all those in Britain and Ireland who witnessed them.

It would also be far too easy and far too dismissive of the Lions' efforts to claim that it was simply a weak New Zealand team that they faced. History has shown before and since that there is absolutely no such thing, especially when they are playing on their own grounds. Meads may have been past his best or, more to the point, the likes of Willie-John McBride and company no longer feared him as Lions teams had once done. Syd Going and Bob Burgess were a half-back combination as good as any in New Zealand history, and the idea that New Zealand had suddenly become feeble is ridiculous.

This was still well before the days of mass communication and few of the Lions really grasped the sensation they had caused back in the home countries by their exploits. Many of them only realised the impact they had when they returned to Heathrow to find that thousands of people had come to welcome them – the conquering, history-making heroes.

It was no exaggeration to say it: rugby would never be the same again.

IAN McLAUCHLAN (Scotland)
Toured: 1971 & 1974

I didn't have much of a clue about what the Lions were. I put my name down because somebody told me I should, but I didn't think about it again until a month before the tour when a London journalist told me that he'd heard they were going to pick me. Then I went to Paris for the France match and met this funny little man called Carwyn James, who invited me out for a cup of tea. So I spoke to him for a while and he finished by saying, 'I'm looking forward to touring with you in the summer.' And I didn't know what to make of that. Then, later, Norman Mair of *The Scotsman* said to me, 'How did you get on with Carwyn James?' And I said, 'Fine. He's quite a funny little man, isn't he?' And Norman shot back, 'Don't say that – he's the coach of the Lions.'

MERVYN DAVIES (Wales)
Toured: 1971 & 1974

Some people laughed at us for even daring to dream. Being invited to be a Lion brought with it considerable fear. It may sound melodramatic, but the only comparison I can give to getting ready to face the All Blacks is preparing for some kind of war. So many of the All Blacks forwards were heroes of mine, men like Colin Meads and Ken Gray. There were 30 of us and a whole nation of them, no Barmy Army to give us comfort from the side. The last Lions team that went to New Zealand, in 1966, had been massacred.

PETER DIXON (England)
Toured: 1971

I was sitting in the Bodleian Library writing my BLit social anthropology thesis –

'Some West African Mortuary Rights' – when someone told me I had been selected for the Lions. It was a complete surprise, as England had not shown much interest in me, and, by the time of the tour, I was 27 and had won just one cap (in the RFU Centenary game against a President's XV). I was playing for Oxford University as a postgraduate – and Harlequins after Christmas – and recall that John Reason had written in the press that I was the sort of 'rugged NZ-style forward' the Lions ought to look at. I knew a little about New Zealand rugby because we had a good team at Oxford with Chris Laidlaw at scrum-half. He had already played for the All Blacks and was a superb player, helping Oxford to victories over Northampton and Leicester. I imagine that Doug Smith, the manager, and Carwyn James would already have done their homework by the Varsity match.

WILLIE-JOHN McBRIDE

I remember Carwyn James came and talked to me because I wasn't going to go in 1971. I thought it was time I gave my career a bit of attention and I remember Carwyn came over and it was one of those moments that hits you. I'm in my 70s now and it was one of those moments that comes back to you. He came to Belfast and said, 'I want to talk to you about who we should take to New Zealand. Who do you think will stand up to this?' Then at the end he said, 'I heard a rumour you're not available'. I said, 'It's about time I gave it a rest.' I'd been on three tours. He sat back and he took a big puff of his cigarette and looked at me and said, 'But I need you.' And you know, nobody had ever said that to me before. It makes you sit up when somebody says that. I tell you, when I came away from that lunch I was going to New Zealand. He said, 'This time it will be different.' When he said it, it was very powerful and very simple.

JOHN DAWES (Wales)
Toured: 1971. Coach: 1977

Many people outside Wales did not really know much about Carwyn before the tour, but the success of the Lions made people sit up and take notice of him, and then Llanelli beat New Zealand soon afterwards. The coach in those days was not the all-important individual he is today. But going out to New Zealand and winning a massive series as part of a 26-match tour, it was Carwyn who set the standard for those who follow, and all the praise levied on him is still thoroughly

John Bevan.

deserved. You also have to have a top-class manager. Doug Smith managed the tour, and Carwyn never tried to interfere with that side of things. There was never a moment of doubt as to who was number one man on tour and that man was Doug.

WILLIE-JOHN McBRIDE

For the first time we were on the right lines. We said, 'We're going to run at them.' It was a whole new philosophy and, of course, the backline was superb. I wouldn't have gone otherwise. I knew we had it in us. I always had faith. If you look at the back-line: Gareth Edwards, Barry John, Mike Gibson, John Dawes, David Duckham, JPR, Gerald Davies. If you can't win with that you're not going to win anything. I thought, surely to God we can get eight men who can get them the ball!

GERALD DAVIES

Maybe in the past the Lions were a bit slow in admitting that they really wanted to win, maybe they were always a little bit apologetic about that. The early tours had very much an amateur ethos and even though we were still amateur in 1971, there were players who had been there before and they brought in the need to have a professional outlook, by which I mean they wanted to get serious.

MERVYN DAVIES

We were the first breed of professionals with a small 'p' to come out of the United Kingdom and Ireland. We didn't consider the Lions tour to be a bit of a jolly – we wanted to go there and prove ourselves and win this series. We had a genuine desire backed up by ruthless commitment, real determination and no little skill. Everyone

has this image of the 1971 Lions playing wonderful, expansive rugby throughout New Zealand, but the real truth was that the method was not important to us, it was just the result we wanted.

IAN McLAUCHLAN

Glasgow council said that no matter what happened I couldn't get any more time off for rugby. My second son was a week old when I left. Eileen has always said, 'If you get an opportunity take it.' Even when they said they weren't going to pay me, she said, 'Ach well, I'll just get a job.' We sold the car. I said to the bank to leave the mortgage until I got back, and we just made it happen.

Mervyn Davies.

DOUG SMITH (Scotland)
Toured: 1950. Manager: 1971

We went into selection incredibly thoroughly. Carwyn and I must have travelled about 12,000 miles each in the build-up, going to scruffy games, big games, getting to know all the possible contenders. We knew what we wanted and we sought advice from experienced men like Dawes, McBride and Gibson. Carwyn was the rugby brain, I backed the boys to the hilt and they knew it.

JOHN DAWES

Doug Smith said before the tour that we would win this series 2 -1 with one Test drawn. That was a bit frightening to hear at the time and we were all embarrassed by that more than anything else. Everyone was well aware that the Lions never won in New Zealand.

DOUG SMITH

I got respect from the boys and I respected them. Above all, you have to get the right gel, the right spirit. I went on determination, dedication and discipline. The first day in New Zealand I stepped out of the lift and saw four Welshmen with Prince of Wales feathers on their chests. I told them I'd give them two minutes to put on the Lion and when they came back and went to sit together I split them up among players of other nationalities.

GARETH EDWARDS

A lot of the party had been to New Zealand before either with Wales or the Lions, so there were no real surprises. Carwyn James was brilliant at feeding off the experience of those seasoned players. You have to be so mentally strong to prepare for an itinerary facing Canterbury, and then New Zealand, and then Wellington, then New Zealand again and so on.

PETER DIXON

In our warm-up week training in Bournemouth, Willie-John McBride and Ray McLoughlin said it would be tough in New Zealand. So in training they deliberately had people standing on your

Powerful All Blacks winger, Bryan Williams.

feet and holding you down at the lineout, which Colin Meads had been doing for years with impunity. If we hadn't done it, we wouldn't have been prepared at all, but it was still a shock because the physical challenge when we got there was so different to a week in the sun in Bournemouth.

GARETH EDWARDS

There had been a setback in our first game when we were beaten by Queensland – we had to play two games in Australia on the way out. But in all honesty we were so jet-lagged. We had no idea what time, day or place it was.

JOHN TAYLOR (Wales)
Toured: 1968 & 1971

The previous two Lions tours were fairly disastrous… and the worst fears seemed more than justified when Queensland beat us in the very first match. Jet lag, or as we found after our medical lecture from Dr JPR Williams, circadian disrhythmia, was an impressive curtain to hide behind.

GARETH EDWARDS

It meant that we were written off before we had even set foot in New Zealand. A lot of the younger boys like Barry, John Taylor, Gerald Davies and myself had gained earlier Lions experience and along with Carwyn's quiet method of bringing everyone on and building up the winning mentality, there was plenty of self belief.

DOUG SMITH

'Get your retaliation in first' was one of Carwyn's little inventions. We had a side with huge character, you had to be tough, physically and mentally, to take it.

JOHN DAWES

Carwyn like to talk to the players individually and dine with them; his man-management was excellent, and also being a professional man he had a rapport with the media. I can't remember him ever losing his temper and he was also a great listener, especially to a forward like Ray McLoughlin. Ray was a great 'probability man'. To him, rugby was like a game of chess and Ray had to work out all the options on offer in any particular situation, and then explain them to whoever was listening. When he roomed with Barry John, Barry would say that he just used to go to sleep with Ray going on and on about some aspect or other about the game.

PETER DIXON

John Dawes was a very easy captain, who did not need to shout. He was so relaxed, and nothing fazed him, to the extent that he'd even have a joke on the field during matches. He was also a good player, with his weight of pass and softness of hands benefiting the players around him. He always seemed to know what Barry John would do, and he brought out the best in Mike Gibson, forcing him to fade at just the right time when we were bringing JPR into the line. But Willie-John McBride was one of the rocks around whom we stood. The backs scored the tries, but the forwards still had to win the game, and you sense that whatever happened, Willie-John would have punched us home and made us bloody win.

GERALD DAVIES

Dawes was a great passer of the ball, it was a delight to play on the wing outside the man. What he always had was confidence in the people outside him, he was always willing to deliver a good ball to the next man and he would never just shovel it on. If he couldn't give a good pass to you, he would hold onto the ball. And Barry was always on the lookout for something. They were all very special players.

IAN McLAUCHLAN

Carwyn must have spent whole months preparing for that tour. Before one of the games, for example, we played football. The press couldn't believe it – there wasn't a rugby ball in sight, because he wanted to have a change of focus so that the constant intensity of the tour didn't have a negative effect. He also sent boys on holiday mid-tour to take them out the firing line. Before the Otago game we all trained on one side of the pitch and Barry John was over on the opposite side with a bunch of kids. He was the goalie and they were kicking penalties at him. Every now and again we used to go out on a cross-country run, and Barry would just say, 'Oh no, I don't believe in that.' I remember one time we ran into this wood and when we came out the other side to go along a wee stretch of road back into the field where we had started, a flatbed lorry drove by with Barry sitting on the back. If anyone else did that Carwyn would have lost the plot but Barry got away with it. He used to say, 'I play with my brain.' And that was the way it was.

JOHN DAWES

Barry John went from the Prince to the King in New Zealand. People forget that he toured New Zealand with Wales in 1969 and really hadn't established himself. During the Wales Grand Slam in 1971 he was adequate, but in New Zealand, his tactical appreciation and general game were astonishing. He really came of age on that tour, and he developed an incredible self-confidence that he could do what he wanted and he knew that we would react to him. People forget that he played 17 games on that tour, he wasn't held back. He just took New Zealand by the scruff of the neck – and it was the New Zealanders who gave him the title King John.

BARRY JOHN (Wales)
Toured: 1968 & 1971

I was ready to turn down the chance to tour because it had been a very physical Five Nations. We won the Grand Slam but I had been knocked around against Scotland and then broke my nose against the French. I felt I needed the summer off to recover and so when I got the call-up for the tour, I didn't answer it. A concerned Carwyn came to see me, told me how important I was to his plans and eventually his words persuaded me. I am glad they did, because that kicked off three of the most magical months anyone could ever have had. That tour completely changed my career and our victory made the Lions, and rugby union. It was front-page news everywhere, we got national television airtime, we were asked to do magazine interviews and we found ourselves in the gossip columns. The triumph in the Test series was not only historic, but it also made rugby union more appealing to the general public.

JOHN DAWES

Mike Gibson was also so influential on that tour. Barry John and Mike were like chalk and cheese. Barry was a total extrovert and Mike was much quieter, but the way they were similar was in their extraordinary skill levels. JPR and Gerald Davies might have been regarded as two of the tour's real superstars but Barry and Mike were the ones who really stood out for me. Mike went out on tour as the second fly-half and not a centre, and I don't think it was a deliberate thing with Carwyn that Mike ended up in the centre. It just happened. Mike had a very serious attitude to rugby but the main thing was that he and Barry thought at the same level. Their partnership was really key.

BOB HILLER

Above all, the 1971 Lions had wonderful players. It was a great backline – Gareth Edwards, Barry John, Gerald Davies, John Dawes, Mike Gibson, David Duckham, JPR

Williams – all legends in the making. Carwyn was phenomenal, miles ahead of anyone we'd met in coaching. He was a highly intelligent bloke, quite quiet, but a great coach in terms of ideas and how to apply them. John Dawes was easily the best captain I played under.

You were happy whenever you saw Gerald Davies or David Duckham get the ball. Duckham was a fantastic player who could win a match for you. He scored six tries in one of the midweek games when it was pissing with rain, and he ran towards the touch in-goal line on a couple of occasions just to make my conversions more difficult.

Gareth Edwards hands-off Bob Burgess during the Third Test in Wellington.

GARETH EDWARDS

Every New Zealand side has a good pack and set of backs, so whenever you go, you know you are going to be tested and to everyone's credit, we not only concentrated like mad on the Tests but also the huge provincial games, when the home players take such enormous pride in pulling on their provincial colours.

DOUG SMITH

All our games were torrid affairs. After you'd won on the Saturday some clown would spout, 'Wait until you get to Wanganui – we'll kill ya!'

FERGUS SLATTERY (Ireland)

Toured: 1971 & 1974

We had some craic. Do you remember Bill McKay? Great Irish and Lions forward of the 1940s and 1950s. A hard man who emigrated to New Zealand. We were in Napier, I think. He introduced himself, then said, 'Do you fancy hunting tomorrow?' I said, 'How do you mean hunting?' 'Wild boar.' I said, 'God, that would be great.' He said, 'I'll pick you up in the morning at six.' To my surprise Ian McLauchlan said he'd come with me. We got into this jeep and drove over hills and across this river and drove halfway up a mountain and then we stopped and we had to get out. There were Maoris there. They put a rifle over my shoulder and up on a horse I got. We edged along the mountain on these horses and if you fell off you were dead. We got to the top and

Barry John glides through the All Blacks' defence.

Rua, one of the Maori fellas, says, 'Right, now we go hunting.' McLauchlan went off silently and sat on a rock. He said, 'I'm having none of this shit.' I had my rugby boots on me. We were climbing down the mountain into this ravine. We had a pack of dogs with us and the dogs caught a boar. I stuck the ol' knife in and rammed it down and that was the end of the boar. I thought, 'Jesus, look at me, I'm king of the mountains!' Then Rua takes the knife and cuts the boar down the middle and the guts flop out in a big ball. And the smell! Then he ties the two back legs together and he says, 'You kill, you carry.' And he threw it over my neck.

We had to go back up the mountain with this dead boar on me. Eventually we got back up to the top and there's McLauchlan sitting on his little rock breaking his bollocks laughing. The day comes to an end; back on the horses, back across the mountain and we got to one of the stations, or villages, on this farm and they were having this party. The worst part was on the Friday on the front page of the *New Zealand Herald* there's McLauchlan dressed up in a chef's outfit with a big white hat on top of his head and a great big knife and he's standing beside the boar I killed. I said, 'McLauchlan, you shit!'

PETER DIXON

Socially it was great, and I was a single man. As an anthropologist I also liked seeing

Gareth Edwards slips the tackle of Wayne Cottrell and races away from Alex Wyllie and Ian Kirkpatrick as John Taylor moves to back him up.

new places, and I'm only sad that I've never been back to New Zealand. I tried to get out to Maori parties in particular, and I remember coming back from an all-night party one morning and meeting Carwyn, who asked me if I was out for an early morning walk. I said, yes, I hadn't been able to sleep – which in a sense was true.

IAN McLAUCHLAN

In New Zealand you can't do anything without being noticed. I remember going for a walk in Auckland on the night we arrived and at the first corner we came to was a travel agent with two huge windows and both were filled with profiles of the Lions, with photos, age, who you played for, everything. Two blocks further along the road it was the same again. That was a real culture shock to us. Everyone wanted to talk to you. We were asked not to drink midweek, and one night we were stuck in this small town with nothing to do, so John Pullin, Sean Lynch, myself and Mike Roberts went to this quiet bar and said to the guy behind the counter that we didn't want to speak to anyone, we just wanted a quiet drink. We ended up absolutely blotto. But Carwyn knew everything, so the next morning he said we were going to have a cavalry charge, and 'You four are going to lead it.' Of course, the rest of the boys knew we had been on the piss, and they were all shouting to get a move on. We had to charge around six fields about three times. I developed a real admiration for Lynchie that day. He was running and throwing up at the same time. He'd had a bucket load more than the rest of us.

SANDY CARMICHAEL (Scotland)
Toured: 1971 & 1974

Ray McLoughlin is a very senior financier and a very sharp guy, and after our third or fourth game we were beginning to get quite irritated because they were being quite restrictive with what the New Zealand Rugby Union were giving us. So we had a players' meeting and Ray said he had worked out that with the size of the crowds, the cost of the tickets and the number of games we'd played, the tour had already been paid for. So we agreed that we should look to get a little something more from the NZRFU and decided to ask for two bottles of wine on the table at every dinner. So we sent the committee away to do that, and that's what we got. We were delighted. It's the way things were done in those days.

GARETH EDWARDS

We knew we had to get off to a good start with a win against Counties/Thames Valley in Pukekohe, and then we were up and running. Then it was Wellington, who were New Zealand's equivalent of Leicester Tigers. We played some absolutely wonderful rugby against them – we scored nine tries to beat them by around 40 points, and local pulses started racing. They realised that the Lions were not lambs.

JOHN TAYLOR

John Bevan on the wing started off magnificently, he was one of the great players before he left for rugby league. But both he and Chico Hopkins, the scrum-half, began to suffer from homesickness. Both were young and both were from the valleys, John from the Rhondda and Chico from the Llynfi.

FERGUS SLATTERY

When we played Wellington I was playing against Graham Williams, a guy who played for New Zealand about six times and he was at the end of his career. I always obstructed guys at the back of the lineout, pushed them or blocked them. It just meant our fly-half could do whatever he wanted to do and you'd get away with it once or maybe twice, but then a guy might give you a smack. About 15 minutes into the game I obviously pissed this guy off and he just punched me and I punched him back and he punched me again and I started laughing. I thought, 'This is fucking ridiculous, I have no right to be punching this guy and he had every right to punch me because I was messing him around the place.'

IAN McLAUCHLAN

The turning point of the tour was the provincial game against Wellington, with half the Test team, and we beat them 47-9.

DOUG SMITH

They were bastards, the New Zealanders at that time. That game against Canterbury, where we lost Sandy Carmichael, the front of his face smashed to bits, black eyes fit to burst. The New Zealanders made the mistake of trying to smash us to pieces and got their come-uppance by us hitting them back. That was what riled them most.

RAY McLOUGHLIN

Canterbury certainly had a reputation of being harder, as they call it in New Zealand, than

Gareth Edwards spins the ball out to Barry John.

everyone else. New Zealanders are great ones for intimidating guys on the grounds that once you've done that they are a walkover. This was going to be a very difficult match and I had been urging everyone to show their teeth immediately in the face of the intimidation that was bound to happen. That was essential to avoid being psychologically beaten.

JOHN DAWES

Although we never said it, the Canterbury game was pinpointed as the big game before the First Test. However, Carwyn did not play Barry John in that game, he thought that Canterbury might go after him so Mike Gibson was the fly-half instead. That was the one and only time that Barry was protected by Carwyn.

IAN McLAUCHLAN

In any rugby, if somebody hits you then you have to hit them back. It doesn't matter when and how you do it but you've got to make them absolutely understand that you are not a soft mark. Because if you don't they will do it again, and again, and then somebody else will do it and you'll just become a bloody punch bag. I came from a background where the punch bag was always on the other side. When we played Kings Country I had the guy propping against me in all sorts of trouble, and when he dropped his hand I said, 'Don't even think about it pal or I'll put you in hospital. I don't get punched at home and I don't get punched out here.' The New Zealanders believed that the Lions in previous times were all about fair play – but after that Colin Meads said, 'These Lions don't believe in fairy tales.'

SANDY CARMICHAEL

It was the big game going into the First Test and Ray and I were on the pitch, so it looked like we were going to be the props in the Test side. I don't think we realised what we were going into against Canterbury. It happened early on when I got a backhander at a lineout right across the left of my face. I went down and the medics came on the pitch to check it out before I played on. There were punch-ups all over the park, and the story about the ref saying, 'I'll referee the game and you can do what you like,' is true. He denies it, but that did happen. Not long later I drove into a ruck, hit the deck and fed the ball back, then I got kicked in the other eye. I thought, 'Fair enough, that's life,' and I just carried on. It was the backhander that had caused the real damage.

FERGUS SLATTERY

Alister Hopkinson was propping against Sandy Carmichael and he just kept punching him in the face. Canterbury went out to kick the shit out of us. We beat them 14-3 and it was a bit of a hiding. They went out with this thuggish attitude. Gareth Edwards was running across the pitch and Alex Wyllie came up behind him and punched him in the back of the neck. Edwards and somebody else went to the referee and said, 'What are you going to do?' And the ref said, 'I'm only refereeing what I can see.' It's a bit like saying, 'Good luck lads, do whatever you want.'

SANDY CARMICHAEL

By the time I came off the pitch, both eyes were pretty well shut, so they sat me on the bench and put ice packs on my face. McLauchlan came towards me to see how I was just as I went to blow my nose, but it was blocked and because the sinus was cracked the air blew into my eye socket, which inflated like a balloon. That was the first time – and probably the last time – I ever saw fear in Ian's eyes.

PETER DIXON

The Canterbury match stands out as brutal. It was a battle all the time, primarily among the forwards. At the lineout there'd be a fight at the start of it, then the ref sorted it out; you'd have the lineout again, and then there'd be a few sly punches as you were running across the field. There was also trouble at the scrums with their second-rows throwing punches through on our props. I respect Sandy for not retaliating, but if he'd said anything to me I would have swung one in. I was not really aware he was being hit, mainly because everyone was fighting their own corner. I was determined that if anything came my way it was going back again, and there are a few pictures of me trying to flatten Grizz Wyllie, and vice versa. It carried on between Wyllie and myself a few years later when Canterbury were on tour in the UK.

RAY McLOUGHLIN

In that game there was a degree of intimidation that, to my mind, was unacceptable. I was pack-leader and I was tempted to take the team off the pitch on the basis that it was the best way of making a protest and, properly handled, could be presented as not being afraid but as requiring more courage than not doing it. Maybe I chickened out but I felt that with the macho approach New Zealanders had it would have been seen as a weakness.

WILLIE-JOHN McBRIDE

I don't think there was a ball on the field for the first half hour. We lost Carmichael and then McLoughlin hit Wyllie in the head and broke his thumb, so the two props were gone. Slattery got injured, Mick Hipwell got injured and there were others. It was bloody nonsense and the referee was a disaster. There was a premonition that there could be trouble.

Gerald Davies and Bryan Williams in a foot-race for the ball.

FERGUS SLATTERY

Hopkinson came from the front of the lineout and punched me in the mouth, a punch I never saw, so a cowardly act. He smashed my front two teeth and concussed me, but I eventually got back on my feet. Peter Dixon tells the story about me asking him where were we. He obviously was able to reply and say 'Canterbury', but when I, like a drunk, asked him again 10 minutes later he didn't have an answer as someone had punched him in the meantime.

SEAN LYNCH (Ireland)
Toured: 1971

Put it this way, I was injured for the Canterbury match and from the stands it was one of the most vicious matches I have ever seen. They were the heavy mob and you had to go for them because they were going for you. My idea on the field is to take your own man out and if everyone does likewise you'll be all right.

JOHN REASON (writing in *The Victorious Lions*)

The sight of Sandy Carmichael's face as he lay collapsed on the masseur's table in the Lions' dressing room after the match against Canterbury will stay in the memory of all who saw it for as long as they live. His left eye was closed and a huge blue swelling of agonised flesh hung out from the cheekbone like a grotesque plum. His right eye was a slit between the puffed skin above and below it. His right eyelid was gashed and straggling with blood. Another gash snagged away from the corner of his eye. He was quivering with emotion and frustration. His hands shook as they tried to hold the ice packs on the swellings.

WILLIE-JOHN McBRIDE

I remember Doug Smith coming on the bus after the game and saying to me, 'The King is dead, long live the King – we'll beat them All Blacks next week,' and half our team had gone to the hospital. I'm sitting looking around me and saying, 'I'm needing a lot of convincing here.'

SANDY CARMICHAEL

We went to watch carriage racing at the local track that night, and I put my sunglasses on because my face didn't look too well. Some of the New Zealanders were there sneering, 'Why are you wearing sunglasses at night?' And I said, 'So nobody else can see exactly what you have done to my face.' The next morning, big Doug Smith, the tour manager, came to my room and said, 'I'm terribly sorry Sandy, but it will take eight weeks for you to repair yourself and there's only eight weeks left – so, you're going home.' And that was it. I was sharing with David Duckham, who was one of the finest gentlemen I've ever met. He said, 'Now Sandy, it's up to you, we can sit in this room for another two or three hours and when you're ready to go and meet the boys I'll come with you. I'll stay with you.' So, that's what we did – and he stayed with me the whole time. When we eventually went down we discovered that Ray McLoughlin had been sent home as well because he had broken a scaphoid. It had been like Custer's last stand.

FERGUS SLATTERY

I was left behind in Canterbury to get dental reconstruction or whatever.

SANDY CARMICHAEL

I've never named names over that and I never will, and the reason is that if I tell then the story ends. I don't want them ever to forget and if I leave it this way then they can't forget. The only other person who knew is dead, and that is Dr Smith who promised not to tell anybody. I got a phone call from New Zealand the last time the Lions were there in 2005 asking me about it – and that's great because they haven't been able to draw a line under it. For years and years, British teams had gone across to New Zealand and South Africa and had the shit kicked out of them. After what happened in Canterbury the Lions were fairly angry – and the Test side decided they were not going to sit back and take it anymore.

WILLIE-JOHN McBRIDE

It was just sheer nonsense. All sorts of stuff. Hopkinson and Wyllie were the two guys who started it. Hopkinson is dead now. There was a guy Tane Norton who was captain of the All Blacks. He was always a good friend but he wasn't proud of that stuff. There were two or three thugs on the field. They say it's part of the game and they get away with that. We knew they would target people, like Edwards. I'd seen it all before. We won the battle and we won the match and we won it well and it gave me a feeling of what we had. We had guys who wouldn't lie down.

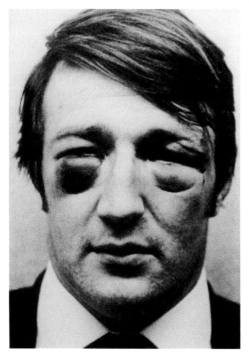

IAN McLAUCHLAN

In the Canterbury game, Arthur Lewis had said to young John Bevan, 'If you get the chance, don't try to run around them, run through them.' And on the way to the clinching try he knocked three of their guys down. It was an amazing try. Two of them converged on him and he blasted his way right through the middle of the pair of them. You don't do that very often in New Zealand.

Sandy Carmichael shows his battle wounds after the Canterbury match.

SANDY CARMICHAEL
Bevan knocked two guys out the way like a bowling ball going through the middle of two pins. He was a very fast man and there wasn't an inch of fat on him – and to this day I'm in awe of that score.

IAN McLAUCHLAN
The First Test, to be honest with you, was over in the blink of an eye. It was probably the most intense game of rugby I ever played in. They just came and came and came at us all the time. The All Blacks are generally pretty clinical – if they have a two-on-one they tend to finish it – but that day they seemed to pass when they should have kept it. Our tackling was ferocious. I don't know how many tackles I made that day, but it was a lot, and when we came off the field we were elated but we were on our knees – really tired. I've never seen my try again. I did an interview in Wales and the guy gave me a DVD which he said was the 1971 tour in colour, so I've got that at home, but I've never really bothered about it.

GARETH EDWARDS
New Zealand made a quite magnificent start to the First Test, we had to defend heroically, but their scores didn't come. When we won the match that really shook them.

FERGUS SLATTERY
The maître d' at our hotel in Dunedin was talking to four of us on the eve of the First Test – Gareth, Mike Roberts, me and somebody else – and he stated New Zealand would win, so we obviously said rubbish and he was so adamant we inquired as to the best bottle of wine he had in store. Chateau Lafite 1934. So the bottle was put up as the wager. The following evening, after the match, the four of us sat at the table and called him over and he spent a few minutes in an emotional state and then proceeded to open the wine and smell it and gaze at it and then we said, 'Pour it out into the four glasses,' and no, no he had to swirl it around in the glass first until we said, 'Pour it out in four quarters!' and he did reluctantly and then we drank the 1934 prize down the hatch. It was gone in seconds after 37 years of care. He cried.

IAN McLAUCHLAN
I have to say I didn't rate Ray McLoughlin as highly as everybody else seemed to. He never did anything outside the scrum. He was totally immobile. It pisses me off that after 40 years people are still saying that he was the first choice loose-head. He wasn't even there. When we won that First Test match he was back in Ireland, and Sandy was back in Scotland. The players who won the Test match, their names are there and anyone who wants to make a song and dance about the players who went home, well, would we have won the Test match if they hadn't gone home? I don't think so. That's what I think and you can write that any way you like.

PETER DIXON

We were in with a shout of winning the Second Test but then Ian Kirkpatrick scored a wonder try running through the middle of most of the pack and then the backs. They scored two tries down the blind-side in that Test. That was John Taylor's side! Although I should also have been covering across.

JOHN TAYLOR

The highlight of the games between the Second and Third Tests was a dazzling performance by Gerald Davies against Hawke's Bay. The match was rather ill tempered, but Gerald was above such things, and scored four of the best tries one could hope to see. Having side-stepped, swerved and outsprinted all opposition on the wing for the three of them, he moved into the centre and split the defence open for the fourth, with his unique ability to side-step at full pace.

GERALD DAVIES

On a Lions tour of New Zealand, probably more so even than in South Africa, the next game is always 'the big one' for the locals and in the press. 'Wait till Canterbury. Or Wellington, or Auckland, or Taranaki.' And so on. At the end of the tour, it was, 'Wait till you get to Hawke's Bay.'

There were strong-arm tactics employed against us that day. But again, we were playing the game in the way that Carwyn James wanted us to play. Run, attack, use all that you have. For all their physicality, what came through in the end was our ability to play rugby and attack from all corners of the field. I think the moves of three of the four tries started from our own half, they were all counter-attacking plays.

GARETH EDWARDS

It was uncanny, because we came off after the Second Test defeat convinced that we could win the series. I was getting back from a hamstring injury in that Second Test and did not have a particularly good game, while the All Blacks played very well, with Ian Kirkpatrick and Syd Going outstanding. We prepared well ahead of the Third Test and Carwyn changed our tactical approach by sticking Derek Quinnell at blind-side flanker with a clear instruction to stop Going. Fair play to DQ, he did. We had a great start with a couple of first half tries from Gerald Davies and Barry John.

JOHN TAYLOR

From the moment we arrived in Wellington for the Third Test, our thoughts were only on rugby. We all knew that this was the most important match of our lives. After 17 minutes, it was New Zealand 0, British & Irish Lions 13. It had been a glorious 17 minutes! The All Blacks managed a solitary try in the second half but we won 13-3 and, suddenly, we had created history.

IAN McLAUCHLAN
The key for us was containing them up front. We beat them in the First Test and that was a big shock to them. In the Second Test they fluked it. The best we played in the series was probably the Second Test, but we were a little bit over-confident. We knew we could easily hold them up front, and we thought if we did that the backs would run riot – but the All Blacks got two breaks and finished them both, while we got umpteen breaks which we didn't finish off.

But in the Third Test their forward effort collapsed and we won it really, really easily, and that killed them off. Bringing back Brian Lochore, which they did, was wrong. There must have been young guys in New Zealand who were fitter and hungrier. We viewed that selection as a sign of desperation.

WILLIE-JOHN McBRIDE
The last Test was a toughie. I knew the referee certainly wouldn't be on our side and the crowd certainly wouldn't be on our side and it was one mammoth game, 14-14. In one way we could have and should have played better. We didn't play all that well and it was a massive relief that we'd won the series when we drew that game. Against all odds.

JOHN TAYLOR
We should have won comfortably but in the end we needed an unlikely JPR Williams score – some fullbacks are renowned for their drop-kicking, others are not and JPR was the latter category. Therefore, when he let fly from the 10-yard line it was not only his London Welsh colleagues who were sceptical. But the ball sailed over. All the records were broken, the series was won and Barry John, with a massive 180 points, was the King of New Zealand.

WILLIE-JOHN McBRIDE
The odd time I'll speak at a lunch or a dinner and I mention that backline people sit and gasp and that's 40 years ago and they still remember those names. I couldn't tell you who played on the last Lions tour. Barry John was top of his game, but it wasn't just him. The miracles of Gerald Davies and Mike Gibson, who was at his peak; wee Gareth and JPR, those guys were all at their peak. Something I'll take with me to my grave, the pleasure and privilege of playing with those guys. It was sheer brilliance.

GERALD DAVIES
My father was a great admirer of the All Blacks, and he could never imagine anyone beating them. His greatest hero was George Nepia, the legendary fullback. My father had watched him play against Llanelli at Stradey Park. One of the nicest things was that on the tour in 1971 I got to meet George Nepia at Hawke's Bay, and had a photograph taken that I was able to take back to show my father.

BARRY JOHN

In New Zealand, I had been given the tag of 'The King'. My face appeared everywhere and the fact that I scored 10 of our 13 points in the decisive Third Test led to 'King John wins game for the Lions' headlines everywhere. It was never something I was comfortable with and the players used to take the mickey out of me over it. When I walked into the dressing room, they would stand up in unison and bow. It was their way of making sure I never got too big for my boots.

JOHN DAWES

Was that series win the highlight of my career? At the time I did not think so but on reflection, it had to be – to go to New Zealand and beat them. However, there was one match that was my absolute highlight – another game involving New Zealand, but this time for the Barbarians, two years later. In pure rugby terms, that has to be the highlight because of the quality of play produced by both sides. We never dropped the ball once and what we achieved was quite fantastic. Mervyn and Gerald both dropped out through injury and as they sat watching from the stands, one of them turned to the other and said, 'Not being out there is the biggest mistake we have made in our rugby careers.'

BARRY JOHN

Nothing summed it up more than the August day we landed back at Heathrow airport. There were so many people to greet us that morning. It was the day the authorities realised they needed to review airport security because a bus load of Welsh fans from Maesteg turned up on the runway about 20 yards from our aeroplane.

That Lions tour raised the profile of rugby union from Division Three South to the top of the Premier League. Our feats in New Zealand have never been achieved since, but winning over a four-Test campaign down there is as close as you will get to an impossible task in rugby. It will only get harder for the Lions given the close proximity of games on tours and how difficult it is to put together the intensity needed to beat New Zealand over, what is now, three successive weekends.

IAN McLAUCHLAN

Doug Smith said at the beginning of the tour that we would win the Test series 2½ to 1½, and that there were two fatal flaws in New Zealand rugby that we would exploit. So in every single interview he did he was asked what one of the flaws was, and he always said he'd tell just before he mounted the plane to go home. So at the end of the tour he was asked again what the flaws were, and he said, 'None – New Zealand rugby is in great shape. We're just in better shape.' That was it. He had played them along.

GERALD DAVIES

We had no idea how big it had become when we were out there, no real sense of history in the making. It was 1971. What were mobile phones? What was the connection between New Zealand and back at home? If you wanted a phone call you had to give 24 hours' notice. The person who drew our attention to it was Cliff Morgan, who came out to commentate for television – when the television people at home realised that something big was happening they sent over Cliff.

I was talking to him one day just after he got there and he told me that I would not believe the interest at home, and that was the first time you really understood. We carried on in the Test series but it was only really when we got back to Heathrow that it hit me. I remember saying at the time, looking at the thousands of people, that this is what I imagine it was like when the Beatles arrived.

JOHN DAWES

Winning the series in New Zealand in 1971 and then with the 1974 team following it up in South Africa, the whole concept of Lions tours changed. Until 1971, the Lions had always been regarded as a group of players who could sing and also play a bit, and although naturally they tried to win, it wasn't everything.

BARRY JOHN

The predictions from New Zealand were that we would be easy meat for Colin Meads and the men in black. As predictions go, it was right up there with Michael Fish: 'There won't be a hurricane!'

WILLIE-JOHN McBRIDE

You sort of get a taste for it. It was because we won in '71 I said, 'Right, I'll have another go at these buggers in South Africa,' in 1974.

John Dawes, Doug Smith, Colin Meads, Carwyn James and Gordon Brown following the Fourth Test.

CHAPTER NINETEEN

THE INVINCIBLES
1974

SOUTH AFRICA

A KEEN *debate is always raged as to which have been the greatest Lions. Was it the 1971 party, for their brilliant efforts in proving that it could be done, in blazing the glorious trail and reversing history, therefore proving to the parties that came after them that to defeat the All Blacks was not an impossibility?*

Or was it the 1974 group, which overran South African rugby in such a devastating manner, which went through the entire tour unbeaten, and which also turned history on its head by taking on South African rugby up front and beating and beasting the goliaths of the game? What is the answer to the debate? Frankly, there are many involved in British and Irish rugby who are simply thrilled to be given a choice. What is certain is that both tours catapulted players into the stratosphere, numbering them as amongst the all-time greats before the tour had even ended, at a time when Britannia, along with Ireland, did indeed rule the waves.

Willie-John McBride's name is indelibly linked in the archives of the 1974 Lions to South Africa. Making a then unprecedented fifth tour with the Lions, he captained an unbeaten team that set numerous new records on its way to becoming the first international side to win a four-match series in the Republic since 1896 (3-0, with a draw in the final Test). Above all, however, he did so much personally to ensure the tour's success, fueled by the scars which previous defeat had left on him.

The political climate was strongly inclined against the tour, the Westminster Government having declared that they could not support the visit. Shortly before the team were due to leave Britain, McBride gathered his party around him in a London hotel besieged by anti-apartheid demonstrators. As the clamour outside penetrated the room he told them of the huge task ahead of them. Aside from the political protests, he went on to recall his past experiences in New Zealand and South Africa. How his team would face intimidation and dirty play, differing foreign law interpretations and referees likely to favour the home side. The fight would be hard, he said, and he offered anyone who didn't feel up to the physical and mental challenge the option of dropping out from the visit there and then.

No one faltered as the party silently contemplated four hard months ahead. The silence was apparently broken by the tough Pontypool hooker, Bobby Windsor, who chimed in his broad East Wales accent that, 'I'm bloody well going to enjoy this!' McBride had set his stall out and his players were going to follow where he led.

He was, in many ways, years ahead of his time. The term 'great enforcer' was a popular press expression used years later to describe Martin Johnson's attributes as a lock and captain both of a

---

Opposite: Tour captain, Willie-John McBride.

successful Lions outfit and England Rugby World Cup team. But the phrase could so easily have applied to McBride a generation earlier.

If McBride was the 1974 tour's enforcer, its brains were his Ballymena clubmate, Syd Millar. The Ulstermen formed an impressive double-act. The uncompromising mental attitude and physical fitness they generated in their talented players should not be underestimated when assessing the reasons for the team's success.

Millar, a triple Lion (1959, 1962 and 1968 vintages) had twice toured South Africa before becoming one of British and Irish rugby's outstanding coaches with an unequalled knowledge of the mechanics of forward play. He had an abundance of talent at his disposal and he set about moulding a winning side with relish.

Was there ever a better quad of props in Lions rugby than Sandy Carmichael, Ian 'Mighty Mouse' McLauchlan, Fran Cotton and Mike Burton? The unlikeliest supporter for this proposition was JPR Williams, the Welsh fullback. JPR so relished the physical engagement of rugby that, on tour, he enjoyed nothing better than offering himself as a tight-head prop for practice sessions. He'd adapted quite easily to the role on tour in New Zealand in 1971 and enthusiastically presented himself for duty again in 1974.

After a particularly rigorous work-out during which he had been popped out of the front-row during a practice in the Kruger National Park, JPR told the Daily Telegraph's *John Reason, 'There seems to have been an improvement in technique [since 1971].'*

In the second-row Gordon Brown of Scotland was at the peak of his formidable powers. His work in the lineout was a rich source of possession for the tourists' pacey backs and he perfectly complemented the skipper in the pack's engine room. Built like a tank he also crossed for eight tries on the tour, establishing a new record for a forward.

Fergus Slattery, Mervyn Davies and Roger Uttley were the ever-present back-row for the Test series but their high-octane performances were fuelled by the knowledge that they were under huge pressure for their places from their 'shadows'. Tony Neary, Andy Ripley, Stewart McKinney and Tom David pressed them hard, Ripley losing out to 'Merve the Swerve' very narrowly, apparently on account of the Welshman's superior off-loading skills in the tackle.

Results and analysis show that modern Lions rugby reached its peak on this tour – no fully representative side before or since has been unbeaten. But looking back, while the stock of forward play was high, there were perhaps signs that back play was entering a recession. The counter-attacking play that had set the 1971 tour on fire was still there, and JJ Williams, JPR Williams and Andy Irvine were as exciting a trio of runners as South Africa has ever seen.

But a preoccupation with set moves and too much use of the crash-ball in midfield meant that the bright, carefree approach seen in New Zealand three years earlier was less evident. Ian McGeechan and Dick Milliken in the centre, however, defended superbly and were the ideal combination.

Gareth Edwards was a commanding figure behind the scrum and revelled in the gilt-edged possession his forwards provided. He himself believed that in 1974 he was at a career high. He had assumed the mantle of playmaker from Barry John and masterminded the side in the Test series. The best of Phil Bennett's dazzling running at outside-half was also seen on this tour, while the level-headed and calculating play of McGeechan and Milliken outside him added to the Lions' edge in the Tests. JPR Williams was reliability personified behind them.

The Lions also had some magnificent characters, notably Windsor, around whom a host of legends grew, Mike Burton, who would have served the Test team well, and Andy Ripley, the one and only. Ripley was a Test match player to his bootlaces though he only ever played one for the Lions. His rescue of a stray kitten on tour, the bulletins in the papers as he nursed it and the picture of a local citizen who agreed to adopt it, made the great man as popular in South Africa as he was with his own party.

It was a ferocious tour, and the ascendancy of the Lions provoked an even more ferocious backlash from the home teams, with provincial opposition trying desperately to soften up the Lions so they could be finished off in the Tests. But this Lions team was too hard, too durable and too fierce in itself. There were some gory punch-ups during the tour, the kind of thing that would have kept a whole battery of citing officers in employment had there been any in that era.

The tour also, apparently, gave rise to the '99 call'. This was meant to be a call used by either McBride or whoever was the Lions captain on any match, as a reaction to an outburst. It meant that everyone should simply throw punches at their nearest opponent, on the basis that a referee might send off a lone puncher but he could hardly send off a whole team.

The call has become legendary. Or perhaps mythical. In fact, you can barely find a Lion who ever heard the call being made, and plenty more who believe that it was simply a figment of the imagination, a legend that grew in the telling. Even McBride himself, at a push, will admit that he may have called '99' once but probably no more.

In the run-up to the First Test the Lions won seven matches, scoring 294 points including 43 tries. Records galore were established in the 97-0 win against the South-Western Districts at Mossel Bay. It was the biggest win by any international touring side in South Africa; Alan Old's 37 points remain the most points in a match by an individual player for the Lions on tour and JJ Williams' six tries matched the Lions record established by David Duckham against the West Coast/Buller Combined at Greymouth on the 1971 tour.

The 1974 tour party.

Then came the First Test, and glory began to beckon. Admittedly, the Lions were forced to battle hard for a 12-3 victory in the opening Test in Cape Town. The Newlands ground was heavy after rain but the Lions forwards gradually overcame their opponents. The tourists came from behind to strangle the Springboks, the pack's quick ball giving Phil Bennett and Gareth Edwards the scope to dictate the tactical course of the Test.

The best performance of the tour came in Pretoria where the Lions went 2-0 up, registering their highest score and biggest-ever winning margin for a Test against South Africa (28-9). Two early tries by the deadly JJ Williams got the Lions off to a flyer and a second half dropped-goal by Ian McGeechan stretched them to a two-score lead before the dominant Lions pack laid the foundations for late scores by Phil Bennett (penalty) and Dick Milliken (try). By now, South Africa, under Hannes Marais as captain, were casting about desperately, shuffling their players and often throwing out the good with the bad. For the Third Test, they were so uncertain as to who might mark the great Edwards, that they called up three players and put them through a bizarre passing test.

The Lions would not be intimidated in the Third Test in Port Elizabeth where a massive first half punch-up threatened to halt their progress. Andy Irvine replaced Billy Steele on the right-wing in the only change in the tourists' Test personnel from the first two games of the rubber. The Springboks had dropped ten players and made a total of eleven changes to their side after losing in Pretoria.

But once again the Lions' technical discipline proved too much for the hosts and a Gordon Brown try gave them a 7-3 cushion at the interval, after a half of monstrous fierceness. Scores came regularly in the second half for the tourists to win 26-9 and thus take their first series in South Africa for 78 years. Famously, the team walked to the touchline at the end, and as a group, waved to their team-mates in the stand, as a tribute to the efforts and support of the dirt-trackers.

Anti-apartheid protestor, Peter Hain, outside the Lions' London hotel.

The evening and next day in Port Elizabeth is meant to have seen one of the greatest parties in Lions tour history, which is saying something. The Welsh journalist and Lions tour veteran JBG Thomas appeared to take refuge in glorious understatement in his tour book The Roaring Lions: *'Some beer was spilled on the carpets and one fire extinguisher was used.'*

Three more comfortable provincial wins followed – only against Orange Free State were they seriously challenged – before they reached Johannesburg for the final match of the tour. As they ran out for the Fourth Test they were nursing a played 21, won 21 record. Gordon Brown had broken a bone in his right hand in the Third Test so his place went to Chris Ralston for the fourth international, the only change to the Lions Test side. Ralston had had an unlucky tour suffering with influenza, bronchitis, dental problems and a shoulder injury. He was knocked out playing against the Leopards, ending with an enormous cut to his head. Moreover, he, along with Bobby Windsor and Stewart McKinney, had been the party's most nervous flyers and experienced his worst moment when a bird had flown into an engine of the plane carrying the team out of Port Elizabeth.

Ellis Park was full to the rafters for the last Test to see if the Lions could emulate the 1891 tourists and finish with a 100% record. In the eyes of many they did, through Fergus Slattery. The Lions scored two tries (Roger Uttley and Andy Irvine) to one, but Slattery was controversially denied a winning score by the referee, Max Baise, in the last minute. The Lions left the field disgusted at the decision.

JPR Williams had joined the three-quarters line near the end of the match and had looked as if he would score himself. But he was held up on the line before unloading to Slattery who drove over. His team-mates swore that he had grounded the ball between his legs and over the line. But Mr Baise didn't see it that way and so while Willie-John McBride ended his Lions career with a record 17

Racial segregation gates.

*Tests to his name, the tour log showed the 13-13 Ellis Park draw as the only blot on the 1974 Lions'
22-match copybook.*

*The Lions had departed London as political outcasts. They returned to London airport on
the Tuesday after Johannesburg to a heroes' welcome and were feted by the government for their
outstanding success. Millar has since written that he regarded this as rather two-faced.*

*For South Africa, it was beginning to dawn on them that the high-level competition denied them
by the sporting isolation caused by apartheid was to the detriment of their rugby at international
level. It was their most convincing defeat. And for British and Irish rugby, a glorious summit.*

*The party was strong, rumbustious, full of character, devil, class, resistance, unity and purpose.
And there is no doubt of their status as all-time greats.*

GARETH EDWARDS

All three of my Lions tours were tremendously demanding, a non-stop schedule of
midweek games followed by Saturday matches, and it is no exaggeration to say that it
took me nine months to really get over both the physical and mental demands of the
1974 tour – that is how tough it was playing a 22-match tour. And things had changed
– the expectation was that if we could go to New Zealand and beat the All Blacks then
we could go to South Africa and beat the Springboks. Easy!

In 1971 Carwyn James said that if we had 30 to 40 per cent of possession then we
would win – and the backs did make the most of that hard-won possession – while
in 1974 we had such a powerful set of forwards who dominated the games and
controlled the set pieces that we had closer to 60 per cent of the possession in most
games, and sometimes more. The confidence of winning in 1971 was carried through
– along with the backbone of that winning team – and we had what it took to play at
altitude on the high veldt, on hard grounds and with a dry ball.

A lot of the boys had been to South Africa before and we knew there was no such
thing as a bad Springboks side, so this would be a different mountain to scale. Willie-
John was making his fifth Lions tour, and you cannot get more experienced than
that, while players like Phil Bennett were coming to the fore. And we were incredibly
fortunate with injuries. We only used 17 players in the four Tests and that settled side
and continuity of selection certainly contributed to our success. What a tour.

FRAN COTTON (England)
Toured: 1974, 1977 & 1980. Manager: 1997

The first time I had ever really become aware of the Lions was in 1968, when they were
on tour to South Africa. The tour was covered by television and I remember, as a youngster, training at Newton-le-Willows Rugby Club and then crowding into the clubhouse
with the rest of the players to watch the games. I marvelled at the quality of the rugby
and the huge crowds and, in my case at least, it really did fire a young man's imagination.

To be selected years later was a dream come true and having toured both South
Africa and New Zealand with the Lions I felt I had measured myself against the best

in the world. I believe you have no claim to being labelled as a world-class player until you have made your mark on a long tour to the southern hemisphere. And I don't care what anyone says to the contrary.

WILLIE-JOHN McBRIDE

South Africa can be a brutal environment, so one of the things I kept preaching was that we had to be better than all of it. Bigger and better than the crowd, the referee, the linesmen and the players. We had to be bigger and better than all of that.

IAN McLAUCHLAN

Syd Millar was a brilliant coach, but his man-management skills outweighed everything. I don't think there is any doubt that in 1971, it was Doug Smith, the manager, who was in charge. In 1974, it was clearly the coach who was in charge.

BILLY STEELE (Scotland)
Toured: 1974

Willie-John was a father figure, which was quite important because you had a lot of experienced guys there, but there were a few boys like myself who had never really toured before.

SYD MILLAR

The captain has to be a psychologist because the players are all different. Some don't like being away from home, for example, so the captain has to identify that and spend some time with them. Even though tours are now down to six weeks, that is still a long time compared to national tours today, which are just a few weeks.

Wille-John McBride leads his pride into battle.

Others lack confidence. It's a big deal going on a Lions tour, especially for young players, and the captain has to make sure everyone feels involved. Sometimes it can be simple things like receiving letters. There was one player like that in 1974 and we made sure we didn't hand out any letters until his had appeared.

The main difference between captaining the Lions and captaining your country is of course that the captain has to unite four different sets of players. To do that, he has to be a motivator and a leader of men. The captain has to develop that pride in the Lions. He has to have the respect of the players, so you want to be sure the captain will hold his place in the team. That's not absolutely critical but it's very, very important.

I made Willie-John McBride Irish captain and I made him Lions captain too. He was my choice because I knew how he thought and he knew how I thought so it wouldn't take long to get us working together.

IAN McGEECHAN

People these days would be amazed to learn that even on a tour as recent as 1974, there was still no medical back-up available on the tour, no doctor or physiotherapist accompanied the party. If you needed treatment, the injured players had to find the nearest physiotherapist or whatever in every town we visited, and if the injury was a slightly more serious one, then they would have to start from scratch with each new appointment.

I was very lucky to have been part of it in 1974. It was a fantastic tour, and every player would say it was a life-changing experience, not just a rugby experience. We are all incredibly close and have a bond unique to the Lions that I have never experienced with any other team. It is the highest accolade to become a Lion, and then to become a Test Lion is still the ultimate measure of a player.

MIKE BURTON (England)
Toured: 1974

When it came to selection for England I always seemed to be chosen for the nasty away games in Paris – for an afternoon out against Gerard Cholley and his friends – but never for the easier games at Twickenham, when the college boys would always be selected. When I was chosen for the Lions, I felt like a boxer who has had his arm hoisted as world champion.

ANDY IRVINE (Scotland)
Toured: 1974, 1977 & 1980. Manager: 2013

It was my first tour so I was bound to be a wee bit starry-eyed – and when you are winning then everything becomes even more enjoyable. I was the second youngest in the team and I had never been on a tour before – so I had no idea what it was all about. It was a fantastic experience – and I'm obviously immensely proud to have been part of a team that created history in the way that we did.

ROGER UTTLEY (England)

Toured: 1974. Assistant coach: 1989

I was just starting off, and had only played four England Tests, and when I got picked it was massive for me. In retrospect, Africa generally was still a dark continent – we knew about apartheid, but not really what it meant. The prospect was fantastic, and as a youngster I had seen footage of Frik du Preez take a kick-off and run in a try from his own 10 yard line, so I knew something about the history. I had also watched the '71 Lions in New Zealand on the black-and-white pictures coming back from afar, and been inspired by the heroic win. So the Lions had been there for me from an early age, and the prospect of being one of them was a fantastic achievement and a massive privilege.

ANDY IRVINE

I gave up my honours year at university because I felt that there was a good chance of me going on the tour. So I went and got a job and I explained to my new employer that I needed a contract where I could disappear for three months in the summer of 1974 if necessary. I was very fortunate that my boss was a pretty keen rugby fan so he understood just how momentous a Lions tour was, and I got paid leave. But I never got another day's holiday apart from that.

IAN McGEECHAN

We had to suspend payments on the mortgage for several months at the time of the tour because, although Judy was working, I was not being paid in my absence from teaching.

ROGER UTTLEY

I had started teaching in '71, and when I went on the Lions tour they gave me a leave of absence and paid me. The tour allowance was about 75p a day, but you didn't need to spend any money. The proceeds of my daily allowance, added to my share of the money from black-market tickets, bought me a second-hand Austin Maxi on my return to the UK.

MIKE BURTON

On the flight out, Willie-John was tacking on to various groups and sharing a drink in the relaxed atmosphere of the flight… Willie eventually reached a group which included myself and Geoff Evans, the clever Coventry centre. He sat down and puffed on his pipe and opened a can of beer. 'You know, it's going to be hard,' he said. And he gave me that look – his head bent slightly forward, so that the whites of his eyes were showing… He held up two great fists, one in front of the other, Marquess of Queensbury style. 'It may come to a bit of this,' he said, looking around us. I nodded once… I was trying to tell Willie that I would follow him through the thick of it and right out the other side.

GORDON BROWN (Scotland)
Toured: 1971, 1974 & 1977

In rugby you get bankers and brickies, doctors and dockers, teachers and tearaways. Bobby Windsor was a hard-as-nails Welsh steelworker. When he came to your house you put away all the cutlery, when he shook hands you had to make sure you still had your watch and rings.

I remember when we all gathered in a London hotel, Willie-John McBride made one of his famous rousing speeches: 'If there's anyone here with any doubts go home now. Not a word will be said. But if you don't leave within the next two minutes then you're here for four months. I've been in South Africa before and there's going to be a lot of physical intimidation, a lot of cheating. So if you're not up for a fight, there's the door.' There was a brief silence until Bobby, who loved fighting more than anything, jumped up and shouted, 'I'm going to bloody well love this, boyo…'

BILLY STEELE
Bobby, who only had a few caps for Wales at that time, spoke up at a meeting when we were asked if we had anything to say. 'Yeah, I do,' he said. 'When I'm down on the deck and these bastards start kicking me and stamping on my head, I don't want to look up and see the numbers on your back. I want you right there with me.' Talk about a key moment. That was the tour on the road.

ANDY IRVINE
Willie-John had been on two previous tours to South Africa and had been on the receiving end of a bit of a doing. He was determined that this tour was going to be different.

He hammered home two things. Firstly, that we were never going to take a backward step when it came to confrontation – and things did get violent. Secondly, that our forwards were going to attack their scrummage. Syd Millar had also been on the receiving end in South Africa as well, and with Ian McLauchlan being an influential figure in 1974 too, there was a very, very strong emphasis on scrummaging – and it did make a difference.

ROGER UTTLEY
The brains trust of Syd Millar and Willie-John between them knew what had to be done. They said when the squad gathered in the UK, 'If you don't want to go toe-to-toe you can leave us now.' Syd attended to the forwards and we did lots of scrummaging, really brutally hard sessions. We had a lot of blokes who were really not very nice people on the rugby pitch. Whether it was Fran Cotton, the 'Mouse' McLauchlan, Gordon Brown or Mervyn Davies – Merve the Swerve was quietly determined – we were uncompromising. Bobby Windsor may have been amusing off the pitch, but on it he was a very tough piece of work.

IAN McGEECHAN

When Syd Millar and Willie-John sat down together side-by-side, the great warriors with battered faces and stiff movements, they looked as if they would be more at home on Mount Rushmore.

ROGER UTTLEY

It was the best three sporting months of my life. I went out as fourth choice second-row forward, and played in all four Tests at blind-side. I played in 16 of the 22 matches on that tour, and it was sensational not only to be part of the Lions, but part of a winning Lions team. There was no doubt, we wiped the floor with them. Sure, their selectors panicked – but we forced them to panic.

The dirt-trackers and Test team stuck to it – there was no split, and we worked hard and trained very hard. We were pros for those three months and it was great not having to worry about things like laundry or food. We also saw a magnificent country, and were treated very well.

FRAN COTTON

There were three factors that we had in 1974 that are a common denominator of all successful tours. All 30 players were committed to the cause right up to the last minute. We had a legacy in terms of benefiting from the experience and confidence of players who had also been part of the 1971 team. And we had so many world-class players at their peak who were already Test Lions, such as Gareth Edwards, JPR Williams, Ian McLauchlan, Willie-John McBride and Mervyn Davies.

WILLIE-JOHN McBRIDE

The anti-apartheid demonstrations were a big part of the build-up. But the way I saw it, it was a shambles in Northern Ireland in those years. I lived through it all and it was a disaster and I had no influence over that, so how could I have influence in South Africa? All I was interested in was people. I've always seen sport as a very powerful thing in bringing people together. I still believe that. You had to live here to know how bad it was. I was a bank manager and that wasn't an easy life. I've always been a person that, if I believe something is right, I do it and I don't run away from it.

SYD MILLAR

Basil D'Oliveira came to talk to us about South Africa and the other guy who came was the writer, Laurens van der Post – two South Africans who both said we were right to go. What Van der Post said was, 'If you don't go, it's like people sitting in closed rooms not communicating; you can go and you can communicate and you can be critical and because you are rugby players people will listen.'

ROGER UTTLEY

I played for North-Eastern Counties against the Springboks, against the likes of Piet

Greyling, Jan Ellis, and Dawie de Villiers, so the prospect of playing them again was sensational. But I also knew about the apartheid issues because there'd been a big demo at the Gosforth Greyhound Stadium before we played them. However, for all the niggling political doubts, I wanted to see for myself what was going on. It was a big adventure, and to go with the guys who were legends, like Gareth Edwards and Willie-John McBride – it never occurred to me not to go.

On the political front, if we had gone over there and got whacked then it would have confirmed the white South African status as top dog. But we showed they were not invincible, and the black and coloured people loved us beating the South African whites. So I think it did good, and maybe got the whites to see that they couldn't have it all their own way.

BILLY STEELE

To be honest, I didn't know anything about the situation. And when I got there, I was a bit gobsmacked by signs on benches saying, 'White only'. We were the first to play the coloureds, we were the first side to be on the same pitch with the blacks. Is it a bit naive to say that you have to build bridges rather than ignore it and hope that it sorts itself out?

WILLIE-JOHN McBRIDE

When I was captain of Ireland I was under threat the whole time. I couldn't win. There were guys saying, 'What are you doing captaining a bloody Irish team?' And then I'd go down south and there'd be people saying, 'This bloody Protestant, why's he captaining the Irish team?' And there were all these threats. I lived with security. Every time I went in the Shelbourne Hotel in Dublin there was a guard at my bedroom door. People said, 'What do you do it for?' And I did it because I thought it was right. If I

Willie-John McBride calls a lineout during the Fourth Test.

had stood back from all that there probably wouldn't be an Irish team. You know what I mean?

BILLY STEELE

I don't suppose we really helped the blacks' and coloureds' cause by going to South Africa in 1974, but I'm not sure we damaged it either – and they certainly seemed glad to see us.

Before we left, there was all this protesting going on outside our hotel, and I remember Willie saying, 'My beloved Ulster is in turmoil and I can't do bugger all about that. So I can't be expected to do anything about South Africa.'

DICK MILLIKEN (Ireland)
Toured: 1974

Should we go or should we not go and was it morally correct? Tony O'Reilly spoke at the Ireland-England dinner the previous year and he said, 'My advice to any young man on tour is to go with an open mind, take it all in and form your own opinion, don't let anybody tell you what you should or shouldn't think, judge for yourself.' It was reassuring for somebody like him to say that. There were people here in Bangor who'd stop me in the street to say I shouldn't be going. People saying, 'It's awful you're going.' Local papers had articles and there were letters. The O'Reilly thing was good.

FERGUS SLATTERY

Three groups of people – those who were pro-contact, the second who were anti-contact and the third, which was the biggest group, were the people who really didn't give a shit. And that was the reality. That's the way the world generally is. The biggest group are those who really don't care.

IAN McLAUCHLAN

With a kind of naivety, and very selfishly, I went to play rugby. After we came home I was asked on to a television programme to talk about apartheid and I said that I could not honestly give an opinion on that because I went to South Africa to play rugby and the South Africans showed me the rugby they wanted me to see. We didn't really come into contact with the areas where the blacks and coloured people lived. We went to some townships, but were never in a position to ask them what life was really like.

I went back to play for Natal in 1975 and it was not a nice place to be. You saw a lot of things that you didn't see as a tourist. We got a black girl in to babysit the kids and told her to help herself to anything in the kitchen, but she sat in a corner with her own stuff and she hardly ever spoke. As soon as we arrived she was darting off. She was completely intimidated by us.

Only a couple of people turned up to protest before the tour. Peter Hain and his sister were around, and they told us that we shouldn't be going. Some of them were in the park outside the hotel singing the songs, until Willie-John went out and asked them in for a cup of tea.

SYD MILLAR

The sports minister in the London government was an ex-soccer man and they removed British citizenship from those of us who had passports. The embassies were told to have no contact with us. By removing our right to contact our embassy and the embassy's right to contact us we regarded that as them saying that we were non-citizens. That's the way we read it. At the same time, all this stuff was going on in the North of Ireland. It may well have been that some of our relatives could have been shot or blown up or something and we would need our embassy. But they didn't think about us in that way.

So we weren't very happy when Denis Howell, the sports minister of that time, appeared at Heathrow when we came home and, after having said that we were non-people and we shouldn't have gone, he appeared because we were successful and there might have been a photo opportunity for him.

GARETH EDWARDS

By the time I went to South Africa in 1974 with the Lions, I was so much more aware of the general political situation. It could hardly have been otherwise for I encountered more and more the arrogance of the white man.

How do I view the wider picture so many years later? John Taylor was strong enough and knowledgeable enough to say that going there wouldn't be any good at all for the future. It was his view, I respected that. Others felt differently.

When we went in 1974, given all the fuss which had preceded the tour… we made a point of seeking out black people and asking them for their views. The majority said they thought we were right to tour, a few felt we should have stayed away. But what most said was, 'You give us the will to go on.' That will had increased significantly by the time we had finished our tour unbeaten. Rugby was the game of the Afrikaner, which is why the black people took so much pleasure from our win. It was as if we had delivered a blow on their behalf.

How do I know that? Because Nelson Mandela subsequently made it clear that the tour worked against the Afrikaner in the long run. The Afrikaner believed he was secure in his ascendancy but we proved by thrashing his beloved Springboks that that wasn't the case at all.

I know one thing – the coloured people at the matches used to go berserk with excitement when we were winning. Even if it was only for a short period of time, you could tell that they felt a wonderful pleasure and change from their usual misery. It would be too presumptuous of me to say that the 1974 Lions tour caused major cracks to appear in the entire system of apartheid. I don't believe any rugby tour has the power to do that. What it may have turned out to have done, perhaps in an unexpected way, was provide one more shoulder pushing against the wall of apartheid which had seemed at one time impregnable.

BOBBY WINDSOR
We played against two black sides out there and they were really pleased to play against – if you like – a white side, and afterwards have a meal together, which I thought was a great thing, both for them and for us.

I thought by playing against two black teams we were helping. And when one of those teams (the Leopards) scored a try against us, and the Springboks hadn't scored a try in the first two Tests, well, they went crazy. It was like they had crossed the line first.

JOHN TAYLOR
In '68 I was worried about the whole business of touring South Africa, but I wanted to be a Lion so much that I let myself be persuaded. I'd had misgivings but I was desperate to play. I put all the misgivings to the back of my mind.

The prevailing rugby logic was that you weren't helping sustain apartheid, you were building bridges. As soon as I got there, I realised that was complete nonsense. There was no question, apartheid was more obvious and far worse than I had ever expected it to be.

The night before we left, the high commissioner or the ambassador said something to the effect of, 'Don't get involved in our politics; you won't understand them. But our rugby and our girls are great so go and enjoy them.' And then, when we got out there and had our first night in a hotel in Stilfontein, a group of real Afrikaners came

Phil Bennett makes his dazzling break to score in the Second Test.

to our hotel and, without any prompting from us, launched into an aggressive defence of the apartheid system and how this was the only way to treat the blacks and so on and so forth. I thought, 'Bloody hell! What have I come into?'

Everything was so much more stark and black and white than you could have ever imagined. Apartheid then was essentially being strengthened. They were pretty much finding ways to push the blacks out of the specific areas that they wanted to. So it was really when I came back from that tour that the decision on touring there in the future was made.

The rugby establishment took this attitude that rugby guys were terrific guys, no matter what, that it was bigger than anything and therefore it was wrong in any way to break ranks on that. I obviously took a different point of view and thought man's inhumanity to man was far bigger. I said, 'I will go back to South Africa when Nelson Mandela invites me back,' and eventually that happened, which was wonderful.

I was absolutely convinced that the rest of the sporting world was right and that there was this sort of massive arrogance in rugby that the brotherhood of rugby, the fraternity of rugby, meant more than the brotherhood of man – that they couldn't be bad chaps because they played rugby. It was very much that sort of arrogance that I absolutely deplored in rugby. I had no doubts at all.

MERVYN DAVIES

In those days I was living in London and sharing a flat with John Taylor, who had been to South Africa in 1968 and was quite vociferous about his views on apartheid. We had many arguments about it but I said, 'I'm just going out there to play rugby. You've been there, now give me a chance to go there and make my own opinions about it.'

Andy Irvine after the final whistle against the Leopards.

BILLY STEELE

The blacks were our biggest fans. They were always penned into this little enclosure with the sun in their eyes, and as the tour went on their enclosure got smaller and smaller. After a few weeks we started noticing this and eventually we started to go round to that part of the ground when we arrived to give them a wave, and they would go bananas.

Like all Lions tours, we used to do community visits to schools and local rugby clubs and so on. After training one day, a coloured girl shoved a note into Willie's hand. It asked if we could go to a coloured school. Well, of course we could. I went on a couple of visits, and boy did they look after us well.

DICK MILLIKEN

The non-whites used to be put in the part of the ground that looked into the sun. We always walked to their area and waved to them. It wasn't that we were trying to be provocative or anything, it's just that they were cheering us and we were acknowledging it.

SANDY CARMICHAEL

Peter Hain was protesting against us going, and if I ever meet him I'll shake his hand and thank him from the bottom of my heart, because he did us a huge favour. They were scared he was going to disrupt our training at Eastbourne so they flew us out to South Africa ten days earlier than scheduled – and that was vital to us being almost ready at the beginning of the tour.

We trained in Stilfontein in fairly high altitude for more than a week and Ken Kennedy, the Irish hooker (who was also an orthopaedic surgeon) was doing a thesis on rugby injuries, so he volunteered to be the tour doctor. He checked all our blood levels, made sure our red blood levels were increasing, and if they weren't then we got pills. All that stuff developed a side ready to hit the ground running in South Africa. Even with that, in the first game we played in the high veldt my lungs were on fire – but because of Ken and the work he did, we coped.

Bobby Windsor used to excite the non-white element in the crowd something terrible. Whenever we arrived at a ground there would always be a game being played on the pitch beforehand, and the blacks would always be herded like cattle into an enclosure with the sun glaring into their faces. Well, Bobby would walk down to that part of the ground and he'd be like an orchestra conductor, he'd lift his arms up and they'd all be up roaring, then he'd put his hands down and they'd be quiet, and then he'd raise his arms again and they'd all be up. He was lucky he wasn't arrested for inciting a riot.

FERGUS SLATTERY

At the beginning of the tour the British government told the diplomatic corps in Pretoria not to get involved with us at all, to stay away from the games, not to host functions. Then we landed at Heathrow on the way back and there was an invitation to go to Downing Street. Where did it all change? What happened when we were out there? Apartheid certainly hadn't changed one little bit at that time. But the attitude of the British government had changed.

The whole experience was riddled with contradiction. You had in those days the sections cut off from the terraces, reserved for the Cape coloureds and blacks, the non-whites. They turned up in their droves – and some of the areas they came from were grim – just to cheer us on. If they'd wanted to make a protest in any other way, they wouldn't have gone to the game at all. That didn't mean that they were directly trying to support the tour, of course.

I went in the dead of night on the train on my own with a journalist, from Durban up to Johannesburg. When we got there, the station master – in the middle of the night, mind you – had the red carpet out. He had all his station staff lined up, as a guard of honour for us. And there wasn't a white person in sight. So, here was another extraordinary contradiction. If there was resentment from the black community towards us, I never saw it. They didn't have to do that. That was something that the black station master decided for himself: there's a Lion on this train. Even when you weren't looking for it, there was so much goodwill towards us, no question.

ROGER UTTLEY

When we got to South Africa we spent the first ten days at the Three Fountains Hotel in Stilfontein, which was a little mining town out in the sticks near Potchefstroom. There were three or four of us in a poxy little room with single beds, and kit-bags and boots everywhere. The bathroom and bog were down the corridor, so it was nothing too flash. We didn't really see anyone until match day.

IAN McGEECHAN

I received what was probably my greatest ever compliment on that tour. It came from JPR Williams, who has probably long since forgotten that he ever made it… Dick Milliken and I had worked out between us that the opposition were going to be at least a stone heavier than us but that not only meant that we were going to have to be more clever to make up for it, but that we were not going to let anyone past us in midfield. As far as I can remember, we did not let anyone through us in a Test match and JPR never had to make a tackle on an opposing player who had cut through the middle.

At some point during the tour, JPR addressed us both. 'It's great playing behind you two,' he said. At that point, Dick and I reckoned that we could both die happy.

BILLY STEELE

It wasn't the era of professionalism, but in Willie-John and Syd Millar we had two guys who had seen it, done it, had had their arses kicked in South Africa and were determined not to have their arses kicked again. And we were very serious in how we approached each game. We trained like dogs.

We used to warm up and stretch, then Syd would always get us to run round the whole complex once or twice depending on how big it was – it could be a mile and a half. Then he had it set up so Rippers (Andy Ripley), who was an international 400 metres runner, would get the nod and take off, and we'd be after him like a herd of rampaging buffalo.

Then there were the sprint sessions, and there was a lot of competition: JJ was an international sprinter, Jonny Moloney was fast, I was a PTI in the RAF and as fit as a fiddle, Slattery was quick and he'd join in with the backs, and like a true flanker he'd go like a flyer, so you'd always be watching him like a hawk – it was all good banter, but highly competitive.

Tommy David, another flanker, had a poncho moustache and he used to always fancy his chances – although he wasn't quite as quick as Slats. When the shit really hit the fan you would look round at the finish and he'd have spew hanked on his moustache. So you knew you had to get in front of him.

ROGER UTTLEY

I don't remember '99' ever being called – if there was an incident, all that happened was everyone got stuck in. It was never really my cup of tea, and looking back on film of the Third Test I see myself step in, throw a punch, and step back pretty quickly. Against Northern Transvaal a blond Aryan type slotted me, and I went down in a heap only to see JPR piling into him.

WILLIE-JOHN McBRIDE

The '99' has been overplayed. It didn't happen more than a couple of times, but it stopped the nonsense. I shouted 99, I think, once and I didn't have to do it a second time. The funny story about that is when we were chatting about it (standing up to South African aggression) and what we were going to do, I remember Phil Bennett saying, 'Excuse me, am I involved in this?' I was really talking to the forwards, but I said, 'Phil, we're all involved in this.' The day it happened was exactly the day I thought it would happen: Eastern Province, and afterwards we came in the dressing room and the guys were saying, 'That worked, that stopped it,' which it did. Somebody said to Phil, 'Where the hell were you?' Phil said, 'Oh, I gave the ball boy a hell of a hiding.'

FRAN COTTON

It was an appreciation that the only way you can protect your team-mates was to be all in it together. It was an embodiment of team spirit – don't mess with any of ours, otherwise you'll have to handle all of us. In fact, there were only three or four incidents in 22 matches, and most of them were in the Third Test.

That Test was do or die for the South Africans and they picked big powerful blokes who were lively, and for the first 20 minutes it was an incredibly tough game. At one point you saw someone in a red Lions jersey drop on the ball and all eight Springboks stamped all over him, so we took action. That was when JPR came storming in from fullback to clout Moaner van

Heerden. The balloon only went up when Gordon Brown scored. Then, in the second half, van Heerden came in and thumped Bobby Windsor, and Broony climbed in.

Apart from that, there was a bit of a set-to when we played Northern Transvaal, and also a flare-up against Natal. The Natal incident started when JPR clouted Tommy Bedford, who was the local hero, and it went off to the extent that the crowd started throwing full cans of beer from the top of the stands. It resulted in the referee having to call the players from both teams into the middle of the pitch for safety. That was it in 22 games, so the rest is myth and legend.

BILLY STEELE

To be honest, I never heard '99' being called. It was agreed that if any nonsense started it would be one for all and all for one, but you didn't need to call '99' to make our big boys like Gordon Brown realise that it was time for them to step forward.

FERGUS SLATTERY

The '99', I always regarded it as a load of ol' crap. The principle behind it, and it was really only to do with the Third Test, was that if anything happens there'd be a shout of, '99', and everybody gets stuck in because there's no way the referee can send us all off. My attitude when it broke out was to grab the guy standing beside me and say, 'Stay out of it.' What's the point? I was never going to go and hit a guy who was just standing there. The idea was you'd hit the nearest guy to you. Why? It didn't make sense. I think about two or three guys started swinging punches. I wasn't going to hit a guy who wasn't looking at me. That's a cheap shot. That's cowardice.

IAN McLAUCHLAN

It's rubbish. There has been all sorts of chat about the '99' call but why warn somebody when you are going to hit them? It didn't exist. It's like the story about a Welsh guy who backed £10,000 on us winning all the provincial games. And he was going to share it with us, and if we won all the Tests he was due half a million pounds and he was going to share. We never met him, however, because he didn't exist. All these fantastic stories have grown up in the ether.

All these things like either Carwyn James in 1971 or Willie-John McBride in 1974, saying, 'Get your retaliation in first.' Duncan Paterson was saying things like that in Borders rugby long before I went on the tours. But if you tell a story enough times, then fact gets mixed up with fiction.

DICK MILLIKEN

I don't ever recall this '99' being called although there was a clear instruction that if we were all in fighting they couldn't send us all off. When everything flared up in the Third Test, Ian McGeechan and I, our natural reaction was to step back, then we were pushed aside by JPR who ran 15 yards to land a punch. He was the only back who got involved. He had a Geronimo sweatband and came roaring in to hit some second-row.

ROGER UTTLEY

When we played Eastern Province at the famous Boet Erasmus Stadium in Port Elizabeth, they were a thuggish side who tried to work us over. There was fighting left, right and centre, with Stewart McKinney and Mike Burton in the middle of it – the boys were not going to be messed about.

SYD MILLAR

When we played Eastern Province, the information we had, rightly or wrongly, was that the South African coach, Johan Claassen, had gone into the dressing room and said, 'Let's rough them up a bit to see what's in them.' Well, we were the wrong team to rough up.

SANDY CARMICHAEL

The boys from the '71 tour were so affected by what happened against Canterbury on that tour, and they said if there was any indication of that sort of crap it demanded an immediate response. There were no neutral referees or touch judges, so you had to let the South Africans know. We stood up to them, probably for the first time. We went down to Port Elizabeth to play Eastern Province, and I was on the bench. It was strange because they were in the same colours as Canterbury – black and red – and that triggered something in my mind. And these guys wanted to play like Canterbury had.

But the Lions showed them that if they wanted to start it then we would finish it. There was the biggest punch-up you have ever seen in your life. There was this guy knocking hell out of Broony on the ground, and as he was getting up Stewart McKinney came off the tail of the lineout and poleaxed him with a punch. By the time the referee got to the situation McKinney was back at the tail of the lineout again looking like butter wouldn't melt in his mouth. So the Lions came out on top there, in the fight and in the match, and that told South Africa that a line had been drawn in the sand.

BILLY STEELE

It was brutal. At one point I got the ball near the right touchline with three of their guys coming across and you could see in their eyes that they were desperate to knock me into the back row of the stand. I managed to cut back inside them and I was delighted to score – but I was just as relieved to still be in one piece.

You can't condone violence, but we didn't start anything – we just didn't take a backward step. And that gave them a hell of a shock.

ANDY IRVINE

It was a small back division when you think about it, because it was only JPR and Dick Milliken who would be regarded as reasonably physical – the rest were all quite small, but fast and elusive.

IAN McLAUCHLAN

They called '74 a forwards thing. Rubbish. Tommy Grace scored 14 tries, JJ Williams

13 tries, Andy Irvine 11. It was classic rugby. The coach, Syd Millar, had said he didn't want any miss moves, crisscrosses in the middle of the field or anything like that: he just wanted the ball out to the wings. JJ was absolutely on fire, as was Billy Steele earlier in the tour before he got injured. Billy was one of these guys – against three men in a five-yard area he'd beat all three of them. Give him the ball on halfway with no one in front of him and tell him to run it in, he couldn't do it. He'd always get caught, he just wasn't quick enough. But Billy was the Dancer. And JJ – give him the ball anywhere and he always wanted to score. He was lightning fast, by far the fastest man I ever played against

BILLY STEELE

I was a jinky side-stepper so had very little interest in getting involved in punch-ups. When the trouble erupted us flair players in the backline – guys like Phil Bennett, Ian McGeechan, JJ Williams and myself – would be hanging around looking useless, and JPR would charge past us at 100 miles an hour to get to the fun.

ANDY IRVINE

And there was one or two real geniuses there. In any list of great players, Gareth Edwards would be right at the top, he was in a complete league of his own. A couple of times we really struggled in games until he got going, and then he transformed the whole thing. Against Orange Free State in Bloemfontein we were down and out until he grabbed the game by the scruff of the neck. And I still think that pound-for-pound Phil Bennett was the best stand-off we've ever seen. On hard grounds you couldn't get to him, and he was tougher than people give him credit for. He was almost unstoppable – I learned more from Phil on that Lions tour than anyone else.

He obviously played a lot of his international rugby with JPR and had a big role in bringing him into the game, and he introduced the same ideas to me – but because I was a wee bit quicker than JPR he adapted the moves and angles to make it really effective. We operated these things that Benny had come up with for Heriot's and Scotland for the next ten years!

BILLY STEELE

I would say Gareth Edwards was the greatest player ever. He was a gymnast and pound-for-pound he was the strongest player in the squad. I remember one training session when he said to Syd that he would have to stop because he had blisters. Now, they weren't that bad – but he didn't need to train. It was a case of, 'Take a break Gareth. Enjoy yourself and have a few gin and tonics. But do the business on Saturday.'

ROGER UTTLEY

The list of great players on the tour starts with Gareth Edwards. He just did everything right, and was such a threat. JPR Williams was a rock at fullback, and as combative as any forward.

IAN McLAUCHLAN

For me, the key guy in South Africa was Mervyn Davies. He was the perfect No 8. He won ball in the back of the lineout, steadied everything, always took possession forward. He was a fantastic player. Fergus Slattery didn't stop running from the time he got off the plane to the time he got back on it. He was like a dog after a bone. And Phil Bennett was at the peak of his game.

FRAN COTTON

We trained very hard, and the scrum practice was far harder than that on any of the modern tours. We would put down 60 to 70 scrums every single day, and it was live scrummaging between two packs in which every player wanted a Test place. It was fiercely competitive, and at the end of it you were absolutely goosed. I went out there 16st 12lb and came back close to 18st. My neck was 17in before and 19in after. None of my clothes fitted when I went home. That's how tough it was.

I have a huge amount of respect for the determination of the South Africans, but power is too important to them. They tend to be too one-dimensional.

STEWART McKINNEY (Ireland)
Toured: 1974

The scrumming practice. God, it was hard! There was no scrummaging machine, so it was all live stuff – eight against eight, 60 scrums a day.

WILLIE-JOHN McBRIDE

Scrummaging. Every day and when it came to the game it was easy. The forwards in 74, you didn't mess with those guys. Cotton, Windsor and McLauchlan, myself and Gordon Brown, Roger Uttley, Mervyn Davies and Slattery. Hell of a pack of forwards. I knew we had the men to stand up to anything that was going to be thrown at them.

IAN McGEECHAN

We had so much reserve strength. Geoff Evans and Roy Bergiers were the other centres on the tour and at the very start, I was looking at them and I could not believe that I would become a regular in the Test team… We also had Alan Old, a strong contender for fly-half.

MERVYN DAVIES

The great finisher on that tour was JJ Williams on the wing. He had always been rapid, he was an international class sprinter as a young man before he devoted himself to rugby, but he was also a really good all-round footballer. His trademark was the chip ahead. JJ would be running at top pace then he would dink the ball over the defenders with his boot and chase it and almost every time it would pop up into his hands. His influence was amazing. He scored two tries in the Second Test in Pretoria, he scored another two in the Third Test in Port Elizabeth, one was so brilliant that they never laid a hand on him and he scored in total isolation. There was one great picture of JJ with both arms in the air after he scored a try with thousands of delighted black followers behind him joining in the celebrations. He was so sharp.

IAN McGEECHAN

It was JJ Williams who scored some of the signature tries, especially with his party trick of chipping the ball ahead and using his great pace to get to it first. Fran Cotton was a fantastic rock at tight-head... the list of great players was endless. Fergus Slattery was at the peak of his abilities, and was an amazing figure because he played it ferociously hard on and off the field. On the field he was absolutely brilliant, he underlined the defensive principle I have stuck with ever since, and driven into all the teams I have coached. It is that the most important defender is the man just inside the ball and just inside you. When Dick and I were going up in defence, Fergus would be bawling, 'I'm on your inside! I'm on your inside! If he comes this way, I'll smash him.'

SANDY CARMICHAEL

We were a squad of 30 men who had gone there to win the series, and there was never any griping about selection from me or any of the other guys who missed out on the Test team. I realised that I had a job to do with the dirt-trackers, and they were now short of a loose-head prop because Franny had switched to the tight. There weren't many props who could play both sides, but he was one and I was another. So I went to Syd and said that I could play loose-head if he gave me an easy game against Rhodesia to bed in, so that's what we did.

That must have been the strongest Lions squad that ever toured, and just to be part of it was astronomical. We meet up now and then and it's as if we have never been away – the banter is still there – and it's great to be part of a family like that.

ANDY IRVINE

I knew I was going out as number two to JPR, but they ended up playing me on the wing on Saturday and at fullback on Wednesdays. I ended up playing 14 games, which was brilliant.

We didn't train twice a day, so we had a run out in the morning and the afternoon was free to play golf, go surfing or do anything you wanted, really – but like any holiday it can eventually become a wee bit

Ian McGeechan.

tedious, whereas if you are involved in nearly every game it gives you something to focus on. Players nowadays like to be rested because they are knackered, but in those days you wanted to play in as many games as you could.

SANDY CARMICHAEL

I was in charge of allocating rooms. I had this complicated, colour-coded chart, and it was my job to make sure that you didn't have two guys from the same country rooming together, you didn't have two guys who had roomed together before in the same room and you had the guys playing in the next game all rooming together. We'd set off on a plane to a new town and they'd give me the team while I was in the air, and by the time we had landed I had to have them all roomed.

One of the big problems was the snorers, and Broony [Gordon Brown] was one of the worst. Hotels shook with the noise he made, so you had to break one of the rules if he was playing and get a player who was not involved in the next game to room with him because that person was going to have a hard time sleeping. You'd be saying, 'Look son, it's for the good of the team. You're not playing, you're not even on the bench, but you're with Broony – because the rest of the team need to sleep.'

ANDY IRVINE

Bobby Windsor was one of the real characters of the tour. One of the great stories about Bobby is that his boss at the steel works where he worked in South Wales wouldn't let him go on the tour, but because there was thousands working there they never checked and he got one of his pals to clock him in and out. And when Bobby got back he found he had earned more money than usual because his pal had put him in for overtime. Whether it's true or not, who knows? Nothing would surprise me with Bobby.

BILLY STEELE

The management didn't want us to phone home too often. I think there had been problems on previous tours with people getting homesick, so they wanted everyone to focus on what was going on in South Africa. But unbeknown to the rest of us, Bobby had been sneaking into the manager's room to phone his wife, until one day before training Alun Thomas came onto the coach and said he'd just received a telephone bill from the South African Rugby Union for x thousand rand. He said: 'I suspect it's one of you boys so I would like the culprit to own up.'

Nobody moved. Everybody was looking at each other wondering what the hell he was on about. Then he said, 'Well, I'm a bit disappointed because I know they have been ringing Newport 321456.'

Bobby jumped up and shouted, 'Which one of you bastards has been phoning my wife?'

SANDY CARMICHAEL

Andy Ripley was just from a different world. I remember one night when four of us were sitting having a meal, and Rippers got up and said, 'Sandy, do you fight in bars?' I said, 'No.'

And he said, 'You've got a face that looks like it fights in bars.' And then he just walked off.

We had to go to this cocktail party and we were supposed to be in our number one dress code, but Rippers turned up in flip-flop sandals, trousers and his blazer with no shirt. So he got a row from the management, who told him to wear a tie next time. So at the next function, he still had no shirt but he was wearing a tie.

ROGER UTTLEY

I still have this image of Rippers on our final day in Cape Town when we were going over the Chapman's Peak Road for a braii with his feet hanging out of the car window on one side, and his head out of the other.

IAN McGEECHAN

Andy did not even take a case. He crammed everything into the Lions duffle bag that we were given. Into the duffel bag went his blazer, his kit, whatever. When I shared a room with him, I discovered that he just tipped everything out in a pile in the corner.

ROGER UTTLEY

During the tour there was no curfew, and there were big G&T sessions by the swimming pool at most hotels led by JPR. But when it came to training you would be there on time ready to go – and any signs of weakness due to the overindulgence were not tolerated by Syd. There were plenty of training ground punch-ups, and there was one big bust-up between the front-rows at Seapoint, when the dirt-trackers had a go at the Test team, so we had to go in and beat them up.

GARETH EDWARDS

The strength of the '74 tour was the unity of the whole squad. I'm sure most of the lads

JPR Williams puts in a booming clearance kick.

would tell you that some of the hardest moments on that tour were training against, dare I say it, the B-side, which was a shadow side more accurately. They were as tough as any team we played.

It's hard to put in so many words what is special about the Lions. Suffice to say every player aspires to play for his country. Then you realise there is a further step to take. You read about it and, OK in later years, you're able to see these tours on TV. But we grew up reading about them, Cliff Morgan, Jeff Butterfield, Tony O'Reilly and all those guys on these long, long trips to the far side of the world. It's a gathering of the clans, isn't it? And there's the uncanny factor, too, that you battle and try to tear each other apart only weeks before and, all of a sudden, you are standing shoulder to shoulder against a common enemy a long way from home.

BILLY STEELE

The greatest team talk I ever experienced was before the First Test. A meeting was called in the team room before we left for the match, and when I walked in there was a few guys already sitting there with Syd and Willie at the front of the room. It took five to ten minutes for the room to fill up, and during that time nobody spoke. Then we all sat there for another five to ten minutes and still nobody spoke. The hairs on the back of your neck were standing on end. Eventually, after 20 minutes, Willie-John stood up and said, 'Right, we all know what we need to do. Let's go and do it.' I was petrified when I went into that room and I felt invincible when I came out.

DICK MILLIKEN

The First Test was played at Newlands on a very heavy, muddy pitch on a rainy day reminiscent of the usual conditions back in Ireland. One of the crucial scores that victorious day was a drop-goal by Gareth Edwards. There was nothing on, no real danger to South Africa and we were running on a particularly heavy part of the pitch. The genius stopped, looked up and dropped one of the most magnificent goals I have ever witnessed. It wasn't a beautiful or typically classical drop-goal that flew high through the posts, but remarkable because I am convinced that when he dropped the ball to execute the kick he was momentarily stuck in the mud. Only his immense strength, grit and grim determination overcame the laws of gravity.

MERVYN DAVIES

I managed to set down my own marker early in the first half when their flanker Boland Coetzee took an inside pass from his wing. It was one of those unearthly occasions when time stood still and I unleashed the perfect hit. It was the tackle of my career and it gave me terrific pleasure. You can keep your 50 yard runs and wizard little sidesteps. The sensation of me catching Coetzee under his ribs, driving hard and sending him wheezing 10 yards backwards onto his arse was bliss. As soon as he hit the dirt the boys rucked over him and won turnover ball. All around us, we heard the South African crowd let out a collective, almost wistful groan.

GARETH EDWARDS

When we won the opening Test at Newlands it was like throwing a grenade into South African rugby – it created so much confusion the Springboks did not know which was their best side and that confusion kept going right to the end.

In all honesty we were very fortunate to win that Test, we dug in and squeezed out the result, but after a really tough game against Transvaal ahead of the Second Test we turned the screw at Loftus Versfeld and played at a different level.

I was 27 years old at the time and probably playing as well as at any time in my career and playing behind that pack was a pure pleasure.

FERGUS SLATTERY

When we played the First Test we played against what was a Western Province-biased side. It was played in Cape Town and when we went up to play the Second Test in the Transvaal in Pretoria they reversed it and they put more Afrikaners in there and they got taken apart. But when they went back to the coastline they decided Plan A didn't work and Plan B didn't work so now they'd go for Plan C and put all the gorillas in there to eat the Lions alive. They picked Gerrie Sonnekus at scrum-half but he was more a No 8 and they brought in two gorillas into the second-row.

WILLIE-JOHN McBRIDE

I remember leading the team out in the Second Test. Of the moments in life that I remember vividly to this day, that was one of them. The sun hitting me and I was carrying that bloody old mascot thing and the ground was like a rock and 50-60,000 South Africans all around us, and I knew, I just had that feeling, that there were 14 players with me who were not going to lose. It was just a wonderful feeling. It still hits me today. They picked that guy Moaner van Heerden. He didn't last very long. Moaner was kicking guys and hitting guys. He was carried away. He came out with the idea of sorting us all out. There was no way he was gonna survive.

GORDON BROWN

The referees were giving us no protection whatsoever. In the Third Test at Port Elizabeth, the 'Boks had brought in some heavies to try and sort us out, the main one being Moaner van Heerden. Willie-John had singled him out and warned that he would have a go. The nearest Lion would then wade in and give van Heerden a doing. Sure enough, after ten minutes, van Heerden belted Bobby Windsor and I was the nearest man; that's how I broke my thumb.

During that fight I hit Johan de Bruyn, who was a fearsome forward from Northern Transvaal. A fearsome man with a glass eye. And when I punched him, the eye flew out. So there we are, 30 players plus the ref on our hands and knees scrabbling about in the mire looking for this glass eye. Eventually, someone yells 'Eureka!' whereupon de Bruyn grabs it and plonks it straight back in the gaping hole in his face. And when he stands up I can't believe what I'm looking at… there's a huge dod of grass sticking out of his eyeball.

SYD MILLAR

Max Baise, the referee who did the First Test had refereed us in 1968 and I knew him, and when we went to South West Districts and he was reffing I said, 'Oh, you've dropped a bit in the rankings, haven't you?' He said, 'I'm not too popular now.' Anyway, the South African union put him on the list of four referees for the Test and we could choose. I said to the guy, 'If we pick you we just want a fair deal and if it's a fair deal, you'll get more.' So he was straight as a die in the First Test.

BILLY STEELE

We didn't have neutral referees. For the Test matches, they would give us a list of four South African referees and we would get to choose one. For the First Test we chose this guy called Max Baise, because we'd had him during the provincial matches and we liked him, and I'll always remember he penalised the Springboks for not being back ten at a lineout and Phil Bennett kicked it. The Lions just didn't normally get decisions like that.

After the game, I went out to see a friend of mine behind the stand before I got changed, and Danie Craven was there giving Baise a real dressing down.

So, before the Second Test they asked us who we wanted to referee, and we said we'd have Max Baise; but we were told we couldn't have him because he wasn't on the list.

SYD MILLAR

This guy de Bruyn came to me. He'd refereed in a provincial game and had not refereed very well and he came to see me and apologised and said, 'I'm sorry, I haven't had a good game today, I made mistakes.' I said, 'Ah, don't worry about it.' They put de Bruyn on the referees list for the Second Test so I picked him and he was straight as a die as well. And we picked him for the Third Test as well.

They took de Bruyn off the list for the Fourth Test and they gave us another four who we didn't know much about and we said we're having none of them. We compromised and said we'll take the first guy again. Baise. He disallowed Slattery's try.

SANDY CARMICHAEL

South Africa were always trying to muck up our preparation. We called it 'the fifth column'. When we arrived in Pretoria for the Second Test, we found there were two dozen cans of beer each in every room, and 200 fags each because a lot of us smoked in those days. They must have thought we would drink and smoke ourselves stupid before the match. So we quickly called a team meeting and decided that we would hire another room and we'd lock all 60 dozen cans of beer and all the fags in there – and we'd take it all to Kruger National Park with us when we had our break the following week.

So that's what we did. We won the game, and the next morning we piled it all onto this ancient Dakota plane which was built in 1948 and flew to Kruger Park, and we were worried about the weight with all that beer plus a squad of burly rugby players. We flew all over South Africa in these old Dakotas, and I remember one stewardess telling us that it took an hour to get the blasted things going before a flight.

By one o'clock in the morning of our first night in Kruger Park we'd finished all the beer. The party fell apart when the dust fire extinguisher went off. The whole place ended up white. I remember Geoff Evans asking if anyone had a corkscrew, and nobody did so he smashed the top off the bottle, and emptied the contents into his glass.

We were wandering around with wild animals all over the place. We had one training session while we were there, and while we were running up and down the pitch passing the ball I saw something moving out the corner of my eye. It was a pride of lions settling down to watch us. I said, 'Should we be here?' And one of the guys looking after us said, 'You're okay, they've eaten.' That didn't reassure me too much.

STEWART McKINNEY

They go and shoot paint at each other these days to build team spirit, and all these other organised bonding things, but we had none of that. We would sing songs. At first everyone was very shy, they didn't want to get up and sing. Bobby Windsor got up and told a load of jokes, the funniest half hour of my life, and we just went from there. Willie-John sang, Fergus Slattery sang, Billy Steele then sang, for the first time, 'Flower of Scotland', which became our tour song, way before the Scots took it up.

We had a week up in Kruger National Park, the largest game reserve in South Africa, and we had a hell of a good time. We were on the drink for a week. Imagine that on a modern-day tour! Today you'd be watching videos of the other team. We had every afternoon free to do your standard leisure things, fishing or shooting or wee cruises up the Zambezi. I'm not jealous of the players these days. Ours was a different game from a different era. I think we had a lot more enjoyment. I'm actually jealous of the guys who toured in the fifties. They went by boat for a month there and back. They were gone for six months; that would've been my idea of heaven!

ANDY IRVINE

The Welsh are always good singers; Willie-John McBride could carry a tune, and Franny Cotton was actually pretty good with some songs from the Bible belt in America – but it was Gareth Edwards who demanded the Scots sing a song, and Billy Steele came up with 'Flower of Scotland'. I have to admit I had never heard it before. Nowadays it gets criticised for being a wee bit dour, but back then it really took off. It was easy to learn the words and it became the Lions tour song.

BILLY STEELE

I've always been a big fan of folk music – The Corries, The Dubliners and so on – and 'Flower of Scotland' ended up as the tour song. We changed the line about 'Proud Edward's army' to 'the Springbok army'. I remember rooming with Bobby Windsor on one occasion and he had the song stuck in his head. He kept waking me up to ask what the next line was. He woke me up about six times.

Before the Second Test at Loftus Versfeld we were singing 'Flower of Scotland' on the bus on the way to the stadium, but we had only finished the first verse when we arrived and I remember the officials coming on and trying to get us off the coach, but nobody moved until we had finished. And when we finally walked off the coach and walked through the crowd we felt ten feet tall.

Willie-John said afterwards that he realised at that point that there was no way we were going to lose.

DICK MILLIKEN

For the Third Test the 'Boks were two down in the series and they came out so fired up. Their eyes were glazed after being locked up in a prison camp and for about the first 25 minutes Geech and I did nothing but tackle. We had a great understanding, just met force with force and we were black and blue. Then we got up near the Springbok line and Gordon Brown caught the ball and fell over for a try and for them it was like the air going out of a balloon.

IAN McGEECHAN

The Third Test was the hardest game I have ever played and the first half was even harder than that! The Springboks were on a mission from history and the pressure they put on us was incessant and for a long time there was nothing we could do to stem the tide of their attacks.

The psychology of it was difficult for me. Every time I played on that tour, I was up against guys who were comfortably a stone or two heavier than me. Sometimes I wondered how long I could keep defending against it all. But this happened so often in my career of playing for or coaching the smaller team, and we were able to lay our honey trap. South Africans are always intent on coming out and making their hits. They are very focused on pushing up in the straight-line to smash the opposition. The honey trap we laid involved trying to get them to come up and then we'd spring it and shift the ball late.

FERGUS SLATTERY

There was huge physicality in the first 40 minutes of the Third Test and you just had to stand up to it and give as good as you got. We got a bit of a break when their hooker threw it straight to Gordon Brown who just fell over the line. Try! We kicked it so it was 9-0 at half-time and that was the end of the game. Thier Plan C hadn't worked. We hammered them.

DICK MILLIKEN

They just collapsed. They had marmalised us and it was like being in the trenches, but we were ahead and they looked as if they believed that we were invincible. We ran amok in the second half.

MIKE BURTON

The night after the Third Test when we took the series was one of the greatest ever. Willie-John's wild side surfaced again. There was damage to the hotel, fire extinguishers were set off, beer was spilt, glasses were broken, doors were knocked off hinges. There was quite a trail of destruction.

ROGER UTTLEY

We saw the wondrous stalactites in the Kango Caves, flew through the mountains in a Dakota down the Garden Route and spent a day in the Kruger Park chasing rhinos in little Nissan pick-ups. Alan Old was in the back of one of them with his broken leg still in plaster and, like the rest of us, bouncing everywhere. Health and safety wouldn't allow it today. After winning the Test in Port Elizabeth a fishing trip was arranged on a little boat with a few crates of beer on board. We hadn't even untied when Billy Steele said, 'I'm not feeling too good'. Then we got to the mouth of the estuary into a big swell, and I remember Swerve and Burto eating boiled eggs while Gareth and I were hanging over the side dying of seasickness.

Then there was the showdown at the Marine Hotel in Port Elizabeth when we were having a bit of a ruck and the manager got excited. That's when Willie-John, in Y-fronts and socks, after being informed the police were coming said, 'Tell me, how many will there be?'

MIKE BURTON

Next morning arrived with the whole party in the anguished stages of re-entry and they savoured a day and a night to remember. Down in the foyer, Alun Thomas, the manager, was fretting. He was studying a list of damage handed to him by the hotel manager. 'Look what the boys have done,' Thomas said. And he went down the list: 300 rand for this, 500 rand for that, 600 rand for something else. It had been quite a night. Willie took the list and looked down it, with the inevitable pipe puffing away. He looked at the two managers. 'Are there any dead?' he asked, and walked away towards the revolving doors for some fresh air... As he passed me, he stopped. 'Last night was priceless. They will never be able to buy that again for a million, let alone what they are talking about back there.'

SANDY CARMICHAEL

After we won the Third Test I was rooming with Stewart McKinney, and it was dangerous, dangerous stuff. We started drinking at six o'clock that night and went to bed at quarter to one on the Monday morning. We were taken down to a barbeque at the beach in Port Elizabeth, and everyone was in swimming. We looked at the water, looked at each other, looked at the water and looked at each other. Eventually Stewart said, 'Sandy, we'd just drown.' So we turned round and walked back up the beach for another drink.

ANDY IRVINE

In fairness, the South Africans did improve a lot for the Fourth Test – so they deserve credit for that. But did we deserve to win that game? I would say, marginally, yes. I don't know about Slats' try, but my gut feeling was that it was a score. So, it was a wee bit disappointing – but there was an element of relief because if we had lost it that would have spoiled the record. What we have done is left a wee scope there for another team to go one better than us. The challenge is still there!

FERGUS SLATTERY

I put the ball down on the ground but I didn't score because the referee didn't award it. The referee didn't see it and to be fair the result was correct because Roger Uttley was awarded a try in the first half and it wasn't a try. He never got his hand on the ball. The problem with the Fourth Test was that on the Tuesday I saw that all the guys had packed their bags and had completely switched off. That's a big mistake and we made it. We went into that Test ready to tick box 22 having won 21. The guys weren't really thinking about it. You play an international match and the closer you get to it the more you commit mentally to it. You have to be 100 per cent mentally attuned when that whistle goes whereas we would have been 10, 20, 30, 40 per cent. It was a mental thing not a physical thing.

IAN McLAUCHLAN

Relations between the two teams weren't that great and Morné du Plessis said once that the Lions were a bit stand-offish. That's not true. I went for meals with my opposite number, and spent a whole Sunday with him and his family. I met one of their guys when I was over following the Lions in 2009 and I asked if the old wounds had healed yet. 'No. I hated you in 1974 and I still hate you now, but I will buy you a drink.' That's the sort of attitude it was.

GARETH EDWARDS

South Africa is an extremely hard place to go and win, take it from me. They will take the skin off your back and never give anything less than their all.

In 1974 they also had outstanding players like Jan Ellis and Morné du Plessis so I did not have exactly an armchair ride. But behind such a dominant pack and with Big Merv controlling things at No 8, we were playing on the front foot with time to size up our options.

MIKE BURTON

What we did to the Springboks represented the biggest hammering ever given in a series between two major rugby-playing nations. If the players had been racehorses when they retired, they would all have gone to stud, and they would have won the Derby. Many people said that our second string, midweek side would have been far too strong for the Springboks.

DICK MILLIKEN

Geech told me when he was Lions coach in 1997 they arrived and the then minister for sport said, 'Mr McGeechan, it's great to meet you,' and Geech said that he proceeded to recite the entire Test team from 1974. He said, 'It's because I was on Robben Island when you were playing and our white guards had their radios on listening to the match and we cheered when South Africa were being beaten to annoy the guards and it was a great uplift for us.' If anybody ever asked me who would I like to spend a day with, it would be Nelson Mandela. I was a 23 year old in 1974 and since then I have taken a lifelong interest in South Africa and what happened there and to think that in that cell Mandela was listening and maybe acknowledged the name Milliken; that he would have known of me, that's just incredible.

IAN McLAUCHLAN

They took myself, Willie-John, Gordon Brown, Mervyn Davies, Fergus Slattery, and JPR Williams from the 1971 team and made us the core of the 1974 team. If they had taken the nucleus of the 1974 team on the 1977 trip to New Zealand, I firmly believe we would have beaten New Zealand again.

IAN McGEECHAN

I never thought for a moment that we would not beat the Springboks, even though we had never beaten them before. Dick Milliken and I struck up a great partnership on and off the field on that tour, and it is a friendship which has continued all down the years. After we won, we both looked across at the two massive Irishmen, Willie-John and Syd. It wasn't anything that they said or did. It was just a look that passed between them. It was a look that was completely different, a look of elation, a look that I had never seen before.

The meaning of the Test wins and the tour to two first-time Lions playing in a great Lions team, and wide-eyed at it all, and the meaning to two old warriors

who had suffered and grafted for it, was something on a different plane altogether.

FRAN COTTON

The great thing about Willie-John as a captain was that he knew when to work, and knuckle down, and when to play. One of my most vivid memories is on the Sunday after we won the Third Test in Port Elizabeth. We had a big barbecue on the beach as a tour party, the sun was shining, we had steaks and cold beer, and life couldn't have been better. There

Gareth Edwards in action against Natal.

was a British journalist covering the tour, Chris Lander, who had a habit of turning up everywhere on a bike, and there he was on his bike in the surf!

Afterwards we continued celebrating at a hotel nearby, where the manager was a right idiot who shouted at his black and coloured staff, treating them very poorly. Micky Burton and Bobby Windsor came down the stairs each with a fire extinguisher and covered him from head to toe in foam, while all his staff applauded.

SYD MILLAR

Attitude is the first thing a team needs to have. If the attitude is right, the other things fall into place.

You will always have guys who are disappointed when they don't get in the Test side. They may be star players in their own country but they could be only number three in their position in these islands. Those guys can turn off a bit.

The second team is very important on Lions tours; it's vital they keep their side of the tour up. The captain has to make sure those guys know how important they are to the team and to the final result.

WILLIE-JOHN McBRIDE

The sheer belief in ourselves, the loyalty of those guys to each other. I remember the last moment in the Third Test and we'd only used 17 out of the 30 players in the series and the immediate reaction was to stand on the touchline and applaud the players in the stand because they were part of us, they kept us in the Test side because they worked like hell to get in the Test side themselves and they made us all the keener to stay there. A remarkable bunch of men.

Glorious Victorious. The Lions return home.

CHAPTER TWENTY

HISTORY IN REVERSE
1977

NEW ZEALAND AND FIJI

THE GREAT *satisfaction and even joy for rugby in Britain and Ireland during the 1974 tour of South Africa lay in the evidence that after years of losing the physical confrontation on so many tours, the Lions had grown up and, as Colin Meads once said in New Zealand, 'They had stopped believing in fairy tales.'*

The process by which the Lions were able to stand up physically and even to dominate New Zealand and South Africa in the two tours in the first half of the 1970s continued at such a rate that during the 1977 trip to New Zealand, the Lions pack were in almost every significant phase by far the superior unit, giving New Zealand a real going over up front in what was, in many ways, the most humiliating sight ever suffered in New Zealand sport. Indeed, they inflicted so much pressure in the Test series that the All Blacks were forced to resort to a three-man scrum.

Yet, incredibly, things went too far. The Lions – and British and Irish rugby as a whole – had become so obsessed with scrummaging and forward dominance that they had begun to ignore their age old strengths in back play, individual genius and the ability to cash in on possession. There are some Lions teams of the past who lost in their Test series who, had they been given as much possession as the 1977 Lions, would have won at a canter.

The Lions were pushed off their rugby pedestal as a result, by three Tests to one, with the series slipping away in the dying seconds of the Fourth Test. For years the tourists had travelled in hope – the hope of winning sufficient possession; but it was now the New Zealand backs that prayed for a beggar's share of ball to outplay their visitors. The New Zealand side of 1977 were not a great outfit, but they were allowed to escape.

British & Irish back play had become stereotyped and on this tour it struggled to put into practice the simple tenets that Carwyn James had held so dear in '71. The visiting backs were simply unable to transfer the ball at speed to their wings. Their preoccupation with set moves that were clearly telegraphed to their opponents in the Tests left the All Blacks defence with the simple task of shepherding the Lions sideways in a rudimentary form of drift defence.

Perhaps the biggest irony of all was that the coach on tour was John Dawes, the wizard who had inspired such glorious attacking rugby for London Welsh, Wales and the 1971 Lions. Dawes appeared somewhat out of sorts on tour, apparently engaging in battles with the visiting press party as well as the All Blacks, and he could not conjure a return from the Lions' possession.

The outcome was that the Lions' match-winners JJ Williams and Andy Irvine, two of the few tour successes, were unable to find the overlaps and spaces that had opened up on the '71 visit. With Phil Bennett, in some ways a reluctant tour captain, forced out of his comfort zone by the New Zealand

---

Opposite: 'Mud Man' Fran Cotton: the iconic photograph from the 1977 tour.

back-row, centre Ian McGeechan once observed that all too often when we was given the ball, he was running towards the touchline.

Wales generally ruled the Five Nations in the seasons between the 1974 South African and 1977 New Zealand tours. Champions in 1975, Grand Slam winners in 1976 and Triple Crown holders in 1977, they supplied the majority of the tourists when the original party of 30 was announced.

Sixteen of them – a record contribution for the Principality – were named under the captaincy of Phil Bennett. Not all of the contingent were deemed to have justified their selection.

Given that Gerald Davies and Gareth Edwards had declared themselves unavailable, and that no concession was made for JPR Williams having to stay behind until June owing to his medical commitments, the size of the Welsh contingent did raise eyebrows. Uncapped Welsh players Elgan Rees (for Gerald Davies), Brynmor Williams (for Gareth Edwards) and Alun Lewis (a replacement scrum-half when Williams was injured during the Third Test) leapfrogged established internationals from the rest of the Home Unions. John Bevan, moreover, Bennett's rival for the number 10 shirt in the Welsh squad, went as Lions understudy to the skipper.

Arguably Gareth Edwards' individual brilliance, his experience as a tactician and ability to take pressure off his fly-half could have turned the series in the Lions' favour. Bennett had to stand deeper to cope with the passing of inexperienced scrum-halves so that in attack the Lions were invariably starting off on the back foot. Edwards' style would undoubtedly have helped with the backs' alignment.

George Burrell of Scotland, a Lions contender in 1950 and later an international referee, was the manager, with Dawes, Wales' guiding genius through the three seasons of Five Nations successes, the automatic choice as Lions coach. In the aftermath of a series defeat, many critics argued that maybe Dawes had misplaced confidence in some of the fringe Welsh players who had gone on the trip.

David Burcher pipped Scotland's experienced centre, Jim Renwick, for a place among the five centres in the party. Only three out-and-out wings were selected, though Bruce Hay, a fullback, and Gareth Evans, a centre whose sole Wales cap had been as a replacement wing for Gerald Davies during a defeat in Paris, could deputise. Burcher had replaced Ray Gravell in the Welsh side that season. Gravell had been a Lions prospect but had suffered a shoulder injury that had put him out of contention for the tour. The best crash-ball exponent in the Home Unions, his absence was a bitter blow to John Dawes' plans.

Burcher was a different type of centre who had enjoyed a successful Five Nations, but Renwick, with his burst of pace, was judged unlucky to miss out. On tour his priceless acceleration in midfield would have been a valuable asset playing alongside his Scottish co-centre Ian McGeechan who, with Bennett, was probably the only certainty for the Test side.

Before the tour party flew out, a couple of changes were necessary. Welsh lock Geoff Wheel failed a medical that discovered a heart flutter and Roger Uttley suffered a back spasm after the tourists had convened. They were replaced by Moss Keane and Jeff Squire. The England lock Nigel Horton sustained a broken thumb in the seventh match of the tour, against Otago, and significantly, Bill Beaumont, his England team-mate, flew out to replace him. The burly England lock established his credentials quickly on arrival and was arguably the find of the tour, his clean lineout catching and power in the rucks and mauls making him an integral part of the pack for the last three Tests. 'Why wasn't he chosen originally?' critics asked.

There simply could not have been a greater contrast between this trip and the previous Lions odyssey to South Africa, which took place in sunny weather and fast conditions, proceeding with a certain glamour and with the respect of the South African rugby people and the nation. On the 1977 tour, the tourists were unlucky to hit one of the wettest New Zealand winters on record. Rain and mud seemed to afflict every match and the depressing conditions did nothing for the Lions' back play.

Furthermore, there was a harshness and a lack of civility in the reaction to the team on the part of the home media and public, something which many put down to the thirst for revenge after 1971. 'The bad news tour', it was called, the result of what seemed to amount to a hate campaign waged by New Zealand tabloids that labelled the Lions 'lousy lovers', louts and animals.

It induced a defensive reaction from the Lions and the tradition of fun that had gone hand-in-hand on previous long tours was missing. Public relations deteriorated. The Lions became stand-offish and were often obstructive and uncommunicative with their own media, some of whom – Clem Thomas among them in his role as rugby correspondent for the Observer *– fell out with the Lions management. Burrell and Dawes became very protective towards their players and ultra-sensitive to criticism, the upshot of the pressure of trying to live up to the high standards set by their immediate predecessors.*

Even so, there was only one defeat in the matches outside the Tests in New Zealand. The tourists' midweek side lost 21-9 to the New Zealand Universities four days before the First Test. The Lions played their walking wounded in this match and faced some bizarre decisions from a referee working through the law book for reasons to award penalties. The Universities kicked five altogether and their sole try was the result of an unseen knock-on.

It proved a poor omen to take into the Test in Wellington at the weekend. The Lions went one-down, losing 16-12 at Athletic Park where all the scoring took place in the first half. Grant Batty, then past his best and carrying an injury, scored the match-breaking try just before the pause, intercepting in his own half to run 60 metres to the posts. The Lions forwards were surprisingly unable to win possession in a scoreless second half.

Despite losing narrowly, morale was low and the team lacked direction. It was at this point that Terry Cobner, the Pontypool and Wales flanker, brought the pack together to forge a new spirit of

The 1977 tour party.

commitment and developed the game plan that brought reward in the Second Test. He effectively rescued the Lions from impending doom after that First Test defeat. If there was one reservation it was probably that Cobner did not demand enough quick ball after his men had won it.

The Lions made significant forward changes for the Lancaster Park Test. Derek Quinnell, Bill Beaumont and Gordon Brown were immense in the Lions engine-room, blazing the way for the pack to raise its game. The tourists regrouped admirably to level the series and win their first-ever Test in Christchurch. The highlight of the match was a corner try by JJ Williams, taking a beautifully-weighted pass from Ian McGeechan who had drawn the defence. The score gave them an early 13-0 lead, Phil Bennett having kicked three penalties. All New Zealand could muster were three Bryan Williams penalty goals as the Lions ran out 13-9 winners.

Spirits were lifted and good wins against the Maori (in a cliff hanger), Waikato, NZ Juniors and Auckland were excellent preparation for the vital Third Test at Dunedin's Carisbrook ground. Here New Zealand scored a try in the first minute and never surrendered their lead. The irony was that the Lions' forwards completely dominated the All Blacks in this match, but through poor decision-making and weak kicking their backs threw away countless opportunities in attack. The Lions were never more than a score behind until the final quarter of the match when Bruce Robertson shone in the centre for the hosts. It was, like some other games, an encounter with far too much rough play.

A tight series was decided agonisingly in the last minutes of the final Test in Auckland, when the Lions thought they had grafted out the win to draw the series. Yet they lost 10-9 when No 8 Lawrie Knight, with the help of a lucky bounce, stormed over from ten metres for a try in the corner four minutes from time. The Lions had only themselves to blame. They had won the majority of the possession and exercised a stranglehold over the All Blacks for 60 minutes during which they established a 9-3 lead. They were so dominant up front that one New Zealand newspaper reported that the All Black pack 'had been shoved about like cows'.

But the Lions surrendered the lead in the last quarter by opting to throw the ball around. Their backs were unable to pierce New Zealand's tight defence and the All Blacks capitalised on trifling errors to haul themselves into a position from which they won the game and with it the series.

For the first time a Lions tour abroad attracted a considerable travelling following of British and Irish fanatics. They fell into two categories: the package tourists and the shoe-stringers – students, mostly, who hitch-hiked their ways around the main match centres or, if their pockets were deep enough, hired camper vans.

It was little wonder, then, that the entire party are said to have roared with delight when their plane took off from New Zealand for a stopover in Fiji. As founder members of the International Board, the Home Unions strictly adhered to its laws and regulations. Until 1981 the IRB forbade recognition of matches outside the Five Nations and Tri-Nations as major Tests. For that reason Lions games against the likes of Fiji, Canada, Ceylon and Argentina were never accorded full, official Test status. This was also the first Lions tour to New Zealand which did not have a segment in Australia.

It was just as well that match did not have Test status as the tour ended with an international in Suva where the Lions were beaten 25-21 and, just to pile on the anguish, the party was held up by an air-traffic controllers' strike at Heathrow before arriving home 12 hours late. It was a defeat that caused severe soul-searching amongst those charged with giving a technical lead back at home. The truth was that the team winning possession lost the match. An unwanted rugby first.

MOSS KEANE (Ireland)
Toured: 1977

I packed a modest bag, big enough to hold two pairs of underpants, four pairs of socks with holes in five, a jumper with no elbows, a pair of jeans, pants for good wear and three bottles of Lucozade, just in case they didn't sell it in New Zealand.

ANDY IRVINE

It was regarded as an unhappy tour because the weather was terrible. It really did rain a lot. And we also had a lot of injuries.

IAN McGEECHAN

Absolutely nothing on that tour seemed to turn out quite as British & Irish rugby supporters had hoped. It was not the glorious moment; it was a grim, doomed, endless slog. It was interminable, not enjoyable in the slightest.

MIKE GIBSON (Ireland)
Toured: 1966, 1968, 1971, 1974 & 1977

I injured my back in about the second training session and it affected my hamstring, and thereafter I was rarely in a position to compete for a Test place. I spent more time on the physiotherapists' couches than on training grounds. You often used to think that if you had an injury you could have a super time on tour, but you didn't. You just wanted to play rugby.

ANDY IRVINE

When you're not winning you tend not to bond as well as a team. It's pretty obvious that it's easier to build up a rapport on the back of victories. In South Africa we had a very stable Test side, whereas in '77 it changed a lot – partly because of injury and partly because of players losing form. And if you look at successful sides, the one thing they always have is consistency in selection.

BILL BEAUMONT (England)
Toured: 1977 & 1980. Manager: 2005

The Lions had been in New Zealand for a month before I arrived as a replacement, and I was sharing a room with Fran Cotton before my first tour game in Timaru against Mid-Canterbury. Fran told me that I would always remember Timaru for the rest of my life because it was the place where I played my first game for the Lions. He was right.

PHIL ORR (Ireland)
Toured: 1977

It just rained all the time and you couldn't really get out, which wasn't much fun. It was the tour of the famous Fran Cotton mudbath photograph against the Junior All Blacks in Wellington. He was one in the lineout, I was three and in a matching condition.

PETER SQUIRE (England)
Toured: 1977

Because of the Lions' success in 1971 the pressure was on, and New Zealand were out to ensure that they won the series. You had a sense the whole way through that the country was against us. There was pressure on them to win, and also on us to do as well as the 1971 Lions. That team had outstanding world-class backs, with Gerald Davies and Barry John scoring fantastic tries, and we were expected to play like that. We were also expecting to play an expansive game, but when we found ourselves in New Zealand's wettest winter for 20 years, playing on bog-heaps, it moved more towards a forwards game. The conditions were captured in the classic photo of Fran Cotton covered in mud.

FRAN COTTON

All 30 players looked the same, it just so happens I was the one immortalised by Colin Elsey, the photographer. It poured with rain throughout the match and for the last quarter of an hour you could only recognise people by their mannerisms or the way they ran. Obviously I had no idea of the significance of that picture until a few weeks later when I arrived at Twickenham to play for the Lions against the Barbarians to celebrate the Queen's Jubilee. When we drove into the West Stand car park, everyone, and I mean everyone, was waving the match programme on which yours truly was featured on the back cover!

PETER SQUIRE

Moss Keane was the outstanding character. He was a big, generous monster of a man, and a great storyteller – if you could understand what he was saying! He had a very strong Irish accent, and he liked a drink or two, and sometimes would get a bit wild, although usually he would collapse when he'd had his fill. His tour number was 33, but no one laughed when he said 'Tirty Tree'. I roomed with him and Willie Duggan, who

Phil Bennett emphasises a point during a break in play.

was another big character. Willie tended to keep his own hours, and the only way you knew he was back in the room was because he was a chain-smoker. By the end of the tour you knew these guys better than you knew most of your England team-mates. You had spent longer in the trenches with them and you developed lasting friendships.

MOSS KEANE

Willie Duggan was a very good rugby player and he was an enigma. He never believed in training and his brain was unreal.

WILLIE DUGGAN (Ireland)

Toured: 1977

I always smoked before I went out because I was of a nervous disposition. I had to try to relax.

PETER WHEELER (England)

Toured: 1977 & 1980

The classic schoolboy error on tour was letting someone know your room number because your bar bill could grow to epic proportions. Hotel telephone operators were always buttered up by everyone in the tour party because calls home were so important, but there was always ducking and diving to get away with not picking up the bloody great telephone bills to the UK.

PHIL ORR

We didn't see a great deal of New Zealand and there was much too much rugby. It would be nice to go and see New Zealand properly. I'm not a rugby fanatic and I like to get away from it but one of the problems of being on a Lions tour is that it is difficult to do that. It's relentless and the intensity of interest is incredible. I remember in one town waking up in the morning and switching on the radio – it was the morning of the match – to find that the station which was broadcasting was doing so live from breakfast in our hotel. When you wake up on the morning of a match the last thing you want to do is be interviewed over your cornflakes. So everyone ordered breakfast in bed, which didn't go down too well with the public, but you can understand why we did it. That sort of pressure you didn't need.

PETER WHEELER

The press guys were part of the tour, and there was no reason not to trust each other, however in 1977 it changed a bit when the New Zealand tabloids got stuck in. One week it was 'Lions are Lousy Lovers' and then the next week it was 'Lions are Thugs'.

PETER SQUIRE

We were not prepared for the 'Lions are Lousy Lovers' stuff in their tabloids. We didn't have media training in those days and it did get to everybody a bit. The siege mentality got stronger the longer the tour went on.

ANDY IRVINE

The captain almost certainly would have been Mervyn Davies, but he had to retire the previous season so Benny [Phil Bennett] became the Welsh captain and it must have been seen as logical for him to take on the Lions job. I thought we were really unlucky. We maybe got a wee bit more than our fair share of luck in '74 but that evened itself out three years later. That '77 team was definitely better than the results showed. We had a great front-five.

WILLIE DUGGAN

It's my view New Zealand have never seen a pack of forwards like that before. The eight guys we had were so physical but we also all had rugby skills. We were able to match them up front for strength, aggression and will to win.

IAN McGEECHAN

John Dawes disappointed me as a coach. I was looking forward to learning from him. It may seem remarkable to say now that he was the first backs coach I had ever had. I was expecting a lot and, strangely, he didn't say a lot. He talked mostly in generalities, and he was never really specific about what he wanted.

FRAN COTTON

In 1977 we did not have the same collective attitude to fitness that existed in 1974, and there were not as many world-class players. However, the one that I would have to pick as world-class on that tour is Graham Price. Pricey really came of age, and at that time was the best tight-head in the world.

BILL BEAUMONT

The style of play we had in New Zealand was too forward-orientated. Forward power wasn't enough to win us the series.

ANDY IRVINE

The coach was John Dawes, who tended to concentrate more on the backs. Phil Bennett, the captain, was also a back. So the forwards were lacking in decision-making and organisation. Terry Cobner emerged as the forwards coach and he did a very good job. He was a school teacher and had done a bit of coaching so he was highly respected and regarded, but relative to the calibre of the likes of Mervyn Davies and Fergus Slattery, our back-row wasn't nearly as strong.

BILL BEAUMONT

I've always liked John Dawes and there was no doubting the record that he had achieved as a player and then as a coach with Wales, but he wasn't up to coaching a Lions tour. He let events overwhelm him – and he's not the first or the last person who has had that happen to them on a tour of New Zealand. As a player who had been there and done it, he assumption was that he would be able to handle the situation, but the intense pressure of coaching is very different to the pressure of playing. The media spotlight got to him and I think that by the end it had totally distracted him – I think it's fair to say that, as players, none of us learned anything from him while we were on that tour, which is very sad because he had a lot to offer. A tour like that needs a big, focussed personality in charge as coach, someone who would have kept rugby at the forefront and not allowed himself to be distracted. I think that if someone like Carwyn James had coached that tour we would have won the series.

IAN McGEECHAN

Some of the Welsh lads on the tour were not really up to the challenge. They did not have the mentality of a winning Lion.

PETER SQUIRE

Andy Irvine played outstandingly in a not very outstanding backline. Andy was very much an individual talent, and he did make mistakes, but he would also do the unpredictable. He was always looking to counter-attack, and he had the pace and skill to do something about it. Phil Bennett was a great player, but didn't play his best rugby on that tour.

PHIL BENNETT (Wales)
Toured: 1974 & 1977

I should never have accepted the captaincy for that tour. I have long thought about what would have happened had it gone to someone else. The pressure of those three months on tour was just too much for me and when the matches were over, I just wanted to leave New Zealand as soon as I could – I had a young family at home that I hadn't wanted to leave and every weakness that I had as a player and a tourist was subsequently exposed. It was a very difficult period in my life.

IAN McGEECHAN

Terry Cobner took charge of the forwards after the First Test and they became a superb unit. But we never got the ball back from the forwards at the right time. They would take the ball on and on but then they would wait until the momentum stopped before giving the ball back. I kept chipping away at Cob. I told him that he had to let the ball go when we were on the front foot, they shouldn't wait till they couldn't do anything with it any-more, and only then give it back… It must have been humiliating for the New Zealand forwards – and old All Black forwards were probably turning in their graves – but we never cashed in on our forward superiority. Typically, as they always were, the All Blacks were incredibly smart… They didn't bother committing too many forwards, they almost gave up on it and not just when they did the famous three-man scrum. Their back-row held off and that meant that when we won the ball we were outnumbered.

BILL BEAUMONT

We lost 21-9 to the New Zealand Universities and John Dawes blew his lid. We were only three or four days out from playing the First Test, but he made us do one of the most brutal training sessions I've ever experienced. It made no sense at all to be doing a fitness session that close to the First Test. The midweek side had played the day before and although they had lost they certainly didn't need to do a fitness session, and the Test team (none of whom had been involved in the loss) should have been rested or preparing for the Test. But instead we were all run into the ground. I remember that after we had been sprinting around for about an hour we had a two minute rest and then split into backs and forwards to go through our unit drills. Everyone just collapsed during the rest and lay on the ground – no one could speak; there wasn't a joke cracked, or anything. No one could even swear.

We did some unit drills and then the forwards were made to do a huge scrummaging session. When it was finally all over we headed back to our hotel. We were down in Christchurch and had to cross a bridge over the River Avon to get back to the hotel, but some of the boys were so knackered that they just waded through the water in complete silence rather than walk the extra distance to the bridge.

To make matters worse we did another sprint session the next day. It was ludicrous. By the time the Test match came around, we were all still reeling from it all. Everyone's legs were so heavy and our bodies were all stiff and sore. It was pretty much the worst preparation for a Test match you could imagine.

PETER WHEELER

I never had a problem with the management on that tour – it was more the way we were treated by the Home Unions. We knew that the game was strictly amateur so we wouldn't get paid, but it was damn difficult to get anything out of them – there was never any decent kind of entertainment budget, so we often had to get the New Zealand liaison officer to pick up our drinks tab; there was a very limited telephone allowance; and we didn't even have enough shirts to allow us to exchange and keep our match jerseys. I played in seven Tests in my Lions career over two tours, but I only managed to keep two shirts.

IAN McGEECHAN

The rain almost created a state of siege. The golf courses were flooded and there was almost nothing to do. Andy Irvine, Bruce Hay, and Doug Morgan, the three Scots, and myself spent our time playing snooker, usually in army or navy clubs, potting away while back at the hotel our training kit was steaming on the radiator. My snooker improved out of sight but I am not sure that our rugby did.

MOSS KEANE

I must have been playing well against the Universities because I got a dunt from one of their players. (Willie) Duggan came down from the stands when they brought me in. I thought I was in Vancouver with Lansdowne. This paramedic says I shouldn't play again for at least two weeks and Duggan was very strong on this. Yet there I was, playing a Test match four days later, against the All Blacks, for f***'s sake. I remember being inside in the dressing room. Terry Cobner was leading the pack, saying we're all Celts – there were five Welsh and three Irish. I just had this feeling of unreality, 'What am I doing here?' type of thing. Most of the match is a blank. That ruined the tour for me, basically.

ANDY IRVINE

We definitely deserved to lose the First Test. Ironically we played with the wind in the first half and lost a few tries, and when we turned into the wind we actually played a lot better and managed to get ourselves almost back into the game.

PETER WHEELER

The environment in New Zealand was fairly hostile wherever we went and the weather was horrendous the entire time we were there. It rained incessantly. There was huge pressure on both side to perform in the Test series – we had a huge burden of expectation on our shoulders after '71 and '74, and the Kiwis had a lot to prove: they had lost in '71, of course, and they had also lost to South Africa in '76, so they were desperate for the win. That whole feeling of desperation spread across the entire country, from the All Blacks to all the provincial players, to the media and the public – they were all hostile towards us and there was a sense of hysteria about the whole thing. They were on a mission and when they won the First Test, the pressure really began to build further. We knew that if we lost the Second Test, that was the series gone.

It's amazing when you look back and consider that before that match, no Lions side had ever won the Second Test in New Zealand – and no Lions side had ever won a Test match in Christchurch. The weather, predictably, was dreadful – absolutely

The First Test in Wellington.

torrential rain, gale-force winds, the lot. And our changing room was grim; I can still picture it so vividly – a cold concrete room with poor lighting that was completely empty except for some little wooden benches. Psychologically the whole experience either breaks you or drives you to shove it back at them, to prove that the environment doesn't affect you. The whole thing is a battle.

PETER SQUIRE

Bruce Robertson and Bryan Williams were class acts, and Grant Batty was effective, but could be a petulant, stroppy character. He threw a punch at me in the First Test and after a few pints at the post-match dinner we had a wingers' union convention with players from both teams where he was warned of future conduct and told not to strike other wings. He took it in good part. Batty was a difficult opponent, tigerish and a good footballer, but I would rather have played against him than Bryan Williams, who was big, powerful and quick with a very good hand-off.

BILL BEAUMONT

I was selected to play in the midweek game against Marlborough-Nelson Bays four days before the Second Test and was amazed to see that Gordon Brown had been picked along-side me. The sectors obviously wanted to see how we played together and the general chat in the changing room was that if I played well, we would be partnered in the Second Test. For a change on that tour it wasn't raining – in fact, it was a warm afternoon – and we flat-tened them 40-23, but I remember being absolutely whacked after an hour or so because of the pace we were playing at. I pulled Gordon aside and said, 'I can't keep this up, I'm knackered.' He turned to look at me and fixed me with those big blue eyes of his and said softly, 'We are going into the Test team together – and if I see you drop off anything in the next twenty minutes, I'm going to belt you as hard as I can.' And that was that – I kept go-ing and so did he and he drove me all the way through that last twenty minutes – and, as he promised, we were partnered together for the Second Test.

PETER WHEELER

There were five changes in the pack from the First Test and Terry Cobner emerged as a binding influence as pack leader. I remember before we ran out he took us into the shower room and told us that we were not alone out there in New Zealand, that the lights would be coming on in the Welsh valleys in the small hours as people listened to the radio reports. It was very emotional stuff. You could see the raw emotion in the eyes of some of the hardest men I know – Fran Cotton, Graham Price, Willie Dug-gan, Derek Quinnell, Gordon Brown – tears were running down their faces. At that stage you had to hold us back from just charging out there. The intensity of the mo-ment was just incredible.

WILLIE DUGGAN

The Second Test was the most physical game of rugby I have ever played in; a real humdinger of a game. It was a game we had to win and when I say it was physical, it came to fisticuffs and whatever had to be done was done. It is what I would call a good old-fashioned game of rugby where the referee didn't get involved. I believe there shouldn't be a referee on the field. Let the lads sort it out themselves.

BILL BEAUMONT

The Second Test will not go down in the annals of history as one of the great games. It was niggly, hard, with lots of off-the-ball incidents, but the Lions had never won in Christchurch before, and we were very determined.

PETER WHEELER

There was a general understanding that we wouldn't take any nonsense from the All Blacks – we had to defend ourselves and if there was any nonsense then you reacted. Phil Bennett had been targeted throughout the tour with late tackles – they knew how important he was to us and that in form he could win any match for us on his own. Kevin Eveleigh hit him with a shocker in the Second Test and I just laid into him. That was such a tough match. It was my first Test for the Lions and it was the hardest game I'd very played. I learned a lot about myself with that Test – the intensity and the emotion that surrounded it left me drained afterwards and I slunk into a real low in the days that followed.

Graham Price attmepts to charge-down Sid Going's clearnace kick in the Second Test.

ANDY IRVINE

We deserved to win the Second Test, and we had our chances to win the Third Test as well but we missed our kicks at goal.

FRAN COTTON

After we beat them in the Second Test the New Zealanders did the unthinkable and dropped Syd Going and brought in Lyn Davis, a passing scrum-half. They also introduced a very quick openside, Graham Mourie. Those changes won them the series because from then on they moved the ball very quickly away from the forward contest, where they were coming second.

We had an exceptional pack of forwards, and we were really dominant, especially in the Third and Fourth Tests. But the conditions were atrocious and the backs lost confidence. It was almost a bit of an event if they got the ball along the line without dropping it. The minimum we should have got was a drawn series, and we were good enough to win it.

BILL BEAUMONT

Technically you won't get better than the Lions front-row of Fran Cotton, Peter Wheeler and Graham Price, and we dominated the scrums to the extent that in the Fourth Test New Zealand were forced into a three-man scrum after losing a prop injured and putting a back-rower in the front-row. It was ignominy for them to do it given the tradition of All Black forward might, but they were smart, and had worked out that it was the best way for them to win their own ball cleanly.

ANDY IRVINE

In the Fourth Test they put three in the scrums at some points because we were just so dominant. Of course, we didn't have the common sense to keep the ball in the scrum and drive them back. We dominated that Test, and they got one try from a speculative kick – three of our guys were after it but it bounced over all their heads and into the arms of Lawrie Knight, and he just touched it down. That was just sheer bad luck.

FRAN COTTON

For an All Black pack to swallow its pride and go for a three-man scrum sounds unthinkable, but it got them quick ball, and it was not the only area where they out-thought us. The lowest point in my rugby career was the 1977 final Test. To dominate and then lose to a soft try right at the end was hard to take.

JOHN DAWES

We had a pack to take on the world, in fact we had two packs that could, and did, lick the All Blacks and by the final Test New Zealand were reduced to pitiful three-man scrums. I have never seen opposition forwards so humbled in the tight. But I took my eye off the backs, didn't show them the attention to detail that I should have.

BILL BEAUMONT

Two lapses of concentration undid all the magnificent work of the pack.

WILLIE DUGGAN

The First Test they won by an interception by Grant Batty, the Second Test we won and in the Third Test we were annihilated. And in the Fourth Test I got over in the last minute but couldn't get the ball down.

BILL BEAUMONT

I never felt more frustrated after a match than I did after that final Test. I remember coming off the field at Eden Park and just thinking, 'How did we lose that?' Their score to win it was tough to swallow, but we should have been out of sight by then. We'd gone for a pushover try on their line earlier on and were moving forward – it was going to happen – and then Willie Duggan picked up at No 8 and was held up. It was so frustrating. I just thought, 'Why? We were about to push them over their own line!'

WILLIE DUGGAN

Basically the Test series hinged on an interception and a silly mistake.

BILL BEAUMONT

It was hard to believe we had crushed the All Blacks up front in two successive Tests, only to lose both.

PETER SQUIRE

I remember the shout of relief and pleasure when the flight home left New Zealand soil. We lost to Fiji on our way back on a three-day stopover, but by then the players had had enough and just wanted to relax. That was when Fran Cotton said, 'Why couldn't it have been 14 weeks in Fiji and three days in New Zealand?'

Bill Beaumont presents the ball to Dougie Morgan in the Fourth Test.

CHAPTER TWENTY-ONE

EXTERNAL PRESSURES APPLY
1980

SOUTH AFRICA

T HIS WAS *a tour which took place against a heavy and difficult backdrop. As a protest against apartheid in the Republic, sporting contact with South Africa and the outside world had almost ceased through a whole range of sports by 1980. As far as the Lions were concerned, early tours to South Africa had proceeded as if the divisions and tensions between the races were simply a fact of life; scattered misgivings were expressed but it wasn't until much later that rugby was drawn squarely into the firing line and consciences were pricked as contact with South Africa became a ferocious problem.*

It was a particular issue for rugby in several ways. First of all, the bond and the friendships between South African rugby and rugby in Britain and Ireland, not to mention New Zealand, meant that the firmest friendships had been established over the years and some people in rugby dearly felt that to abandon contact with South African rugby would be to renege on a friendship.

Yet unquestionably, South African rugby, white-dominated to an almost total degree, was seen by the non-white population at large as almost as significant an instrument of apartheid as the government itself and the police. This was why the 1974 team had been so riotously supported by the tiny, uncomfortable, non-white enclaves in the big grounds.

Certain changes had come about in South African rugby in 1980, notably the fact that the central administrative body absorbed the coloured rugby federation, giving limited access to a form of multi-racial rugby. But many non-whites in South Africa refused to take part, seeing it as a charade for the wider sporting world – and there is no doubt that tokenism played a large part in the selection of non-white players for several teams and tours of the era. Opinion in the world outside was unconvinced. The Olympic movement and the British government were brought into the dispute, with even Conservative administrations urging the Home Unions not to go ahead with tours and not to issue invitations for incoming tours.

Perhaps ironically, one of the administrators who pleaded with the Home Unions not to make their planned tour of South Africa in 1980, was none other than Dickie Jeeps, the magnificent Lion of 1955, 1959 and 1962, who by now was chairman of the Sports Council.

Perhaps the only distraction, and it was a happy one for the unions, was that America's boycott of the 1980 Olympic Games in Moscow was for a time a bigger issue. In the end, the Lions continued the tradition by departing for South Africa, although it was to be the last Lions tour to the Republic for no less than 17 years, a situation which, happily, led to the return of Australia to the Lions itinerary as a touring venue in itself.

At least the rugby authorities could agree on something – that Bill Beaumont, the English lock, would be the tour captain, and remarkably, he was the first Englishman to lead the Lions for 50

---

years. He had led England to a rare Grand Slam in the 1980 Five Nations, was highly respected throughout the game and was to do a splendid job on tour.

Perhaps even better news was the fact that, at long last, the principle of neutral referees had come into rugby. Surviving Lions and the ghosts of Lions long dead must have deemed it a move long overdue. Francis Palmade and Jean-Pierre Bonnet from France travelled to South Africa to control the Test series.

It was a time of depression in the economy, and a time when the demands on top players were becoming almost astronomical. So even though fast air travel was now available and there were almost infinitely improved internal communications in South Africa, it was obvious that the days of the long tours were well in the past. The 1980 trip was the first shorter tour of the modern era with only 18 games arranged – and, by the standards of 2013, even this was something of a monster trip.

Within this period of transition for rugby, and also for rugby in a wider landscape, what no one could do was legislate for the hand of fate. This was a tour savaged by injuries, with no fewer than eight replacements being called on. Poor Stuart Lane, the fast flanker from Gwent and Wales, tore his ligaments with the tour just one minute old, as the Lions kicked off against Eastern Province.

If anyone hoped that this was not to be a portent for the future, then they were sadly mistaken. At fly-half, just to give one more example, the Lions had to play three different men in the four-match Test series – Gareth Davies, Ollie Campbell and Tony Ward. Perhaps the only good news was that, again at long last, the Lions actually took a doctor with them in the party in the shape of Dr Jack Matthews, the Lion of 1950. They needed him.

The rest of the management team was made up by Syd Millar, the coach of the celebrated Lions of 1974, and Noel Murphy, the flanker and former Lion, whose coaching pedigree never quite matched that of Millar.

One sad echo of the previous Lions tour, to New Zealand in 1977, was that the Lions pack was powerful enough to stand up to the home teams in all the primary phases and ruck and maul and even, as it proved in the Tests, to get the better of the Springbok pack. But the Lions backs could not cash in. This was such a sad reversal of history that not even the heavy toll of injured players behind the Lions scrum could provide a complete excuse.

The shorter tour brought out another problem – with the First Test on any Lions tour being of absolutely overwhelming importance, there were now far fewer Saturday games to groom the selection and performance of the Test team. There were still some very fine Lions performances. John O'Driscoll, the blind side flanker, played in every match of the Test series, relished the physical challenge of the Springbok pack and scored the winning try in the Fourth Test with a surging run to the posts. Peter Wheeler, the hooker from Leicester and England, was also ever-present in a Lions Test front-row that provided a solid platform.

A single try in a match against a South African invitation team might appear at first an odd thing to single out as a highlight – even though it was the score which saved the Lions from an almost certain defeat, having trailed 15-6 at one stage. But this extraordinary try saw the ball transferred between around 30 pairs of hands in all, beginning with David Richards, the Swansea centre, making a break from a lineout; the ball went through ruck after ruck after ruck, often with Derek Quinnell maintaining continuity, before Mike Slemen escaped the covering defence to score under the posts. The whole move lasted not far short of two minutes and has been included in all Lions compilations ever since.

The Springboks at the time were an excellent team, with Morné du Plessis as captain – a worthy opponent in terms of international stature for Beaumont. They also had at fly-half Naas Botha, another

n a long line of outstanding Springbok kickers, the kind who had tortured the Lions since the days of
Bennie Osler. Botha was never a great all-round rugby player, but often, he did not have to be.

Elsewhere, Louis Moolman was a gigantic second-row, so huge that one British writer observed
that when Beaumont was standing next to Moolman in the lineout, it seemed as if Big Bill was
standing in a large hole. Another superb player was Gysie Pienaar, an excellent attacking fullback.

To their credit, the Lions won all their provincial games on tour, with highlights being victories
over Orange Free State, Transvaal and Western Province, this latter in the shape of a thumping 37-6
victory in Cape Town. However, in the Tests they simply lacked firepower and steady organisation
behind the scrum, with Davies, Ward and Campbell all alternating at fly-half. They were hindered
by a lack of any real bite in the outside backs and injuries compounded their problems further,
forcing the team to play in a constant state of flux.

Perhaps the most worrying time on tour came in the match against the South African Federation,
which was a rough battle up front. Fran Cotton, the titan of the 1974 and 1977 tours, was suddenly
led from the field with chest pains, and was clearly in some distress. The obvious anxiety was that
he had suffered a heart attack, although the problem was eventually diagnosed as pericarditis, an
inflammation around the muscles of the heart. Cotton made a full recovery but was not to play again
on tour. He was badly missed.

The First Test took place at Newlands in Cape Town, with the Lions at one stage 16-6 down
before they came surging back to draw level at 22-22 just six minutes before the end, and apparently
with momentum now very much on their side. Tony Ward scored 18 points with some splendid
kicking, and Graham Price, the Pontypool prop, scored a try. Yet South Africa had scored three tries,
and at the end, they seized the game when Divan Serfontein scored a dramatic winning try.

In the Second Test, Andy Irvine, another hero of 1974, had arrived as a replacement and was chosen
at fullback. The Lions controlled long periods of the game, but even then the only Lions try, by the fierce
O'Driscoll, could not prevent South Africa building a 16-6 lead. Yet again, the Lions came back and
trailed only by one point with 15 minutes remaining. But they made too many errors, and with Gareth
Davies badly damaging knee ligaments to disrupt the flow, the Springbok wing, Gerrie Germishuys,
the 1980 tour party.

and fullback, Gysie Pienaar, scored tries, and the Lions found that they had passed up another wonderful opportunity. The powerful and popular Ray Gravell did score a consolation try for them at the end.

This tour was the first involvement with the Lions of Clive Woodward, eventually to pilot England to World Cup glory 23 years later. Woodward was replaced in the centre by Paul Dodge for the Third Test, with Woodward, in turn, replacing John Carleton on the wing. The Lions led 10-6 in the second half with a try by Bruce Hay but again, and even though some South Africans admitted that the Lions were superior, there was another late try by Germishuys and a Lions team which had won plenty of possession, had disastrously lost the match and the series.

There was consolation of sorts in the final Test, won with courage by 17-13, and so the 1980 party did not after all become the first Lions to be whitewashed in the Republic. A mini-burst of two tries in under five minutes from Irvine and O'Driscoll gave the Lions the victory, but even then the margin did not reflect in any way their forward dominance.

The Lions were left to rue their luck; they were also left to rue their own failings in their painful failure to cash in on possession. They were left to wonder when next they would travel to South Africa, the place which above all had put Lions tours on the map of the sporting world; and to wonder what they could have done on their tours, if only one of their grand forward packs of history had more frequently managed to team up with one of their illustrious back divisions. The heady optimism of the early 1970s was fading away.

SYD MILLAR

In those days apartheid was a raging subject and we got a lot of abuse, but I had a very simple philosophy. Rightly or wrongly I felt that politicians should not interfere with sport. We asked the South Africans to play mixed teams, which they did. We asked for mixed crowds, which we got. So we thought that was a step forward and more than the politicians were achieving. I remember one press report at the time which said the UK had improved their trading position with South Africa by tens of millions and thinking, why isn't that causing as much fuss.

You could argue for hours about the rights and wrongs of going on that trip, but my point of view is that we did achieve various things and I along with others spent a lot of time speaking to blacks and coloureds and finding out how we might help them in rugby terms, so it was a positive experience and I have no regrets.

OLLIE CAMPBELL (Ireland)
Toured: 1980 & 1983

In my innocence, and it's no defence at this stage of my life, I was cocooned in this sort of rugby world that I was living in and all I wanted to do was play rugby. I was that innocent. I was almost oblivious to the political controversy that was raging at that time. It's a very weak defence, it's almost uncomfortable, it's almost embarrassing saying it now to be so unaware of the repercussions but I was so immersed in the game I was virtually oblivious to the whole issue, strange and unbelievable though that may sound.

MIKE SLEMEN (England)

Toured: 1980

When I first went to South Africa in 1978 with North West Counties, the black and coloured players I talked to after games wanted contact, and we were young guys who wanted to go and play against one of the best rugby nations. I was invited to talk on a current affairs programme on BBC2 before the 1980 tour, on which there was a black speaker talking against apartheid. I said that a Lions tour was a great sporting experience, and that there was nothing we could do about apartheid. I also argued that a sports boycott by the British government was a double standard because wherever you went in South Africa all you saw were international companies, many of them British.

JIM RENWICK (Scotland)

Toured: 1980

I was only there to play rugby, but you can't help notice what's going on around you. If I really thought we could change it by not going to play rugby there then I might have had a different attitude. But I felt: if you stop dealing with them is that the solution? Does that make the situation better or worse? Maybe if you can see how bad it is then that helps the situation because it's in your face. I always think that if there's a problem you speak about it – that's what I was taught to do. When we stopped trading with South Africa it was like we were doing our bit and we didn't have to think about it anymore – out of sight out of mind.

Graham Price, Peter Wheeler and Phil Orr.

JOHN ROBBIE (Ireland)
Toured: 1980

I made an early decision to go and see everything that I could. I used to get up in the morning about 7.30, have breakfast and then just go for a walk I walked the streets of every town we visited. When in Durban I walked on the beach, I chatted to fishermen, guys who had been up all night, at Umhlanga; policemen in Johannesburg; coloured dustmen in Cape Town. I was fascinated by life in South Africa and I wanted to see it all.

OLLIE CAMPBELL

I went to Soweto and the chills still go down my spine as I recall it. Was that an eye-opener! It was a beautiful day, not a cloud in the sky, but there was a cloud over Soweto which stretched as far as the eye could see. And the squalor, the smell, the kids in bare feet. That was my wake-up call, that was my sobering moment. 'What is going on here? This is what it's been all about. There is something wrong here.' It was one of the defining moments in my life. From then, I started questioning.

ALAN TOMES (Scotland)
Toured: 1980

Some of us went on a trip to a place called Sharpeville, a township near Johannesburg. They had us in the back of a truck and one of the guys threw a pocketful of change. All the kids were crawling around the street after the coins, so we all started throwing cash. Thinking about it now I'm a bit embarrassed – big shots throwing scraps to the kids – but at least they got the money I suppose.

JOHN ROBBIE

Once we arrived at our hotel in Cape Town there was a black soccer team also booking in. One of their players spoke to Billy Beaumont and said they were all very disappointed in the Lions. Billy assumed he was talking about the defeats in the first two Tests, but the guy went on to explain that he thought we should have refused the invitation to tour. He was a little bit rude and must have been overheard. Anyway, when we came back from training the soccer side had been moved to another hotel.

SYD MILLAR

I worked closely with Doc Craven of the South Africa Rugby Board, and I met with the president of the black union and the president of the coloured union. The guy from the coloured union came to the hotel and I met him and I said 'Come in.' He said, 'I can't.' I said, 'Come in.' He said, 'I'm not allowed.' I said, 'You're my guest.' And he sat down and he was very uneasy. That sort of thing did make me very uncomfortable.

PHIL BLAKEWAY (England)
Toured: 1980

Right from the start, things began to go wrong. Instead of a week's preparation in

Eastbourne, which had been standard practice for Lions parties of the past, we were whisked straight out to a training camp at Vanderbijlpark, not far from Johannesburg. In theory, it wasn't a bad idea – especially as there were plenty of groups back in Britain anxious to voice their opposition to anything connected with South Africa. The trouble was that we were on the high veldt, some 6,000 feet above sea level. You need time to acclimatise – and the management didn't give us that chance.

Noel Murphy, one of the few non-drinking Irishmen I've known, immediately proposed a 'light work-out' although all of us were still feeling the effects of a 24-hour journey. In reality, he proceeded to run the living daylights out of us. Even the fittest boys – let alone the little fat lads like me – were poleaxed. I recall Allan Martin, 'the Panther from Aberavon', taking off in a sprint around the athletics track, which made him extremely unpopular with the rest of his struggling colleagues. But we were soon struggling because, on the second time round, we discovered him spread-eagled on the ground gasping for breath.

Very soon, we were training for three hours morning and afternoon. In that heat and at that altitude, it was a suicidal policy. It knocked the stuffing out of us before the first game and I am sure it took its toll in the Tests.

MIKE SLEMEN

The main reason we lost the series was the injuries. For instance, Gareth Davies was injured in the first game against Eastern Province when he threw a long pass to me, and was hit late and hard. It meant that I scored the first try of the tour, from about 15 metres out, but it put him out for three weeks, and he only played three more tour games after that. We also lost Terry Holmes, a scrum-half who had good skills and power, and was like Mike Phillips in 2009. Flanker Stuart Lane was injured from the first kick-off in the first game. We kicked long and he was so psyched up, and chased it so well, that he put pressure on the fullback who caught it. But when he side-stepped, Stuart tried to change direction so quickly that his knee went. He didn't touch a ball in a competitive match on tour. We should have known then that it wasn't going to be our tour, but it was a series we could and should have drawn.

JIM RENWICK

I was on the bench for the first game and when Gareth Davies got hurt Syd turned to me and said, 'You're on.' But I had been watching the game and sunbathing at the same time and I couldn't find my boots. So they had a meeting about it and decided from then on boots had to be worn at all times by the subs and you had to be ready to get on as soon as anybody goes down. I maybe didn't make a very good first impression!

OLLIE CAMPBELL

Early on the tour I tweaked a hamstring and missed the first couple of games. My first game was against Natal in Durban. If I hadn't played I was going home. I couldn't touch my toes in the dressing room before the match, but I played. We sneaked a win in the hottest conditions I've ever played a match in. The following day all the blood congealed in the back of my knee and I was out for the guts of four weeks – but I wasn't sent home. I was left behind in Joburg. The doctor who was looking after me gave me as a cure for my hamstring: a zube [cough sweet]!

MIKE SLEMEN

In the non-Test games I got a lot of the ball, and there was the 'wonder try' in the game against the SA Invitation XV. This was a hard game, because it was almost a trial match for the opposition, who drafted in units like the Western Province pack *en masse*. We were losing, but this try showed what we were capable of. We kept the ball and kept moving it – I touched it three times on my wing, and Elgan Rees had it three times on his wing – before it broke down. However, from a hack into our half, Jim Renwick revived it by counter-attacking from our 22 and linking with me. About seven pairs of hands later Bruce Hay gave me an inside pass as I came infield, and I cut through from about 20 metres out to score. They always talk about the Gareth Edwards try for the Barbarians, but this went on much longer, about 90 seconds as opposed to 30 seconds. The press actually stood up and applauded.

ALAN TOMES

I was speaking to our liaison officer when we were in Bloemfontein for the Orange Free State match and he was asking what we fancied doing. I said that I had always wanted to drive a train, so he told me to meet him in the hotel foyer at half-eight the next morning. I kept it quiet and I only told Jim Renwick. The next day this guy took us along to the depot and we got to drive a train. And this wasn't any Mickey Mouse train – this was a proper piece of machinery. It was a steam engine so we had to pull the levers and the power of it was unbelievable. It was a great experience.

JIM RENWICK

Toomba became known as Casey Jones after that.

FRAN COTTON

I realised in 1980, when I had to leave the tour early, that it was the end of my international career. I had to leave the pitch during the match against the South African Federation team with chest pain as a result of pericarditis – an inflammation of the fluid lining the heart. It turned out not to be life-threatening, but I didn't know that at the time, and the doctor who did tests on me that day said he thought it was a heart attack. The diagnosis left me with a sense of disbelief given all the training I had done throughout my career. I was also newly married to Pat, we had just had a daughter, and I was 6,000 miles from home, so there were a few emotions running through my mind that night

I was transferred the next day to the Groot Schuur Hospital in Cape Town, where the heart transplant specialist Dr Christian Barnard worked, and I was sitting in a wheelchair waiting when he came past, recognised me as part of the Lions squad, and asked what I was doing there. After I'd told him, he said if there were any further complications to come upstairs and he would give me a new heart – which was not really what I wanted to hear. After the tests came back with the pericarditis diagnosis it was a huge relief, but I still had to return to the UK, and I watched the First Test at home.

PETER WHEELER

Poor Fran, we had some great times together and South Africa 1980 was no exception. On one occasion we were hacking our way down a golf course in four-balls. I missed a green and when I went to chip back I found my ball nestling next to a snake. I retreated hurriedly before my caddie told me the snake was dead. When we had all holed out I gingerly picked up the snake and popped it in the hole for the next four-ball to discover. As it happened it was Fran who first putted successfully and went gleefully to reclaim his ball, only to find the unwelcome guest I had left for him.

SYD MILLAR

In the First Test we murdered them up front. The cardinal sin on a rugby field is to miss touch and put it in opposition hands where they can run it back at you. We allowed them to stay in the game because of our mistakes.

JIM RENWICK

There's no doubt in my mind that the management wanted to play ten-man rugby, they wanted to take the 'Boks on up-front then bring big men down the middle – and to be fair I think we did beat them up front, but we didn't win the series.

Some people might say the backs let us down and I wouldn't argue with that. But they didn't put anyone in charge of the backs, we were more or less left to do it ourselves, and we had a lot of injuries to key players. None of the backs who played in the First Test had played in a Lions Test match before.

OLLIE CAMPBELL

Tony Ward kicked a record 18 points, but we lost 26-22.

JIM RENWICK

We should have won that game, but the Springboks scored a try in injury time. It was a bad try to give away. A guy called Dave Smith, who was playing in the centre, had a go at us. He broke a few tackles and set up a good ruck, and Divan Serfontein, the scrum-half, dived over the line.

OLLIE CAMPBELL

Like every Lions tour everything depends on the First Test. You win the First Test and your tour is alive until the final whistle of the final game. You lose the First Test and suddenly the dynamic just changes. It was a match we really should have won.

MIKE SLEMEN

My wife, Eileen, was six months pregnant with our second child when I left for South Africa. The problem was that our lad became sick with croup, and because she was looking after him, she became ill. The medics were worried that she would lose the baby girl, which wasn't moving, and I found out she had gone into hospital on the morning of the First Test. She had kept it from me, and it was upsetting when she broke down on the phone, and, after speaking to her mother, I knew I had to go back. I told the management I had to go straight away, but there was nothing that I could do. I couldn't get a flight immediately, and Bill Beaumont persuaded me to play.

I was in hospital seeing my wife, and we were listening to the Second Test on the radio, when I saw she was crying because she felt guilty. It was strange not to be there, but she supported me in everything I did in rugby, and this was more important – our daughter now has children of her own. The Lions had replaced me, and under the rules they could not bring me back, so my tour was only five matches long. It wasn't until quite a few years afterwards that I realised I was the top try scorer.

ANDY IRVINE

I picked up an injury at the Hong Kong Sevens a month before and really struggled to get fit. I thought I had made it in time and got on the plane to London, but I got a fitness test there and they weren't happy with my hamstring and sent me home.

I remember listening to the First Test match on the radio and they lost, with one of the boys getting injured – and I thought to myself that I might have a wee chance of getting called out. Then, within ten minutes the phone rang and I was told to pack my bags. But it wasn't because of the injury, it was because Mike Slemen's wife had taken ill and he was having to come home.

Fran Cotton is assisted from the field with worrying chest pains.

I ended up playing in three Tests but I was a bit of a basket case, because I could play on the Saturday but would then be on the physio table all the next week – they were just patching me up to keep me going.

SYD MILLAR

The Second Test was a wet day and at half-time Doc Craven said to me, 'Look at the pitch.' I said, 'What do you mean, Doc?' He said, 'Three-quarters is green, one quarter is mud. You have been playing on the Springbok line and they haven't been out of their half.' And he was right.

OLLIE CAMPBELL

We should have won. When I came on with about 15 minutes to go there wasn't much between the teams. Ray Gravell, the one and only, was playing in the centre. He always looked like he was a man of such incredible confidence when in actual fact he was quite insecure. A fantastic character, life and soul of the tour. I'm running on and in my head I'm expecting Grav to say, 'Well done on your Test debut,' and offer me a bit of encouragement as to what we might do and the way the game is going, but none of that at all. What does he say to me as I run on? He says, 'How do you think I'm playing?' and, 'Do you think I'm playing well enough to get selected for the Third Test?' Knowing Grav, I said, 'Grav, you are having a stormer!' But that was another one that slipped through our fingers.

JOHN BEATTIE (Scotland)
Toured: 1980 & 1983

I got really friendly with Rodney O'Donnell. He was really superstitious: he refused to come out of his room on Friday 13th; if he walked along a pavement and stepped on a line he'd have to go way back and start again; and when I roomed with him he had to jump into his bed and hit the top and bottom sheet at the same time – it would take him 20 efforts.

He broke his neck playing against the Junior Springboks. He did it tackling Danie Gerber, their number 13. He broke his sixth and seventh vertebrae which, of course, added up to 13 – which he was quick to point out to everyone. He is an amazing man.

He had an operation while we were there and a big frame bolted onto his head and neck. He's still around now, coaching St Mary's College – so he was a lucky guy after all, I suppose.

OLLIE CAMPBELL

The Third Test and we're playing in Port Elizabeth in the torrential rain. It had rained for a week. They had put up these temporary massive stands and it was jammed. We arrived at the ground and Wardy (Tony Ward) had forgotten his boots. Can you believe it? Now that wasn't something he was going to say to Noel Murphy. So he goes around the dressing room, 'Anybody have a spare pair of boots?' The only one who had a spare pair was Colin Patterson and Colin wore size seven and a half and they were training boots with moulded soles, just for the hard grounds. They were not meant for that kind of day. Shortly before we got out, the subs are asked to leave the dressing room and they are up at the back of the highest stand so it takes them an age to get up there. By the time they sat down we've kicked-off. I have one scar on my face from my playing career and it happened within ten seconds of the start of that Test match. I kick off, ball goes loose, I go down on it and Rob Louw comes in with his boot. There's blood pumping out of my face. Meanwhile, Tony is making himself comfortable in the stand. The first thing he sees is me down on the ground.

JOHN ROBBIE

Wardy asked me what the hell he should do now. I said, 'Pray as hard as you can.' It must have worked because Ollie somehow continued.

BILL BEAUMONT

The weather was terrible, with lashing rain and a howling gale. With about ten minutes left to play, we were 10-6 up after Bruce Hay had scored a try and Ollie Campbell had kicked two penalties. Then disaster struck... Clive Woodward normally played centre but had been selected on the wing and made the kind of mistake that is typical when someone plays out of position. He chased after a loose ball and side-tapped it into touch and then turned his back and ran off to get back into position. I was about 30 yards away and hammering across the pitch and it was one of the worst moments of my career because I could see exactly what was about to happen. Clive was jogging away and his opposite number, Gerrie Germishuys, picked up the ball and took a quick throw-in to their flanker, Theuns Stofberg, who passed it back to him, and Germishuys belted up the wing to score in the corner. Naas Botha kicked the conversion and for the third time in three Tests we had been the cause of our own downfall.

PETER WHEELER

The situation seemed unreal. We felt we were playing well enough yet there we were, three-nil down and the series gone because of lapses in concentration, no more.

JOHN BEATTIE

You'd turn up at a new ground, with the smell of barbeque smoke, sun, short grass, rock hard pitches, and huge blokes with suntans against you. And it was that artificiality of people hating you, and waking you up the night before a match by blasting their horns outside your hotel, everywhere you went they were against you.

They really didn't like you, they really wanted to beat you, and that was fair enough, I suppose. But then a few days later I would be amazed at how social they could be. You would drive to a farm and this guy would have slaughtered a beast the night before for a barbeque, and he couldn't do enough for you.

ALAN TOMES

Jim Renwick and I had a bed marathon after the last provincial game. I think we'd just had enough by then. The Griqualand West game had been a really dirty match. We were knackered after two months of tough touring. We were sick of eating steak all the time. We weren't going to get in the Test side. It was wind down time for us really, so we decided to stay in bed for two days, and all we ate was beans on toast. Word got round the hotel that we were doing a bed marathon so guys kept coming up to see what the chat was. It was good fun.

JOHN BEATTIE

I actually went AWOL halfway through the tour. I realised it wasn't working for me and that I wasn't going to make the team so I switched off. I remember going to watch a black folk singer perform in a pub. He sang 'Nkosi Sikelel' iAfrika' and I thought it was a beautiful song. It was all about freedom, and now it's the national anthem. But back then going to see a black man singing in a pub was deemed weird. We had to smuggle ourselves in there. I had more fun doing those things than doing the usual tour stuff. Maybe I felt more comfortable there because I was with the South African beatniks, who were in their early twenties so much closer to my age than the vast majority of the tour party.

BILL BEAUMONT

I believe that we would have won the Test series if South Africa hadn't played two warm-up matches just before we arrived against the South American Jaguars, which was effectively Argentina. In the second of those matches a terrific fullback called Gysie Pienaar emerged. He was destined to play a significant part in our downfall, but if it hadn't been for the visit of the South Americans he may well not have been considered.

OLLIE CAMPBELL

The star of that South Africa team was Gysie Pienaar, the fullback. Everything he touched turned to gold. Jack Kyle always said that the 1950 Lions would have won the series had it not been for the New Zealand fullback Bob Scott. I would say that if it hadn't been for Gysie Pienaar I think we could have drawn or won that Test series. He was that good. It was a tour of what could have been.

PETER WHEELER

It was unthinkable, after all the hard work we had put in and the pleasure we had in each other's company – and despite the number of players who had been forced out of the tour by injury or, in the case of Fran Cotton, by illness – that we would return without one win with which to console ourselves.

BILL BEAUMONT

Wherever we went as Lions we were there to be shot down because of 1971 and 1974 – it was always revenge – and that's why it was such a massive effort to win that last Test in 1980. There had been virtually nothing between the Springboks and us during the series, and virtually all the Tests could have gone either way. On that tour we won all our provincial matches, and that is the mark of a very good team. I was glad for Noel's sake that we delivered the goods in the final Test.

PETER WHEELER

It was a different tour to New Zealand in '77 and though we got a lot of injuries early on, and also lost the series 3-1, it was thoroughly enjoyable. However, a number of stars made themselves unavailable and just as there was no hard-core from 1974 left in 1977, the same was true from 1977 to 1980. The South Africans were big powerful units, but I didn't consider them to be a dirty side – just difficult to combat. I remember Maurice Colclough was being marked by the giant Springbok lock Louis Moolman, and at the lineout it was difficult to get a throw through. We eventually managed it with a hard flat throw to the middle, and Maurice, who was not lifted, was a good player and very athletic. We gave as good as we got, but lost out narrowly because we were a bit disjointed around injuries.

It was very close, and we lost the series because of small things around each Test match. Naas Botha proved for South Africa that he was a better player than simply a goal-kicking machine, and my view is that on Lions tours you had to be eight points better than the opposition before a match to win a game because of home pressure and home town refereeing. They are just a fact of life on tour.

JIM RENWICK

We had a plan to play ten-man rugby, and that is what we were going to do. But if you arrive with two or three different ways you can play then it makes life easier for you when plan A doesn't work. On a tour like that, plan A is not going to work all the time. You are coming up against different teams every three days and sometimes it might take something a wee bit different to get the result you need. Remember they are getting to see plenty of how you are playing so you have got to have something else tucked away to keep them on their toes. I'm not saying we didn't have another plan, but we didn't have it prepared like we should have.

Clive Woodward played in the centre in the Second Test and got in on the wing for the Third Test. He was probably a bit like me from the point of view that he wasn't happy with the way the back play was going, and I think he felt there should have been a backs coach. At Leicester, where he was playing, Chalkie White was the backs coach, and he was actually in South Africa at the time and there was some chat amongst the players about trying to get him involved, but it never came to anything. Most teams had two coaches. Scotland would have had Nairn McEwan and Colin Telfer doing the backs, but the Lions only had one and it was maybe time to think about changing that.

JOHN BEATTIE

I shared with Clive Woodward and he was a Rank Xerox trainee at that time. I remember he accepted a call, and then immediately said, 'Hang on,' and laid the phone down for 30 seconds, then went back on the line and finished the conversation. I asked him afterwards what that was all about and he said, 'We've been told to always be in control of every situation so that's me getting my time to think, and he's on the defensive.' So he was a guy who had been taught how to be a leader. He was a really nice man – but I remember thinking, 'Wow, you're different.'

BILL BEAUMONT

Syd Millar, Noel Murphy and myself, all of us forwards, decided that we would take on the Springboks up front. During that period our rugby had probably become too preoccupied with forward domination at the expense of back play, and as captain in 1980, I hold my hands up. When you are on top in the forwards it is easy to say, 'Let's keep it here,' and one or two of our backs got frustrated because there is no defence against quick front-foot ball, as the Springboks showed us. In South Africa we were a bit one-dimensional – the forwards kept the good ball to ourselves, and then gave the backs the bad ball and said, 'Do something with it.' I accept responsibility.

When you look back at the Lions coaches who have been successful, the ground-breaking tour was in 1971, and Carwyn James was a backs coach, and his captain was a back (John Dawes) – and that influence remained in 1974 through players like Gareth Edwards and JPR Williams. However, it is also true that we had eight different half-backs in eight games, whereas in the front-five of the pack, apart from Fran Cotton's heart problem, we stayed intact all through. Derek Quinnell said to me that we had to put more pace in the back-row, but after Stuart Lane was injured we had no real out-and-out No 7s, so in the last two Tests we played three blind-side wing-forwards in the back-row in Colm Tucker, Jeff Squire and John O'Driscoll.

PETER WHEELER

The South Africans were quick to see that the Lions were short of pace in the back-row after Stuart Lane was injured, and that it would help their cause to move the ball

wide, away from the main source of Lions strength, knowing that big flankers like Rob Louw and Theuns Stofberg would be pounding up in support. It is no coincidence that Louw scored tries in the first two Tests, and Stofberg scored in the Second Test and played a vital role in the decisive Springbok try in the Third Test.

JIM RENWICK

They had been waiting six years for us and when we got out there they were ready. I didn't think we were as ready as they were. Having said that, the Wednesday side never

Ollie Campbell clears his lines against Orange Free State.

lost a game and we were up against good opposition. I don't think many teams will ever do that in South Africa. I played in the First Test because many of our midfield backs, including Ollie Campbell and Gareth Davies, were injured. Tony Ward was fly-half and they had to play Dai Richards in the centre. He was more of a runner than kicker – so I was more involved with the decision-making. But once Ollie was fit again and Tony joined the squad, they could do their own kicking and I knew that I wasn't going to get in the Test side because of the type of game they were wanting to play. They were always going to be better off with Ray Gravell and Paul Dodge crashing through the middle. But I never stopped trying because we wanted to keep the Wednesday team going – we didn't want to lose a game. I ended up playing in 11 games, and only Graham Price and Clive Williams played in more matches, so I got plenty of rugby and did my bit for the squad.

JOHN BEATTIE

Jim Renwick became a cult hero. He was this wee unassuming bloke who nobody could understand and who would sing cowboy songs – and suddenly he had John Carleton and the English guys dribbling at his feet. They could see he was his own man – and a great player who should have been in the Test team throughout the series.

I thought the Scots weren't treated that well. Alan Tomes should have been in the Test team too, and I felt I should have been in the Test team. I've never said it before, but I felt badly done by on that tour. As a junior player, I didn't feel I had the ear of the coach. I was a student and perhaps a bit of a reactionary, so I didn't want to feel like I was crawling to Noel Murphy – but that was what I needed to do.

Ray Gravell was a wonderful guy, but he would finish a game and straight away be in the coach's ear asking what he thought of his performance. I could never be a part of that sort of stuff because I was this quiet, inexperienced student.

The tour was full of these big ebullient characters like John O'Driscoll and Maurice Colclough, who had plate fights in the hotel corridor – and I just felt so out of it.

JIM RENWICK

I used to get stick because of my accent – nobody could understand what I was saying. My number was 22, so I used to shout, 'Twinty-twae,' and they all used to take the mickey. Bruce Hay got it as well because he kept on saying 'ken' – everybody wanted to know who Ken was.

The first night I shared with Peter Morgan, he could speak Welsh but he didn't have a clue what I was on about. So I had to try and speak a bit properly but I soon got sick of that; I wasn't going to change and neither were they, but they soon got used to it. They used to send guys out to schools to speak to the kids. So I got sent along to this one school and they couldn't understand a word I was saying. So I didn't get to do that anymore – which was a shame because I liked that part of it. Sometimes we'd have to go and open a local shop or something, get your photo in the local press and things like that. I used to volunteer because it meant you got to go out and meet folk and have a blether with them and just see what was going on. It was a good tour, a good experience and a good set of guys – but I suppose when I look back I wish I'd been more organised. It's the chance of a lifetime, and I suppose it rankles in the back of my mind that maybe I should have taken it more seriously and maybe I should have said more. But I didn't at the time because I didn't know what was in front of me. It's like playing a game of rugby, you assume that you're going to get the ball at the lineout, but it's not always that cut and dried and if what you've got planned doesn't happen then you have to adapt and make the most of the situation.

BILL BEAUMONT

It was a great honour to captain the Lions, and it was also different because the sense of responsibility meant you became much more focused on the tour as a whole. In 1977 I only had myself to worry about, and never thought I would get into the Test team, so, having achieved that, I came back with a great sense of satisfaction. But in 1980, as captain, you had to prove you were worth your place in the Test side, and lead by example. I had never been fitter than when I went to South Africa because I wanted to make sure I hit the ground running. To get myself in condition I purposely did a lot of road running to get myself prepared for the hard grounds, because if you don't your calves can get very tight. I played all ten Saturday games on the tour, and my only injury was having some blood drained from my knee after the Second Test.

JOHN BEATTIE

Bill Beaumont was an incredible captain and an incredible player, if everyone in the pack had been like him then it would have been great.

FRAN COTTON

Two things decided the outcome of the series. A string of key Lions players were injured, including Terry Holmes, Gareth Davies, and our only open-side, Stuart Lane. And, as happened with the All Blacks in 1977, the Springboks out-thought the Lions. Rather than being confrontational they played a counter-attacking game, using incisive runners like Gerrie Germishuys, Gysie Pienaar and flanker Rob Louw. They never kicked the ball back to us, but ran it back instead, using a classic Lions game to beat us.

We were outsmarted and outplayed, and we really missed a quick open-side of the calibre of Fergus Slattery or Tony Neary, neither of whom were able to tour. Louw was a good player, but he was not in the same class as Slattery.

In terms of conditioning I don't think the 1980 Lions trained very hard at all, and there was no comparison to 1974 in terms of intensity. I don't think they worked the boys hard enough. It was also a whole new group, and although there were a lot of very good players, there were not any who at that time were world-class.

JOHN BEATTIE

My Lions tours were disappointing because we lost. I'd heard all these stories about these fantastic tours of the seventies, but I didn't enjoy my 12 weeks in South Africa in

1980 or my ten weeks in New Zealand in 1983 at all. I actually hated them – genuinely hated them. I really thought we were so far behind the times.

I trained really hard with Bill Dickinson before going to South Africa, I gave up smoking and when I turned up at this hotel near London the first thing we did was go out on the piss. I thought, 'This is madness.' I was anticipating living the life of a monk, but everybody was drunk out their brains and I ended up having to put Graham Price to bed. And that was a portent of the next 12 weeks. It was remarkably self-destructive and amateur. I couldn't believe the drinking that went on – I still can't believe it. If you weren't in the Saturday team you got pissed on the Friday night, and if you weren't in the Wednesday team you got pissed on the Tuesday night – it was crazy. We didn't have a drinking culture like that with Scotland – we couldn't afford to because our backs were always against the wall. I went on the tour thinking I would learn a lot, but all we did at training was run and run and pass the ball and run. So we were very fit but we didn't have the same kind of bulk that the Springboks had. They had been beaten in '74 and this was revenge for them. We heard stories that they had been in the gym, which was an alien concept to us.

The South Africans were just stronger than us. They were more developed people, like Danie Gerber. We were just these skinny Europeans. And there wasn't much art to the way we tried to play. It was tackle, tackle, run, run – and we had a good scrum.

JIM RENWICK

We trained in the morning, had a bit of light lunch, then played a bit of golf or did different things depending where we were in the afternoon. Then it would be onto the beers depending on whether you were playing the next day or not. And when we went drinking we did it in style. Some boys didn't drink or didn't drink much, but some boys drank a lot – and I think I was in that second category. We always had big nights after the games – basically it was back to the hotel where we'd have a bar organised and we'd take it from there.

Some of the boys like John O'Driscoll and Maurice Colclough were wild with drink. They'd get hell of a drunk at the after-match functions and throw food about. I remember at one dinner Syd was speaking and Colclough poured a tub of beans over the top of him. It was schoolboy stuff that you wouldn't get away with in Scotland where it was always far more disciplined. It was quite a laid back tour, I suppose.

Then there was the Sunday School which was basically going out for a couple of beers and having a bit of fun after our lunch on Sunday. Beaumont was the leader, and you had to be invited in. I was in it, Toomba (Alan Tomes) was in it, so was Bruce Hay, John Carleton, Pricey, Jeff Squire, Colclough, John O'Driscoll and a few other guys. We ended up getting T-shirts made.

JOHN BEATTIE

It was the first time we saw sponsorship. We got given training tops with the name of a cigarette brand emblazoned across the front. And there were Coca-Cola stands at the side of the pitch, so they were way ahead of us in terms of the way the money worked.

You'd go to places and have lunch with a gathering of businessmen, and you'd have to tell a joke or a couple of stories, and the businessmen would chip into a pot. I went to a couple of those things. Then at the end of the tour that pot was used to buy uncut diamonds, and there would be somebody waiting at Heathrow airport to buy the diamonds at twice the price, and we'd all take our cut.

It wasn't a lot, but there was this separate business going on about trying to profit from the tour, and I had been totally naive to this. I was 22 and had thought it was all about the rugby.

PETER WHEELER

A Lions tour is like a three-year university degree crammed into three months. It is a test of character to get to know 30 blokes intimately, who become lifelong friends. For instance, after the 1980 tour I had not seen Colm Tucker for 20 years, but then I saw him in Dublin at a match and it was as if we had never been apart. When you are living so closely together, sharing such an intense experience, you cannot hide anything. Whether it's strengths, weaknesses or foibles they will be found out and examined. It is up there with my best achievements and it means an awful lot. It was also the amateur era, and no one got annoyed if you enjoyed yourself. You wouldn't swap those memories or tours for anything.

Bill Beaumont is carried from the field following the Lions' victory in the Fourth Test.

CHAPTER TWENTY-TWO

MONTHS OF MELANCHOLY
1983
NEW ZEALAND

I F THE *melancholic 1966 tour to New Zealand is reckoned to represent the low point of Lions history in terms of results and unfortunate selections, then those who followed the 1983 tour would be forced to admit that this ill-starred, badly-planned odyssey ran 1966 very close.*

The Lions were whitewashed in the Test series and since this was now the era of the shorter tours to one location, they did not have the consolation enjoyed by the 1966 team of some Test success in Australia. There was only one leg in 1983, a rather grim and often (compared to previous vivid tours) even featureless passage around New Zealand, where the confidence and excellence and resistance and brilliance of the 1971 Lions was by now something of a distant memory.

The tour, in the eyes of many, was crippled by the selection of its hierarchy. The great Willie-John McBride applied for the post of coach but in the end was made tour manager, a role which he never appeared to be happy in or enjoyed. Perhaps a ceremonial position was not the old warrior's style, and nor, demonstrably, was dealing with the mass media which now followed every tour.

Jim Telfer, the great Scottish Lion, was appointed as coach, a measure which received general acclaim – and Telfer was, in the next year, to coach Scotland to a Grand Slam, one in the eye for those who attributed most of the blame for the 1983 disaster to him.

Yet again, however, the choice of captain repeated some of the Lions' mistakes of history – not least in the fact that too much attention was paid to the game immediately before the final selection, in this case an Ireland win over England at Lansdowne Road. For this and for other reasons, Ciaran Fitzgerald was named as captain, even though he lacked the world-class attributes and physical stature to make an impact in the Lions Test series, and even though Peter Wheeler, a magnificent Lion in 1977 and 1980, was available and favoured by many. Indeed, Wheeler was omitted from the tour entirely.

Perhaps Fitzgerald's supporters did themselves few favours with their assertion that the opposition to Fitzgerald was some kind of pro-English coalition. It was nothing of the sort; it was an assertion of the obvious realities of the contenders at the time. Also affected by the dispute was the steely Scotland hooker, Colin Deans, who was relegated to the role of dirt-tracker, when almost everyone on tour bar McBride regarded him as the better of the two touring hookers.

Fitzgerald's own performances reached an early nadir when he threw the ball in crooked six times in the Second Test match in Wellington, conceding six priceless pieces of possession. At the end of the tour, Lions supporters were re-acquainted with one of the realities which the previous 98 years of touring had stressed – that to play and to lead an individual country was by no means

Opposite: Tour captain Ciaran Fitzgerald and Graham Price tackle Dave Loveridge.

incontrovertible evidence that you were a Lions captain or a Lions Test player. As Telfer was later to write, he wanted Deans to be his Test hooker, and said so repeatedly, only for McBride and Fitzgerald himself to outvote him on the tiny tour hierarchy.

Yet again, the Lions were badly afflicted by injury, losing dynamic players such as Terry Holmes, in fine form at scrum-half, Nigel Melville, who was injured soon after arriving as a bright replacement, Ian Stephens, a world-class prop, and Jeff Squire, as good as any All Black in the back-row all succumbing. This left them dreadfully short of true class and power.

However, it is extremely doubtful if, given their inbuilt disadvantages, the Lions would have won more than one Test match even if all the chosen team had been available until the end. New Zealand had some pedigree players, notably the splendid Dave Loveridge at scrum-half, Stu Wilson on the wing, Jock Hobbs and Andy Haden up front. There were few weaknesses in the team, and if the All Blacks of 1983 were workmanlike rather than stellar, they were also too organised, committed and strong for the tourists.

As Clem Thomas wrote of the tour, 'The Lions were to win little, for the problems which faced the coach Jim Telfer were daunting, due to poor pre-tour selection. Imagine leaving out Paul Dodge, amongst many other terrible errors of judgement! Why do the Lions selectors, time and again, pick captains who are not certain of being the best in their position on tour?'

Thomas also made another salient point, which sprang from the rather graceless nature of the tour and the lack of any real rapport between the hosts and the touring team: 'Players of all nations were beginning to question their role as cannon fodder on the world stage, as once again on tour we saw players in a game which is supposed to be of fun and enjoyment, involved in scenes of attrition.'

There were very few vintage performances, with the tour provincial games bringing defeats at the hands of Auckland and Canterbury, this latter game being notable not for the usual rough play between the two teams which had marked history, but for the fact that the Lions missed kick after kick at goal after the management bluntly refused to choose a proper goalkicker. Dusty Hare was available and kicked beautifully during the tour, but for some strange reason, the Lions did not seem to grasp the overwhelming significance of goalkickers in the game at that time, or indeed at any time.

One of the other features of the itinerary was a realisation on both sides that in the new 18-match tours, playing four Test matches was simply unviable. So for the next Lions tour, to Australia in 1989, only three Test matches were arranged and the tour became slightly less brutal as a result.

Despite everything, there were some outstanding successes in the Lions ranks. John Rutherford, one of the greatest Scotland fly-halves of all time, had to move to centre to make the Test team, chiefly because no one in authority appeared to realise that the iconic Ollie Campbell was nowhere remotely near his best at fly-half, and that Rutherford deserved a chance. Rutherford added considerable class to the midfield, notably in the Third Test in Dunedin, and his craft was in sharp contrast to the blundering of some of the other Lions backs.

Up front, Peter Winterbottom, then a tyro England flanker, was absolutely magnificent in the resistance, with a courage that was scarcely believable. His high tackle rate and aggression in broken play impressed New Zealanders so much that Winterbottom was inundated with invitations to return for stints in New Zealand's domestic rugby. Gwyn Evans, from Maesteg, eventually forced his way into the Test team at fullback and up front, Graham Price managed to hold on in the scrums to give the Lions some kind of fingertip hold on proceedings.

To their credit, the Lions at least avoided any crushing defeats in the first three Tests of the series, only for them to go down humiliatingly by 38-6 in the final Test in Auckland, the biggest Test defeat in Lions history.

The First Test, as usual, had given the Lions their best chance. And they blew it. Even when the tour of Terry Holmes ended with a serious knee injury in the 21st minute, the Lions still could and should have won, as a good place kicking effort by Ollie Campbell gave them a 9-6 lead at half-time.

However, they were completely unable to cash in on periods of authority due to some poor back play and, eventually, the Lions payed a heavy price when a try by flanker Mark Shaw gave New Zealand the match, 16-12. There was to be no way back.

The Second Test was played in typically horrendous conditions at Athletic Park, Wellington, and the Lions performed wonders in the first half to restrict New Zealand to a 9-0 lead when the home team were playing down a hurricane-force wind. But some absolutely masterly play in the second half by New Zealand, when their accuracy and discipline were quite wonderful, meant that the Lions were denied possession and could not score a single point. It was a crushing 9-0 win.

The series was lost in Dunedin in the Third Test. Again, the match was played in dreadful conditions, but Roger Baird and John Rutherford both scored tries to give the Lions some hope. However, in the end, a try by Stu Wilson cooked their goose, and yet another Test series had slipped by as New Zealand closed it out.

In the opening stages of the Fourth Test, one of the New Zealand fans up in the stand produced a trumpet and blew a loud exhortation to his heroes to go on the charge. They obliged. New Zealand were outstanding that day, with Loveridge operating at his world-class best, with Wilson scoring a hat-trick and with further tries from Hobbs, Haden and Alan Hewson. It was a relentless performance by the men in black, and brutal evidence, if any were needed, of the sad regression of British & Irish rugby.

There had been a lack of wisdom in the preparations and selection, and a lack of class on the field. Sad but true, and the domination of the southern hemisphere had been re-imposed.

The 1983 tour party.

CIARAN FITZGERALD (Ireland)
Toured: 1983

There was a lot of media hassle on the tour which probably distracted from the rugby side of it. All of that came from who the captain was going to be, Peter Wheeler or myself. A lot of the English media prior to the tour had him anointed and appointed. That was a big sideshow all the way through.

COLIN DEANS (Scotland)
Toured: 1983

What really annoyed me was that they picked the wrong hooker. I thought Peter Wheeler would have been picked because of his experience with the Lions, and he would have been a great captain. But they left him at home. They took Ciaran Fitzgerald as captain and I was the other hooker. Ciaran clearly did a good job for Ireland – but he just wasn't a Lions captain. He wasn't the dominant figure in his position and everyone knew it.

PETER WHEELER (England)
Toured: 1977 & 1980

In the Five Nations before the 1983 tour, the Irish beat us so that put me on the back foot, and I knew I'd not had the best season. I stayed in Dublin after the match and had a drink at O'Donoghue's with Fergus Slattery at 11 a.m. on Sunday morning, but when it closed at 2 p.m. the landlord decided he would do a lock-in, and he brought sandwiches round and we just sang songs. It was a fantastic time and went on into the evening. We caught the early ferry back on the Monday morning, the day the Lions

squad was announced, but before we left I was called by the journalist, Ian Robertson, who told me, 'You're not the captain, and you're not in the tour party.' I was extremely disappointed, but I'd had so much go right with my career that I couldn't let one setback get on top of me. We crossed the Irish Sea in the pouring rain, and then my wife Margaret and I drove back home from Anglesey. She tells me that all I said was, 'Oh well,' a few times – but by the time we got back I'd sorted it out in my own mind.

I had no axe to grind with Ciaran. I just didn't think he was good enough as

Coach Jim Telfer.

a player, although he clearly had something as a captain. The questions over his Test credentials showed on the tour in the friction with Colin Deans, who many people thought was a better hooker. I got an invite to go back to Dublin while the tour was on to do some coaching, and Ciaran's brother was on the same course. Word had already come back that things were not so good and I remember him saying that Ciaran had been singled out, using the term, 'Yes, they've put a saddle on him, haven't they?' At that time it wasn't so much the coach and captain selecting the team as it was the Four Home Unions divvying it up.

WILLIE-JOHN McBRIDE
The Fitzy decision didn't go down well in England and they [the media] started up. We had enough guys in New Zealand to contend with without our own starting up. When the New Zealand press saw one or two of the English journalists going for Fitzy they rubbed their hands with glee and jumped in as well. Fitzy played well amid all that controversy.

COLIN DEANS
Despite Ciaran being captain, I was still confident that I was going to get picked for the Tests. I had discussed it with Jim Telfer before we left and as far as I was concerned the team sheet was a blank piece of paper with no names pencilled in – so I had every opportunity to play all four Tests.

JIM TELFER
It is no secret: I was out voted. I never told anyone that until it was printed somewhere else, so I can say it now. I wanted Colin Deans in the team.

Ciaran was supposed to be a natural leader, an army officer; he had led Ireland to the Triple Crown, and he was a big pal of Willie-John's. I'm not saying he wasn't good enough to be on the tour, but he shouldn't have been in the Test team.

I used to sit and say that I didn't think he was good enough. And he would say he wanted to play, and Willie-John would go with him – so I had to accept that. His throwing-in was all over the place. Certain players develop as Lions, and he didn't do it.

I've met him since and he's a nice enough fellow. He was a hard little bastard. But he wasn't good enough – and that coloured the whole tour.

ROGER BAIRD (Scotland)
Toured: 1983
I did feel sorry for Ciaran Fitzgerald, but not as much as I felt for Colin Deans. Fitzgerald wasn't playing well, his throwing-in was struggling, and he became more of a recluse the longer the tour went on. So much so that I met him at Ravenhill a few years back when we were both involved with the under-21s and chatted for an hour – and that would be more than I spoke to him for three months.

PETER WINTERBOTTOM (England)
Toured: 1983 & 1993

I don't remember having a one-to-one conversation with Ciaran throughout the tour – we were only there for 11 weeks!

DONAL LENIHAN (Ireland)
Toured: 1983 and 1989. Manager: 2001

Fitzy was an insular fella anyway. There were nine Irish fellas on the tour by the end of it but he wouldn't be spilling his guts to us either. He was aloof in some ways. An outstanding captain – but he wouldn't be a fella to pour his heart out. I had huge respect for Ciaran and the way he dealt with situations. He never dropped the guard. We had 30 players and only two hookers, so he was togged out for every single game and had no reprieve: Wednesday, Saturday, Wednesday, Saturday – every single week either playing or on the bench.

HUGO MacNEILL (Ireland)
Toured: 1983

Ciaran is the best captain I have ever played with. Not just for his words but his thoughtfulness in dealing with players as individuals was fantastic. I think inadvertently Willie-John, in protecting him from the media, ended up protecting him from his team. Had Ciaran been given the opportunity to stamp his mark on the tour early on it would have made it easier for him. Willie-John spoke a lot at the early meetings. He didn't need to. Even if he sat in the corner and said nothing he was still Willie-John the legend.

OLLIE CAMPBELL

We were supportive of Ciaran but we needed to do it in a more proactive, more verbal way. I don't think we did enough at the time in standing behind him and supporting him. In our own way we all did support him, no question. But it should have been done at some stage by some of the senior players, of which I was one. With the wisdom of years and looking back it was one change I would make. We should have made it clear, as a group at a meeting with everyone there, that he understood that he was our man. I regret that.

JOHN BEATTIE (Scotland)
Toured: 1980 & 1983

I'm not sure about the Ciaran Fitzgerald thing because he was quite a good player and a good lad. I always thought he got a terrible press from us Scots because he kept Colin Deans out, but he wasn't that bad. When you start losing you like to pin excuses on someone and he was convenient because he was a decent bloke, an army captain and Irish. He maybe didn't look the part but he was a battler. Colin was possibly better but Ciaran was a good captain and a good bloke.

JIM CALDER (Scotland)
Toured: 1983

I just remember how hard Colin trained to get… well… nowhere, really. It was pretty tough for him. I shared that angst because I wasn't originally in the Test team. We used to do extra training together, and I remember one night in Canterbury when Johnnie Beattie, Deano and myself agreed to meet at 5 a.m. the next morning to go for a run, because we were all hacked off about not being picked and really wanted to push our case.

Well, at 5 a.m. the next morning I really couldn't be bothered, but at 5.05 a.m. the phone rang and it was Deano at reception saying, 'Come on, let's go.' So I got up and went downstairs and there was Beattie as well, who I suspect had received a similar call from Deano. And I don't think I had ever run so hard and so fast before. Deano was like a man possessed. After half an hour, Beattie gave up, but Deano and myself just kept going and kept going – we were just so pissed off.

Fortunately for myself, I got in for the Third Test. I broke my thumb so I didn't make the Fourth Test, but at least I got some satisfaction from having got my full Lions cap.

COLIN DEANS
Looking back now, I should have helped the guy, for the good of the team. Nowadays they'd have analysts and specialist coaches giving him all sorts of advice, and he would have been helped – but back then he was on his own, really.

There was a hell of a lot of pressure on him – especially given the way results were going – and there was none on me.

The only pressure on me was that my second son, Ross, was born two weeks into the 12-week tour so I had that to contend with. But that just threw me more into the limelight and I got a heck of a lot positive publicity, not to mention generous gifts and well-wishes from the locals. It really was very special that there were these people in New Zealand who didn't know me, and they would come along with these little gifts for me.

JIM CALDER
In 1966, Mike Campbell-Lamerton had captained the Lions but really struggled to justify his place in the team. He had said to Creamy [Jim Telfer], 'What do the boys

John Rutherford.

think?' And Creamy had said that they thought he should drop himself. So he did. And I think Telfer was trying to get that sort of discussion with Fitzgerald.

I remember he took me aside at one point and bounced this idea off me that Fitzgerald might be persuaded to do the same thing, but at that stage I was a midweek player, and not really in a position to be making my voice heard on something like that.

CIARAN FITZGERALD

You had to make the decision very early that that's the way it was. You accepted it and got on with it or else you let it get to you. Not for one minute was I going to lose the opportunity I had. One of the strangest things is that normally you'd take a lot of flak from the home media but a lot of the New Zealand media were flummoxed by all of this and so they were coming out with articles in support of me. I was in the eye of the storm all the time. English journalists would take me aside saying, more or less, did I not realise that I was in the wrong place at the wrong time.

PETER WINTERBOTTOM

I never really felt the split in the squad over Ciaran Fitzgerald, but no one was talking to me about it because I was only a kid. However, Colin Deans was playing very well, and Iain Milne was also good at tight-head. There was a selection dilemma, too, at fly-half, where John Rutherford was the better running No 10, but Ollie Campbell had been part of the Irish Triple Crown side, kicking goals and putting balls in the air.

Rutherford was a great player, and if he had been given more of a run, and Jeff Squire, Ian Stephens, Bob Norster and Terry Holmes had stayed fit, it would have made a big difference. Holmes was a main threat to New Zealand, and without him we were fighting a losing battle from the start.

COLIN DEANS

Iain Milne also suffered with the selection on that tour. Over the years he was a joy to play with. He just gave you that sure-fire feeling that the right-hand side of the scrum was going nowhere. You can look at people in the street and know what role in life people are made for. You know the Bear is a prop. New Zealand were laughing their socks off in '83 when they knew the Bear wasn't being picked for the Tests because we were just ripping teams apart in midweek.

David Leslie was left behind as well, which was sad. I think if he had gone he would have pushed Peter Winterbottom; I think he would have been in the Tests. You need someone with that mental toughness.

JIM CALDER

The All Blacks said that they couldn't believe that Deano and the Bear were not being picked. As Clive Woodward said: 'If you don't pick your best team then how do you expect to win?'

WILLIE-JOHN McBRIDE

I went over to London first of all to be interviewed as the coach and ended up as the manager because they made Jim Telfer the coach. It was a great challenge, but it was a sad time to do it. England got the wooden spoon that year, they had a dreadful season, Wales weren't a good side and Scotland weren't a great side either. Plus we had all sorts of injuries. When we put the team together I remember saying, 'God, will we get away with this?' There were one or two players we had to pick hoping they would get fit on the tour. We had to because there really weren't any other choices.

JIM TELFER

It was wrong to take people like Maurice Colclough. He had been a big star in 1980, but he was coming off a bad injury. He came up to Scotland for a fitness test and he had lost a lot of definition in his leg. We were desperate to get him to go because he was a huge man and he had been a big part of Bill Beaumont's team in 1980, but he could hardly run, and when you passed him the ball he was handless. Nice enough fellow, but I have never been so disappointed by the quality of a player he was, especially given the position he held in the English camp.

PETER WINTERBOTTOM

We were closer than the results of the series indicate. We trained bloody hard, and there was virtually no let-up from Jim Telfer. As a 22-year-old that was fine, and I

Andy Dalton throws the ball in during the Second Test at Athletic Park in Wellington.

just got fitter and fitter – but some of the older boys really suffered. Going to New Zealand you need to give yourself every chance, and I don't think we did. Jim flogged people too hard. We had a week's holiday in Waitangi, and the guys thought it would be great to have a break, do some fishing, and give the body a rest – but we trained every bloody day in a park. Jim developed as a coach, and probably now realises he was flogging us.

ROB NORSTER (Wales)
Toured: 1983 & 1989

Being picked for the 1983 Lions helped me realise a goal I had set myself as a kid. It was a real pinnacle playing for Wales, but the next target was always to play for the Lions. Going to New Zealand in 1983 was a huge highlight in my career.

I was in the mix in 1980, and got a letter asking about availability, but it was a bit early for me. I fell short that time, probably quite rightly because I was a young buck, and Alan Tomes went instead.

Roy Laidlaw tries to clear the ball in dreadful conditions during the Third Test.

Going to New Zealand was a daunting prospect, but we had a strong party. Not quite as strong as it might have been because of selection, but good enough to be in with a shout.

We were criticised for possibly being a little bit too forward orientated, but what do you need to win in New Zealand? There was a view at the time that our manager Willie-John McBride fancied more of a tracksuit role as a coach and perhaps there was some tension created through that.

But Jim Telfer was someone I was really relishing working with. He had a fabulous record as a coach and was a tough guy on the park. He was obsessive about his rugby and a real disciplinarian. He carried some mental and physical scars from the Lions' appalling tour to New Zealand in 1966, but he had stood up then and had a good name and reputation in New Zealand.

But while I was happy to train flat-out, twice a day in sleet and snow, not all the senior pros appreciated the drilling he gave us. A few of them objected to his methodology.

PETER WINTERBOTTOM

We were hard-hit on the injury front as a result. Ian Stephens, Bob Norster, Jeff Squire and Terry Holmes were nailed on for the First Test, but none of them were fit for it. Then Nigel Melville was shipped in for Holmes, and looked very sharp, including scoring a couple of tries – and he would have played in the First Test but for a cheap shot by the North Auckland flanker, 'Wuzz' Phillips, which put him out of the tour with fractured neck vertebrae.

JIM TELFER

I thought at the time I was good enough to be the coach. I thought I had enough experience to take on the All Blacks. But I learned that I just wasn't good enough at that stage to get the best out of the players.

I don't know who would have been good enough because New Zealand were streets ahead of us in terms of how they developed players and played the game. We deserved to be beaten. And it was a pretty sad tour by the time we finished.

I was the only coach, which meant I had to take charge of the backs. I had never coached backs in my life so I had to delegate a lot to guys like John Rutherford, Roy Laidlaw, Clive Woodward and Ollie Campbell.

CIARAN FITZGERALD

There was a clash of styles between Jim Telfer and myself. In the Irish set-up the captain ran a lot of the show and it's always my belief that to run the show on the pitch you have to run it off the pitch in terms of trying to get guys to listen to what you say. The guys had to be able to respond to your voice when you say something. It had to mean something and I don't think Telfer was used to a captain like that. Telfer's captain would have tossed the coin and that was it. I think he was a bit taken aback when I used to ask him what the plan was before the training sessions, how much he was going to make us do. I would voice fairly strong opinions and there was always an edge there. He wasn't used to it and it was an issue all the way through. I wasn't going to give and Willie-John had to step in a few times. Telfer was a good guy, though. He knew everything about rugby.

JIM CALDER

Telfer was a professional stuck amongst amateurs. There was nobody better at preparing a pack of forwards to go out there and give the opposition hell. You could see he'd get frustrated by it, because the depth of his thinking was so much greater than anyone else's.

JOHN BEATTIE

Poor old Jim Telfer – he was badly treated. I'll swear to my dying day that he would suggest stuff in training and then some players, who I can't name, would wait until he was out of earshot and then say that we weren't going to do that in the game. We'd practise a certain way of playing, like rucking, for hours and then these guys would say, 'Nah, we'll just maul.'

It was because he was Scottish. If you were Scottish you were a minion, I felt.

Jim is a fantastic man and was the best thing on the tour, but he couldn't get everyone to buy into what he was trying to do. He was way ahead of everybody there, but they all believed they knew better than he did. They were wrong.

ROB NORSTER

There was definitely a tension between the senior players and Jim and once we had lost the First Test you just felt we were on a slippery slope and there was no way we were going to recover. Players started getting injuries and I'm not sure whether they were always genuine.

We did rucking drills the length of the field, running under a white stick to get our body positions right. We had some torture sessions and also did a lot of heavy scrummaging work. This was often done on sand and we'd rip the skin off our knees – it was hard and tough. If I'd been in my thirties, at the tail end of my career, on an 18-match tour of the toughest rugby-playing country in the world and having just come out of a long, hard season at home, I might have had a different view of things. The tour certainly became a huge test of character.

But to be fair to Jim, he was the sole coach in charge of 30 players – it was bonkers. I used to liken him to Howard Hughes of an evening in the hotels because he would leave his door open and paw over the videos of our matches. If he saw you he would call you in and get you to work the pause and rewind buttons and get you to go over the tapes with him. That's why we all used to tip-toe past his room.

ROGER BAIRD

I think it was unfair on Jim Telfer that he didn't have an assistant. He is an out-and-out forwards coach. There is no one better at getting forwards rucking and kicking shit out of folk, and he was so hell-bent on that that he started getting resistance, especially from the English guys. He needed a foil.

By 1983 everybody had two coaches so it was terribly short-sighted. We ended up orting the back division out amongst ourselves, and consequently I felt we had the alance wrong in the side. John Rudd (Rutherford) should have got a run at ten, and oodward should have had a chance to play in the Tests – but you needed a back in ere to push both those selections.

LLIE CAMPBELL

e had six games before the First Test and the backline that was selected for the First Test d never played together before. Not only could we have won that match but we should ve won it. Had we won that First Test the whole tour would have taken on a different mension and character. We knew then that suddenly we had a mountain to climb.

IARAN FITZGERALD

he First Test was critical and we had a chance of winning it. New Zealand would ve had to change their side had they lost. There was a lot of talk over there that the ll Blacks were ageing so it was an opportunity.

OGER BAIRD

e had a two-on-one and Rob Ackerman dummied when he should have given to evor Ringland; we also had a failed drop-goal attempt near the end, and the list goes 1. History shows that when you go on tour the First Test is your big opportunity – d if you lose the First Test you are in a bit of trouble. The tragedy for us – and for ew Zealand too – was that if we had won that game the series would have been live until the Fourth Test, but after it went 3-0 after the Third Test a number of guys ere just looking to get out of there.

UGO MacNEILL

he night before the First Test, Ollie Campbell and I practised drop-goals from erywhere on the pitch in Canterbury and they were all going over. Near the end of e game, 13-12 down, there was a ruck near their 22 and I called the ball from Roy idlaw. It had rained overnight and just as I went to kick it my left leg went from der me and it still only missed by a couple of feet.

OGER BAIRD

r David Irwin was completely bonkers, and he was picked against Steve Pokere, who is this very nice, religious guy who would not play on a Sunday. At the first lineout e Doc was pointing, and shouting: 'Pokere, you're f**king dead.' He was known om then on as 'the Dirty Doc'.

OLIN DEANS

the Second Test Ciaran Fitzgerald had six squint lineout throws. Against the All acks every piece of possession is vitally important and that was us giving them the ll for nothing six times. To me, that's what lost the Second Test.

CIARAN FITZGERALD

I lost a tooth. A certain All Black at a ruck. I could see this fella coming and I got an elbow straight into the mouth.

OLLIE CAMPBELL

We're playing against a gale force wind in the first half and its 3-0 coming up to half-time and Dave Loveridge scores a try. But it's only 9-0 and it's a 15-point wind! The All Blacks played against the wind in the second half as only the All Blacks can. We didn' see the ball. It was a template on how to play against the wind. Final score: 9-0.

HUGO MacNEILL

We never got a coherent pattern in our backline. It was like a car that was firing but not firing on all cylinders. We didn't have a backs coach. The Lions at our best might have beaten them but we didn't have proper organisation in the backs. New Zealand were jus so good at the little things and when you added them all up it amounted to a big thing.

JIM CALDER

Halfway through the tour we started to lift weights. They booked a room on the top floor of the hotel, and we all went up and started bench-pressing – as if that was goir to make a difference against the All Blacks on Saturday. It was that amateur.

ROGER BAIRD

After the Second Test we went up to the Bay of Islands and had a party, and the cake was hijacked and put over somebody's head. I couldn't name names – but I know tha Roy Laidlaw and Clive Woodward were in the vicinity.

PETER WINTERBOTTOM

John O'Driscoll was a top bloke, but we had to add his 'brother' to the roll-call because he'd go a bit mad after a few beers. In Whangarei after a match he was throwing beds and TVs out of windows, and Willie-John said in the next team meeting, 'We can't be having this, who did it?' We said to John, 'It was you,' but he denied it outright – and that was when we added his brother to the team roster.

Steve Boyle was another character. He played the first two games of the tour and then said to Jim Telfer, jokingly, 'I think I'm being overplayed.' He did not play again for another three weeks.

Boyle's nickname was 'Foggy' (as in Fog-horn), and he was the unofficial leader of the midweek side. On the eve of the Dunedin Test he took them out for a night on the town, forgetting that Jim had arranged a training session for the Saturday mornin No one turned up until Nick Jeavons strode into the hotel lobby at 8 a.m. still in his blazer after a night out.

We had a great time socially, and there was always a Saturday night party after 'Foggy's Tours' had handed the invites out on Friday night. The Kiwis were very hospitable everywhere other than on the pitch.

DONAL LENIHAN

arrived out as a replacement on the Tuesday they were playing Canterbury just before the Third Test. I'd been at home for the First and Second Tests and we'd been reading all the papers. I was very close to Ciaran. He was on the bench for the Canterbury match and I was in the stand but I remember having a bit of a run on the pitch after the game was over. I was on the pitch five minutes and Fitzy called me aside in the in-goal area and started throwing balls to me and I thought to myself, 'Jesus, this is a sign that he needs some reassurance.'

COLIN DEANS

t really became apparent to me that I wasn't going to get my chance when they picked the team for the Third Test in Dunedin. We had played Canterbury midweek and beaten them with me being voted man of the match. Virtually everybody – apart from some of the Irish boys – said that they had to pick me now. We were 2-0 down in the series and we had to win the game, so it was now or never in terms of making the big decision. At the team announcement, when it came to the hooker everybody was looking at me, and my name didn't come up. It was devastating. I got Jim on his own afterwards, and he just said he couldn't say anything. I respect him for that, I suppose.

CIARAN FITZGERALD

remember training before the Third Test and one of the scrums collapsed and I swear to God you'd take a deep breath when you'd go down because it had been raining so hard in Dunedin that the water was up over our boots. We had a shot at that Third Test as well and it didn't happen. It was the first time I ever saw guys wearing thermal underwear. The All Blacks had their thermals on. It was really cold and really

Graham Price, Ciaran Fitzgerald and Staff Jones.

wet. People were blue. It was okay for forwards but for backs it was horrendous. Poor Ollie Campbell might have had hypothermia after the match.

OLLIE CAMPBELL

Might! What does he mean might?! Oh my God, without a second's hesitation, those were the worst conditions I ever played a match in. I think I thawed out at Christmas just about The New Zealanders had these special wetsuits that they wore underneath their jerseys, some of the players wore mittens, some of them cleverly wore a plastic bag between their socks and their boots for insulation. We ran out in the same gear that we would have run out in three years earlier when we were in South Africa on the high veldt. I'll never forget it. We ran out and as soon as my foot landed on the grass the water immediately came ove my boot. It was like putting your foot in a bucket of ice. It felt like minus 50. Maybe it was only minus 10. It couldn't have been colder had it been played on the South Pole.

Five minutes in, everything had gone numb – hands, feet… brain. Everything. I'm telling you, Scott of the Antarctic wasn't even close. Ten minutes of the match and your brain was almost going. None of us had ever played in conditions like it so to lose by just 15-8 was heroic.

But it was the lowest point of the tour. No contest. As I lay in my hotel bed the following morning, my teeth were still chattering. And this pit in your stomach. You'v lost the match, the series. There's no way back.

JIM CALDER

Despite the weather, we probably played our best rugby, with Roger Baird and John Rutherford – who was picked at centre – scoring. But even then we didn't really get close to winning. It finished 15-8.

PETER WINTERBOTTOM

There was no socialising with the All Blacks because we had no time to. However, there was a post-Test dinner in Dunedin which turned into a big bun-fight, and I remember Haden just lobbing food at our table. The officials didn't bat an eyelid… Willie-John couldn't exactly say, 'Don't do that!'

JIM TELFER

Saturday, 16 July, 1983 – the date of the Fourth Test – remains one of the saddest day in my life. A 38-6 defeat, a 4-0 series loss, there was no coming back from that. The dreams I had held three or four months earlier were in tatters. I was very disillusioned with coaching and with rugby and I was also totally against the whole Lions concept by this stage: it was so difficult to get the team together and prepare properly before going into the biggest Test matches these players would ever experience.

I couldn't fault the players, because they'd given everything, but they'd come through system that wasn't good enough to prepare them for the levels of excellence of that All Blacks team, who were just better – both technically and tactically. But for all that I still felt that the fault lay with me because I'd failed to work around those deficiencies and differences, I'd failed to find a way for us to win – and there is always a way to win.

ROGER BAIRD

There had been a couple of boys trying to sell their blazers before the last Test, and one of them was playing in the Test team. I was thinking, 'If that's the attitude then where are we going here?'

OLLIE CAMPBELL

I think the only thing I can say about the Fourth Test is that we came second. That's not a good memory. When the New Zealanders smell blood they go for it.

ROGER BAIRD

I made a cock-up with the first try when I stayed out and should have come in and somebody came through the middle. Then, not long after that, Stu Wilson came in on a short ball to score and before we had a chance to draw breath, they kicked off and Andy Haden caught it and romped right up into our 22 and I thought, 'This is going to be a long afternoon.' They were walking away with it.

Then Stu Wilson came in on another short ball and I came in and stopped him dead in his tracks but I got his knee right in my forehead, so much so that he thought he had killed me. I was completely poleaxed.

They eventually brought me round and I got carted off and Peter Winterbottom walked up to Roy Laidlaw and said, 'The lucky bastard.'

CIARAN FITZGERALD

We had nothing left. During the second half, I'm not saying we had one leg on the plane but it was over before the match was over. I could sense it. Everything the All

David Loveridge breaks free during the Fourth Test.

Blacks did worked like a dream. Every kick bounced into their hands. They got cock-a-hoop and let fly.

OLLIE CAMPBELL

I couldn't agree more. Our bags were packed mentally and we were gone. In fairness, it was literally last man standing at that stage. I scored my only try of the tour against Waikato in the midweek match beforehand and in scoring it I pulled a hamstring. In any other circumstance there is absolutely no way I should have played in the final Test. No way. There are injuries you can play with, but you can't play with a hamstring pull. But it was last man standing.

I couldn't train the week of the Test and I think I only lasted around 30-odd minutes.

It was a bitter-sweet experience, certainly one of my most fulfilling but tinged with disappointment. To be one of only two teams who were whitewashed in New Zealand was difficult to swallow. You regret that we didn't play any memorable rugby. Unlike the 1971 tourists, we left no legacy.

At the same time, it was such an invigorating experience to play against New Zealand. You go through club, province, country, you win a Triple Crown, then the Lions – you think you're at the pinnacle. Then you go to New Zealand. You come up against this wave after wave of attack. You're thinking, 'There is another level.'

You could say I've become a student of New Zealand rugby. I'd get second-hand books in Greene's bookshop on Clare Street. I'd have read over a hundred by now. So you can imagine how magical it was to go there with the Lions, 20 years after you'd first seen them play.

The night of our first game, in Wanganui, Colin Meads was there at the post-match function. Colin Meads. It was like: Welcome to New Zealand. I had to ask him if it was true he used to train by running up and down the hill on his farm with a sheep under each arm. He said it was a myth, which was almost a shame. You didn't want to shatter the illusion.

ROGER BAIRD

They were a better team than us, but I think 4-0 was a bit harsh. If we had gone with a better balance of coaches, and got our selection right, then I think

Michael Kiernan.

we might have grabbed one win in the series. I've spoken to a few other guys over the years – particularly the Irish boys when I met up with Ollie Campbell, Trevor Ringland and Dave Irwin one night – and one of our greatest regrets was that we didn't win that First Test because it was there to be had. If it had been 3-1 that would have been so much better – but it ended up 4-0 and we've never had a reunion or anything like that.

JOHN BEATTIE

The All Blacks by then were on a different planet: John Ashworth, Andy Dalton, Gary Knight, Gary Whetton, Andy Haden, Mark Shaw, Jock Hobbs and Murray Mexted – probably the best All Black pack of all time. Their backs weren't bad either with guys like Dave Loveridge, Stu Wilson and Bernie Fraser. That was a great team – really abrasive.

JIM TELFER

After that tour I vowed not to coach again. It was the lowest moment of my career. I was devastated and no matter what anyone said, I felt like a failure.

Willie-John McBride spoke to the press at the end of the tour and said he hoped the Lions would pick me to coach the next tour, as this experience had been invaluable. But I remember my own response to the media. In reply to one question about my future involvement, I asked them, 'Is there life after death?' It summed up how I was feeling.

I remember being asked what I thought the Scottish press would say about me – but I was more concerned about what the people in the street would say.

I'd really looked forward to being the coach, I'd prepared well and the feedback I got was that the training sessions went well – but it just didn't go how I'd expected it to. I had to be persuaded – mainly by Roy Laidlaw and John Rutherford – to come back to coaching.

Willie-John is a great guy and we toured twice together, but he never really discussed rugby with me. He had been put forward by Ireland as either coach or manager, and when he got the manager's job he maybe didn't want to step on my toes, so he distanced himself from that side of it.

My closest mucker on tour was Donald McLeod. We used to sit in the bar and talk about rugby and have a good drink – but he wasn't there as a rugby expert.

I got myself into a hole and all I could do was keep digging.

I came home and I was totally disillusioned about the Lions. I wanted nothing to do with them. That lasted until Ian McGeechan asked me to help him in 1997.

JOHN BEATTIE

There is nothing worse than being on a losing Lions tour. It really is the worst feeling in the world. You'll hear wonderful stories about the hospitality – but that's bollocks. You are there to be in the Test team and to win the series, and unfortunately I didn't achieve that. To me, it was an unmitigated disaster. I hated it. I don't look back on either of my Lions tours with any sense of affection.

Don't get me wrong, I believe in the Lions hype. I think it is the most magical concept in world rugby: Britain and Ireland decamp to another country and the team you pin your hopes on are wearing a combination of colours from all four competing nations. But for the people in it… well… it's an all-male, bullshit-dominated cabal of blokes – so if you win it must be great, but if you lose everyone hates it.

I could name you the whole '71 team, the whole '74 team, the whole '89 team and the whole '97 team – but I couldn't name you any of the losing teams, including the ones I was involved in.

COLIN DEANS

In '83 they picked the players who were supposed to be good. Players were picked on past reputations. Colclough was big and bulky, but soft underneath when the crunch came. I firmly believe that if the nine Scots on that tour had played in the last Test we wouldn't have been hammered by 30-odd points. We knew Jim Telfer, we were fit and we were prepared to push ourselves to the limit. Some of the other players were not. To train as hard as we did, it was a shock to them. There were occasions when I trained three times a day.

On the last day all the Scots got together and were talking and we decided that we were as good as any of them. And it was quite enjoyable sticking two fingers up at those who had not rated us out in New Zealand when we won the Grand Slam the following year.

JIM CALDER

I remember sitting in an airport on the way back and we all agreed that we were going to go home and really push on as an international team. We had seen inside the other nations and realised that they weren't any better than ourselves. So we came back and

Roy Laidlaw and Dave Loveridge in the aftermath of the Fourth Test.

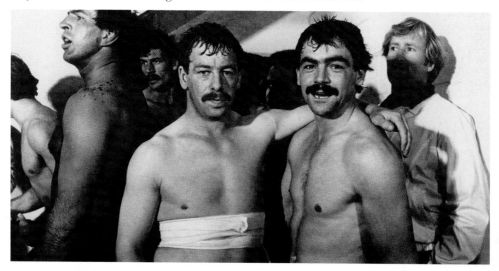

we drew 25-all with the All Blacks and won the Grand Slam in 1984.

There was a bunch of us who were seriously pissed off that we hadn't achieved on that trip what we thought we should have, and that was a big factor in what happened the following year.

ROB NORSTER

New Zealand is a wonderful place to tour, but I'd love to go there in their summer. The fact we headed Down Under after a full season of thrashing about in our own winter conditions and got another three months of the same made it a real physical and mental challenge – and one that we failed to meet.

The captains: Ciaran Fitzgerald and Andy Dalton after the Fourth Test.

CHAPTER TWENTY-THREE

THE COMEBACK KINGS
1989
AUSTRALIA

IT MAY *have been accompanied by a certain grinding of the gears, but even before this tour began there was a sense, at last, that those presiding over Lions tours were catching up with the modern game, and therefore there was a chance that the Lions would catch up with their southern opponents. At least occasionally.*

The first priority was to fill the yawning gap in the Lions itinerary caused by the absence of the South Africans from international sport due to apartheid. After a great deal of discussion, the Lions committee decided to take the plunge and instigated a tour of Australia and Australia alone for the first time since 1899.

It must be remembered that this was before the great surge in Australian rugby which saw the Wallabies win the World Cup in 1991 and 1999. It must also be remembered that the tour came two years after the inaugural World Cup, part of which was held in Australia, when for the semi-final between Australia and France in Sydney, Australia could not even fill the capacity of 18,000 at the Concord Oval stadium. At the time, international rugby in the country was by no means profitable or thrusting.

There were considerable doubts, indeed, that Australia could really stage a successful Lions tour. Clearly, three Tests against the Wallabies would provide a sound centrepiece. Clearly, so would matches against New South Wales and Queensland and, possibly, the Australian Capital Territory. It was years before the days when Australia had five major provincial teams.

Western Australia were not strong, but at least they would provide some opposition and a staging post as the Lions made their way to Perth en route to Sydney and Brisbane in the east. In the end, to fill out a fixture list of 12 games, the Lions had to arrange matches against Queensland B and New South Wales B, against New South Wales Country and against an ANZAC team at the end. To some, as the Lions prepared, it looked a rather thin list.

Such anxieties were in the future as the Lions opted for their coach. Boldly, they chose Ian McGeechan, a great Lion of 1974 and 1977, who, while he had been appointed Scotland coach at the time of his Lions appointment, had never yet actually coached his country. He had one season with Scotland in 1989, and then took up the Lions challenge.

His pedigree had grown since his playing days, notably in a successful tenure with Headingley and with some of the other Scotland international teams. But if it was a bold gamble back in 1989, it was to look slightly less of a gamble in 2009, 20 years on, when McGeechan coached on his fifth Lions tour, and his fourth as head coach, a staggering record and a staggering tribute.

Opposite: The decisive moment in the Test series: Ieuan Evans and Greg Martin dive for the ball as it crosses the try-line during the Third Test.

They even gave him an assistant, another first. Roger Uttley, who toured with McGeechan with the Lions in 1974, was appointed as forwards coach, a wise move bearing in mind that the core of the forward pack would be Uttley's England charges – at the time, England were developing the most formidable pack in their history. The choice of captain was Finlay Calder, the tough Scottish flanker who had the respect of the playing community in Britain and Ireland. The tour manager was Clive Rowlands, a robust and voluble Welshman who had coached Wales between 1968 and 1974 before becoming their manager at the 1987 World Cup. Rowlands had the priceless gift of dealing with matters under his own remit while also clearing the way for McGeechan to operate. 'The Lion is growing,' Rowlands would say after every victory. At the end, the Lion was very big indeed.

And the other upshot was the triumph of a Test series victory. If that was rare enough, then it was even more rare that the series was won after the loss of the First Test, and this in only a three-match series.

But while Australia lost on the field, it was far from all bad news. Just two years after they had so miserably failed to sell out a World Cup semi-final involving their own team, the Lions tour helped galvanise the international game in the host country. The First and Third Tests had been switched to the Sydney Football Stadium, with a capacity of 44,000, and they were both sold out.

Perhaps even more significantly, there was a strong view that the defeat of the Wallabies in the 1989 tour focused attention on the deficiencies in the team, weeded out some weak links and therefore forged the team which, in 1991 under the driving coaching of Bob Dwyer, won the Rugby World Cup.

In one sense, this thoroughly modern tour had overtones of the past. It was a highly controversial tour with some of the incidents of rough play causing a sensation in Australia, with the only difference being that this time it was the touring team, and not the home sides, who were accused of starting the trouble.

At the end of the tour, as eminent a rugby figure as Bob Templeton, Australia's much-loved and admired assistant coach, commented that Australia should not have complained, and that by doing so they were admitting that they were beaten by the harder side in the series. Not that that should excuse some of the excesses on both sides. Dwyer himself, angry at his team's defeat, later declared that his team had been 'beaten up by the English coppers.' This was a reference to the fact that three of the core Lions forwards, Wade Dooley, Paul Ackford and Dean Richards, were all policemen back at home. At one stage, the Australian Rugby Union sent a protest letter to the Four Home Unions committee; it took an informal meeting between Templeton and McGeechan to calm the situation.

The severely truncated tour, with a small number of build-up games before the First Test, made it essential for the Lions to develop rapidly. The fact is that while they developed their forward play, with a pack built around their policemen, the Lions never had time to develop their back play and as Ian McGeechan was to admit with a certain sadness, the Lions never had the opportunity to become an all-round attacking force.

What they did do was develop a powerful pack, with a small but busy front-row, and a back-five forward unit that ranked with any in the history of the Lions. Calder often struggled with injury niggles but with Dean Richards alongside him and Mike Teague in the form of his life on the blind-side flank, they made up a magnificent back-row, and after Dooley had forced his way into the Test team for the Second Test above the estimable Robert Norster, linking up with Ackford, the pack became outstanding.

Teague, the hero of Gloucester, had a magnificent tour, breaking tackles continually with his power and becoming the Lions' focal point. He was voted the official player of the tour, on an aggregate vote from the three Test matches. The extent of his brilliance is that he only played in two, missing the First Test because of injury. He was christened 'Iron Mike'.

There was a problem at fly-half on tour, with Paul Dean, the Irishman, joining the sad list of Lions to be injured in the very first game of the tour. But eventually Rob Andrew, the Englishman who had not enjoyed a great home season, arrived as a replacement and formed an excellent half-back partnership with the fiery Robert Jones of Wales, whose battles at scrum-half against Nick Farr-Jones of Australia were to become notorious.

Gavin Hastings at fullback had a superb tour, but in the centre, there was a significant new figure. Will Carling withdrew from the Lions party due to injury, and in his place, McGeechan drafted in young Jeremy Guscott, who had played for Bath since the age of seven and who had only just won his first England cap, momentously scoring three tries in an away match in Bucharest against Romania. His raw talent was beyond doubt, but it was still an extravagant gamble by McGeechan.

Or so we thought. Guscott was quick to earn the respect, and then the admiration, of the Lions and the world game, becoming one of that breed always coveted by McGeechan throughout his Lions career: 'The Test match animal.' Guscott was never to let McGeechan down in three momentous tours.

The Lions showed excellent form in the early games, disposing easily of Western Australia, and then defeating a strong Australian B team 23-8 in bad weather in Melbourne. They eased their way past Queensland and New South Wales, the latter win gained by a late drop-goal by Craig Chalmers, and they entered the First Test full of hope.

Significantly, even the game against Queensland B at Cairns, in far North Queensland, had the ring of authenticity, with a decent crowd and a competitive game, and a new venue to put on the map of Lions rugby.

Australia fielded the great David Campese on the wing, and they had Farr-Jones and Michael Lynagh at half-back, arguably one of the greatest combinations the world game has ever seen. The

The 1989 tour party.

pair were superb in the First Test in Sydney, against a Lions team which lacked focus, accuracy and tempo. Greg Martin at fullback was one of four try scorers, with Lynagh adding 14 points. The Lions did not score a try in a salutary 30-12 defeat, and such was the shock to the system that McGeechan was forced back to the drawing board.

In some ways, the tactical course which McGeechan and Uttley decided upon was bound to lead to conflict. They suspected that there was a soft heart to the Australian team and that they should wind up their forwards and try to overpower the Australian team at source. The temperature of the tour was already hot, especially after an incident in the match against Queensland when Mike Hall, the Lions back, was kicked many times on the ground at the back of a ruck. There were further incidents in the match against New South Wales.

When it came to the Second Test in Brisbane, with the whole tour clearly at stake, Dooley was brought in to add strong arms to the pack alongside the athletic and steely Ackford; Andrew replaced Chalmers as the controller at stand-off, Teague returned and Guscott came to the fore for the first time. McGeechan, the master, plotted, and there was the scent of cordite in the air, even as the teams took the field.

Part of the game approached carnage, with Robert Jones and Nick Farr-Jones clashing and, as Clem Thomas observed, 'rolling on the ground like two ferrets in a sack.' There was another incident when Lions prop David Young seemed to stand on Steve Cutler's head, with another huge punch-up breaking out.

However, the Lions were the superior team; Australia could not handle their rumbling power and even though they still led inside the last eight minutes, the authority of the Lions forwards was obvious and Gavin Hastings put the Lions ahead when a sweeping movement made space for him to score down the right.

Then came Guscott. The Lions launched another sustained attack and when the young man was given the ball in midfield in a move going from right to left, it would have been easy for him not to take responsi-

bility and to pass the ball. But instead he grubbered the ball through, sprinted with electric pace, gathered the ball as it bounced up and scored the try which decided the Test and rescued the series.

Guscott was an apprentice bricklayer at the time and it is said that one onlooker taking in the scene as Guscott became a Lions legend in one run, said, 'That boy will never lay another brick again.' Back in Bath, another scene was being enacted. Henry Guscott, father of Jeremy, was watching in the early morning on the television. Such was his sense of excitement and elation that he picked up a sledgehammer, walked the deserted streets to Jeremy's home, let himself in and demolished a wall of the house. Happily, the wall had been due for demolition as part of improvements.

Tour captain, Finlay Calder leads his team out.

The furore about the dirty play raged like a forest fire through the week preceding the Third Test, with a barrage of former Australian gunslingers and street fighters produced to condemn the Lions – with some justification. But with McGeechan largely keeping his own counsel, it was also clear that the Australian camp was alarmed at the new momentum.

Despite all the protestations that it would be a clean game, Jones and Farr-Jones clashed in the very early stages, although matters did quieten down a little later, despite the incredible tension of the play. The result was famously decided by the match-winner, Campese, but not this time in favour of Australia. Andrew dropped for goal but missed badly and the ball bounced up to Campese, deep in his own goal area. Campese shaped to kick then started to run the ball out. He changed his mind and then threw a dreadful inside pass to Martin, his fullback. The ball eluded Martin and Lions winger Ieuan Evans made it to the loose ball to touch down for the decisive score. Although Australia threw everything into attack in the final quarter, with hair-raising scenes, the Lions held on at 19-18, the first time they had ever won a Test series after losing the First Test.

The Lions beat New South Wales Country and the ANZAC team and then happily savoured the feeling of joining the touring parties in 1971 and 1974 as the only post-war victors in the deep south. Despite the lurid incidents, it had in many ways been a richly-successful tour. With respect to New Zealand, the sun and climate and wide open spaces of Australia were attractive to the touring party after the New Zealand winter tours, and also good news for the television producers back at home, beaming pictures to the United Kingdom and Ireland.

The tour felt like a real Lions tour, and ensured that Australia would now take their rightful place on the Lions rota, and would stay there, even after 1997, when South Africa returned to the Lions fold. The tour may have helped Australia for the future, in terms of their crowds and their team. But in that moment, it had ended in a Lions triumph.

FINLAY CALDER (Scotland)
Toured: 1989

That was the highlight of my rugby life – without a doubt. We were the best team in the world. We would have beaten anybody. We had quite a mobile pack with Brian Moore, David Sole and myself there, but we also had a fantastically physical English presence with guys like Wade Dooley, Paul Ackford, Dean Richards and Mike Teague, not to mention Dai Young, the Welsh prop who was 21 years old and as strong as a horse. So we were able to develop this hybrid between a 100 mile an hour Scottish rucking game, and an English mauling game. With that pack we would have taken anyone to the cleaners.

IEUAN EVANS (Wales)
Toured: 1989, 1993 & 1997

It was a sensational tour – I loved it from start to finish. We had an outstanding captain in Finlay Calder. He was quietly spoken, but there was an iron fist in his velvet glove. He was intelligent, inspiring and a great man to play with and under. I had huge regard for him.

There were those who decried the fact we were playing a full series against the Wallabies before we went, but the Australians certainly deserved their shot at a full tour. The 1984 Aussie side was an outstanding team and 18 months after our tour they became world champions. So any preconceptions from past Lions about this not being a worthy trip were proved to be totally disingenuous.

GAVIN HASTINGS (Scotland)
Toured: 1989 & 1993

We did not know how good Australia were going to be. It turned out that it was one of the hardest tours I have ever been on. We knew that Australia had achieved the Grand Slam in 1984 and that, in 1988 when they again came over again, although England had beaten them convincingly by 28-19 they had easily beaten Scotland 32-13. In the summer of 1988, England lost both Tests in Australia fairly substantially, so we had a shrewd feeling that life with the Lions in Australia was not going to be easy.

Looking back, it was a lovely country to visit on a tour and it was hugely enjoyable, largely because the man in the street in Australia knows little about rugby union. You can walk around town without being recognised, nobody knows who you are, so it was a great deal more relaxed, off the field, than touring somewhere like New Zealand.

ROBERT JONES (Wales)
Toured: 1989 & 1993

To play for the Lions had always been one of my ambitions. It is the next thing you hope for after playing for your country, proving yourself to be one of the best in your position in Britain and Ireland.

To be recognised in that way was a wonderful feeling. It made me a member of the best team I ever played in, and led to the single incident which is most remembered from my 16-and-a-half years in senior rugby.

JOHN JEFFREY (Scotland)
Toured: 1989

Before we left we had a training camp at Pennyhill, where Finlay and Roger Uttley had a stand-up row in front of the players about what kind of rugby we were going to play. Roger wanted an English style mauling game, while Finlay was convinced that we needed to play a Scottish style rucking game. I'm not sure it really resolved itself, but we certainly rucked more than we would have done otherwise, and there was an uneasy truce from there on in between Roger and Finlay.

Wade Dooley couldn't make that session because he was at his grandfather's funeral, and the English boys joked – perhaps unfairly – that he always had a funeral to go to when there was a tough training session on the cards.

When Wade finally pitched up we were in this lovely pub in Staines, and they made him down two pints of beer and do the bleep test on the lawns outside the bar in front of everybody. Fair play to him, he pulled it off – and managed a phenomenal score.

MIKE TEAGUE (England)
Toured: 1989 & 1993

Finlay wanted to play a certain combination of rugby: it was a big English pack – and he could see a big English presence – but he wanted to play a rucking game. Looking back, I think we adapted well to top of the ground conditions, and the results reflected that.

ROBERT JONES

Ian McGeechan did not dictate to us. Everyone had his say. I had as much input as someone like Bob Norster; Steve Smith, the reserve hooker, had as much say as I did. Ian wanted everybody to be involved, to be able to work closely together. It worked. At no time on that tour did I feel I was playing away from my strengths or doing things because I had been told to do them. Geech and Finlay Calder knew they had the best players in the British Isles in their squad and allowed them to be themselves rather than try to fit them into a preconceived pattern.

SCOTT HASTINGS (Scotland)
Toured: 1989 & 1993

Finlay was fantastic right from the start: demanding that there would be no cliques, demanding that the players' fitness levels increased from the first time we got together, and demanding that we all enjoy the experience.

   And Geech was able to impart his knowledge on the Welsh, the Irish and the English guys – which Lions coaches hadn't always managed to do in the past, so that was a huge plus.

BRIAN MOORE (England)
Toured: 1989 & 1993

We were not quite then into the bitterest years of the England-Scotland feud but enough roots of that feud were showing to make all the English contingent at least a little sceptical of the Scottish captain. Yet in the months of the tour I developed a tremendous respect for Finlay Calder. He is one of the most direct men I have ever met, direct to the point of non-diplomacy. On the field, and off the field, he had an iron-hard competitive edge and attitude. When you play against someone like that, it is easy to hate them. You use it to build up an active dislike to take you into a mindset to return the aggression. When you play with a man like that, it is very reassuring. You could rely on him in the most difficult moments. That is a massive factor in the minds of fellow players.

FINLAY CALDER

I'm so glad that people now see in Brian Moore the man which I have known all this time. He's an extraordinary human being. I've never seen a man as driven about anything and everything in my life. He's just a compulsive winner. Scotland is a funny nation because if he was one of us we would have been so proud of him, but because he wore an English jersey he became this figure of hate.

He had a lot of Scottish traits – not particularly big, thrawn, bad tempered and with this phenomenal desire to win.

With the Lions I quickly recognised that this guy knew a lot more about rugby than me, so I put him in charge of the forwards, and he revelled in the role because it was recognition for him and it showed he had the respect of his peers.

The contact in international rugby is unbelievable. It is like a cartoon, you see stars, and to think clearly through all that muddle takes some doing – but a few guys have the ability to do that and Brian is one of them. Somebody with an incredibly astute rugby brain like Brian, and who is able to get to the nub of any decision in the heat of battle, is worth their weight in gold.

ROBERT JONES

Everything felt right from the moment we arrived at our hotel that May. That sense of four national groups, men who were usually opponents on the field of play, coming together with a single purpose adding to the feeling of excitement.

I have never felt so relaxed. For nine weeks we were away from the pressures of playing in Wales and from the need to earn a living. We were, in effect, full-time professionals.

I realised the quality of the players we had in the squad and I remember thinking, 'I can't wait to play with this team. They are going to be so good to play with.'

BRIAN MOORE

The first two games of the tour had been quiet – too quiet and, probably, too easy. Queensland at Ballymore, in Brisbane, was our first big game and suddenly the tour seemed to take off from there. It was a tough and, at times, brutal game. Julian Gardner

and the rest of the Queensland forwards trampled all over Mike Hall at a ruck, when he was clearly nowhere near the ball. And it wasn't rucking, it was kicking. While Mike was lying on the ground being treated, Finlay called us all in. 'That is the last time something like that's going to happen on this tour,' he said. 'Nothing like that's going to happen to one of us again.' And with that, the whole feeling of the tour changed. There was a palpable shift in the attitude among the whole party. We wouldn't start anything; but if it started, we would finish it.

Brian Moore.

MIKE TEAGUE

I remember Bob Norster dishing it out in retaliation to Queensland after Mike Hall had been trampled on about 20 times. When René Hourquet blew his whistle it seemed as if Bob had been caught red-handed and was going to be sent off. All he said was, 'Penalty Lions.'

FINLAY CALDER

Were the Lions dirty? It depends on which side you were on. We were pretty rough, but I don't think we were dirty, and there is a huge difference. Dirty is kicking somebody's head when they are on the ground, and we didn't do that – certainly not intentionally.

But did we go out to set our stall down? Of course we did, from one to fifteen. And ultimately I think we earned their respect.

JOHN JEFFREY

There were two training sessions that stick in my head as being crucial to the success of that tour.

The first was in New South Wales in absolutely awful wet conditions, and it went on and on and on. Every time we made a mistake the coaches told us to start again, and I never hit as many rucking pads in one session as I did that day. But the guys kept going, and it became this thing about proving the coaches wrong and getting it right for ourselves – and afterwards there was this great feeling of achievement. It really strengthened the squad.

The second session was during a mini break up in Cairns on the Queensland Coast. We had a huge night out and even the coaches were drinking cocktails out of test tubes. Every time certain songs came on the jukebox barmaids would jump on the bar and dance. It was that kind of place and that kind of night.

The next morning we were all really suffering and Robert Jones didn't even make training – but a taxi was sent back for him. His father-in-law was the tour manager, of course, so he wasn't going to get away with anything. We did this really long session in the 90 degree heat. It was torture, but we all made it through – even Robert, who had to do extra. It was a test of commitment – and it was another one of those moments which strengthened the squad.

SCOTT HASTINGS

It was the first time the Lions had toured Australia – in its own right – in nearly 100 years. On previous trips it had been a stop over on the way to New Zealand. Having played against New South Wales and Queensland we went up to Cairns to play a Queensland B team, which was certainly a stark contrast to going to the Northern Transvaal or Waikato, which is what we would have been doing at that stage if the tour had been to South Africa or New Zealand – but that was the tour schedule we had, and you could argue that it made it tougher for us when we made the jump into the Test matches. We certainly seemed to get caught on the hop in the First Test.

IEUAN EVANS

It is the only Lions tour in which we lost the First Test and then went on to win the series. After a very good opening few weeks, in which we played some good rugby, we went into the First Test full of confidence and got bullied off the park. We were comprehensively out-muscled and lost heavily to an outstanding Australian side that two years later would win the World Cup. They had some brilliant players, but still we weren't expected to lose 30-12 – and certainly not in that manner.

ROBERT JONES

I have watched the match on film several times since and they were sharper, quicker in thought and scored some excellent tries. Perhaps we were over confident.

MIKE TEAGUE

Clive Rowlands came in the dressing room and kicked the door hard after returning from the First Test press conference. He said, 'I'm not going in there as a loser again.'

FINLAY CALDER

It didn't take long for the press to start calling for heads to roll, my own included. I called a management meeting and offered to stand down for the Second Test. 'If you go, I must go also,' was all Clive Rowlands said. The matter was closed.

SCOTT HASTINGS

I withdrew from the First Test with a hamstring injury. In 1987 I had gone to New Zealand for the World Cup and played with a tweaked hamstring and made a real mess

Finlay Calder walks his team out before the First Test at the Sydney Football Stadium.

of it – so I didn't want to repeat that mistake. But I was told that I would have to play the following game or I would be on the plane home, so the pressure was on.

We went down to Canberra to play ACT the following Wednesday and we found ourselves 21-11 down and seriously under the cosh at half-time. With the Test team having been thrashed in the First Test it was a real thunderbolt to the confidence of the whole squad, and we knew we were all staring down the barrel. But we produced a fantastic second half performance to run away with it, and when we came off the pitch after the final whistle the Test team were standing there to applaud us into the changing room. The unity which the dirt-trackers found that day was brought into the whole squad, and I have no doubt it was inspired by Donal Lenihan's captaincy.

Clive Rowlands always spoke about the badge getting bigger, and it was moments like that which made the badge grow.

JOHN JEFFREY

At half-time it had looked like the tour was coming off the rails. They had this infuriating Kookaburra song and we really wanted to shut them up – which we did in the second half. The forwards really stuck it to them, and we ended up comfortable winners. That was the turning point in the tour.

FINLAY CALDER

Donal Lenihan was a great talisman in the midweek team. He made them believe that they had every chance of playing in the Test team. You need these guys to keep the tour going. He was like a father figure for everybody, and instinctively knew how to manage each individual. It's hard to put a finger on it, it's hard to replicate – but he just got it right.

He was judge of the court and presided with this Irish benevolence and charm that made it all just click together.

Jo Maso used to talk about it being fine to have a salad but you need someone to bring the dressing. Well, Donal brought the dressing.

I think it was Roger Uttley who christened the midweek team 'Donal's Donuts' after the ACT game, and from there they made up T-shirts and it became a badge of honour to be one of the 'Donuts'. It sounds a bit childish but you need things like that on tour to keep everyone feeling a part of it.

JOHN JEFFREY

Every town or city we stopped in, Donal would somehow find the Guinness rep and get a tap installed in the bar we were going to be drinking in.

DONAL LENIHAN

The Donal's Donuts thing is a complete and utter pain in the arse to be honest with you.

The bottom line is that by 1989 the 6ft 8in second-rows were becoming the norm so I was struggling to make the Test team and I knew that from an early stage. I had no issues from that point of view and to be fair I got on well with Ian McGeechan and Clive Rowlands and I recognised early on that I had a role to play but it wasn't going to be in the Test team.

Having gone out as a replacement myself on the 1983 tour I went out of my way to make the replacements feel part of the group. The Donuts thing, it was exaggerated. Now, they were a great group, don't get me wrong. We played ACT on the Tuesday before the Second Test and we were losing at half-time, but we got it back and won well and that was a key game for the spirit of the tour. The Donuts thing grew legs but it came out of that game.

That midweek spirit had happened naturally but it's been forced on other tours and I'm not sure it's worked. The 1993 midweek team was a complete and utter disaster. They were so bad I think it exaggerated what happened in 1989.

JOHN JEFFREY

The selectors stuck with Finlay, but they had to make some pretty tough decisions before the Second Test, which was only a week later.

They replaced several players, including Brendan Mullin, Mike Hall and Bob Norster. These guys had never been dropped before in their lives, and they were obviously bitterly disappointed. I was pretty gutted too. Before the tour everyone thought that Phil Matthews, the Irish captain, would be the first choice number six, and I fancied myself as the second choice, with Mike Teague an outside chance. So when they selected the squad, and Matthews wasn't in it, I have to admit that I thought I would walk into the Test team.

Then I scored two tries in my first game against Australia A and felt pretty pleased

with my performance – but for some reason they selected Mike Teague for the two big games against Queensland and New South Wales leading up to the First Test and he played well. All of a sudden he was the main man, Iron Mike and all that stuff, and I was chasing him for a place in the Test team.

And it got even worse for me when Mike was injured for the First Test and they went for Derek White at blind-side flanker instead of me. I was left thinking: 'Jesus Christ – what have I done wrong?'

Finlay still takes great delight in telling me that he had the casting vote in that selection. With friends like that…

So, on the evening after the team had

Player of the series, Mike Teague.

been named for the Second Test, we had to go to a governor's reception in Brisbane, where a lot of drink was taken – especially by the boys who had been dropped.

On the way back to the hotel, the bus dropped the dirt-trackers off at a night club, which was the norm in those days, and as we disappeared into the night I remember Clive Rowlands, the tour manager, saying, 'JJ, look after those boys.' And I thought to myself, 'Thanks a bunch – leave me out the team and then leave me with this lot to look after!' Talk about adding insult to injury.

IEUAN EVANS

In the build-up to the Second Test Finlay spoke softly and calmly to us all and gave us a very firm understanding of what was necessary. His message came across loud and clear about how we had to confront Australia in Brisbane.

FINLAY CALDER

There was such desperation in the changing room before the Second Test that it was palpable. It was indescribable – very, very tense.

It was a Scottish-type environment, with David Sole, myself, Scott and Gavin Hastings getting everybody up and building adrenalin, which is what the Jocks were used to doing to survive – because we didn't have the power to match the likes of England.

And then there was this slightly surreal moment when Dean Richards came up to me – he might have been the hammer of the Scots but he's just a lovely, gentle person – and he said, 'You know Finlay, I don't really like all this noise, would it be alright if I went and stood outside?' I said, 'Of course, of course.' There was no point in him standing there feeling awkward. And if he wasn't man of the match that day then he was dash close to it.

That Second Test in Ballymore has been given a lot of hype over the years, but I have to say we were pretty hyped up ourselves at the time – and you could see in the Australians' eyes that they maybe weren't frightened of us... but they were pretty intimidated.

If you are going into a difficult situation then you want to know exactly where people stand, and that was one of only two occasions in my international career when I just knew we were going to win because of the personalities we had in the changing room.

MIKE TEAGUE

What the Australians expected from northern hemisphere sides was for them to turn the other cheek – 'soft Pommies' was the phrase, I recall. However, we had some pretty handy guys on the tour like Dean Richards, Wade Dooley, David Sole and Finlay Calder. We were in our late twenties, the right age, and coming to the height of our powers. We were battle-hardened 'circuit men' who had been around. Finlay was a fantastic captain – a hard boy, uncompromising, and wasn't going to be brow-beaten.

IEUAN EVANS

There were lots of red shirts in the crowd and plenty of support for us at Ballymore and, right from the start, there was an attitude and a readiness on the pitch to go to war.

And it was little Rob Jones who kick-started it all. It set a tone. It wasn't so much that we set out to start a fight, more we wanted to set a tone and let the Aussies know that this time we weren't going to sit back and let them dominate us as they had done in the opening game of the series. The scrum-halves provided the spark and the fuse was lit.

ROBERT JONES

All through the week before the match, Ian McGeechan was playing mind games with me. He kept reminding me how important Nick Farr-Jones, their scrum-half and captain, was to them. He was the key influence in their team, the man who called the shots and made things happen. He was also extremely good at influencing referees, chatting to them, saying things like, 'Sir, sir, wasn't he offside?' We had the feeling that if we could knock him off his game, it would knock Australia off as well.

On the morning of the match, 8th July, I got up, dressed in number ones – the blazer, shirt and tie in which we went to matches – and watched the First Test again on video. I don't think I have ever been so wound up before a match, and that was before Finlay Calder's special line in pre-match oratory which was likely to have you bursting with adrenalin for the first few minutes. I was aching to get to grips physically with Farr-Jones.

An opportunity came at the first scrum. There was nothing premeditated in the sense that I had decided exactly what to do beforehand, but I had gone out with the intention of doing something to unsettle him. It was a spur-of-the-moment decision to stand on his foot and push down.

He came back at me, and within seconds there was a pretty lively punch-up going on. Before the match, Finlay had emphasised that we were not to take a backward step: that we would tackle hard, put on physical pressure up front, ruck hard and drive the lineout. I knew that if there was any trouble, four men would come instantly to my assistance: Mike Teague, the Gloucester builder, and the three policeman, Paul Ackford, Wade Dooley and Dean Richards. And that is exactly what happened.

IEUAN EVANS

Rob threw about 14 punches, almost none of which landed on Nick Farr-Jones. But he did it safe in the knowledge that he had some pretty mighty beasts backing him up. That pack in the Second Test, based around England's forwards, was very tasty and needed no second invitation to jump in and sort things out. We had Brian Moore, Mike Teague, Dean Richards, Paul Ackford and Wade Dooley from the English pack alongside Dai Young, David Sole and Finlay. They weren't going to take a backward step – and didn't!

ROBERT JONES

That punch-up set the tone for the match. Nick was very upset by the incident and kept chatting to the referee. The Australians in general were upset about our physical approach and it has to be said that things got quite brutal at times.

PAUL ACKFORD (England)

Toured: 1989

When Australians start whingeing about intimidatory tactics, then you know you've got them on the run.

ROBERT JONES

Today, I would probably have been dismissed and suspended for six to twelve weeks for what I did, but not in 1989. I can't say that I regret it, though. It was probably the turning point of the match and the series. Nick Farr-Jones was distracted from his normal game and was not nearly as effective as he had been the week before. We won that game 19-12 and established something of a physical and psychological edge over the Aussies.

SCOTT HASTINGS

It was a simple fact that the Lions felt they had been bullied in the First Test and they wanted to get even. We didn't go to fight, but when Robert Jones decided to stand on Nick Farr-Jones at the first scrum there was only really going to be one outcome – and the fists certainly did fly.

I didn't know what had happened to spark that incident until afterwards when I watched a video of the game with Robert Jones and he turned to me and said, 'Look at what I do with my right foot!' Basically, he lifted his boot and with the long studs on he stepped down on Nick Farr-Jones's foot.

Farr-Jones shoved him and Robert responded by throwing a half punch, meanwhile Mike Teague came off the side of the scrum and absolutely melted Farr-Jones with this monster punch. And the whole thing erupts into this massive fight. All the while I'm giggling away in the backline because us glamour boys don't get involved in that sort of rough stuff – unless you are JPR Williams!

IEUAN EVANS

I moved very slowly towards the encounter from my wing, but never got to the heart of it. That was where the big elephants hang out and I know my limitations. It was a very tasty fight, but it was over relatively quickly.

JEREMY GUSCOTT (England)

Toured: 1989, 1993 & 1997

There was another massive punch-up when Dai Young kicked Steve Cutler in the head. There was a huge fuss made about that incident in the press afterwards – and quite right, to be honest – but the furore was also fuelled by the fact that the Wallabies had lost and the series was going to go down to the wire. Everyone was at us – from the press all the way to Bob Dwyer, the Aussie coach – but I think it was because we had them worried. They wanted to undermine us, to try and put us off, because our forwards had grown stronger and stronger as the tour had progressed, and they had been sensational in the Second Test. The Wallaby forwards had been bullied and the whole country was starting to panic. They said that we were deliberately harking back to the '74 tour and the '99' call, but that wasn't true. Nothing was premeditated. Sure, we had identified Nick Farr-Jones as the key to disrupting their backline and Robert Jones had instructions to niggle him to try and get under his skin and put him off, but that was all. The actual fighting wasn't planned and Dai Young's kick certainly wasn't. It was a ridiculous thing for him to do, but he was only 21 and was playing in the biggest match of his life; there had already been a fight and his blood was up. I'm not condoning what he did – far from it – but it certainly hadn't been premeditated before the game.

MIKE TEAGUE

I would describe it as the most violent game of rugby that has ever been played. We can't be seen to condone what went on, but needs must. There were some hard players on that tour; hard men and they all came together and sorted the job out.

JEREMY GUSCOTT

We got a rocket after the First Test. Looking back we had a few players out of position and inexperience at fly-half with Craig Chalmers. We also thought we would win and when we didn't Ian McGeechan made changes – and with that came a different mental attitude. We knew it was the last chance. McGeechan and Roger Uttley gave the squad the belief that we would win if we stuck to the plan. Put simply, we knew we could win if we beat the Aussies up. The Lions forwards didn't need a rugby ball in that Second Test, because it was a question of let's have a scrap and see what they are made of. Robert Jones did his business with Nick Farr-Jones, and away it went. Australia were always unsettled after that – and they weren't as close as a team as we were.

MIKE TEAGUE

Geech was the finest coach I'd ever had – the best. His tactics and analysis were fresh, and refreshing. He was also hard edged, and that idea of going after the Wallabies in the Second Test was his.

In the end we reacted to the way the Aussies made us play. They had dished it out early in the tour, and when we returned fire with fire they didn't like it. They may all have thought, 'You soft Pommie bastards' – but we were a side that fronted-up, and they had probably changed their view by the end of the tour.

The aim was to face them down, but also to play rugby. Geech wanted a balanced game, and he wanted it played at pace. We were very fit, and David Sole, a prop, was as quick as any of the backs, and the likes of Paul Ackford and Brian Moore were also very mobile. The only one of the pack who wasn't fast was Deano, but he could play rugby.

JEREMY GUSCOTT

When the Aussies bleated about the roughhouse tactics we were too busy celebrating to listen. If it's not refereed, you do it all day long. There were no assistant refs and no citing, and both sides were able to muscle it. They were big men – just look at the size of Tom Lawton – but they couldn't handle it.

FINLAY CALDER

For me, the selection of the pack for the Second and Third Tests, with Mike Teague and Wade Dooley brought into the side, was the key. That set the platform, and everything else fell into place.

The Australians didn't like Wade Dooley, he was a big bully of a man in the second-row and they had nothing to compete with him.

JEREMY GUSCOTT

Teague was immense on that tour – it was the best I'd ever seen him play. He had come in as a bit of a wild card and I think guys like Finlay Calder and John Jeffrey saw him as a one-dimensional English forward who just wanted to arm-wrestle his way through the game by being stuffy and tight and mauling everything. But he worked like a maniac out in Australia to change that perception; he got himself fitter than he had ever been, stronger and more dynamic. He would train until he dropped. He was just sensational to watch in action. He would leave nothing out on the pitch. Blood, sweat and tears was Teaguey; you couldn't ask any more.

MIKE TEAGUE

I had hit a bit of form, and so when they thought I'd done the A/C joint in my shoulder against New South Wales it was a bit upsetting. In fact, I'd torn the tendon off the bone.

Having been carted off against Wales in the Five Nations I'd come back to play well for the Lions in the provincial games, and was established as part of the Saturday side. Anyway, Clive Rowlands said they would give me two weeks to get fit, and that they'd give me a cortisone injection, and if that didn't work then I'd be sent home.

Because I was playing well, the management wanted to keep me, but they also brought in a replacement. So, because of the tour regulations on the number of players, I had to sit on my own at matches like a punter, away from the team. However, I was still wearing the Lions blazer and as a result I spent

bert Jones and Nick Farr-Jones come to blows.

a fortnight getting heaps of abuse from these obnoxious Aussie bastards in the crowd. It was the best team talk I've ever had. I was seething. All these crap comments about soft Poms, which I thought were a bit rich coming from a bunch of convicts. They were much worse than The Shed [the infamous stand at Gloucester's ground]. After that, I was a man possessed.

When I was selected for the Second Test I still needed that injection, but we came through to win, and the rest is history.

FINLAY CALDER

Rob Andrew was just outstanding, as well. He wasn't selected originally, which I think was a political thing because Ireland only had four in the original selection, but then Paul Dean got injured in the first match so Rob came in and immediately made clear who the top dog was. He was a great guy to have in your team.

SCOTT HASTINGS

In the Second Test, Gavin scored the first of our two late tries to win it from my pass, which I must confess was a bit of a Barnes Wallis bouncing bomb. He was concussed at the time so he had the choice of grabbing at one of three balls, and fortunately he went for the real one. As he ran back into position he said to me, 'Thanks for the pass – what's the score?' Because he didn't have a clue what was going on.

GAVIN HASTINGS

I don't remember it because Farr-Jones had just smacked me really hard.

SCOTT HASTINGS

Gavin and I became the first pair of brothers to have play together in a Lions Test match since the Joneses in 1908. And it was a very special moment because our elder brother Graham was living in Melbourne at the time, and he came along to support us with our Mum and Dad, who had travelled out from the UK. As Ian McGeechan always says: family is the most important thing.

FINLAY CALDER

Jerry Guscott scored the match-winning try from quick ball which put the Australians on the back foot and allowed him to send through this wee grubber kick, which he collected himself and touched down. What a class act!

JEREMY GUSCOTT

It was a great passage of play – Ieuan Evans chased a kick ahead, the ball ended up in Finlay Calder's hands and he went on a great run that took him about five yards from the Aussie line. The forwards piled in and the ball came out relatively quickly, with Brian Moore keeping things going by coming in at scrum-half and passing the ball out to Rob Andrew. We had a lot of space out to the left, but because of the chaos of the build-up play neither the defence nor the attack were properly aligned. I took the ball from Rob and saw that the Aussie centres, Walker and Maguire, pushed up to take me. I'd been watching a lot of rugby league while we were out on tour and I loved the way they slid grubber kicks through the defensive line on the sixth tackle. Because their defence was scrambling, I saw there was space behind them so I dropped the ball onto my foot and pushed it between them and went through after it. The bounce was perfect and I didn't even have to bend down to gather it – and I was in under the posts. It was the most amazing feeling to know that we had clinched the match and were still alive in the series – and I had scored the try that had secured the win.

FINLAY CALDER

That was the moment when the destiny of the series changed. Nobody can match the Australians when it comes to hanging on in there – but at that point you could sense that the whole thing had shifted in our favour.

Jerry Guscott is the only man to win two Lions series' himself. He turned that series round for us with his late try in the Second Test, and then eight years later he sticks that drop-goal between the posts to beat South Africa. What a sublime rugby player!

SCOTT HASTINGS

Jerry and I were always rivals but we became good friends through that Lions tour and I always felt he played more rugby for the Lions than he ever did in an England jersey. He was absolute class, and that moment summed it up.

JEREMY GUSCOTT

The Lions means many things to me. As a kid, a ball-boy at Bath, the Lions were the great Welsh players – Gareth Edwards, Phil Bennett, Barry John – and a smattering of Mike Gibson and 'Broon from Troon' [Gordon Brown]. It was almost unattainable, but then, as I

Jeremy Guscott chips through the Wallaby defence to score an exquisite try in the Second Test.

progressed through club, county and divisional rugby it became a possibility, especially after getting into international contention. It went on to hold a very special place in my heart.

SCOTT HASTINGS

It was a massive relief to win a really tight Test match – but I don't think anyone believed we had turned the series. What we had done was save the tour because many a Lions trip has gone completely off the rails on the basis that they weren't winning.

We knew we still had a hell of a long way to go, however, because one thing you can be sure of with the Aussies is that you can catch them out once, but you won't do it twice. They were going to come back at us with everything they had – there was nothing surer.

RORY UNDERWOOD (England)
Toured: 1989 & 1993

That has to be one of the most memorable moments of my career. The sheer relief and joy at having turned round the fortunes of the tour in a week.

The Grand Slam is a longer drawn-out affair, whereas in Australia we went from agony to ecstasy in a few short days. It was brilliant.

Even better, we had the time to enjoy it because the tour schedule provided for a break of a week, part of it on Queensland's Gold Coast, before the Third and deciding Test back in Sydney. Everyone enjoyed the moment, even those in the stand, and we realised that we were back on course to take the series.

MIKE TEAGUE

Watch that interview with Finlay at the end of the Second Test, it's great. He's had a smack in the eye, one in the mouth, and he says to Australia, 'You'll get a physical game again next weekend.'

BRIAN MOORE

By the Third Test our confidence was high. I remember going off to warm up on my own; it used to take me a while to loosen up, but I stopped after five minutes because I felt completely loose. It was a feeling I had never had before and never had again, but I was absolutely ready to play. It was not just a physical thing; it was an inner feeling too. I knew that we were all ready and we were not going to lose that Test match.

IEUAN EVANS

The Third Test turned into a game of chess – it was very nervy and tense. Nobody wanted to blink. It was physical and intense, but having responded to the beating we had taken in the First Test we were back on a level playing field.

SCOTT HASTINGS

At one point during the Third Test, the Australians were attacking and purely out of instinct I changed my body position to tackle David Campese and stopped him scoring under the posts. Bob Dwyer, the Australian coach, has spoken about that being the turning point in the game, but it didn't seem like anything special to me at the time. That shows the intensity of rugby we were playing by that point on the tour, we were doing these impressive things by instinct and thinking nothing of it. It was just incredible.

MIKE TEAGUE

What sticks in my mind most about the Third Test is that leading into half-time, while we were still playing, they played 'Waltzing Matilda' and 'Advance Australia Fair' on the tannoy to try and swing momentum their way. We got the series win by the skin of our teeth, but we kept the pressure on them, and did it.

EUAN EVANS

Games like that turn on tiny margins. Moments of genius or errors dictate who comes out on top and, in this case, it was an error by David Campese that proved the difference between the two sides. I can't take any credit for the try because I was just doing my job – chasing a kick ahead, hoping to pick up the pieces if any presented themselves.

We had a scrum in front of the posts on the edge of the 22 and Rob Jones fired the ball back to Rob Andrew for a drop-goal attempt to try to put us back in the lead.

It was one of the worse drop-goals ever. It came off the side of his boot and was heading to the corner flag. David Campese caught it behind his line and, like any dutiful wing, I chased what seemed to be another lost cause.

You can be chasing all day and get nothing, but sometimes the bounce will go your way. Early on in the game he had thrown me a dummy and I had taken it. I had 40 metres to think about what was going to happen this time and I just knew he wasn't going to do the same thing again.

I'm not sure why he tried to run out from behind his own line. But he didn't try the dummy and his pass to Greg Martin went to ground and I dived on top of it. I have to admit, I gave him a bit of verbal after the try, which wasn't like me, but it all stemmed from me taking his dummy earlier on.

We played against each other five times on that tour and, to me, he was a rugby genius. The best player I had ever played against – a truly wonderful, wonderful player.

In terms of significance and importance, that try helping the Lions to win a Test series after losing the first game, it was the most important try of my career. What a shame given all I had to do was dive on the ball over the line!

FINLAY CALDER

David Campese probably had the worst series of his life. He had that slip-up in the Third Test and it was down to frustration. We had choked him of possession and for somebody like that, who thrives on loose ball and having opportunities to express himself, that must have been torture.

He got a lot of stick in the Australian press afterwards, but his mistake wasn't the reason we won the series. We would have beaten any team at that time.

MIKE TEAGUE

Campo's schoolboy error was unreal. But there are all different levels of rugby, and there are some players, like him, who had something extra, and then there are others who look to players like him to make things happen. On that occasion, it simply didn't happen the way Campo wanted it to – but we also put him under pressure. Ieuan Evans was probably a bit quicker than Campo, and in the last two Tests Ieuan gave him no space at all.

JEREMY GUSCOTT

It was pretty shocking to see the amount of abuse that the Aussie media and fans rained down on Campo after the match. He turned up late to the post-match dinner and left early – and I can understand why: he was taking the blame for the loss – from himself, from his teammates, from his coach, the fans, the media, everyone. But in many ways, how could they blame him? The man was a bloody genius and he tried things. It just didn't come off for him on that occasion – but his pass might have gone to Greg Martin who might either have cleared up field, or they could have started a counter-attack that might have taken them anywhere. We had bugger all defence at that stage – Ieuan had pushed up and if he had been beaten by the pass then Campo and Martin would have been in the clear; the rest of us were still covering across and there would only have been Gav at the back to try and stop them. To lose a match like that is devastating, but it could have been very different. I've always tried to be philosophical about these things. Campo certainly won more matches than he lost because he tried things.

MIKE TEAGUE

If Campese had one of his good days and the sun was shining, you were stuffed. It didn't work out for him on that tour, but he was the best player I've ever seen.

IEUAN EVANS

It isn't just the try that sticks in my mind from that game. I actually caught a rabbit in the middle of the game. I looked up at the big screen and saw I was in shot. There was a brown thing cowering at my feet and I looked down to find it was a rabbit. I picked it up and carried it to someone on the side while the game was going on and then went back to the match.

MIKE TEAGUE

I got the match ball after the game, but I threw it to John Jeffrey. Getting that man of the series was the highlight of my career, and I remember Roger Uttley saying to me, 'You won't realise what you've achieved until years from now.' We went around the field and thanked the fans, and it was also good to see in the press box that the UK press was delighted with the result, showing that they were human after all.

For years we had been hearing about how the southern hemisphere were fitter, stronger and faster, but for once we had beaten them, and on their own territory. There was tremendous satisfaction in that.

JEREMY GUSCOTT

A sight I will never forget was that of Clive Rowlands. He had tears flooding down his cheeks as he greeted every player and he told us, 'The lion is getting bigger!'

SCOTT HASTINGS

Bizarrely there was a fourth Test match back at Ballymore against an ANZAC XV – which was a combined New Zealand and Australian team. Only two New Zealanders – the great Frano Botica and the prop Steve McDowell – turned up, so they played alongside 13 Australians. We won that match as well.

FINLAY CALDER

Nick Farr-Jones is on record saying that the Lions coming over and beating them up in 1989 was the best thing that ever happened to Australian rugby. His point was that if it hadn't been for the experience they wouldn't have won the World Cup two years later.

Professionalisation was the best thing that ever happened to rugby at the top level, by a mile; because the strain on players, on their families, and on their employers, was becoming more and more and more. It had started at the World Cup in 1987 when people began to realise that the commercial aspects were changing, and reached its inevitable conclusion when they made the announcement in 1995 that the game would go open. I suppose the 1989 Lions were an important step in that process. We were playing in front of full stadiums and it was great fun – I wouldn't change those seven weeks of my life for anything – but money was pouring into the game and the players weren't seeing a penny of it, so it was obvious that it wasn't going to be long before there had to be a change.

Ieuan Evans screams in delight as he scores the clinching try.

CHAPTER TWENTY-FOUR

THE TWILIGHT OF THE AMATEUR
1993
NEW ZEALAND

THE LAST *Lions of the amateur era took off in the aftermath of a mediocre Five Nations Championship which had ended with a thumping win by Ireland over England in Dublin, a win against the odds. The uneven nature of the tournament gave rise to a degree of uncertainty as to whether this team really could become the second Lions to win a series in New Zealand.*

The good news was that Ian McGeechan, the master of 1989, became the first man ever to coach two Lions tours, a welcome recognition that the post as Lions coach should always go to the best man, and not simply be informally rotated around. Gavin Hastings, the regal Scotland fullback, also seemed to be a wise choice as captain, although the party seemed to be less strong in key areas. Significantly, the committee system of selection meant that McGeechan was not always allowed his preferred choices.

Predictably, the 13-match tour of New Zealand was to be mired in controversy – over refereeing, as ever, with the First Test being decided by one of the most controversial calls of all time – and also because the pressure of the tour exposed shortcomings in the original selection and, as the tour developed, a clear division sprung up between the Test team and the midweek team. The split reached a nadir when the Lions lost embarrassingly against Hawke's Bay and Waikato, robbing the tour of momentum at a crucial stage.

To this day, some of the '93 party still have a bitter taste in their mouth and are adamant they would have won the series. The fact that they came so close after a mediocre Five Nations suggests the coaching party could not be improved upon and McGeechan's diary of the tour was titled So Close to Glory. *As journalist Clem Thomas noted, it 'could just as easily have been called* Same Old Story.' *By the time the Lions arrived back home they were being viewed by New Zealanders as potentially one of the best Test sides to have toured the Land of the Long White Cloud, but they still came up short by 2-1 in the Test series, despite a tremendous win in Wellington in the Second Test.*

The barricades surrounding the 'play for the love of the game' ethos were crumbling during the early 1990s, and it would be two years later that they would be fully dismantled. An old-style controversy arose when Wade Dooley's father died during the tour; the England second-row immediately flew home for the funeral and an appropriate period of mourning. Dooley wanted to re-join the tourists but under the agreements for the trip, he was not allowed to, as he had already been replaced.

This did not help the mood of the Lions camp, although the silver lining was that it did give a fresh-faced lock called Martin Johnson, who had honed his game during an 18-month stint of club rugby in New Zealand, his first taste of action in the red jersey. It would not be his last.

Opposite: Tour captain, Gavin Hastings.

That this was an amateur tour played by policemen, builders, bankers, lawyers and pilots was underlined by the fact that the players received £22 a day communication allowance which at the time would buy them 25 minutes on the phone to their family back in Britain. Some were also force to claim a £40 a day hardship allowance to make up for lost earnings.

McGeechan was part of a management team that also including tour manager Geoff Cooke, the man whose organisational skills helped transform England's rugby fortunes in the late 1980s and early 1990s, and assistant coach Dick Best, another man of pedigree.

There had been three outstanding candidates for the captaincy – Will Carling, who had led England to two Grand Slams by then and a World Cup final, the Scottish fullback Gavin Hastings and the Welsh winger Ieuan Evans. Hastings was given the nod on the grounds that he had toured New Zealand three times, the Kiwi supporters knew who he was, and he was a racing certainty to start at fullback. Carling was a massive public figure, but not necessarily a popular one amongst officialdom or with the Celts, and as things turned out would not last the Test series as a first choice centre and would withdraw from possible selection for future tours – the only major player ever to do so in the modern era.

Hastings ended the adventure with his reputation enhanced both as a player and as a leader. His boot rewrote the record books as he scored the most points by a Lions player in a series, the most penalty goals in a match and became the tourists' leading scorer in Test matches. This was also the fir Lions tour where a try was worth five points and many observers thought it would end up in a free-running touchdown festival, but Hastings' boot and that of Grant Fox, the home fly-half, turned out to be the main protagonists.

It is to Carling's credit that he took his demotion on his very famous chin and knuckled down in the midweek games, which is more than can be said for some of the dirt-trackers. Of these games, there wer losses recorded to Otago, Auckland, Hawke's Bay and Waikato.

Half of the 34-man party were English, their largest representation for years, but there were just two Irishmen – prop Nick Popplewell and lock Mick Galwey – in the initial selection. To say that that put Irish noses out of joint would be an understatement, particularly as the Irish had beaten Carling's England in the final match of the Five Nations.

The Irish press had a field day but Best was quoted as saying after the tour that selection had been a dog fight with every home faction trying to get their own men into the party. For example, Best fought for Jeff Probyn, the English prop, to be taken but was outvoted and still thinks the defeat to Ireland was a factor in this, and that Probyn would have made significant dents in the All Black front-row. Peter Wright and Paul Burnell, the chosen tight-heads, lacked authority and the Lions were forced to switch Jason Leonard over to the tight-head during the series.

The final selection headed off to New Zealand from London and started with wins over North Auckland, North Harbour, the New Zealand Maoris and Canterbury, playing with a rare verve and style, with the comeback win over the Maoris particularly impressive. Ben Clarke in the back-row and Jeremy Guscott in the centre were supercharged.

Then the team hit their first road block. James Robson, the medic from Dundee, was on his first Lions trip and after seeing the state of some players after the game against Otago, which ended in a 37-24 defeat, it is a wonder that he ever toured again. Scott Hastings ended up under the surgeon's knife with an horrendous fractured cheek and there were also worries about Carling and the giant

English lock Martin Bayfield, who was taken out in mid-air and crashed to the ground from a great height – opinion varied as to whether this key Lion was deliberately targeted. He recovered but remained shaken.

But centre Hastings, a hero of 1989 and a superb tourist, was off the trip. The ship was steadied with a 34-16 win over Southland in Invercargill before McGeechan had to pick his side for the First Test at Lancaster Park. Surprisingly he opted for Carling in the centre although up to then the England captain had been short of form, and gave Kenny Milne the nod at hooker over Brian Moore.

What followed in Christchurch would have knocked the stuffing out of many touring sides as Australian referee Brian Kinsey made at least three decisions that Lions supporters and their Kiwi counterparts still argue about to this day. Kinsey gave the All Blacks a try when Frank Bunce and Evans tussled for the ball over the line, with television pictures showing that Evans had a grip on the ball as they crossed the line and the ball wasn't grounded. Then he called the Lions back for a penalty when Carling was odds-on to score, despite being held by flanker Michael Jones after being released by Jeremy Guscott, turning seven points for the tourists into three.

But still McGeechan's men were leading 18-17 with seconds on the clock. Then Kinsey controversially penalised No 8 Dean Richards when it appeared that Bunce had held on to the ball after a tackle – this presented Fox with the chance to win the game. There was no danger of him missing and the Lions had a hard job containing their disappointment or disgust.

To win the Second Test after such a setback is a testament to the fighting spirit of the squad, or the Saturday part of it at least. Captain Hastings was suffering from a hamstring injury and volunteered to miss the game reckoning all 15 players had to be fully fit to face such a fierce examination. McGeechan had other ideas and Hastings played, as did the newly-landed Johnson – one of seven Englishmen in the back and 11 in the starting line-up. Carling was omitted. McGeechan spent the week carefully going through the game plan and, as he later admitted, sent out a team with far less licence than usual.

The 1993 tour party.

The All Blacks scored early when, horrendously, Hastings dropped a high kick and centre Eroni Clarke scored, but the Lions led 9-7 at the break before winger Rory Underwood scored a stunning try: New Zealand captain Sean Fitzpatrick knocked on, scrum-half Dewi Morris counter-attacked and Guscott drew John Kirwan to send Underwood flying down the left-hand touch line at the gaunt old Athletic Park, to score.

Underwood's try sealed only the sixth Test win ever by the Lions on New Zealand soil and although the midweekers suffered a dispiriting loss to Waikato, by 38-10, hopes were high that Hastings could emulate John Dawes, 23 years previously, by captaining a winning Test side against the All Blacks.

Surprisingly, the hosts left out No 8 Zinzan Brooke and re-constituted their lineout by calling in the veteran Andy Haden to do some coaching sessions. The Lions, encouragingly, took a 10-0 lead after a Scott Gibbs try and five points from the boot of Hastings.

But the All Blacks were to prove convincingly superior, and led by Sean Fitzpatrick, they launched a ferocious assault on the tourists. With the lineout misfiring and a lack of composure across the park, the Lions conceded tries to Bunce, Fitzpatrick and Jon Preston, leaving them on the ropes and eventually on the wrong end of a 30-13 defeat. It was a bitter end to another bitter series.

It was a shame that allegations of excessive drinking by party members not in the Test squad damaged morale, and the fact that in the olden days, such behaviour would not have been quite so out of order, is no excuse. Yet this was also a tour conducted in an oppressive environment, in which affection and even respect for the Lions appeared to be in short supply from the New Zealand public and media.

It might have been an amateur tour but McGeechan conducted a thoroughly professional inquest into the events in New Zealand. In his report, he made 13 recommendations, stating that the coach should have the final say on selection of the squad and that the tourists needed more time together before they left the United Kingdom. He also had some salient points to make about the difference between referees in the southern and northern hemispheres.

GAVIN HASTINGS

Without doubt, the pinnacle of my rugby career was to be selected as captain of the British & Irish Lions on their 1993 tour of New Zealand.

It was something that gave me a marvellous sense of personal fulfilment, but at the same time I was also aware of the enormous honour that the selectors had conferred on me, by recognising that I was the best man to lead the Lions. It was, therefore, an extremely unnerving responsibility and a severe challenge.

It was a fabulous honour to captain the Lions in New Zealand, for I like the country and I respected New Zealand rugby players. At the same time, I would like to think that they respect me as a rugby player because I performed to a level in New Zealand that I am proud of, and I am similarly proud of the way that the Lions performed in the Test series. We held our heads high, we conducted ourselves well, both on and off the field, and you cannot hope for, or expect, anything more than that.

I had the benefit of having been on the previous Lions tour in 1989 and I think I had the even greater benefit of being known to New Zealand and its rugby people.

I had been out there in 1987 for the World Cup with Scotland and stayed to play club rugby for Auckland University. I went back with Scotland in 1990 and returned in 1992, this time with a World XV to celebrate the centenary of the NZRFU.

I think all those factors were extremely important in advancing my claims for the captaincy and I think it was a decision seen as a good one out in New Zealand. I also believe that I had huge support in the British Isles.

MIKE TEAGUE

The success of Lions tours is that you meet these men in a very special cause, and you become lifelong friends. Ask any player and they all want to say, 'We were Lions.' However, in 1993 there were too many players living on reputations, past their sell-by-date, who had gone on one tour too many. Also there were too many political selections, and I do not believe it was the best side that could have represented the Lions.

JASON LEONARD (England)
Toured: 1993, 1997 & 2001

My first Lions trip was a fascinating experience, although it would have been much better if we'd won, of course. What I found particularly enjoyable was the tour mentality – everyone sticking together, the cross-nation banter and the breaking down of national stereotypes.

Even as a player, you end up believing what is written about other players a lot of the time, so when you meet them and tour with them for eight weeks, it can be a real shock to discover they're actually OK.

It's also good to get to know some of the non-England players in a friendly environment because, routinely, we tend to see people only when we're about to play them or have just played them. You're all on the same side on tour, which produces much tighter bonds and allows you to get closer to other players.

BEN CLARKE (England)
Toured: 1993

It was the pinnacle. Everyone remembers Lions teams, and it was just a wonderful experience that I will always cherish. It all began well before the tour because of the selection build-up, and the Five Nations season before it was massive because you were playing against your Lions rivals. So, the first thing was to get selected, and then you wanted to get in the Test team. I was driving my car through Bath, and my mum called – it was about 10.30 in the morning, and she'd heard it on the radio. I knew I had half a chance, but you don't expect it, because that would be the wrong thing to do with a Lions selection. It was a fantastic feeling.

PETER WRIGHT (Scotland)
Toured: 1993

I knew before I went that I was a controversial selection. Most people expected Jeff Probyn to get the call, but he missed out and I have no doubt that politics had a lot to do with that. He was a seasoned international prop at that stage and I was at the end of my first season, but there were already 16 Englishmen in the squad so that maybe counted against him.

JEREMY GUSCOTT

Probyn should have gone – there is not a doubt in my mind about that. He was hugely respected by every front-row player in the Five Nations and all the England guys knew how good he was – and how important he had been to the success that we were enjoying during those years in the late eighties and nineties. I remember thinking at the time that he hadn't been selected because they were looking for quicker, more mobile props. But the ones that were selected were hammered up front and it soon became apparent how much we could have done with having him there to shore the whole thing up. The selectors had gone for a balanced squad which encompassed all four countries rather than just selecting the best players available to them; there were too many other English guys, so Probyn missed out. But as a result, ultimately so did we.

PETER WINTERBOTTOM

One of the problems was that although Gavin Hastings was captain and was Geech the coach, the majority of players were from England, and dominated Test selection. However, the English didn't think it was an England tour, even though we were the most successful team at the time, and it showed in the way that Nick Popplewell, Ieuan Evans and Scott Gibbs all broke through into the Test side. It was clearly a problem for some of the Scottish players, who were demotivated and didn't participate in the midweek games as they should have.

MIKE TEAGUE

I have the utmost respect and time for Gavin Hastings – the best fullback of my era – but whether he was the best captain, I don't know. Gavin would be one of those guys I would go to battle with, but political considerations shouldn't have got in the way. He was probably not the right man to lead the tour. Will Carling was a natural leader of men, and should have been picked as captain. He was underrated as a player and as a captain – but he was also the first rugby superstar, he was getting married, and he had too much off-field stuff going on. There were a lot of English on the tour, and so Carling was probably the right choice, but he didn't get the nod due to the English contingent being so big and the danger of them dominating everything.

WILL CARLING (England)
Toured: 1993

I didn't need to captain the Lions from an ego point of view. I'm not belittling the Lions. The 1993 tour was a unique experience. But, at that stage in my career, it was nice not to be given that responsibility. Maybe I was being selfish… The Lions were looking for an emphasis away from the English bias. Two of the three-man management team were from England. And English players were obviously going to provide the majority of the squad. To be Lions captain is a great honour. No one would ever turn it down. But, after five years of leading England, I was looking forward to the responsibility being with someone else. So I spoke to Geoff Cooke and said I was tired. Gavin Hastings knew how I felt. We had discussed it when we worked together for ITV... I didn't head out to New Zealand thinking, 'It should have been me.'

PETER WRIGHT

When we ran out for our first game against North Auckland, Stuart Barnes – who was captaining the side – did the usual thing of laying the Lion mascot next to the flag on the halfway line. They had this guy dressed up in a stupid costume dancing around, and he came over and stood on our mascot, which I thought was highly disrespectful – so I shouldered him to the ground as he ran past.

JEREMY GUSCOTT

I was in prime position to get a Test spot, and thought that if people didn't want to train and put it in, then that was one less competitor for a Test place. I was wrong – I should have said, 'Get going and put the work in.' I went to New Zealand as a bit of a namby-pamby runner, but was determined to show that I could defend. I think I did that, and came back with a lot of confidence. I was pleased with how I played.

PETER WINTERBOTTOM

I told Will Carling at one stage that he was a fucking disgrace, because he was a good player, and was letting himself down – although Scott Gibbs was playing better.

The New Zealand Maori throw down their challenge to the Lions with their Haka.

It's hard to take the disappointment when you're an international and you don't get selected, but it's quite sad they let themselves down. How people handle that is not just the key to how they perform, but how everybody performs.

SCOTT HASTINGS

One of the great things about touring with the Lions is that you get to meet some of the game's great legends, and when we went to Wellington to play against the Maoris our liaison officer was Bernie Fraser. Richard Webster revealed that he had been a ball-boy at Swansea when the All Blacks had toured Wales in 1980, and he told Bernie that the thing he had admired most about him was his amazing mouser. I don't think Bernie was very impressed by that.

BEN CLARKE

A lot of the players felt for Wade Dooley, and the whole thing must have been heart-breaking when he had to return home for his father's funeral. New Zealand offered to pay his way back, and where they did the right thing, I don't think the Four Home Unions did in refusing the offer. Jeff Probyn must have been a very close call at tight-head, and he must have felt hard done by. He had very good technique, and we would have benefited from him being there without a doubt. As a tourist Richard Webster is the guy I remember because he was great fun and always saw the lighter side of things. He always had a smile and lots of positive energy.

JEREMY GUSCOTT

We went clay pigeon shooting and Richard Webster, who was completely hyperactive, was given a pump-action shotgun – the least responsible person in the whole tour

Gavin Hastings beats New Zealand Maori's Sam Doyle to score the winning try.

squad to be given charge of something like that. When it was his turn he did quite well and hit some of the clays, then started to celebrate, holding the gun casually in one hand – and it went off, hitting the ground about two inches from Peter Winterbottom's foot. Wints went completely pale but he handled it OK, until the reality of the situation hit him later and he realised that he had almost lost his foot, or some toes – which would have been bad enough, but he would have also lost his Test spot… to Richard Webster.

PETER WINTERBOTTOM
As soon as Martin Johnson came out it was clear that he would be in the Test side – and it was clear he should have been on the tour from the start.

WILL CARLING
We had all known Wade Dooley's dad. It was a chance for this great amateur game to show the world what a great amateur game it is. If rugby had been a professional game, I might have understood – it would have cost a lot of money to have paid an extra man. But this was a player who had won 50 caps for his country, whose father loved rugby and would have wanted him to come out, who had announced that he was quitting rugby after the tour, who had been invited out by the host union. Even now I can't believe the Home Unions behaved like that.

SCOTT HASTINGS
The first half against the Maoris was a disaster. I remember looking up at the score-board at half-time and thinking we were in real trouble. We were 20-0 down, but we had the sun and the slope in our favour after the break and things eventually started to go our way and we managed to come back to 24-20. It was a big relief, because if we had carried on like we did in the first half we would have been humiliated.

PETER WRIGHT
The Maoris had a guy called Alan Prince who scored a great try – but as he dived over he gave Rory Underwood the bird, which was completely out of order. To show that sort of lack of respect is bad, but to do it to someone who was a world-class player and a great ambassador of the game was shocking. The Maori management handled it really impressively. They came out and apologised and said how disappointed they were with their player. They turned what could have been a really negative situation into something which reflected really well on them.

JEREMY GUSCOTT
Rob Andrew played well in the Test matches, but in the build-up to the series, I really hoped that Stuart Barnes would make it in ahead of him. We were playing together at Bath and I felt that we were a better fit. But it wasn't to be. Barnsie is a big

red wine drinker and he started off the tour taking it fairly easy on the booze front, but after a few weeks the split between the midweek side and the Test team began to show and it was evident that the selectors were going to go with Rob at ten – so Barnsie began to indulge in some of the produce from the local vineyards. He would turn up on the bus for training looking pretty grey and with his sunglasses firmly in place. He coined a new phrase, having stuck to just 'two quiet ones' early on, it eventually became 'two quiet ones – followed by twenty loud ones'.

There's been a lot made about the midweek side going AWOL on the rugby front and ended up just partying – and there's no doubt that some of them did – but there were those of us who played in the Test side who also had some pretty big nights out. I remember going on a fairly big bender after the Maori game where a whole load of us went out until the early hours and were crashing all over the hotel when we got back. There was a team meeting the next day and Geoff Cooke stood up and had a real go about there being so much noise – and he told us that those responsible were to own up and go and see him after the meeting. I wish I could say that I was big enough to go and see him, but I didn't. In fact, none of us did.

SCOTT HASTINGS

I remember thinking after the Maori game that Jerry Guscott was almost certain to be in the Test side, which left me, Will Carling and Scott Gibbs battling it out for the other centre spot – so I knew I needed a big performance before the Test team was announced. I was on the bench against Canterbury the following Wednesday and against Otago on the Saturday after that – and for some reason I knew I was going to get on in that game. While we were walking around the pitch before kick-off a seagull landed on my head and shat all over me, I was absolutely covered, and somebody said it was supposed to be good luck. And sure enough, ten minutes into the game Will Carling had to come off with a leg injury and I thought, 'Great, this is my chance.' We were playing pretty well, but Otago scored a try just before half-time so it was really tight. Then, at the start of the second half, I went to smash Josh Kronfeld and his knee must have hit my face. The next thing I remember is trying to close my mouth but it wouldn't shut properly. I knew there was something serious wrong so I just stood up and walked off the pitch. And that was it – my tour was over in an instant.

MIKE TEAGUE

Against teams like Waikato and Otago you want to be at your best, and although guys like Richard Webster were outstanding for the dirt-trackers, not everyone was as motivated. The other problem was that New Zealand is a very hard place to go and win in. You can catch them napping once, but you will not catch them again. Sean Fitzpatrick, the All Black captain was also very good at psyching out the opposition, and finding their weaknesses, and New Zealand were in the process of building a really good team.

PETER WRIGHT

As the tour progressed the squad became more and more divided. The Saturday team was clearly the priority, which was absolutely understandable. Meanwhile the midweek team was left to its own devices.

PETER WINTERBOTTOM

It was very unfortunate that the tour party split in two. You felt for some of the boys in the midweek side, because quite a few of their team-mates didn't do the shirt justice. Some of them had given up. The key to a successful Lions tour is you have to have quality players, but you also have to have team spirit running right through it. Whether you are in the Test side or not, everyone has to pull in the same direction. In 1997 Geech and Fran Cotton had clearly identified that non-Test players had to pull their weight, and before the tour they got the guys to say before they left how they would contribute if they didn't make the Test side. In 1983 and 1993 we didn't do that, and the Waikato and Hawke's Bay matches in 1993 were embarrassing.

PETER WRIGHT

I've heard all the chat about the Scottish front five, and myself in particular – worst Lion ever and all that crap – and that does grate. People are entitled to their opinion – but I know that I did the best I could. I played on both sides of the scrum for the team, and we had a couple of pushovers when I was on the park. What doesn't kill you makes you stronger, and I came back from that tour, re-evaluated my game, and became a better player as a result.

Power players: Dean Richards grapples with Michael Jones.

PETER WINTERBOTTOM

In the First Test we got so close, and then the penalty given against Dean Richards ended it. It was harsh, the referee didn't have to give it, and it was the last play of the game. It was rough justice to lose like that, especially as Frank Bunce had also been awarded a dodgy try. But what's the point of moaning and being characterised as a sore loser? It was the First Test and we still thought we could beat them.

JEREMY GUSCOTT

To this day I still don't know what that penalty was for at the end of the First Test – but it was a decision that turned the game. We were robbed. We had gone well up to that point, but that decision killed us, and we did well to come back and win the Second Test in Wellington.

BEN CLARKE

We had quality throughout the squad, but Scott Gibbs was very powerful and really took the game to the New Zealand midfield. For the All Blacks, the talisman was Sean Fitzpatrick, who was a great leader and player, and we also had to contend with Michael Jones, who not only had great ball-playing ability and real physical presence but was also incredibly athletic.

ANDY NICOL (Scotland)
Toured: 1993 & 2001

In 1993 I didn't make selection. Gary Armstrong was originally in the squad but he got injured and I felt I was in with a good shout for being his replacement, but they went with Rob Jones instead – which was fair enough. So I went to the South Sea Islands with Scotland instead, and we had just been beaten in Apia in Samoa, and I was lying on the deck absolutely drained because it was really hot, as you can imagine. Then, Allan Hosie, the tour manager appeared next to me and said, 'Chin up – you're going over to New Zealand tomorrow to join the Lions.' Robert had taken ill and been taken to hospital for blood tests, and they had sent for me as a temporary replacement. So, whereas the rest of the Scotland squad were going home via a three-day stopover in Fiji, I was going to New Zealand to join up with the Lions, which seemed to me like a great deal.

When I got to New Plymouth, Peter Winterbottom said to me, 'You had the chance to go to Fiji and you came here instead – what is wrong with you?' I think he was joking. I was there for six days, by which point Rob had recovered, but they gave me a special dispensation because we had quite a few injuries, and I sat on the bench against Taranaki. These were the days before tactical substitutions, so with six minutes to go Rob clutched his shoulder and came off – and I got on. Willie-John McBride played 68 games for the Lions, and I doubt he can name every opposition side he faced. Well, I can tell you exactly what I did in my Lions career: ten passes, two kicks and stood on one New Zeaander. And we won! Geech wanted to keep me as a training member of the squad, and New Zealand agreed to it, but the Home Unions blocked it.

WILL CARLING

Auckland was a shock. It was the first time in my life that I had been dropped. I had no inkling about it. Nobody had spoken to me or warned me... I had this terrible sick feeling in my stomach. It wasn't that I thought it was unfair; Scott Gibbs had been playing really well and deserved his chance. But I wondered what I was doing on the tour. I had drifted along for four weeks, and had just paid the penalty.

JEREMY GUSCOTT

I was in the stand for the Hawke's Bay game and it was pretty tough viewing. There were guys out there who were trying their best – guys like Barnes and Carling, who were pushing to get into the Test side – but there were others who were just awful and had clearly given up trying. I can still remember how angry I felt about that; the honour of wearing a Lions jersey should never be taken for granted like that – the tradition is too important and you just think about all the work done by the guys who never get to wear it, but would give their left arm to be out there. We all went out and had fun and had some pretty big benders, but the tour failed right there – when players stopped caring about the jersey and what it meant.

BEN CLARKE

It was galling watching the midweek team because we, as Lions, should have dealt with those New Zealand provincial sides. Too many people were looking around for excuses, and although I can understand a huge amount of disappointment if you don't

Dewi Morris dive-passes to clear the ball from a ruck.

get in the Test side, some players did not deal with it very well. The best way is to prove to the selectors that they've got it wrong by playing out of your skin.

PETER WRIGHT

The Saturday team always sat at the back of the bus, but on one occasion towards the end of the tour we finished training before them and got changed quickly so that we could take their place at the back. When the Saturday team eventually turned up they gave us a suspicious look then must have thought better of making a scene and decided to sit down at the front. Little did they know that somebody had got hold of a box of over-ripe mandarins, and half a mile down the road we all jumped up and bombarded them with this rotten fruit. The driver was obviously in a hurry so wasn't for stopping, and it was like the scene in 'Bugsy Malone' when all the kid gangsters get covered in cream pies. Martin Bayfield was too tall to duck his head down behind the seats, so he got the worst of it. It was all done as a bit of fun – but there was a message there as well. Guys like Will Carling and Mike Teague were in the midweek team, and I don't suppose they were entirely comfortable as marginalised figures, which is what we all basically were by that point.

PETER WINTERBOTTOM

In the Second Test we had the edge up front and played well tactically, and a combination of Rory Underwood's try and Rob Andrew kicking his penalties won it.

JASON LEONARD

Playing New Zealand is always difficult. Playing New Zealand as a forward is more difficult still. Playing New Zealand in New Zealand as a forward is about as hard as it gets.

Frank Bunce is awarded a controversial try despite being held up in the tackle by Ieuan Evans.

As I prepared to do just that, with the Lions shirt on my back and in a Test match for the first time, it felt like one of the most important moments in my career. I knew how much it meant to win. If we lost, the series would be over, and if we drew, we'd have no hope of winning the three-match series. We had to win.

I had a good game in what proved to be quite a comfortable win for us, 20-7, which the Lions' biggest Test win in New Zealand to date. The local fans were getting quite upset at the fact that the Lions were winning – they really don't like losing at home – and someone threw a beer can at Brian Moore.

I didn't see it at the time but when we went into the next scrum I could smell this awful stench of beer and Brian kept burping. He told me afterwards that when he'd picked the beer can up to throw it to the side of the pitch, he realised it was full, so he opened it, toasted the baying crowd and took a slurp before throwing it aside.

BRIAN MOORE
At that point in the game if we had been pushed over there we would have lost the Test. We scrummaged more for the ball and that was obviously a dent to their psyche because they had gone for it expecting to do us. No one who's not a forward understands the huge significance of these small events and that one was almost imperceptible to most people. But it was a big turning point because shortly after that there was a turnover and Rory Underwood scored.

I remember going back to the halfway line and waving to the crowd nicely and cans

Brian Moore spills blood for the cause against Auckland.

rained down. One that landed on me was actually full. Now I don't know why I did this but I opened it and drank it and threw it away. That upset everyone more.

JEREMY GUSCOTT
I got the ball after the turnover and we swept up the left flank. There was a two-on-one with me and Rory against John Kirwan, with John Timu covering across behind him. I knew that I had to fix Kirwin, otherwise he would just push Rory into touch or at least be on hand to slow him down until Timu made it over to make the tackle. I didn't do anything special to fix him, but sometimes you just need a look and you put doubt in the defenders mind. I looked up and our eyes met and then I glanced back inside him and that was it – I knew I had him. I straightened, he turned inwards slightly and I gave the pass. Rory had hardly any space, but it was all he needed – he didn't have to break stride, all he had to do was catch the ball and put on the afterburners. He literally had a yard or two of space but he left Timu absolutely for dead – and then pulled off one of the most ungraceful dives ever seen on a rugby field as he went into score.

RORY UNDERWOOD
The All Blacks kept coming but we smashed them back, we held them at a critical five-metre scrum where Jason Leonard proved his worth at tight-head, the two Martins [Bayfield and Johnson] dominated the lineout and, when a bit of loose ball appeared, I was able to help the tabloid headline writers into 'Rory Glory' mode.

When Sean Fitzpatrick dropped the ball, Dewi Morris saw the space on the blind-side immediately. We had depth to our attack, Jerry Guscott drew the cover and gave me the space to get round John Kirwan and beat John Timu for pace.

All I could think of in those 40 yards was the need to get the ball down because I knew how important a try was at that stage, so when I could see the line I took off into the worst dive for the corner ever. Whether I could have got nearer the posts to help the conversion I don't know and to be honest, it didn't seem that important.

As I was running back I raised an arm in salutation to the boys in the stand. I knew how tough it had been for them. They had been putting in the work, they had been beaten, the press was starting to give them a lot of stick and they, as much as us, needed the tonic of a Test win.

We retreated to a brilliant atmosphere in the changing room; there was relief, delight, the knowledge that we had achieved the win we felt had deserved in the First Test and how well everyone had recovered after the traumas of the previous fortnight.

MIKE TEAGUE
I played in the Second Test, but I was carrying injuries. Frank Bunce was pretty impressive, and when he tackled it was like being hit by a train. For the Lions, Ben Clarke was absolutely on a roll. He has not had the credit for how well he played,

probably because we did not win the series – but what you need is young players like him hitting a purple patch. On Lions tours you want young hungry players combined with a handful of senior pros, but not too many.

There were a lot of players on that tour who should not have been there, simply because they were not good enough to be Lions. I remember Peter Winterbottom coming into the changing room after the Waikato game, and he was disgusted with the performance of some of the front-five forwards. I had been the pack leader that afternoon, and it had been a very long one, with John Mitchell orchestrating the demolition of the Lions. Right in front of the players in question, Wints said to me, 'I refuse to play with them again.' And that was very much the state of the tour at that stage – a bit of mumping had come into it when some players had missed out on Test selection, and the tour party had split down the middle.

WILL CARLING

I don't understand how we could be so focused for the Tests, and so poor in midweek… I know that the Tests are the thing… But I was shocked to find out that guys who were internationals were not mentally strong enough. I don't think I've been in a side that hasn't competed before. It was about character more than ability: Waikato were a good side, but Hawke's Bay were not. Once my Test chance had gone, it was down to personal pride. The tour was going down the tubes, but I was still keen to play. The results might have been disastrous, but I got a lot from the last two midweek games. I was under pressure – I had to show a bit of character. Certainly, the Carling silver spoon image took a battering. It did me no harm to see life from the downside.

Nick Popplewell, Martin Johnson and Martin Bayfield in action against Auckland.

PETER WRIGHT

People talk about us losing the Waikato game, but what they forget is that Waikato had won the First Division Championship the previous season and were about to win the Ranfurly Shield from Auckland a few months later – so we knew it was going to be one of our toughest provincial games and it was being played by the midweekers right at the end of the tour. It was crazy scheduling! People also forget that we played that game with a few guys injured. Will Carling wasn't fit but we needed to keep Scott Gibbs fresh for the last Test, and Richard Webster had a bad arm as well. So there was a lot of mitigating circumstances. But it was the only game the whole Scottish front-five played together, so I suppose it was easy to pin the blame on us.

PETER WINTERBOTTOM

Mike Teague told me about an incident when he walked into a stadium urinal after the Waikato game and overheard an exchange between an elderly Kiwi fan and one of the Scottish Lions who had played in the defeat. The pensioner said, 'Mate, you were a bloody disgrace,' to which he got the reply, 'Shut up old man, or I'll give you a good hiding.' Teague responded, 'My money's on the old man.'

WILL CARLING

I had a varied series: I played the First Test, commentated on the Second, and sat on the bench for the Third. The bench was easily the hardest. In the commentary box, I accepted that I would not be involved.

GAVIN HASTINGS

It was a fascinating experience and I am sure that everyone who went on tour was richer for it. To me, that is what playing top-level rugby is about. It is not playing in front of your home crowd or 50,000 people at Murrayfield; if you really want to test

Rory Underwood finishes off a brilliant individual run to score in the Second Test.

yourself, the place to do it is New Zealand because, as far as I am concerned, it is the hardest place I know to play rugby. There are no easy games in New Zealand, the pressure is intense, there is no hiding place and you just have to get on with it.

It was a great credit to the Lions that we came to the third and deciding Test match with the series squared at one-each. The highlight of the tour was the Second Test victory in Wellington, but it was extremely difficult to raise our game to that level two weeks in a row.

PETER WINTERBOTTOM
In the Third Test New Zealand made changes, bringing in Aaron Pene at No 8. He and Jamie Joseph at blind-side and they got New Zealand going forward. Michael Jones also played a lot looser, and we knew that New Zealand would come back firing. However, I don't think we quite understood how far we had to step up to win it.

JEREMY GUSCOTT
The All Blacks had worked us out by the Third Test, and when they got into Martin Bayfield our game was gone. I didn't have a huge sense of disappointment, but the whole scenario would have been different but for that First Test result. I thought we were struggling in a few areas, but we still went out and beat them in Wellington, and we went into the last Test believing we could win the series. However, having done judo as a kid, I know that there are certain floor moves and holds that are almost impossible to get out of, and the Third Test was a bit like that. It took them 30 minutes to work us out, and when they did there was no coming back. They were a better team, but we gave them a good run for their money.

PETER WINTERBOTTOM
Ben Clarke was a revelation, and the outstanding Lion. Ben was right on form, and played as well as he ever played. He was really fit, quick, and a very good ball-carrier because he was a big, physical man who did not go down easily in contact. For the All Blacks it was Michael Jones. He was a great player, who had everything: quick, great hands, fantastically fit, and very athletic. He was difficult to play against.

JEREMY GUSCOTT
Ben Clarke was unbelievable. He said, 'I'm having them,' and when he got the bit between his teeth against the All Blacks he was unstoppable. All he had to do at blind-side was get hold of the ball, smash into people, and not worry about his hands. He was immense on that tour, almost head and shoulders above everyone else, which is pretty difficult to do. He was on a different plane to the rest of us.

BEN CLARKE
It's flattering being told they would have adopted you as an All Black, and kind words from a very well respected rugby nation – and one that doesn't give too many compliments either.

PETER WINTERBOTTOM

We played 18 games with an average of 23,000 spectators a game in 1983, and we got a communications allowance – but it was a nightmare trying to phone home anyway. Roy Laidlaw didn't get anything from his employers. He said the local butcher would give his family free meat, but when you consider something like that, and gates of 23,000, it's a disgrace.

Everything was far more professional by 1993, and the whole organisation of the tour was at a different level. It seemed in 1983 that we were just a bunch of blokes going out and giving it our best shot. Before we went to New Zealand there was one training session at the Honourable Artillery Company, and medicals at the St Ermin's Hotel, and we were given a tracksuit and a waterproof and off we went. In 1983 I was still farming up in Yorkshire, so financially there was no benefit, whereas in 1993 I was working in the City for Tullet & Tokyo and I was given paid time off. Most companies had started paid leave by that time because the game had become bigger from a commercial aspect.

The Lions is the biggest thing you can be involved with as a rugby player – although if England had won the 1991 World Cup, I would probably have put that as my biggest achievement. But we didn't. It is very difficult to be successful with the Lions, because, as the records show, it is nigh on impossible to win a series with such short preparation time. A Lions tour is very unforgiving because you have no time in which to remedy mistakes in selection or tactics. It is especially difficult on tours to New Zealand and South Africa, where the game is a religion, whereas it isn't in the UK and Ireland – although it is probably more achievable in the professional era than it was then.

I had my 33rd birthday on the 1993 tour, and I retired from club and international rugby after the Third Test at Eden Park. I'd had a fantastic career, but it doesn't always end as a fairytale.

Scott Gibbs powers through the New Zealand defence.

GAVIN HASTINGS

The reality of a Lions tour is probably far less glamorous than the expectancy before it all happens. It is, however, a tremendous experience for young men. There is an immense amount of hard work and application, and even, at times, moments of boredom. You have to live with new people and if the relationships are going to be happy and successful, there has to be a lot of give and take.

The coming together of the best players from all the Home Nations is something very special, and I think that people treat it as such and regard it as a great honour. I certainly did. I would not have missed the experience for anything.

SCOTT GIBBS (Wales)
Toured: 1993, 1997 & 2001

I've got massively fond memories of 1993 even though we didn't win the Test series. It was initially strange to be away for nine weeks in New Zealand. Looking back now, it was probably even stranger as there was no real telecommunications through mobile phones and so on so it was old-school touring.

I went on that tour as an underdog and ended up playing the Second and Third Tests. That was a great highlight for me because I remember Ian McGeechan was delighted to give me the jersey because I'd earned it. I played hard, trained hard and I deserved to get there.

BEN CLARKE

What makes Lions tours so unique is trying to pull together a team, and my feeling is that it's important to concentrate and develop teamwork in terms of knowing how each other play. Geech achieved that in 1997 and 2009, and I think we achieved similar cohesion in the Test side in 1993.

The First Test was bloody close, but we made too many errors when we had the beating of New Zealand. It was hard-fought and rugby then was a massive territorial battle with the lineout a crucial area and in the last ten minutes we got momentum. There were two controversial incidents on which the result hinged, with Frank Bunce given an early try despite Ieuan Evans also having his hands on the ball, and then the Dean Richards penalty. To this day I don't think it was a penalty – no player would give away a penalty in that situation. New Zealand is an intimidating place to play rugby, and to referee, but I thought Kinsey's decision was outrageous. It left you very much with a sense of having been robbed.

New Zealand played the same game both weeks, and we should have beaten them both weeks. Our lineout was very powerful, as they found out in the Second Test, but there were signs they knew that already when Martin Bayfield was definitely taken out by Otago the weekend before the First Test. For the Second Test we brought people in, and tightened up as a squad because we realised we really had a wonderful opportunity to win the Test series. We knew we could command territory, and just had to be careful of them on the break. Jason Leonard coming in at tight-head paid dividends when the scrum had to hold up on our line, as did Brian Moore being selected at hooker.

We dominated the lineout in the first half to the extent that they 'replaced' one of their locks, Mark Cooksley, at half-time. He just about remembered he had a hamstring injury as we walked off, and he obviously strained it further eating an orange at half-time.

In the last Test they changed their team, bringing in Lee Stensness at inside-centre, and also concentrated on putting right their lineout and attacking ours. They were under pressure from their own media, and it was a great finish to the series with it reaching a climax at 1-1 going into the final Test.

I watched it again for the first time 14 years later – I couldn't bear to watch it before that – and you could see that by the last Test we had run out of steam, and they raised their game. They deserved to win that one, but the other two are another matter.

JEREMY GUSCOTT

Playing in New Zealand in 1993 was a completely different experience to Australia in 1989. In '89 we played on hard, fast tracks and we won the series, but in many ways 1993 was a better tour because in Australia we were pretty anonymous during the build-up to the Tests and the country only really seemed to wake up to us for the Test series, while in New Zealand every game you play is a challenge and everyone you meet has an incredible understanding about rugby and respected us players – especially after coming so close to winning the First Test and then thumping them in the Second.

BEN CLARKE

The thing about the Lions is that you have a group of guys who live together so closely for nine weeks, and then are never together in the same room again. At the time I'd just

Ben Clarke.

started working for NPower, and was on paid leave plus the tour allowance of about £20 a day – which was not enough when you have to play three card brag for eight weeks with Dean Richards, who was king of the cards. We were well looked after, and I loved New Zealand. It is a great country, and the ultimate testing ground for a rugby player. There was no let-up on or off the field, and I made sure I enjoyed the tour and the country. It was a tough tour, but that's what made it good.

Gavin Hastings tries to put on a brave face after losing the series to Sean Fitzpatrick's All Blacks.

CHAPTER TWENTY-FIVE

GLORY DAYS
1997

SOUTH AFRICA

THIS ERA *in rugby was both heady and dangerous. The Lions departed for South Africa less than two years after the game had been declared open, and therefore professional, at the famous International Rugby Board meeting in Paris in September 1995.*

Rugby authorities had spent decades battling against the spectre of professionalism and so when it became a reality, very little had been put in place to deal with the profound changes in culture that would clearly now eventuate. Indeed, sometimes rugby appeared to be thrashing around desperately trying to catch up.

To a considerable number of people, the whole concept of Lions tours was now at stake, so wedded were they to the old years of amateurism. To some, the very concept of a professional Lions team seemed to be anathema, a contradiction in terms, however curious was their reasoning.

That is why this magnificent, ferocious and compelling tour was as important as any in Lions history. Not only did the Lions fight aggression with aggression, not only did they win where so few visiting teams had won, but they triumphantly re-emerged as a gleaming professional outfit and as the team which secured the future of the Lions concept long into the future. For that, the masterly Ian McGeechan, making his third tour as head coach, his steely assistant, Jim Telfer, Fran Cotton the manager, and the great English lock and tour captain, Martin Johnson, must all take vast credit.

Any cynics were put firmly back in their places when the tourists completed a memorable 2-1 series win over the reigning world champions in front of tens of thousands of travelling fans – yet another remarkable aspect of the more recent Lions tours has been the incredible numbers following; in red hordes in their replica jerseys they added an unforgettable backdrop to many of the games and especially to the Tests, which were mega-occasions played in Cape Town, Durban and Johannesburg.

Even the tour song suggested an updating, a break with a sometimes hoary past – it was not one of the grand old traditional hymns not, thank goodness, one of the raucous 'rugby songs' but 'Wonderwall', by Oasis. Another new development was that the team was followed by a fly-on-the-wall documentary team, and while not every traditionalist and not every player was entirely happy with this, one of the fruits was a vivid off-field DVD of the tour, including a speech by Ian McGeechan before the Second Test, which was so inspiring that it even moved great Lions such as Johnson.

Bookmakers in Britain had the Lions odds-on to lose all three matches against a Springbok side that contained several of the 1995 World Cup winners, including the likes of James Small, Joost van der Westhuizen, Mark Andrews and Andre Joubert. But shrewdly managed by big Fran Cotton, who

---

Opposite: Scott Gibbs displays the defensive power that epitomised the '97 Lions.

as a player knew what it was like to beat the 'Boks in their own backyard, and brilliantly coached by what could be called the good cop/bad cop double act of Ian McGeechan and Jim Telfer (whose scrum sessions became legendary and who saw the tour as the high point of a distinguished coaching career), they pulled it off.

On his retirement, Lawrence Dallaglio, who announced himself on the world stage during the trip and later won a World Cup with England as well as two Heineken Cups with Wasps, said the tour was the best experience of his career. There were stars all over the place but probably the signature player was Welsh centre Scott Gibbs who sent a shiver down spines all over South Africa when he smashed into the giant South African prop Os du Randt in the Second Test and sent the massive man tumbling to the ground. It was the defining image of the tour.

Elsewhere Irish hooker Keith Wood, Scotland's Tom Smith and Ireland's Paul Wallace formed a Test front-row that was expected to be hammered by the home opposition; but they burrowed underneath their huge opponents and McGeechan's innovative work across the park bewildered the inexperienced Springbok coach, Carel du Plessis. Du Plessis wasn't long for the job and was soon replaced by Nick Mallett.

The influence of a group of rugby league converts should not be underestimated. Players such as Gibbs, John Bentley, Alan Tait, Dai Young, Scott Quinnell and Allan Bateman had all spent time in league and brought their professionalism with them to the squad, to the aid of those still in the transition period who had begun their careers in the amateur years.

It seems strange to relate now, but at the time there was a lively debate about who should captain the squad with Ieuan Evans from Wales, Ireland's Wood and Rob Wainwright, the Scotland flanker, all being considered. England's captain at the time, Phil de Glanville, was not deemed worthy of a spot in the extended 62-man provisional squad but it was Johnson who was to justify totally his selection. Johnson, who admitted he was no big fan of the formal stuff that went with captaincy off the pitch, was picked as much for his physical presence as for his leadership abilities.

A 35-man squad –which would swell to 40 after the inevitable injuries – left Britain after some team-building exercises designed to get players from different nations to bond with each other. Cotton also organised some more traditional team bonding when, two days before the squad flew to South Africa, he laid on a free bar for the squad at a pub in Weybridge, Surrey. Nothing bonds rugby players like a few beers and by the time last orders had been called all national barriers had apparently been broken down and the squad were united.

The players laid down their own rules – and there were none about drinking, so if a Lion fancied a pint at lunchtime the day before a Test, he could have one. But as centre Jerry Guscott wrote: 'If someone was playing on Saturday, the chances of him having a drink after Wednesday were virtually nil.' The team also resolved to go out as a group at least once a week, for a meal, to watch a film or even, as they once did, a Harlem Globetrotters basketball exhibition match. Great care was taken by McGeechan to keep the party together, even after the Test team had been named. It worked triumphantly.

So, with what was estimated to be two and a half tonnes of luggage, the first paid Lions were 30,000 feet up in business class. The reason the excess baggage bill was so astronomical was the result of yet another McGeechan masterstroke. A year before the tour the Scotsman sought out the advice of John Hart, then the coach of the All Blacks who became the first New Zealand side to win a series in South Africa.

Hart's advice was that the Lions would get no favours from the 'Boks so they had to be self-sufficient. That meant the Lions should carry over their own training equipment, including scrum machines, tackle bags and even their own drinks bottles. Hart also advised that McGeechan should pick players who were similarly self-sufficient in that they should be able to make their own decisions on the pitch and not be fazed by the odd knock back. Talk about a meeting of rugby minds.

As usual with McGeechan-led tours the coaching staff had no preconceptions about the make-up of the Test side when they left Britain. Many thought Englishmen would dominate the pack but by the time of the First Test Johnson was the only red rose man in the front-five.

The first four games were all won – against Eastern Province, Border, Western Province and Mpumalanga – but the victories were not without incident. In the 38-21 victory over Western Province, Bentley was accused of gouging by winger Small, albeit to media men after the game, and the rivalry would simmer throughout the tour.

Infamously, second-row Doddie Weir was stamped on by Mpumalanga's Marius Bosman and his tour was over. Cotton was incandescent, saying the South African should have been banned for six months. As it was all the Lions received was a three-point penalty; but the disgraceful incident only served to knit the Lions together more tightly.

There was a hiccup with a 35-30 defeat to Northern Transvaal, but a week away from the First Test against the Springboks in Cape Town there was still no clear delineation between the midweek team and the Test side until McGeechan revealed his hand. With Paul Grayson injured, Scotland's Gregor Townsend was picked at fly-half with instructions to play flat in the South Africans' faces and with the aim of moving the big South African forwards around the pitch. The back-row was to comprise Lawrence Dallaglio and Richard Hill flanking the giant Tim Rodber, an inconsistent performer for England but who was monumental in that series.

As the home propaganda machine cranked up, McGeechan countered by compiling a video of tour highlights that was played on the eve of the Test and Cotton read out letters of goodwill that had been sent by rugby fans back in the United Kingdom.

The 1997 tour party.

The match was not the easiest on the eye but an outrageous try by scrum-half Matt Dawson, in because Rob Howley had been injured out of the tour with a broken collarbone, where he dummied the entire South African cover defence, and a late try by Alan Tait got the job done in a famous 25-16 win. Tait celebrated his score with a gunslinger salute and the entire South African press went into firing squad mode as they criticised du Plessis.

Critically, the so-called dirt-trackers kept the momentum going, something they had failed to do in 1993. They had set the tour back on the road after the Northern Transvaal reverse with a great win over Gauteng, the leading province, in a match in which Bentley scored an amazing try, weaving his way over from long range.

Then after the Test, they thrashed Orange Free State by 52-30 – although the win brought a worrying incident when centre Will Greenwood swallowed his tongue after a collision and very nearly lost his life. The quick thinking of team doctor James Robson saved him.

The whole host nation was dreaming of the most ferocious backlash in Durban for the Second Test. It came. In an oppressive atmosphere the Springboks threw everything at the Lions, pounding them up front and scoring three tries, but missing out on extra points through poor kicking – with Henry Honiball, Percy Montgomery and Andre Joubert all trying their luck and failing miserably.

By contrast, the consistent Neil Jenkins, out of position at fullback, kept banging them over – scoring five soaring penalties in all, and gradually, incredibly, the Lions clawed it back until it was level going into the closing stages.

Cue Jeremy Guscott. Who else? There was always an element of great drama and even Hollywood about Guscott the player and he duly delivered the killer line. Keith Wood initiated an attack down the left, the Lions drove on and the ball reached Guscott to the left of the posts. His drop-goal boomed over.

The brains trust: Fran Cotton, Jim Telfer and Ian McGeechan.

Unlike most of Guscott's career it was not a thing of beauty, but it did not have to be. The hair-raising closing stages were played out under the Springbok hammer but the Lions held on to secure the series.

For the record, a Lions team savaged by injury lost the last Test match at Ellis Park 35-16. As the players eased themselves into their luxurious seats on the flight back from South Africa they may not have realised that they were already Lions legends.

As Telfer had said to his forwards before the First Test, 'To be picked for the Lions is the easy bit. To win for the Lions is the ultimate.'

JIM TELFER

I had given up coaching at Melrose when I became director of rugby at the SRU, so when Ian asked me to take up the Lions job in 1997, I hadn't coached for four years and I was actually quite frightened when I thought of all these guys like Martin Johnson, Lawrence Dallaglio and boys like that. They were professionals and I was an administrator – and I think they were a wee bit worried about my reputation as well. But I quickly got them together in the forwards and explained to them that we were in this together. They were the players, so, if they made a decision, we would agree on it, and go for it. There were a lot of experienced guys so I was honest with them. 'I haven't coached all that much for a while, so we have to decide on a way we were going to work, and once its decided I'm in charge.' And that's the way it was. They did everything I asked of them. I thought the Lions in 1997 were absolutely great blokes.

FRAN COTTON

It was a unique tour because of it's timing at the end of the first season of pro rugby

Tour captain, Martin Johnson, secures the ball against N-E Transvaal.

in the northern hemisphere. It will never happen again in the same way. It was the first time a Lions squad was paid to go on tour, there were rugby league returnees to union selected, and all the players had been amateurs before and now they were professionals, so they were guys with a broader life experience. There was also a massive change because the tour was only played in the main centres in South Africa, so they saw less of the country.

NEIL BACK (England)
Toured: 1997, 2001 & 2005

I was in bed eating my breakfast when my wife, Ali, brought in the envelope. It was a letter from Fran Cotton congratulating me on my selection to tour South Africa with the Lions. For a moment I just sat there, staring at it. Then I let it fall to the covers and burst into tears, sobbing my heart out. A huge reservoir of tension and passion and desperation had built up inside me in my wilderness years in international rugby and those few words from Fran burst the dam.

RICHARD HILL (England)
Toured: 1997, 2001 & 2005

At the turn of '97, I was playing for England A and I felt that I was pushing for potential England selection, but you never knew. The thought of a Lions tour or a Lions Test series was certainly not something that was playing on my mind.

It's only after you've got one or two England games under your belt that you suddenly start thinking, 'Well, actually, I've played against two of the four teams that make up the Lions and I think I've fared okay, therefore I must stand a chance of getting involved in the squad at least.'

I found out by letter. It was in a hotel in Birmingham that we had to meet for the very first time. We gathered as a squad of about 60-something and all of a sudden you're looking around the room and thinking, 'This isn't a bad room to be in!'

JEREMY DAVIDSON (Ireland)
Toured: 1997 & 2001

I never thought I would be able to play with my childhood heroes. I would watch people like Will Carling and Jerry Guscott playing on television, and then there you are meeting up with Jerry Guscott in the Lions hotel. It was a bit of a shock to the system but I always just looked at the next game every time and I think that might have helped me. Some people maybe looked too far ahead.

JEREMY GUSCOTT

I was really pleased to be selected because, although I had been playing well for Bath, I wasn't in the England team. I had seen Geech a few times before the squad was announced and he had hinted that not playing for England wouldn't damage my chances, but I didn't now for sure if the Lions would pick me. Once the squad was announced I just wanted to get out there and start playing because the competition for a Test place was huge.

JOHN BENTLEY (England)
Toured: 1997

To play rugby union was a huge step and I never expected to be called up to play for the Lions – it was a different world. To play for the Lions was never even a dream. It was a place where legends existed, not the likes of me.

I'd signed for Newcastle in September. My year was going to be spent playing eight months for Newcastle and four months continuing to play for Halifax in the Super League. Fran rang me in the January – I'd been under his guidance at Sale in 1988 prior to going professional – and he said, 'Are you available to tour with the Lions in the summer?' Technically, I wasn't but I said, 'Yes.'

Fran said they needed to look at me playing against slightly better opposition and that he'd contact England and see if they could get me a game for the second string. He rang me back and said, 'The news won't come as a surprise but they won't touch you.' So when I got selected for the tour, I think the majority of people had never heard of me.

But when people ask me if it was a surprise in the end, it wasn't because Fran had told me they were watching me. It was a great honour, though, and I had never expected to be involved at the start of the season.

John Bentley makes a break against Border, with Tony Underwood (left) and Mark Regan (right) following in support.

I sat down with my wife, Sandy, and we puzzled over how we would cover the direct debits while I was away. If I had played rugby league that summer I would have earned more than twice what I did with the Lions. There are some things in life that money cannot buy, but the payment for such a high profile event was very poor.

NEIL JENKINS (Wales)
Toured: 1997 & 2001. Kicking coach: 2009

Just getting on tour was the biggest challenge for me. I broke my left forearm in the Five Nations against England and from that moment to passing a fitness test to make the trip to South Africa, it was the longest eight weeks of my career. I even resorted to putting my injured arm into a special magnetic coil three times a day to try to speed up the healing process. When we met up at Weybridge for a week of preparation I tweaked a calf muscle to heighten the tension and then had to go through a 40-minute full contact session the day before we got on the plane to prove there were no problems with the arm. To say I was nervous would be an understatement. I was within touching distance of achieving my dream of going on a Lions tour, but had to put my arm to the test with tackles, falling on the ball and getting knocked over.

RICHARD HILL

There's no doubting that we had a mutual bonding around one fact: not only did the South African players, media, and public not think that we had the ability to win the Test series, many people in Britain and Ireland didn't think we could win it either.

There was a point to prove – an acknowledgement of the ability we had in our squad and of the fact that we could win. It would take a lot of hard work but the most encouraging part was that everyone was committed to that.

I think we did a good job in the first week. We had the set-a-side team-bonding activities as well as a couple of training sessions and the impromptu social. It was nothing staged. It wasn't like speed dating or anything like that!

FRAN COTTON

We were written off from the moment our plane landed. They were world champions and the Super 12 was perceived as a vastly superior and more professional competition to anything in the north. That new generation of Bok players had possibly forgotten, or just didn't know, how big a deal an incoming Lions tour was.

Coming after their memorable World Cup triumph in 1995 and the excitement of those early Tri-Nations tournaments, it didn't resonate as loud as it should have. South Africa installed a new coach who had never worked at the highest level before – we just couldn't believe that – kept their Test players out of the provincial teams which gave us an easier run-in and then didn't select a first choice goal kicker. We even persuaded them to give us the first two Tests at sea level.

Perhaps the '97 Lions didn't boast so many huge names as '74 but my God they made every last ounce of their ability count. Like '74 they were totally together as a unit and I have never seen a group train so hard. But they got the balance absolutely right: we relaxed when the opportunity presented itself and we enjoyed each other's company.

Sometimes in sport, as in life, you get your just rewards for all the hard work you put in. South Africa 1997 was one of those occasions.

IAN McGEECHAN

How much more momentous could that tour be? The Lions toured the Rainbow Nation of South Africa just a few years after the African National Congress came to power... And two years after South Africa had won the 1995 World Cup. The tour also took place less than two years after the sport had declared itself open... taking steps into the unknown. The 1997 Lions were the first professional Lions, the first tour when the players signed contracts. The old days of the tour allowances, the few pennies a day to be used for making telephone calls home, and the rest of the paraphernalia of amateurism had all disappeared.

KEITH WOOD (Ireland)
Toured: 1997 & 2001

Was I thinking about my father all the time? I was, when people asked me a question about him and the 1959 tour. But was I the rest of the time? No, I wasn't. From his Lions time, Dad gave virtually everything away and before the South Africa tour I said that I had little or nothing of his. I'm not a great one for memorabilia anyway. But when I said it, a whole load of stuff came back to me. I got Dad's Lions cap, a guy

Rob Howley breaks away from Western Province's Percy Montgomery.

had minded it for years, wrapped it in tissue paper and looked after it reverentially. A guy sent a towel from the '59 tour which doesn't sound anything spectacular but this thing is a work of art, hand-stitched with the Lions and the silver fern, absolutely phenomenal. These were all things that Dad would have given to people. Jeff Butterfield gave stuff into the RFU museum and part of the collection was footage and the RFU cut it down to 13 minutes and gave it to me. It's colour footage of Dad from 1959. Incredible stuff.

You're trying to get rid of the Irish colour when you're on a tour like that. The Irish press kept bringing up, 'How many do you think we'll have on the Test side?' And I said, 'Who cares? That's not what we're supposed to be now. We're trying to get away from how many English, Irish, Scottish and Welsh are on the team. We're Lions.' There is an element of trying to condition yourself into that as a thought process. It's the most important element of a Lions tour.

GREGOR TOWNSEND (Scotland)
Toured: 1997

I believe the Lions is a four-legged stool and if you cut one leg off it will affect the whole balance. We had five Scots and four Irish, and eight of that nine were involved in the Test matches – with the other one, Doddie Weir, being sent home injured.

Looking back, the core of England's World Cup-winning team was there. Richard Hill had only played a few games for England, Matt Dawson was third choice for them, and that was the first international rugby team Martin Johnson had captained – so I would imagine that was an important moment in the development of that English team.

NEIL BACK

They chose my kind of captain. Martin Johnson was a surprise to some people, but not to me. I had followed him into battle with Leicester many times and never found him wanting. Selecting a 6ft 7in, 18 stone bruiser as a skipper sent the Springboks an early message of our intent. I also knew Johnno's personality – very straight, very fair, hard-working on the pitch and relaxed off it – would unite the side drawn from different nations. It was also important that the fans and the media would take to the captain. Selecting Will Carling, for instance, would have been a disaster because, rightly or wrongly, he was associated in too many people's minds with English arrogance. Everyone respected Martin.

ALAN TAIT (Scotland)
Toured: 1997

It was the first time I had met Martin Johnson but I was immediately impressed with him as a rugby player and as a man. He didn't say much – he did all his talking on the pitch, and I'm a big admirer of that way of operating.

JOHN BENTLEY

Cautious and non-committal, Johnno showed no leadership qualities whatsoever on tour until he got into the dressing room or onto the pitch. Then what he said went. He commanded the respect that a captain needs.

GREGOR TOWNSEND

Making Martin Johnson captain was a masterstroke. He was a man with no ego and a huge determination to win. Him and Jim Telfer together – it was what you wanted leading a hard-working pack.

IAN McGEECHAN

The tour will always be remembered for its prodigals who were returning to their original code now the game had gone professional. We chose six, all of whom had been cruelly missed by their country. John Bentley, the Yorkshireman had a huge personality and ability which appealed to me – Bentos was to become a signature player on the tour.

JEREMY GUSCOTT

John Bentley was one of the tour characters. 'Bentos' had the hearts and minds role for the Lions as social secretary – and he was a good one – but, make no mistake, he wanted that Test profile for himself more than anyone.

JOHN BENTLEY

The last thing I wanted as social secretary was to be suggesting options for the lads and having Guscott sat at the back taking the piss out of them. So I approached him to come onto the entertainments team. He burst out laughing and gleefully accepted, knowing full well why I had done it. In meetings we would spend 20 minutes mulling over a certain plan and then he would wade in and write off the whole thing, refusing to do it. To make matters worse he would instantly come up with a better scheme. That's Jerry for you.

I thought about co-opting Rob Wainwright but decided against it because his idea of fun wouldn't have gone down well with the rest of the team. One day he took a lot of them out for a two-hour ramble! Falconry was his scene and myself and Dai Young used to make budgie noises when he walked past. I don't think he sussed it.

The job was quite easy. All we had to do was to keep a constant flow of activities available. Golf, go-karting, cinema… Very little was compulsory – only a team trip to a restaurant every Thursday night. The traditional tour court session also sat, though in a less alcoholic fashion than in the amateur days, with Judge Keith Wood delivering summary justice in an appalling wig. Only the coaches suffered with alcohol – poor old Geech had to down the largest whisky you've ever seen in one gulp. Fran, who was accused of giving the same speech too often, was tried and found guilty for being boring on tour after some poor work from his defence counsel, Mark Regan. Austin Healey was tied up with tape and had an apple stuffed into his mouth – for being Austin.

On previous Lions tours they seemed to have proper singers but as we didn't, we had a tour tune – 'Wonderwall' by Oasis – which we could all wail. It was an okay song and it helped to bring us together, but we could have chosen a better band. I hate Oasis. They seem to think everybody owes them something. Who do they think they are? They don't give a damn. In my opinion they could do with a right good hiding. Rather like James Small.

JEREMY GUSCOTT

When we got to Johannesburg airport we were greeted by Louis Luyt, the South African RFU president, and he gave an awful speech. It was a very disrespectful, 'Thanks for coming, but we'll win 3-0 and wave you goodbye' speech. It was also fantastic for us. We knew we were better than that, and didn't pay much attention to the media talk. If you get the right blend of harmony with sheer willpower and determination it is a very powerful concoction, and the 1997 Lions had that blend.

JIM TELFER

When we arrived in South Africa we had a function, and at the top table was Fran Cotton, 1974 undefeated Lion; sitting next to him, Ian McGeechan, 1974 undefeated Lion. You could see how much that meant to the Springboks. They couldn't seem to get away from the fact that they had been beaten by the Lions in 1974, and the victors were there in front of them. They really respected that pair – so they were great choices as manager and coach. It was important psychology.

We played some superb rugby on that tour. Rugby I've never seen from a Lions team before. The way we cut defences apart... We could get beaten in the forwards, but the quality of our back play was just superb.

Scott Gibbs used to intimidate his opposite number. They'd be lined up for a scrum or lineout and he'd be lined up shouting at their inside centre, 'I'm going to get you. I'm going to rip you apart.' And the rest of the team lifted, because he was on their side. The rugby league guys – Quinnell, Bentley, Young, Gibbs, Bateman and Tait – brought a professionalism to it. Not through telling everyone what to do, but just by the way they conducted themselves. It was a magical ten weeks. There were never any rifts.

ALAN TAIT

All the rugby league guys had a head start. I'm sure we were picked on form first and foremost but Geech would also be aware that he was going to get a lot of professionalism from us. They had just turned professional whereas the likes of myself, Scott Gibbs, Allan Bateman and John Bentley had been professional for eight or nine years, so we definitely added an edge. But we mixed in really well. There was no divide because the rugby league guys appreciated that they were rubbing shoulders with class players like Jerry Guscott, Lawrence Dallaglio and Martin Johnson. The determination of the group was the key to our success. People talk about defence winning you matches, and guys like myself and Gibbsy knew about defensive structures, about how to hold the line, and how to put pressure on the attacking team. There were just a lot of good players there showing a huge amount of desire.

LAWRENCE DALLAGLIO (England)
Toured: 1997, 2001 & 2005

There were times when our coaches would stand aside and let Gibbs, Tait and Bateman tell us how they defended when playing top-level rugby league… it was clever of our coaches to tap into these lads' expertise.

GREGOR TOWNSEND

Geech led all the team meetings and he was very inspirational in how he painted a picture of what we needed to do. It was quiet motivation. Telfer dealt solely with the forwards and he really had a grip of what made them tick. That was Jim at his best – they would have done anything for him by the end of the tour. Before the tour they were not as open to Jim as they needed to be. I remember the guys at Northampton had heard stories about Jim and how he coached – they would have been exaggerated or even apocryphal stories – but the likes of Tim Rodber would say that there was no way anyone could do things like that with us. But as soon as he started coaching them they realised that he was so knowledgeable and passionate, and that he was there to improve them and win – and they got right behind him.

JIM TELFER

They knew that if we were going to survive then we all had to be on the same wavelength, and they had to make their contribution. It was early in the professional era – but they were professional. And I was lucky that the core of Englishmen in that team were rugby nuts, like Dallaglio, Johnson and Rodber. Eventually I was dictatorial, but not initially – by the time I started shouting the odds I knew that they were with me.

JASON LEONARD

The first game of the 1997 tour was against Eastern Province in Port Elizabeth and I was chosen to captain it because of my previous Lions experience. It was an important game as you have to get tours off to a good start and I knew that I had been selected because they needed someone who understood what they were doing, to get out there and ensure us a win. Even though it was the first game of a long tour, I knew that for the sake of the rest of the tour it was vital that we came away with a victory.

I was pleased with the way I had captained the side. We stuck to our guns and had played the sort of rugby that we believed would beat the South Africa side in the Test matches.

JIM TELFER

We got badly beaten in the scrums during our third game against Western Province, and we were due to play Mpumalanga on the Wednesday, so we decided that the guys who played in that match wouldn't be asked to come back and do a scrummage session. But the guys on the bench would, alongside the Saturday team.

So, after the game we all went back on a minibus to Pretoria, where we were based, and did this absolutely brutal scrummaging session. Tom Smith must have been about 5ft 10inches when we started that session and 5ft 8inches when we finished, because the machine didn't move – but they didn't want to give in, and they didn't want me to beat them. We got beat in the next game, but that didn't matter, we had set the scene.

I mellowed a lot before the 1997 tour. I was a real bastard beforehand, but I learned that I had to delegate – so I did and I got my reward from the players.

RICHARD HILL

I think we also bonded on the training pitch. Sometimes it was done through extremely hard work. Having someone like Jim Telfer as your forwards coach, a man who doesn't take any stick and doesn't accept standards below the best, meant that when we had a couple of scrummaging performances that were below par in the first three games, we received a severe scrummaging beasting.

It went beyond scrummaging technique. It turned into scrummaging technique, scrummaging fitness and a severe beasting, but that's a way of bringing people together. You live people's experiences. You live their pain and you live their joy when it's over.

You knew that they had the capacity levels for hard work. You knew that everybody that was there was prepared to go to the last breath, because you'd seen it. You knew how far they could go and you also knew that if you weren't putting it in, you were letting them down.

SCOTT GIBBS

When that squad was announced in '97, I think there was an element that this squad was different, this management was different, and all those elements came together to create one playing entity.

There was never anyone who felt alienated in any way. That's a true strength of a squad, that inward support from everybody. That was there in abundance in '97 and that was why it was so successful on the field and off the field. We made a lot of friendships and there was never one clique.

I've got my lists of Lions laws, and togetherness was on it. There was never any question of us against them. It was all 35 preparing to beat the Springboks. Everybody played their part in that and that's why everyone can share in the delight that we won the series because it wasn't done by just the team on the day.

I think the Lions has meant more to the rugby fraternity than any other team because it brings people together and there's a common goal. It galvanises and brings all the Home Unions together. It's the best of the best.

NEIL JENKINS

I was playing at fullback for Wales at the time and got picked in that position for the tour, although also as back-up at fly-half or centre. I knew Gregor Townsend was Geech's first-choice No 10 and I had a battle on my hands to get a look-in at fullback with England's Tim Stimpson and Nick Beal in the party.

It wasn't until I got the chance to play at outside half, though, that I really got back into the swing of things. That was in the fourth match, a midweek game against Mpumalanga, when I scored one of our ten tries and converted seven.

That game gave me the confidence to move forward and showed the management I could deliver on the goalkicking front. Then I landed six penalties and three conversions in the big win over Natal. That was the big breakthrough for me.

JEREMY DAVIDSON

The midweek team went to Transvaal [Gauteng] and we were told it was the real heartland of South African rugby – and we played well. The tour took a turn and the coaches' eyes were opening a bit and they were thinking possibly, 'We've got more contenders for positions than we thought.'

IAN McGEECHAN

That game against Gauteng was so important, because we had just lost to Northern Transvaal. I had learnt hard lessons from previous tours that the midweek team is essential to morale and momentum. Nigel Redman had only just arrived on tour, joining us from the England tour of Argentina as a replacement for Doddie Weir. He soon proved to be the real thing and we pitched him in against Gauteng. He was marking the massive Kobus Wiese, who had said in the press that he was going to give us all the trouble in the world... We scored one of my all-time favourite Lions tries in the game through John Bentley and then a brilliant team try touched down by Austin

The pack prepares to put all the hours of training that Jim Telfer had put them through into practice against Natal in Durban.

Healey. And Nigel did a spectacular number on Kobus, playing wonderfully well. We won 20-14 and South Africa was starting to open its eyes.

NIGEL REDMAN (England)
Toured: 1997

Jack Rowell, the England manager, took me aside in Argentina. He told me that I was going to South Africa. I said, 'Jack, I don't believe it!' Jack replied, 'Neither do I!'

JIM TELFER

We were beaten 35-30 by Northern Transvaal on the Saturday, and we were due to play Gauteng in midweek and Natal the Saturday after, which was typical – in seven days we were due to play three of their top teams. So, we picked a second team to play Gauteng, hoping like hell that they would do well, and they were getting a wee bit of a stretching in the first half, but they weren't losing by much, when a kick went right into our corner. Well, Tony Underwood caught it and drove and kept possession, the next man came in and rucked it, and we cleared our lines. If they'd scored at that point they would go on to dominate the game, and we'd have been in trouble.

After that, there was a great John Bentley try and Austin Healey scored as well, so we won quite comfortably in the end. Afterwards I remember walking up from the pitch, and the first team, which had been beaten on the Saturday, clapped in the team which, in my opinion, saved the tour. It's moments like that which you never forget.

I went out with an open mind about the Test team, but Tom Smith had only played three Test matches for Scotland and was seen as a surprise choice. We still had Jason Leonard, Graham Rowntree and Dai Young, who were scrummaging forwards, but as time went on it became apparent that they couldn't play the fast moving type of game we wanted to play. So, I suppose we were quite brave in going with Tom Smith and Paul Wallace in the front-row, and for Jeremy Davidson ahead of Simon Shaw, who was several inches and a couple of stone heavier, in the second-row.

JEREMY DAVIDSON

I got a lot of games at the start of the tour because they were trying to see what level of player I was. Because I was a young international player I didn't really have a big brand name like a Rodber, a Dallaglio or a Guscott. Two or three games and you know Guscott is ready for the big match against the Springboks, you know you can throw him in there. So they played some of the younger players a bit more so they could have a look at them and see whether they were up to it or not. Before the First Test I played a midweek against the Emerging Springboks and I think that was another big test for me and I came through it reasonably well.

My room-mate Graham Rowntree woke me up. Handed me the letter. He told me he hadn't been picked and he asked me to open my letter to see if I'd been picked, which was quite strange considering I didn't know him that well. He was shaking me in bed saying, 'Out – open your letter.'

JIM TELFER

We knew that they would try to bully us in the scrum, so we wanted as low a scrum as possible. We never dominated in the scrum, but they didn't pulverise us either. Tom Smith is not a bad scrummager, and Paul Wallace is an awkward bugger – he got under Os du Randt. If we'd played Graham Rowntree and Jason Leonard, we would have had the same result scrum-wise, but these guys had a little bit extra around the park.

PAUL WALLACE (Ireland)
Toured: 1997

Some guys – John Bentley and a lot of guys – were waiting up all night for the letter coming in under the door before the First Test. I slept very soundly.

JOHN BENTLEY

The nearest anyone came to going 'off tour' was probably me after the disappointment of missing out on the First Test. I was in charge of a mini video camera for the *Living with the Lions* fly-on-the-wall documentary when the time arrived… I decided to film my reaction to receiving the fateful envelope that would tell me whether I was in the team for the First Test or not. I had scored four tries in five games and thought I must be in with a chance. I could not sleep with excitement the night before so I rose early and waited outside the lift for Samantha Peters, our administrative secretary, who was the bearer of tidings. I filmed the build-up, but, when I found out I hadn't made it, I was crushed. To make matters worse the letter started 'Congratulations', so I thought I was in until I read the rest of it – which told me I was a substitute. The video does not show how I reacted because I did not turn the camera on again for two days.

JIM TELFER

Jason Leonard is a superb guy. He came with 60 odd caps, and on his second Lions tour, he could play tight-head or loose-head, and captained the team in the first game when Martin Johnson was being rested. I think a lot of people would have expected him to play in the Tests, but by the time we played Natal we were playing superb off-your-shoulder rugby, carving the opposition into ribbons with our angles, and we beat them 42-12. After that we decided on our Test team, and Jason Leonard took it like a man. He came in and helped both Tom and Paul. He must have been disappointed, but he never let it show – and that culture we had developed there of everyone working for the cause shone through. He went a long way up in my estimation that week.

JASON LEONARD

Lions tours are not about Test caps, despite what it may seem like from the outside. It's about a big group of players going away together and between them doing what is necessary to win.

Players have bad days and I didn't have a great tour, so it was right that Paul Wallace and Tom Smith were the Test props, which didn't mean that I didn't support them every inch of the way, and do all I could to help them in training.

I am as competitive as the next person but Lions tours are different. I knew I wasn't going to make the Test side so I decided to try and help the other front-row players as much as possible. I did everything I could, whether it be scrummaging sessions, lineouts or rucking and mauling sessions.

GREGOR TOWNSEND

We fought so hard for each other and that went right back to the very start of the tour. We realised that in 1993 there had been a split between the midweek team and the Saturday team, and that was why the tour went off the rails in the last few weeks – so it was a reaction to that. There was a real togetherness, and it was genuine. I remember training sessions when you felt somebody had turned up not that interested, maybe they'd just had a hard game, then somebody would say to him, 'You need to sort yourself out. This is a team session – not just your session.' That to me epitomised all the good things about that tour. The team would be put under the door first thing in the morning or the night before in preparation for the team announcement so you could gather your thoughts and if you were not picked it was your job to go up and shake the hand of the guy who had got in ahead of you. If you played on the Saturday you would be out training on the Sunday holding a pad. Not that the players thought about it much, but the payments were for the whole tour, so you shared the exact same bonus money regardless of how many games and Tests you played in. All these little things were vital to making the tour – and not just the three Test matches – a success.

LAWRENCE DALLAGLIO

It was made very clear right from the moment that we gathered at our base in England that nothing had been predetermined in terms of selection – every position was up for grabs. It was a great philosophy and it rang true – you had guys like Tom Smith, Paul Wallace and Jeremy Davidson who came in from left-field to start and star in the Test series, and you had a guy like Matt Dawson, who was fourth choice for England at the time, who came to the fore after Rob Howley was injured and became key to our success.

KEITH WOOD

Wally [Paul Wallace] wasn't even picked on the original squad. Peter Clohessy was picked ahead of him. When did I realise he was in the frame for the Test side? I won't say very quickly, but it was just a perfect confluence of events for Wally. He was so un-believably powerful and the manner of our training suited him. Playing against Os du Randt, nobody expected anything of him, but because he scrummaged low he ate du Randt alive. Not from the start, but by the end of the game Wally had him inside out, a guy four or five stone heavier. He was showing that form in the last week or 10 days before the First Test, but it was still a surprise he was picked. You see, you don't make presumptions about yourself or about anybody else on a Lions tour.

JEREMY GUSCOTT

We lost to Northern Transvaal, but the Test team was coming to the boil, and having played pretty well in the provincial games – scoring against Northern Transvaal – I got a sense that I had clinched a place for the First Test. I didn't feel we were ever in danger of losing that opening Test. The Bath side I played in was so full of talent and hard mental edge that we hardly lost, and that's how I felt with the '97 Lions. We were the best of the best, and it gave me great belief in South Africa. I thought afterwards, 'Thank you boys for thinking we'll be a pushover, can't thank you enough.'

LAWRENCE DALLAGLIO

I've never discovered whether it was a case smart pre-tour negotiations by Fran and the Lions committee or whether it was just a balls up by South Africa, but the order in which we played the Tests suited us perfectly, with the first two at sea level and the third at altitude. If I had been the organising it as a Springbok administrator, I would have had us bouncing around from altitude to sea level and then back to altitude again.

NEIL JENKINS

I got the nod for the First Test and can still remember the envelope coming under the door in my room telling me I'd been selected. I was sharing with Tony Underwood and he didn't get in – they picked Alan Tait, a centre, on the wing instead. What a contrast there was between my elation and his dejection. I went for a walk to give him a bit of time and space to get over his disappointment.

LAWRENCE DALLAGLIO

I'm never going to forget Jim Telfer's speech to the forwards before the First Test.

Tom Smith, Lawrence Dallaglio and Martin Johnson prepare for kick-off.

It's seared on my memory forever. You could have heard a pin drop. 'The easy bit has passed,' he said. 'Selection for the Test team is the easy bit... This is your fucking Everest boys... to win for the Lions in a Test match is the ultimate... They don't rate you. They don't respect you. The only way to be rated is to stick one up them... They don't think fuck-all of us. We're here just to make up the fucking numbers.'

KEITH WOOD

Jim Telfer speech's before the First Test, it was a slightly out-of-body experience. He was a bit mad. He was. But he got it. Jesus, did he get it. He drove us to the absolute edge of our ability, and it was about weeding out any possible flaws in the squad so you were left with this team that had the mental toughness to go through it. I've said it before, if we were there another day we'd have killed him. We were all falling apart by the very end of it. We hit a level of effort and training that to be honest we weren't fit enough for. We pushed ourselves beyond the limit. It was both technical and mental – and we loved it.

PAUL WALLACE

Os du Randt was down on the programme as 20 stone but he was at least 22 stone. I've propped against a lot of guys who are 20 stone and he wasn't 20 stone. He's a huge man. And also he had a massive back-five behind him. André Venter on the flank was probably the biggest man on the pitch.

KEITH WOOD

There was a fear that they might do damage to the front-row. The first scrum we hit they knocked us back five yards and I had fear myself. We were just a little bit too high. My fault entirely. Six inches too high. We could use their weight against them by being lower, and we did that. It was frightening and daunting to have all your fears come home immediately and then have to realise quickly that you have to be lower and you'll be fine. They thought they were going to destroy us in the pack. I would call it a certainty that they had. We got the height right in the second scrum but still got knocked back a couple of metres. They were just huge men. We had to fight for every single second of every single scrum. But we ground them down. They were bigger, but we were fitter and willing to work – and we knew that every time we went down for a scrum if we didn't get it exactly right we'd be belittled, and that's a great driving force. Was Wally's scrummaging illegal? The referee didn't penalise it, so it was entirely legal. Of course it was illegal! But that's what scrummaging is about. The amount of carping that went on afterwards was absolutely fantastic. Look, it was a confrontational battle, and he was magnificent.

GREGOR TOWNSEND

Matt Dawson was a controversial selection because he hadn't played much for England at that stage, but he turned out to be an inspired choice. Geech knew his players.

NEIL JENKINS

The First Test against the Springboks at Newlands was supposed to be the first step towards them underlining their status as world champions. Everyone in South Africa expected them to win the series 3-0. I saw my Mum and Dad the day before the First Test and my Mum said she thought I looked ill. In the dressing room before the game I was literally sick with nerves. Maybe that's why I put the kick-off out on the full. Not the most auspicious start to my Lions Test career.

JEREMY DAVIDSON

If you go out there for the Lions against the Springboks you've got to have a bit of confidence in yourself, you've got to be able to back yourself in the lineouts and I knew I was capable of winning whatever ball was called to me, and luckily enough, the captain called me a lot. It's not often a captain does that, but it shows you what a good captain Martin Johnson was. Getting so much ball helped me play a bit better.

JEREMY GUSCOTT

As I looked around the other faces I felt a deep confidence in them – there was no one who made me think, 'He's not up to it.' There's no doubt in my mind that despite the drama of the last seven minutes when we scored tries through Matt Dawson and Alan Tait to clinch the game, it wasn't a great spectacle to watch. But it was a great occasion, and a great result. In addition, the try by Dawson was a peach. To beat Ruben Kruger for pace off the back of an attacking scrum and then sucker Gary Teichmann, André Venter and Joost van der Westhuizen with a dummy is no mean feat.

Jeremy Davidson rises to take a lineout during the First Test.

Although the South Africans scored tries through Os du Randt and Russell Bennett, the big hits coming from the likes of Scott Gibbs, Tim Rodber and Lawrence Dallaglio were shaking them up despite their bulk. In fact, the defence was so punishing I remember wondering how some of them got back up.

JIM TELFER

After we won the First Test, Johnson said to Ian, 'We're still on tour – everyone will come out and work on Sunday morning.' And even though they didn't do very much, the team which won the Test match helped the other players in the squad prepare for their next game.

NEIL JENKINS

We had another game three days later against Orange Free State and the next day the Test team were out on the training field helping the dirt-trackers get ready for that game. That is what characterised the 1997 Lions – one for all and all for one.

It was the most harmonious group I'd ever had the pleasure of being a part of and we all worked incredibly hard for each other. Before we'd even left, Geech had instilled in us that we weren't English, Irish, Scottish or Welsh, but one team representing one of the greatest rugby brands in the world. We were all Lions together.

FRAN COTTON

I knew what qualities Will Greenwood had at centre, and he started to show them on the tour until he was injured badly against the Free State. That was a scary moment, and it could have been fatal but for the urgency of our team doctor, James Robson, and the medical staff. They saved his life.

Matt Dawson throws an audacious dummy and slips down the wing to score in the First Test.

NEIL BACK

A hard training session on the Sunday was followed by a split in the camp. The Test side headed off to Durban, where the Second Test was... the rest of us relocated to Bloemfontein, where we were due to meet the Orange Free State. It was the first time on tour that we had been divided like that and it added to a sense of gloom in my mind that I was not going to get a Test berth. Other guys felt the same way. Our answer, on the rock-hard turf, was probably the best game of the tour. Fran Cotton later described it as the best ever performance by a midweek Lions side between two Tests. It was certainly the best game of rugby I have ever played in. We won 52-30 and I felt that our performance, and more importantly our attitude, meant that they might look again at one or two of us for the next encounter with the Springboks. Ieuan Evans was out of the tour with a groin injury. That meant Bentos was named in his place on the wing. The selectors also added new names to the Test bench – among them, that of NA Back. The feeling of being named in the 21 was fantastic... I still wanted to start, but this was a step in the right direction, and I felt as though I was walking on air for hours after getting my envelope.

FRAN COTTON

Another player who impressed me hugely was Allan Bateman, and it would have been an interesting selection decision if he hadn't pulled his hamstring before the Second Test. Bateman was the surprise package, and it was a straight call between him and Jerry Guscott. What a task.

NEIL JENKINS

The pressure on the 'Boks was massive coming into the Second Test in Durban. Their coach was under enormous pressure and their biggest failing was their goalkicking. They failed to convert either of their two tries in the First Test and then missed three more in the Second Test. The atmosphere was electric at King's Park and after we had taken the field I turned to see the Springboks sprint out of the tunnel onto the field. Here we go, I thought, they're up for it! It was a game we should never have won, really, but the defensive work of Scott Gibbs, Lawrence Dallaglio, Richard Hill and Tim Rodber in particular was out of this world. The Springboks scored the tries but I managed to kick all five of my penalties.

JEREMY GUSCOTT

The night before the Second Test, Gibbsy did a TV interview where he said that we would be approaching the game like World War Three and that we were all relishing the prospect of the physical confrontation. He said that if all we did was tackle for 80 minutes, then we would love it. I'm not sure if he was speaking for me when he said that! But it was great to hear him say it – and it was exactly what needed to be said the South Africa and it gave you great confidence knowing that he was on our side

The atmosphere at King's Park was incredible. We came out of the tunnel and were hit with this wall of noise. It was electric – there were huge blocks of fans in red all around the stadium shouting, 'Lions! Lions! Lions!'

Johnno pulled us into a huddle on the half-way line while we waited for the Springboks to come out and Gibbsy started jabbing the air shouting, 'We have to raise our intensity. They're going to come at us with everything they have but we have to smash them back. We have to be better than last week, we have to play harder than we've ever played before.' Then he stared us all in the eye. 'This is ours.'

LAWRENCE DALLAGLIO

The Second Test was the most physically intense game I played during my entire career – and the first five minutes was complete mayhem. The Springboks came out of the traps and just wanted to blow us apart. They smashed into every contact and looked to dominate us completely. It was a psychological as well as physical confrontation and if we had crumbled then, the whole game was gone. We just had to do our best to repel them – and they just kept coming in wave after wave of attack; then, when we had the ball, it was all we could do to try and hold onto it as they smashed us with tackles. It was brutal. But if you can hold out against that kind of physicality and in that kind of environment, then you have a chance. Rugby is a game of confrontation, not a game of containment, and it's virtually impossible to win if all you do is contain. Virtually impossible – not impossible.

JEREMY GUSCOTT

Gibbsy wanted to take on the Springboks all by himself. He was so pumped up that he just wanted to smash anything in a green jersey; he wanted to smash through them, he

Alan Tait scores the clinching try in the First Test.

wanted to smash them to the ground. He's not the biggest bloke in the world, but he would have taken on anyone that day. He was some player to have alongside you.

When he made that break and thundered into Os du Randt, leaving du Randt on the floor and spinning off to carry the ball on again, it was one of the most inspiring moments I've ever experienced on a rugby field. We won a penalty from the ruck when he was eventually brought to ground and as Gibbsy jogged back I heard him say to du Randt, 'Get up, you fat ox.'

KEITH WOOD
People say they didn't go in with recognised kickers. They did. They had really good kickers but they crumbled under the pressure of the series. Whatever it is about the Lions there is a crazy intensity. Crazy. And things happen in that sort of pressure.

GREGOR TOWNSEND
In the second half we played a lot better rugby and that got us the penalties we needed – but it took real nerve for Neil Jenkins to stand up and put those kicks over.

NEIL JENKINS
The pressure mounted with each kick, but every time I took my mind away from Durban and imagined myself back on my training field in Church Village. Same routine and, thankfully, same result. People always ask about pressure kicks, but that is what goalkickers live for. You don't hope the chance never comes, you pray it does. The fifth and final penalty was probably the most important of my career, but I approached it as any other and managed to keep the pressure at bay.

JEREMY DAVIDSON
At the end of the Second Test we knew we needed to get up there, we needed possession, we needed to get the ball back in our hands and we needed to score because time was running out. The throw was called to me and I just wanted to get it for the team. I've got a picture of the drop-goal and you can just see one of my feet sticking up out of the ruck before it. There was nothing on for Jerry. I've watched it on video many times since and it still gives me shivers down the spine.

JEREMY GUSCOTT
At one stage in the Second Test you thought, 'When are these guys going to stop coming?' They were just relentless and it was all defence on our side.

If you'd seen me spraying drop-kicks all over the pitch in training during the previous week – off the outside of my foot, off the inside of my foot, off the end of my toes – you would have bet as much money on me putting it over as you would on a one-legged man in a backside-kicking competition. But I'd played fly-half from the ages of 7 to 19, and the natural decision was made when Matt Dawson passed me the ball. I saw it unfolding and made the decision without anyone saying anything to me.

The moment is frozen in time in my memory. Probably because freezing was what was most on my mind. As the ball drifted towards me through the arc of the floodlights everything seemed to happen in slow motion. I prayed it wouldn't miss. I prayed it wouldn't be charged down. The sense of elation I felt when I eventually looked up and saw the ball soar between the posts will stay with me forever.

IAN McGEECHAN

Of all my rugby moments, the sound of that final whistle in Durban in 1997 was probably the sweetest, perhaps even shading the Scotland Grand Slam in 1990. When we were dissecting the game afterwards we found that in truth, we had not played at all well, we had not set up our own game and on occasions, we had been bullied. But we had stayed the course quite magnificently, and we won the series in the face of a relentless South African onslaught. The hostility of the crowd seemed to be willing us to lose by a large margin, but we didn't. I went on to the field at the end as the players and the followers were united in scenes of incredible joyfulness.

NEIL JENKINS

After the game I remember running around the field with Scott Gibbs, both of us draped in Welsh flags. We'd played for Wales Youth, Wales and now the Lions together and it was a very special moment for the pair of us.

Nothing could take the shine off winning the series. The 1997 Lions team was the greatest I ever played in and I made life long friends with so many great players.

Richard Hill hacks a loose ball.

JOHN BENTLEY

We all have individual moments that we recall but, having been written off as a bunch of no hopers, for us to win the Second Test, and for me to be a part of it, was my biggest highlight. I don't think I realised how big an achievement it was until I got home.

FRAN COTTON

I was tremendously impressed by the players' dedication, but there was also still an element of mischief with guys like Bentley, who gave it what every rugby tour has to have, which is some humour and a sense of when to play, and when not to play. They all had a common purpose that they stuck to, and they worked for each other. It was a privilege to manage them.

They showed their character in the Second Test when after being under the cosh and defending for their lives they had the energy and the will to snatch it. I don't think we were lucky to win, but it could have gone either way.

In 1974 we already had existing world-class players, whereas in 1997 we had a group who were developing into world-class players, and who over the next three years became world-class.

GREGOR TOWNSEND

The more I look back on that tour the more it grows in my mind as the most special thing to have happened in my rugby career. It was special at the time – it is the ultimate honour for a British or Irish rugby player, and I made friends for life. But I think I assumed there would be more of this to come, but I didn't make the 2001 tour. And if you look at the last three tours, they have had nothing like the success of that 1997 trip – so I was incredibly lucky to be a part of it.

The series-winning moment.

ALAN TAIT

I had played a lot of big games – especially in rugby league, which is really hard-nosed about going out there and doing a job – so I think that helped me take it all in my stride. But now I look back at it I can see that I didn't appreciate at the time just how special that experience was. Now, when I see the Lions go off every four years to try and achieve what we managed to achieve and always coming up short, it really hits home how much it means to a lot of people. It was just another day at the office, but I should have been looking at it as a massive, massive achievement. And every four years the size of that achievement gets bigger and bigger.

KEITH WOOD

The thing that still frightens me is that we could and should have lost all of them. South Africa is just so difficult. It's a tough place but that's what makes it so fantastic to play there and win there.

IAN McGEECHAN

I think that we surprised South African rugby in every way. The 1997 Five Nations tournament had been poor, and accounts of some of the games were really scathing. They felt that British and Irish rugby was not constructive, not dangerous in the

The final whistle of the Second Test: a moment that will live in the hearts of the players – and the fans – forever.

attacking sense. They felt that we were not particularly heavy and powerful defenders and the northern hemisphere rugby in general was… limited. That was all to our advantage.

JIM TELFER

There's an aura about the Lions. I lost a bit of confidence in the concept for a while after I coached the 1983 tour, but it's a special team. No other team comes together for a very short period of time, goes on the gruelling tour and then never plays together again as a group.

JEREMY GUSCOTT

Geech has a phrase – 'Test match animals' – it means having the ability to turn on your best performances at the highest level, keeping a cool head while playing at your highest intensity and making the right decisions under pressure nine times out of ten. I think that the whole of the '97 squad had that about them. You had some of the hardest men ever to play for the Lions – Johnno, Gibbsy, Dallaglio, Hill, Rodber, Davidson, Wallace, Smith, Wood – and some real skill out wide. But the real key was that we played for each other – we went to war for each other; and we formed a bond that will never be broken. It's amazing what can happen in the space of just a few weeks.

The squad gather around the Lion Challenge Cup.

CHAPTER TWENTY-SIX

THE NEARLY MEN
2001
AUSTRALIA

A NOTHER LIONS *tradition that was once assumed to be eternal ended before this tour when Graham Henry, the New Zealander who was then coaching Wales and who was later to guide New Zealand to the 2011 Rugby World Cup, was appointed as coach and became the first Lions head man to come from overseas. The reaction was interesting. Some old Lions objected, other people realised that in the new professional era, the Lions should be coached by the best available man.*

On paper, the team looked very powerful, many critics regarding them as one of the finest touring sides to leave the British Isles. But the tour, which raised soaring hopes when the Lions played brilliant rugby to win the mesmeric First Test in Brisbane, ultimately sunk to a desperately disappointing low with defeat in the series. For those familiar with Lions history, it was also a classic tour that echoed so many common traits of the past – pockmarked as it was with great rugby, injury and controversy.

But of all the glorious and not-so glorious failures in the Lions' history this really was, categorically, the one that got away. Even against the Wallabies, the reigning world champions, the Lions had for a long time looked palpably the better side. It was only late in the tour that a rash of injuries, and more particularly an exhaustion factor after a ferocious and almost endless home season, took a heavy toll. In some ways, the tour stopped dead, out on its feet.

England's Martin Johnson was the obvious choice to lead the party, having spearheaded the victorious side in South Africa four years earlier, as he was firmly entrenched as his country's skipper and was a certainty for the Tests in the second-row. The Leicester man duly became the first man to captain the Lions on two tours.

More controversial was the choice of coach. He was supported by manager Donal Lenihan, the Irishman who had captained the midweek side in Australia 12 years previously, and Andy Robinson, another '89 Lion, who was seconded from England duty as assistant coach.

Gradually, the support group was growing after decades when the manager and a secretary were practically the only back-up. Other backroom staff in 2001 included England's defence coach Phil Larder, kicking guru Dave Alred, Jonny Wilkinson's mentor and fitness expert Steve Black, and the almost permanent Lions doctor James Robson from Scotland. Of these, Robson probably had the heaviest workload as the tour unfolded.

Henry's preparations were not helped by the foot-and-mouth epidemic which swept the British Isles in 2001 and which caused the cancellation of the Cheltenham Festival and left the Six Nations unfinished until the autumn.

Opposite: Jason Robinson skips around Chris Latham for the perfect start to the First Test.

His initial selections, in a 37-man party which was the largest ever at the time, initially raised some eyebrows with centre Scott Gibbs, the Welsh talisman of the 1997 tour, left out and England's Martin Corry also surplus to requirements. Both would eventually join the party, Corry with spectacular effect, as injuries took their toll as they usually do on Lions tours.

Henry, however, did include the former rugby league winger Jason Robinson, who had not played a full Test up to then, and the Irish centre Brian O'Driscoll who had announced himself on the international scene so spectacularly a year earlier with a hat-trick against France in Paris, in his initial squad. Both would play significant roles in the Test series.

But in all, eight players were invalided out of the trip including the influential Englishmen Richard Hill and Lawrence Dallaglio (he hardly played any part), the Welsh scrum-half Rob Howley and the young Scottish No 8 Simon Taylor, injured in game one. Seven players were called up as replacements including bizarrely, on the morning of the Third Test, the Scottish scrum-half Andy Nicol.

Nicol had been with a supporters' tour enjoying the sights of Australia and, as he has since admitted, had not kept himself in the best of shape but he was whisked up to the Lions bench after Austin Healey went lame with a bulging disc. Nicol, who can hardly have been expecting to get a game, has made his promotion the subject of his after-dinner speech routine ever since.

As a New Zealander, Henry was always likely to be the target of criticism. Some called his man-management into question, with Welsh players complaining they were alienated by their national boss, and some who thought the Test team had been set in stone before the Lions had even left Heathrow. Henry caused further disarray amongst the party when he publicly prioritised the Test team after a loss to Australia A in Gosford, meaning that when the inevitable injuries hit, players promoted to the Test side were allegedly unfamiliar with its workings. With a World Cup win under his belt he has since admitted that he made errors on the tour – and at the end of it found himself on the wrong end of a stinging attack from the England coach Clive Woodward.

Henry was further undermined by newspaper columns written by Matt Dawson and Austin Healey during the course of the trip, which disrupted the spirit of the party and angered the hosts.

Dawson's tirade, published in The Daily Telegraph *under the headline 'Harsh regime tears us apart', took the gloss off a famous First Test win hitting the streets as it did just hours before the kick-off at the Gabba. Dawson accused Henry of being 'uninspiring', said that training was 'mindless' and added that Lenihan had treated the squad like children. He also revealed that some players had threatened to go 'off tour'.*

Dawson was fined £5,000 for his rant and in his autobiography published three years later still refused to accept that he had betrayed the Lions. He did, however, admit that he regretted the timing of his outburst which was followed up by a complaint about the schedule of the short ten-match tour once the series was lost. The scrum-half also claimed that Johnson had threatened to quit the tour if Dawson had been sent home.

Healey's contribution came on the eve of the deciding Third Test in Sydney and landed in Australia just as he had been ruled out of the match. Printed in The Guardian, *Healey's ghosted column took swipes at Australian second-row Justin Harrison, labelling him a 'plank' and a 'plod' and told the hosts to 'spin this, you Aussies, up yours.'*

Healey and Harrison had clashed in a midweek match with the Brumbies and when Harrison was picked for his Test debut, the winger's alleged views on the lock were given a full airing in his column.

However, despite all the criticism it is often forgotten that in the early tour games, and indeed, in every game up to half-time in the Second Test, the Lions played some of the finest rugby on any tour, any time – thrilling a staggering number of travelling fans who made the Gabba in Brisbane, especially, seem entirely like a home game.

The trip was also affected by tragedy when the Lions' popular Australian Rugby Union liaison man and baggage master, Anton Toia, died after suffering a suspected heart attack whilst swimming off Coffs Harbour in the lead-up to the First Test. Toia, who had previously fulfilled a similar role on Scotland tours, was a popular figure with the players and the New Zealander's death, at the age of 54, cast a shadow over the squad. The Lions cancelled their team meeting and all public engagements in Toia's memory and the Anton Toia Memorial Secondary Schools Tens Carnival was founded shortly afterwards.

The early games were walkovers with the Lions amassing 199 points in outings against Western Australia in Perth and a Queensland President's XV in Townsville. Jason Robinson scored five tries in the second game, but after impressing for a half in the first match Simon Taylor was out of the tour with a knee injury.

The Lions then had three matches against much tougher opposition – the Queensland Reds, Australia A and the New South Wales Waratahs. The Reds were impressively seen off 42-8 but Australian second-string, coached by the streetwise Eddie Jones, a future Wallaby coach, beat the tourists 28-25, with the Lions only getting to within three points thanks to two late tries. England centre Mike Catt was another casualty in that match.

The match with the Waratahs was a brutal affair that ended with the Lions winning 41-24. It was not the scoreline that made the headlines but the five yellow cards and one red that were brandished on the night by referee Scott Young. The yellows to Lions Danny Grewcock and Phil Vickery and to Waratahs Tom Bowman, Brendan Cannon and Cameron Blades were overshadowed

The 2001 tour party.

by fullback Duncan McRae's red for an assault on Ronan O'Gara. The Lions fly-half was pinned to the ground by the Australian who rained blows on the Irishman, leaving O'Gara needing eight stitches in a bloody left eye and McCrae contemplating his violence during a seven-week ban.

As the Lions fans arrived in Brisbane for the First Test Henry played his hand by picking Robinson on the left wing, the Bath fullback Matt Perry – out of favour with England – ahead of Iain Balshaw, the Irish centre pairing of O'Driscoll and Rob Henderson and the newly-arrived Corry on the flank.

Despite the distractions of Dawson's column the Lions turned in one of their best ever displays with Robinson sensationally leaving Chris Latham for dead in the opening minutes and fellow winger Dafydd James touching down before the break. O'Driscoll trumped the lot with a spectacular second half solo try and Scott Quinnell barged over to help the Lions to a 29-13 win. Chants of 'Waltzing O'Driscoll' filled the Brisbane air that night.

The midweek team kept their side of the bargain with a 30-28 win over the Brumbies in Canberra with Dawson making some amends for his provocative column by kicking the winning conversion before the party headed to Melbourne's Colonial Stadium for the Second Test and the turning point of the series.

The Australian Rugby Union had been shocked by the sea of red shirts at the Gabba as 20,000 Lions took over the ground and were determined not to cede the same advantage to their opponents in the cultural capital of their country. Their answer was to hand out gold hats, scarves and placards to local fans to redress the balance.

The Lions led 11-6 at half-time with a try by Neil Back, but had been easily the better side. During the break, one of the best-known Australian rugby writers turned to colleagues and said, 'This game is all over, the Lions are just too good.'

However, there was to be a dramatic reversal of momentum. Joe Roff's interception of a wafted Jonny Wilkinson pass prompted a 29-point blitz that left Henry's men shell shocked and out of the game, which they lost 35-14. The bad news continued when Richard Hill, who had been completely outplaying the Australian back-row, was poleaxed by a stiff arm challenge from centre Nathan Grey just before half-time and played no further part in the series. Lenihan expressed fury that Grey was not cited.

Onto Stadium Australia in Sydney, which a year earlier had hosted the Olympics and two year's hence would hold a World Cup final that

Keith Wood charges ahead against Western Australia.

would end in better fashion for the English Lions than the final Test of the 2001 tour. By this time the Lions were on their last legs, exhausted and injured. Henry later confided that they were not able to stage a single worthwhile training session in the week before the big game and that five of the team that started would not have been available if the game had been just two days earlier.

Wilkinson, who had been doubtful during the week with an injury, scored a try amongst his 18 points and Robinson added to his collection of touchdowns, but with seconds left the Lions trailed 29-23. However they had a lineout close to the Wallaby line and the hosts were preparing themselves not to contest it so they could defend any driving maul attack Johnson's pack would mount.

But showing nerve in his first Test match, Justin Harrison decided to jump for the ball and won crucial possession from Johnson. Harrison's skill won the series for the hosts; he later admitted that, knowing the type of player the Lions' captain was, he had guessed that Johnson would assume the responsibility of such an important lineout and call it to himself.

It was a bitter end to the trip for the Lions and the inquest into how much rugby British & Irish players should play before these demanding tours was immediately opened. The whole home season schedule was being called into question and so was the true commitment of British and Irish domestic rugby to the Lions cause.

The players from the Home Nations were battered by the end, but even now no one has come up with an answer to overcome this issue. 2001 had been a tour of glamour, colour and, eventually, defeat.

History was to provide another slant. The Australia team were never really vintage, they had weaknesses. Did this win postpone the surgery needed on the team, therefore leaving them at the mercy of the England team in the 2003 World Cup final? Would a Lions win have changed history had they won, and made Australia rebuild as they had done in 1989? Who knows.

MARTIN JOHNSON

In all honesty, before I was asked to captain the tour, I had had mixed feelings about the prospect. I was England captain, so I knew that I stood a good chance of being asked, but I also knew the expectations and the pressure and the amount of hard work that was involved with a position like that. I also knew what I would have to put my body through. But at the same time it was a huge honour and when I got the call from Donal Lenihan, I accepted it there and then. The enormity of what it meant to be the first man to captain the Lions twice didn't enter my head – I didn't allow it to. All I was concerned about – as I had been when I was asked in 1997 – was doing the job well.

JASON ROBINSON (England)
Toured: 2001 & 2005

I was a complete wild-card selection. When the initial 67 players were picked for the provisional squad, I wasn't in it, which was no surprise. I had only been playing for Sale for a few months since my switch from playing rugby league and although I'd been fast-tracked into the England set-up, I had yet to start a game. So when the final squad was picked at the end of April and I was named, it came as a bit of a shock. And to be honest, I had no appreciation at the time of what an honour it was to be selected for a side like the Lions. I look back and I realise now just how big it was and how privileged I was to have represented the Lions. The memories are one of the greatest things I have. The shirt just brings so many people together, it is unbelievable. To see a mass of red shirts wherever you go all supporting the same team is just fantastic and something that makes a Lions tour so special.

KEITH WOOD

It's a great release to get the first game of the tour under your belt. We'd been kicking lard out of each other for a few weeks, training really hard and we all wanted to get out there.

You're only a Lion once you've put on the jersey, so there were 22 guys who were suddenly far more relaxed after the Western Australia game – and it was a huge honour for me to captain the side. We scored a lot of tries and did a lot of things well, but we were annoyed about letting in two tries. It was also a real shame about the injuries – Simon Taylor, Phil Greening… they were the first of a long line of guys who were injured out of the tour.

MIKE CATT (England)
Toured: 1997 & 2001

Looking at the squad that was selected, I had no doubt in my mind that the 2001 tour party was even stronger than the one we had in 1997. I was desperate to go, the idea of playing in a backline with Jonny Wilkinson on one side and Brian O'Driscoll on the other was just so exciting. But I knackered my back before we left; I thought it would be OK and made the decision to go. I did all I could to get my back sorted out but I couldn't play in the first three games, and it got to the stage where I began to feel embarrassed about being there because I spent all my time on the sidelines. Eventually I was picked to play Australia A, but I didn't even make it to half-time. The irony is that it wasn't my back that was the problem – I tore a calf muscle – and that was that, tour over. It was such a shame because I had been playing really well for England that year – but it was just such a brutally long season and my body was in desperate need of rest. There were so many injuries on that tour, and I think a lot of them were down to the wear and tear of a long, long season.

JASON ROBINSON

I remember waking up on the morning after our first game and thinking that we would be doing some rehab work, but instead we went into a full two-hour training session. For the guys who had played the night before, it was the last thing that any of us wanted to do. We were stiff and sore and the focus had been on a light rehab session, so it was hard to switch mentally and get motivated for the full-on session. It was then that it dawned on us that this was how it was going to be throughout the tour. After training we had half an hour to eat, have a pool session and do some media interviews before heading to the airport to fly to Brisbane. There never seemed enough time to do anything.

DR JAMES ROBSON (Tour doctor)

Toured: 1993, 1997, 2001, 2005 & 2009

As a medical team you tend to see everybody. The coaches are dealing with the players as a group, whereas the doctor tends to see them as individuals.

So it's incumbent on the doctors as well as the more senior figures to help gel the party together – there are very few tours where someone will have had no contact with the doctor.

There is also more to the job than simply dealing with injuries as they happen. Local conditions can be just as big a factor in the medical team's planning as the ruggedness of the opposition.

One of the main challenges of the 2001 tour were the distances we covered, because for every hour you change through the time zones you need a day to recover.

We also had some pretty reasonable heats to start with, particularly in Townsville, and Australia has some of the most venomous animals in the world to watch out for.

I remember at a training session one of the players sitting down by the side of the pitch and leaping up with a yell, saying they had been bitten.

We found several ants there but you immediately thought of redback spiders! Just because you're training for a rugby match doesn't mean a spider won't bite you.

GORDON BULLOCH (Scotland)

Toured: 2001 & 2005

I was disappointed not to get in the initial squad because I had played pretty well in the Six Nations and believed I had got the better of most of my rivals. But I wasn't the

Rob Henderson dives in to score against Queensland.

only Scot who would have felt hard done by – for instance, the Leslie brothers missed out. Graham Henry took a lot of Welshmen even though they hadn't had a good season – I think it was a case of better the devil he knew.

So I went out to Vail in Colorado to get away from everything and do a bit of training, and after a few weeks there I got a call to tell me to get on a plane to Australia. So I went from Vail down to Denver airport, to LA, to Christchurch, to Sydney, and then on to Townsville. And when I eventually got to Townsville nobody there had even heard of the Lions.

It is rugby league territory so this was a kind of missionary expedition, and the rest of the squad hadn't flown in from Perth yet – so nobody knew who I was or where I was supposed to be staying. To top it all off, my luggage had been lost as well. It was the last thing I needed after 26 hours of travelling. I was stuck at the airport for ages before I eventually found someone who knew what was going on.

I got driven to our hotel and the rest of the squad arrived overnight – and I was straight into the squad to play the Queensland President's XV.

The first half of that game was a bit frustrating. Obviously, we hadn't played together so we were a bit rusty and a few things we tried didn't quite come off. They put us under a bit of pressure and were very enthusiastic early on. But when we got control of the game I think you could see the class come through. It was great to get 80 points in the second tour game.

It went well for me in the second half, I got a few passes away and set up a few things so I was pleased with how it went. Things were a bit dodgy in the first half, I missed a few throws, but once you settle down it was such a great bunch of guys to play with.

I had read the papers on the way over and they said the fans would probably be out in Australia for the First Test or the week before, but there was a sudden invasion at the last minute and there were thousands of them, all with different jerseys and different flags. It was like a home game for all the guys. It was great to be part of it.

MARTIN CORRY (England)
Toured: 2001 & 2005

There was always a mythical status about the Lions. It wasn't a case of 'you can achieve this'. There was a real aura about it and an aura about the players. My goal was always to play for England. Once you've played for England, then you say 'I'd love to play for the Lions', but it's very hard to have the Lions as a goal. I'll always put it up there so, so high.

It did make it easier being called up late. There wasn't any time to dwell on it. It was more a case of, 'How am I going to get to Australia, what am I going to do, is there going to be someone there to meet me, will someone be waiting for me?'

When I got there, it was literally a case of 'Here's your playbook. You need to learn this because you're playing tomorrow.' It was all a massive rush. With jet lag and everything, I didn't really know where I was. I then played the Saturday as well so it was all about trying to focus on the games rather than thinking, 'I'm on a Lions tour.'

PHIL VICKERY (England)
Toured: 2001 & 2009

It was a massive event. In 2001, I was 24 so still reasonably young and it was something I always dreamed of. I watched Lions tours growing up and I never really thought I would be involved in one.

It was fantastic playing with Keith Wood and Tommy Smith. Obviously Dai Young was around and Scott Gibbs came out in the end, Brian O'Driscoll etc. There were a lot of big names and I thoroughly, thoroughly enjoyed it and learnt a lot from mixing with all those guys. We all made friendships that have lasted ever since.

MARTIN CORRY

I think the great thing with the Lions is that everyone realises that you need to get to know each other. You've been knocking lumps out of each other throughout the year and there's got to be a new bond. Everyone works hard to create that and all the players realise that it's something special when you're out there.

MARTIN JOHNSON

Looking back, I can see why some of the payers on the tour struggled with Graham Henry and his attitudes. I've lived in New Zealand, my wife is a Kiwi and in many ways Graham reminded me of my father-in-law, so I got that very dry Kiwi sense of humour that he had and I understood many of his attitudes and ways of thinking – but I think a lot of that was missed by the other players and they reacted in the wrong way to some of the things he said and some of the ways he approached things.

A lot of the guys had complaints about how hard we were worked in training. We had all been through a long, hard season and when we met up together at Tylney Hall before leaving for Australia, we did a lot of team-building exercises, but we also went to Aldershot to the army's physical education centre and were worked very hard. But I agreed with the management that all that kind of thing was important because we had to pull the whole tour squad together and get a sense of understanding across the group about systems, a style of play, defensive patterns, and so on. Modern rugby demands that you work hard – especially when you are a team and squad that has been thrown together with only a limited about of time available to you to prepare and get to know one another. But no matter how hard you are worked, it helps to feel supported and understood by those that are driving you, and I think that the problems stemmed from the misunderstandings between Graham and some of the players.

He said, for example, that people in the southern hemisphere didn't rate our skills or how we played and he knew because he was one of them. He meant that he was from down there and knew how they thought, not that he didn't rate us – but there was a general feeling that was spreading across the group that he did feel that way.

He was very intent on making sure we played in an incredibly structured way, with predetermined moves set for phase after phase after phase. Normally teams will have predetermined plays for two or three phases after a set piece and will then play it as they see it with the scrum-half, stand-off and inside-centre controlling the attack, but he wanted us to have set plays for seven or more phases at a time. Not only did this make us slightly robotic in our play, but it also increased the pressure on all the players as they tried to remember exactly where they were meant to be, rather than just playing their natural games and reacting to what was in front of them. In the end, we realised that this style just wasn't working for us and, as players, we decided to abandon it. And when we made that decision, we started to play our best rugby of the tour.

KEITH WOOD

We made big mistakes on that trip. We over-trained heavily and I remember having conversations with Graham Henry and Martin Johnson about it and we challenged Graham. We said, 'Listen, we're over-training, we're knackered, every one of us, we're wrecked.' And he said, 'We're going to stop in a week's time and that'll be all the really hard work done.' But by the time we stopped it had taken too much out of the players.

I made a mistake and Johnno made a mistake because we went along with it. It's more important to be ready to play on Saturday than to pile up the work. There's a balancing act that has to be done. The difficulty is going through technical areas of the game so that you do it together. Six weeks before, you're enemies and now you have to trust each other and be the best of friends. You have to have a technical defensive system, technical lineouts, technical rucking, technical scrummaging and that requires a lot of training and that is the biggest problem. There is so much work that has to be done but we did far too much work. We had to tick all of those boxes but we were wrecked because of the

Jonny Wilkinson launches a counter-attack.

effort it took. We probably over-ticked them. I should have pushed it an awful lot more with Graham. Absolutely. I should have pushed it with Johnno, too.

DONAL LENIHAN

Looking back, I would accept 100 per cent that we worked the players too hard early on but there were reasons for it. England as a professional entity were two years ahead of the other three countries at the time. England had a defence coach. Ireland, Scotland and Wales didn't have one. So you had Phil Larder who demanded more time because defensively he would say the other fellas didn't have a clue. This was a whole new set-up for three-quarters of the players. So Larder demanded more time and, in fairness to Graham, because it was largely an English management team that were used to working with each other, he was trying to find common ground and so he was keen to give them the time they needed for their specific aspects of responsibility. As a result of that, I'd put my hand up and say we trained too long.

LAWRENCE DALLAGLIO

Contrary to many reports which emanated from the tour, I believe that the fact that the Lions stayed in contention right to the final whistle of the final Test was in no small part attributable to the huge workload we put in as a squad in the first three weeks of the trip. I don't accept the criticism that the training was far too hard and there's been a lot of rubbish spouted on the subject. This is the modern professional era and the players are paid to do a professional job. I firmly believe that the two main coaches, Graham Henry and Andy Robinson, did a first-class job.

MARTIN JOHNSON

Touring can be difficult for players, even when you're representing a team as special as the Lions – and small irritations can really begin to get to you. We were training incredibly hard, playing some tough games and building up to a massive Test series, so we were all aware of trying to keep ourselves in the best nick we could. So it was frustrating when we flew to Brisbane after playing the Queensland President's XV, that we flew on a commercial flight in economy class – with a lot of the players too big for the seats. Scott Quinnell, in particular, struggled with a knee knock and was in a lot of discomfort throughout the flight, but we all stiffened up pretty badly. This is not to sound like a bunch of prima donnas, but when you're playing at the elite end of sport, the smallest margins make a huge difference and it was disappointing that with all the work we were doing, small things like this hadn't been thought out properly by the management.

JASON ROBINSON

I roomed with Rob Henderson in Manly before the Australia A game. He was a great lad, but he was known as 'the Snorer'. It was like sleeping in a room with a real lion. He was hilarious, he would pretty much sleep all day and then come alive at night, trying to speak to you at 1.00 a.m. smoking fags out of the window and ordering pizza and chips from room service.

LAWRENCE DALLAGLIO

Losing to Australia A was a real set back. All credit to them, they played very well, but we made life difficult for ourselves with a lack of any decent first-phase possession, and then handing the ball back to them on several occasions, which put us under enormous pressure. You can't play without the ball. But we were also concerned at the penalty count against us; the interpretation of the laws was definitely different to what we were used to and we suffered – especially me as I was sin-binned.

MARTIN JOHNSON

We were outplayed and out-passioned by Australia A, but very nearly snatched an undeserved draw late on. The one thing that we were really pleased with was our fitness and we had rallied well in the second half. It just hadn't been enough. In the aftermath of that game, though, Graham Henry spoke to the press and said that, following that result, we would have to start concentrating on the Test side and not so much on the other guys. That caused outrage in the press at home and caused further friction within the group. There was a sense that the Test team had been identified before we had even left the UK, meaning that those not involved in that selection felt that they had little or no chance of breaking into the Test side. That statement from Graham seemed to confirm this suspicion and it had a big effect on the morale in the camp.

Things got worse after we beat the New South Wales Waratahs in Sydney. It was a brutal match, best remembered for Duncan McRae's savage attack on Ronan O'Gara which ended in him getting sent off, and we lost a lot of players to injury over the course of that week – Dan Luger and Robin McBryde were ruled out of the rest of the tour and there were serious injuries to Will Greenwood, Neil Back and Lawrence Dallaglio.

LAWRENCE DALLAGLIO

I survived in the midweek game against Australia A in Gosford and everything seemed to be going well and then I played on Saturday against the New South Wales Waratahs. It was shattering for me when my knee gave way in the second half and I realised my tour was over.

RONAN O'GARA (Ireland)
Toured: 2001, 2005 & 2009

The Waratahs game was unbelievable – and a pretty dark memory for me. We were attacking inside their 22, I passed to Woody and he took it up close to their 5-metre line. Two of their guys brought Woody down. One of them was Duncan McRae. As the ruck was forming I followed up and shoved him. Next thing I knew I was on the ground and McRae was pucking the head off me. After the first dig I thought it was going to stop any second but they kept coming. Nine. Ten. Eleven. A frenzy of digs. One after another after another. I just lay there and took it. It was the weirdest feeling. Lying there I felt totally lost. Like I was in a daze. Even though he was on top of me I wasn't pinned down. I tried to protect my face with my right arm and after a couple of seconds I grabbed the back of his jersey with my left. Useless. Pointless. Why? Why didn't I try to push him off? Hit him. Something. Why did I just take it?

Two lacerations under my left eye needed eight stitches but the pain of that was nothing compared to the humiliation. Why didn't I try to defend myself? In the dressing room I was fucking raging. Raging with myself. Raging with McRae. When the game was over I wanted to go into their dressing room and have a cut of him. Rage was useless to me then. Too late. Why didn't I hit him when he was pucking the head off me? I don't know. I still don't know.

DONAL LENIHAN

It was a joke. I have no doubt that the Waratahs went out to take scalps that day. Tom Bowman took out Danny Grewcock from the kick-off and got a yellow card, so there was an underlying tension throughout. We lost Lawrence Dallaglio in the game, we lost Will Greenwood, we lost Neil Back for the First Test. Phil Waugh was the Waratahs captain and there was the post-match reception and he stood up and he said the Lions will 'wake up in the morning feeling sore, they took a few hits today'. You know the type of crap. There were visions of Canterbury versus the Lions in 1971.

Bob Dwyer was coach of the Waratahs. I knew Bob. We're in the hearing the day after the Duncan McRae thing and McRae never looked at Ronan once, he never apologised and never made any effort to shake his hand. This is 18 hours after the game. They tried to say that Ronan caught McRae by the balls and it was a reaction to that, but it was a complete and utter lie. That really incensed me. I had a lot of time for Bob Dwyer but I lost time for him after that hearing.

KEITH WOOD

I was about five yards from it when it happened; I was in a ruck and I never knew it was going on behind me. I ran off in the other direction. I thought McRae should have got banned for two years, three years. I thought it was horrible.

DONAL LENIHAN

I'll always remember going into the medical room after the game and that's where my admiration for Martin Johnson went even further through the roof. We'd won a difficult game and he was being stitched. He said, 'What's the story with Greenwood?' I said, 'He's out.' 'Dallaglio?' I said, 'He's out.' 'Back?' 'Out for the First Test.' He kind of shook himself and said, 'Right we'll just have to get on with it.' He's lying there and three Englishmen he would have soldiered with for a long time and who would have been well in the running for Test places were out and he just said okay. It was like if I said to him 'We've run out of second-rows, you're going to have to play in there on your own.' He'd have said, 'Fine, I'll do my best.'

MARTIN JOHNSON

So we had lost a lot of players by this stage and although we had only lost one match, morale was pretty low all through the squad. But things were really compounded before the midweek team played the New South Wales County Cockatoos. Normally we would split the training sessions, with the Saturday side in one group and the midweek guys in another doing a team-run, but this all changed and we ended up watching videos of Australia before the midweek team were asked to play as the Wallabies against the Test 22 so that we could work on our defence strategies. Essentially the guys in the midweek team felt like cannon fodder for the Test side, that their midweek game didn't matter and that the Test squad had been finalised even with a game to go. It was absolutely the wrong way to run a squad like the Lions, even though I understood that the management just presumed that a team like the Cockatoos didn't pose any threat and so the midweek team didn't require the same level of attention as those that would be involved in the First Test. 1997 worked so well because every player genuinely felt that they had a chance to put their hand up for selection, right up to the very last minute. In 2001 a lot of the boys never felt they really had a chance to make the Test side, no matter what they did, and this treatment just made the chasm that was dividing the group wider still.

GORDON BULLOCH

Lions tours are all about Test results. It doesn't matter what the midweek results are or what is happening off the field – if you are winning the series everything is good. So Graham Henry and his assistants put all their eggs in that basket. We all knew what the Test team was going to be from very early on and there was very little give and take on that.

So there was a real split feeling in the camp. The day before the dirt-trackers played New South Wales County we did a whole session with the Test team – bag holding and then acting as lineout opposition – before we did our own preparation. I can understand the thinking, but it wasn't a great message to send the midweek guys.

The Lions are held up on a pedestal and there is a belief that it will be a great experience – but I think a lot of guys are left with a sour feeling afterwards.

PHIL VICKERY

In the build-up to the First Test, you couldn't go anywhere without being stopped. I think I've got a pretty good relationship with all supporters, whether they are English, Scottish, Irish or Welsh but being embraced and being part of that with the Lions was truly a privilege.

Ronan O'Gara is assisted from the pitch after his brutal attack from Duncan McRae.

DANNY GREWCOCK (England)

Toured: 2001

Getting selected for that tour was a fantastic opportunity. I got lucky in some respects because towards the end of that season I'd broken my jaw. That meant I could do all the training bar the contact work so I got myself in good shape.

The way I looked at it, I was the last-placed second-row on that trip with Scott Murray, Jeremy Davidson, Malcolm O'Kelly and obviously Johnno. There was me and the three other guys all battling for one other place.

They'd all had far more experience than me. But I think the fact that I was a bit fresher legged than the other guys, that I hadn't played as many games during the latter part of the season, gave me a little bit of an advantage.

You need a bit of luck on these kind of tours. I managed to stay injury free on the tour itself and got involved in some of the good games before the Test series and that gave me the chance to play against Australia.

I didn't feel under any pressure because I looked at all the other guys and they were all vastly more experienced than me in terms of the number of caps they had for Ireland or Scotland. It was just a case of going out and giving it my best shot.

I think everyone felt they had a good chance of a Test spot. We all knew Johnno was captain and we would probably all have admitted that he was streets ahead of most second-rows in rugby at the time.

So we all knew we were battling for one place but I think we felt it was relatively open. We all gave it a go but luck came my way and I managed to hold down my place. Thankfully, it all went in my favour.

MARTIN CORRY

It was a real surprise to get selected for the First Test. I found out in bizarre circumstances. I went down to the team meeting and Richard Hill came up and tapped me on the bum and said, 'Congratulations mate.' I said 'What do you mean?' and he replied, 'Oh, don't you know?' I said 'OK, tell me what you know,' and he told me I was in. They tried to do this big presentation of the team but I'd already found out!

MARTIN JOHNSON

We had a team meeting the night before the First Test and I'd never felt so much nervous energy in a room – but it was an anxiousness rather than an excitement. With the mood in the camp, the fact that we were about to face the world champions, the build-up in the media and the knowledge that tens of thousands of fans had paid a fortune to travel across the world to see us, all led to a sense of the enormity of the occasion. But we channelled it well the next evening and had a great warm-up right in the bowels of the Gabba and there was a real sense of togetherness among the 22.

JASON ROBINSON

We warmed up in a large room under the stand and while the intensity was building in there we had no idea how much it was building outside – when we went out all you could see was a sea of red in the stands and the noise was deafening.

KEITH WOOD

We were down in the bowels of the stadium and we could all hear this noise. And we climbed the steps and the whole stadium was just full of red. And it was magic.

NEIL BACK

The atmosphere and the fans were fantastic. They were unbelievable. When we walked into that stadium before the First Test in 2001 you knew, if you didn't know already, what the Lions was all about. That was one of the highlights. It was a sea of red. The hairs on the back of your neck and all over your body were standing on end and you knew it was something special. I think that's why that performance on that day was as it was.

Fans are quite rightly passionate about their own team, whichever country they follow, but when they come together and put the red of the Lions on it's something really special. The great thing about rugby union is that there's no segregation, the banter is fantastic and, on a Lions tour, everyone comes together and they become Lions.

PHIL VICKERY

The First Test in Brisbane at the Gabba is probably one of my greatest rugby memories and experiences. It was just phenomenal and I'd never experienced anything like it. The support, the euphoria, the expectations, the pressure, the history and everything that surrounds the Lions makes it just a phenomenal thing to be involved in.

MARTIN CORRY

That First Test was one of the highlights of my career. When I look back at it, I probably still can't appreciate the enormity of the occasion. Everything about it, the build-up, the crowd, everything was amazing. We were running out there thousands of miles from home and 75 per cent of the crowd were wearing red shirts. Then, with the way we played, everything was just a dream.

MARTIN JOHNSON

The game could hardly have started better. With two minutes and 45 seconds on the clock we were five points up. It was a dream start, giving us the belief we could penetrate what was then the world's best defence.

MATT DAWSON

I was on the touchline right next to Jason Robinson when he ran round Chris Latham and it was quite unbelievable. The guy only had three yards to work in but just ran round Latham as if the Aussie was made of stone.

JASON ROBINSON

I received a pass from Matt Perry and found myself in a one-on-one with Chris Latham, the Aussie fullback. There was only a metre or so of space on the outside, but I decided to take it. He must have thought that I was going to try and cut inside him, so before he could react I was round him. I just managed to keep my feet in touch and to get round towards the posts. It was a great start.

KEITH WOOD

The first day that Brian O'Driscoll turned up at an Ireland training session he just pure class. He stepped on to the field and he was phenomenal. Before the tour I thought he was a certainty for the Test team. I didn't even have a hint of a doubt. The man had it in spades, always. People talk about his try in the First Test, but I prefer to remember what he did for the first try that Jason Robinson scored. All the space that Brian opened up. His first pressurised thing and he does the right thing, that's what I like about it. His try, I'm not dismissing it out of hand, it's phenomenal. But it's what you expect of him.

DONAL LENIHAN

When you put it into the context of the situation, O'Driscoll's try was even better than it looked. We had been under a lot of pressure going into the First Test and were in a reasonably strong position at half-time, but for him to score that try at that stage of

Martin Johnson secures a lineout throw.

the game quite simply closed out the First Test. The try was a totally individual one and to see three or four Australians flailing vainly after him gave the team and the crowd a huge lift.

BRIAN O'DRISCOLL (Ireland)
Toured: 2001, 2005 & 2009

Australia's defensive record was so good in the World Cup and had been so hyped during the tour, but when we broke it comfortably early on with Jason Robinson's try our self-belief grew massively. We became unafraid to try things. My try was donated by Jonny Wilkinson. There were a couple of forwards hanging round in the Australian backline and I shouldered them off and had the gas to beat the last tackler.

SCOTT QUINNELL (Wales)
Toured: 1997 & 2001

A lot of people have asked about the little nod I gave in celebration to my try, the fourth we scored in that First Test – it was an acknowledgment to myself, and to all those that had helped me get to that point, that this was the pinnacle of my career – a Lions Test cap at last and an absolute thumping of the world champions in their own backyard. Australia 2001 will always be the stuff of dreams to me.

BRIAN O'DRISCOLL

The best moment of the tour was the feeling after we had won the First Test. Hearing

Brian O'Driscoll dives over the line to score the try of the series.

that final whistle and knowing that we had just beaten the world champions was just sensational.

MARTIN JOHNSON

That was one of the greatest Test performances I have ever been involved in. It was an 11-month season, we were in Australia a long time and endured some tough times. But a convincing result like that made all the effort and sacrifice worthwhile.

The previous week had probably been my toughest as a player – with all the media sniping, the problems of morale in the camp and then the tragic death of Anton Toia; so to win the First Test was a great feeling. I wanted to make sure that the whole squad felt a part of the win, so I said in the changing room afterwards, 'This is what this tour is all about: winning these games. We're all a part of this.' And it was true – if I learned anything from '97 it was the importance of the whole squad, not just the guys who pulled on the Test jerseys. I wanted to try and bring the squad back together. I'm not sure whether it worked or not, but everyone was in good spirits.

It didn't last all that long though, because I had to go to a press conference afterwards and all they wanted to talk about was the column that Matt Dawson had written for a newspaper at home, where he criticised the management and the training. I was amazed that a player as experienced and senior as Matt would allow something like that to be published under his name right before the First Test – or while we were on tour at all.

I spoke to him later about it and he was embarrassed and pretty upset by the whole thing and was worried about the repercussions. But I said, 'If they send you home, we're all going,' and I meant it. When you play for a team, for any team, people are always hammering home the importance of history, of what it means to people at home, to your family and so on. But I always focused on the guys I was playing with – the 14 other guys on the pitch with me were the most important. It was an attitude that kept my thoughts focused, that shut out the enormity of the situation, and it meant that my loyalty to my team-mates was absolute. I wasn't going to allow him to be sent home. Fortunately, Donal and Graham, who copped a fair bit in the article, were big enough men to let the situation go and Matt was kept on tour.

DONAL LENIHAN

Clive Woodward was sniping all the time. He was at the English players. When we played the Brumbies on the Tuesday after the First Test Woodward was around that week telling the English players they shouldn't be there they should be in Melbourne preparing for the Second Test. He was goading the English fellas.

We had a problem with Matt Dawson and Austin Healey and newspaper columns. I actually liked Austin. I admired him in a lot of ways because what you saw in Austin was what you got. The Dawson thing and the way it came out in the paper was disappointing. If he had an issue he should have come to me and he didn't do that. There was an element where maybe he thought he was a shoo-in for the Test team but Rob Howley was the number one. In fairness to him, on the following Tuesday night he kicked the winning score against the Brumbies and we just smiled at each other and life goes on.

I remember this man tapping me on the shoulder after the Brumbies game and it was Matt Dawson's father and he said he wanted to apologise, that it was not his son's form to do something like that and that he knew it created hassle – and I thought it was a nice gesture from a quiet man. I never said that to Dawson and I don't know if his father said it to him. These things happen. You move on. To send him home would have been completely counterproductive, would have detracted from what we were doing and to be fair he had a fine game against the Brumbies. You move on.

KEITH WOOD

There were a lot of guys who went on that tour who went on the previous tour and they presumed they'd be playing and you can't make that presumption. One Lions tour doesn't lead to another Lions tour. I went to Australia in the box-seat but I never make a presumption on any day.

MATT DAWSON

The win against the Brumbies was a big moment for everyone. I personally got very emotional, but I think there were many others who felt likewise.

The conversion was like a pressure valve being released. It blew out all the emotions of the previous few days. I did break down in the dressing room reflecting on all the negatives of the preceding 72 hours. Dai Young and Scott Gibbs had given a very important and passionate team talk at half-time, reminding us all what it meant to wear the Lions jersey. There were 40 minutes left for me to make amends.

The Test pack readies for engagement.

I realised that this was a great opportunity to put some things to rights. I cleared my head and went through all the routines I'd spent hours and hours doing on the training field. I blocked it all out and let rip. It was a good contact and a good feeling.

MARTIN JOHNSON

Daws had not been kicking well and there had been an earlier instruction from the bench for Ronan O'Gara to take over the kicking duties, but Rog said to Daws, 'No you keep going, keep your head up,' which was a great thing of him to do. When Daws lined up the match-winning conversion, I had complete faith that he was going to redeem himself. In the changing room afterwards he was pretty emotional about the whole thing, and it was great to see all the other guys in the squad slapping him on the back. It felt like things had come back on track and we were all set up for the Second Test.

MATT DAWSON

If ever there was a game of two halves, it was the Second Test. We were dominant in the first half and defended well but we were blitzed by a very good Aussie side in the second half when they made amends. We had two or three good opportunities which we didn't put away in the first half and they may have changed the complexion of the game. We played well before the interval but it is the result that counts. They beat us by 21 points so that really hurt. We were so disappointed. We were disappointed in ourselves, especially because of the stark contrast of our performance in the two halves.

DONAL LENIHAN

Half-time in the Second Test we're ahead and again we'd played unbelievable rugby in the opening half and Australia had done everything on and off the pitch to try and mess us up that whole week. They took all the banners and things off the Lions supporters going into the ground and they handed out scarves and T-shirts to the Aussies. This is where I admire the Aussies: they're winners. There was a walk of about 50-60 metres from the dressing room down a narrow tunnel and you come up to go into the stadium. When we were coming out they put up ads on the big screen so that that Lions team was on the pitch before our supporters even saw them, whereas when Australia came out they had the cameras focused on them 50 metres down the tunnel so the noise and atmosphere was building up. They were so shocked by the colour and support the Lions had in that opening Test. They spread the Lions fans all over the place for the Second Test.

KEITH WOOD

We had played incredibly well in the First Test and incredibly well in the first half of the Second Test. Just after half-time we made a series of errors and Richard Hill got knocked out of the game and if you ever want to see the importance of one player and how his removal from the scene could change something, that was it. We were in control at every ruck until he went off, because he was on fire. And then they got the upper hand from there on in and we just seemed to struggle.

DONAL LENIHAN

Jonny Wilkinson, and bear in mind he's a 23 year old fly-half at this stage, made a shocking error. The emphasis at half-time was to play territory for the first ten minutes. Keep them at bay and we were there. Right from the kick-off we win the ball, he goes blind and he gives the pass to Joe Roff who scores in the corner. He needed to rifle that ball into the corner.

BRIAN O'DRISCOLL

Some people have said Australia's intercept try at the start of the second half was the crucial score. But I don't agree. That only made it 11-11 and the game could still have gone either way. The score after that was the killer. That's when the match started to slip away from us. It was irritating to have played so poorly in the second half. We knew we should have put away more opportunities in the first half. Australia punished us by scoring from their opportunities in the second.

DONAL LENIHAN

Then there was the Richard Hill incident. Nathan Grey took out Richard Hill with an elbow and he was an unbelievable loss. We lost Rob Howley, then Jonny was carried off. The games were late so at 1 a.m. I was told that the independent citing commissioner, whose name was Grey, which I thought was ironic, had cited nobody and I said, 'You must be joking, surely Nathan Grey has been cited?' So, I got his number, a New Zealand guy. I rang him at 1 a.m. and I said, 'Can you let me know on what grounds did you deem it appropriate not to cite Nathan Grey?' All he said was,

'You shouldn't be ringing me, you're not allowed to talk to me and I don't have to answer that question.' And he was gone the following morning. About six weeks later, Australia were in South Africa and David Giffin was cited for elbowing a Springbok but it was nowhere near as bad as the Nathan Grey one. The citing commissioner was our same friend from New Zealand and Giffin got, I think, six weeks.

RICHARD HILL

I bobbled a pass from Martin Johnson and took a hit to the face. At the time

Matt Dawson celebrates his late match-winning conversion against the Brumbies.

you're thinking, 'Well, has that affected me or not?' You almost need a few seconds to gather yourself.

I don't think I was actually convinced who I was playing for because I'm not used to playing in red! It took me a little while to work out who I was playing for and where we were.

I went off just to try and re-gather my thoughts, went back on and played out the rest of that half. I remember walking off the pitch and it was almost like I then woke up in a medical room at half-time.

You go through some of the precautionary tests and, unfortunately, that night I was told I wouldn't be able to feature the next week. That was a horrible thing to take.

I thought from my personal performances that the tour had been going well. I desperately wanted to get out there again and play in the series decider. Unfortunately, that was taken out of my hands.

MARTIN JOHNSON

Australia started to shift our scrum around, which was a surprise, got us on the back foot and kept us off balance. We were totally outplayed in that second half. We self-destructed and let ourselves down badly. From a forwards point of view, we didn't function as a unified eight and that cost us massively. We had dominated them in the First Test and in the first half of the Second Test, but we switched off at a crucial moment: they shunted us back, turned us over and Joe Roff ended up scoring his second try. It was a hammer blow. The momentum was all with them after that and Matt Burke later crossed for their third try. From winning 11-6 at half-time, we ended up on the end of a 35-14 thrashing.

KEITH WOOD

So it's 1-1 and we get to the Third Test and I remember the stats well, I was one of six players who trained on the Monday who played on the Saturday. We were falling apart. We really needed to get the series won in the first two weeks. We were hanging.

GRAHAM HENRY (Head coach)
Toured: 2001

You cannot ever visualise these things happening. We had a lot of class players in the original tour party who were obviously Test candidates, but who never featured in the Test series or featured early and didn't finish the series.

The build-up for the Third Test was far more frustrating than the match itself. We had so many injured players that we probably had only about two-thirds of the side on the training pitch at any one time and not even the same ten players. When you consider it was impossible and impractical to undertake any full sessions in preparation, what they did in that Test was really quite remarkable. We just had to sign up, got them on the field and they gave 100 per cent – more than 100 per cent probably. It was a frustrating week full stop. If the Test had been on the Wednesday, half of the eventual team wouldn't have been unavailable.

DONAL LENIHAN

How we got as close as we did in the Third Test I'll never know because we barely trained for the week.

ANDY NICOL

I had started the Six Nations as Scotland captain so presumably had a fair chance of going, but we didn't have a great championship and it didn't happen. I went on a supporters' tour instead and drank my way around Australia for two and a half weeks. Then I got a call the night before the last Test from Donal Lenihan saying that they had an injury in the squad and might need me the next day.

I was about to go and climb the Sydney Harbour Bridge and I decided I wasn't going to say no to that because it was something I had always wanted to do. So, at half eleven on the Friday night I was standing on top of Sydney Harbour Bridge listening to all the Lions fans singing on the Rocks down below, and thinking they might be singing about me tomorrow. I got a call at nine o'clock the next morning to say that I was needed to sit on the bench that night.

I spent all Saturday with the injured Rob Howley, trying to digest this huge playbook and getting more and more nervous as the day went on. We went to this local park for a walk through before the evening kick-off, where I think I made two passes to Johnny – one bounced first and the other was spot on – and that was it, I was apparently ready to go.

It was an invidious position to be in because I couldn't say no. But if I had got on after five minutes I probably would have been subbed off after 20 minutes and that would have been hellishly embarrassing. But, as it got near the end I started to think I could get through it on adrenalin, and I had said to Matt Dawson that if we are big up or big down then get me on – but there was six points in it so I didn't get my chance.

When I went into the changing room after the game my number was pulled out the hat for the drug test, and I hate to think what the analysis man would have made of that substance!

MARTIN CORRY

While the First Test was one of my career highlights, two weeks later was one of the real low points. We should have won the Second Test and then we allowed too many mistakes to creep into our game in the Third Test. It was a series defeat that hurts because we should have won it. It was very disappointing but, having said that, it was the first time I got to play on that kind of stage so I really enjoyed it.

KEITH WOOD

We felt the Aussies knew a lot of our lineouts and we were trying to change a lot of them but we had an awful lot of changes in personnel and that made it hard. We had three or four lineouts on the trot that had been difficult before the one towards the end. The call for that lineout was to the back and I wanted to throw it to the back and

Johnno over ruled and called it to the front. I threw a pretty good throw but they read it and snatched a hand in front of it. Did the game come down to that throw? After the fact it does and the reason it does is because of Justin Harrison and all the chat, but it didn't come down to that at all. We still had an opportunity to go and score. And it wasn't as if it was five yards from the line, it was 20 yards out. It fits the bill in terms of the story, though.

Was it important? Yeah. Should we have won it? Yes. Could we have scored off it? Yes. But none of those things follow on from one another. I wouldn't be caught up on it. We lost the series because we lost our key player, Richard Hill. And we were like walking wounded at the end of it. I was so unbelievably shattered at the end of it.

DANNY GREWCOCK

I still rank that First Test in Brisbane as one of the best-ever atmospheres for a game. That's what the Lions bring. It just adds that something special.

We got a good start. They were the world champions, they were the Tri-Nations champions and they were a team that had been there and done it all. We'd had a relatively tough tour travelling around Australia and perhaps the expectation on us wasn't too high for that First Test, but the boys pulled out a performance.

But, ultimately, you're there to win a series. You're far more critical when your team loses. Success can smooth over a lot of things.

One try could have made the difference between a series loss and a series win for us. The boys gave it their all and sometimes you can give it your all but, whether it's a bit of luck, an interception or because you're playing as good an opposition as they were, you don't get what you perhaps feel you deserve. That's tough, but that's the way sport goes.

There's no doubt that was a brilliant Australian team at the time. I don't think it was any disgrace for us to have lost the series but would I have wanted to win, do I think we were good enough to win it? Yeah. The series was close and little decisions meant they won it and we didn't.

MARTIN JOHNSON

I was close to tears after the final whistle. We were right in the series up until those last seconds and the realisation that it was all over and we had lost was so deflating. All that effort, everything we had worked for, all our dreams were suddenly shattered – and it was my last time in a Lions jersey. It was a dreadful feeling that will live with me forever.

JASON ROBINSON

The tour was a great experience, but it was also the hardest two months of rugby that I'd had in my life. There was so much travelling and a lot of training with hardly any time off, so I felt like a zombie most of the time. Time is always against you on tours like that – especially in Australia where you have to cover vast distances between each game –

but it never made any sense to me that we had full contact sessions the day after games. There were a lot of injuries sustained throughout the tour and a lot of guys were forced to go home, but the sad thing was that a large number of these injuries happened in training. I know that I wasn't alone in feeling so tired all the time and I honestly believe that if we had been kept a little fresher we would have won the series.

MARTIN JOHNSON

There were all sorts of things that conspired against us. The morale in the group was up and down and there were some big divisions that developed. The management and the playing personnel didn't all gel and there was a lot of carping over what the best tactics were for the games, or the way that we approached training and preparation. But at the core was the selection of the squad from the outset. I didn't feel that the best players that were available were all there, or that the best players in the squad were picked for the Test 22s. We suffered with injury and some guys' form deserting them, but even then I think we could have overcome those difficulties if we had had the strongest squad available to us.

I also think that I could have led the party better than I did. In 1997 I was aware that I was a young and inexperienced captain, but I had a lot of senior guys to help me through things – also, there was a real excitement throughout that tour party about what we were doing and the way we were playing. Four years later, I had captained good England and Leicester sides and perhaps demanded more from those around me. My man-management skills weren't as good as they should have been. I expected people to just work hard and get on with things, no matter how hard they found the whole touring experience, but if I had my time again I would have had more one-to-one chats, I would have tried to appear more open so that the players could come to me and air their issues. I concentrated too much on the job in hand and just presumed that others would follow suit. At the same time, the tour was a brutal culmination of an 11-month season, and I was just trying to get through the training and the games without breaking down – as I'm sure we all were – so my mind wasn't as focused on the needs of the other tour members as it should have been.

We didn't socialise much, either, which is a key part of touring and was a crucial element to the team-bonding that we had had in 1997. Because of the time difference, almost all our games were at night, so by the time we eventually headed back to our hotel, it was midnight. With recovery or training always scheduled for the next morning, we very seldom did anything other than go straight to bed. As a result, there were guys that I never really got to know – and that will have been true for every player across the squad. Without meals out with a few beers, or some nights out in bars and clubs together, it's very hard to get past the initial veneer and get to know another player really well. I don't outright blame the management for this – they weren't scheduling the matches – but they were aware that there were problems and should have done something to address them. Again, as captain, I should have done more to drive that as well and I didn't.

There are many regrets I have about that tour. There are some great moments to remember too – such as the First Test win and some of the attacking rugby that we played; but the regrets are freshest and most vivid in my memory.

DONAL LENIHAN

We made mistakes with the training and I hold my hand up to it, but I'm proud to this day of the quality of rugby we played and I think it will stand the test of time. I think people look back now and think maybe we were a little harsh in our judgement of the tour because the quality of the rugby was outstanding.

Martin Johnson after the final whistle of the Third Test.

CHAPTER TWENTY-SEVEN

BLACKOUT

2005

NEW ZEALAND

SIR Sir *Clive Woodward has never been one to shrink from massive challenges. When he was appointed head coach for this tour – which was to end in almost unrelieved sporting disaster – it must be remembered that there were very few dissenting voices against a man who had dominated the southern hemisphere and also the Six Nations during his time as England coach, and had also won the World Cup.*

Woodward realised that New Zealand were developing a special team, with Dan Carter and Richie McCaw nearing career peaks and also that, as usual, the players he chose would be exhausted even before they left Heathrow by yet another overbearingly testing home season. He knew he would find few friends. Certainly, everyone in the southern hemisphere would wish him ill, and there were unquestionably people in British and Irish rugby who were not exactly averse to see him fall flat on his face. And that is almost exactly what happened.

He made another bold decision – that they would maintain the tradition of Lions tours and play games in midweek all around the country. Many were calling for Lions tours to be drastically truncated, so that apart from maybe a couple of warm-up games, they consisted only of the three Test matches. Woodward, and many other traditionalists, believed that this would remove all the colour and history from a Lions tour, and also removed the whole point of the activity.

Yet he then decided that the only way the midweek games could be played was if you took enough players to run two teams, and enough back-up staff to service those two teams. Accordingly, when the party gathered at Heathrow, they were one of the most populous sporting squads ever to assemble, and even a man with his organisational capabilities was never able to dispel the notion that it was all impossibly unwieldy, and almost bound to end in disaster.

It was perhaps natural that Woodward would call upon some of those Englishmen who had done him so many favours over the years and had ultimately won him the World Cup, but some critics felt the 44-man original party was top-heavy with Englishmen who had been injured or out of form. Welshman John Dawes, who captained the Lions to their only Test series success in New Zealand back in 1971, was the first to voice his concerns proclaiming that some of Woodward's picks were 'baffling'. Even the talismanic Jonny Wilkinson was to struggle on tour.

In truth, even Dawes' brilliant side of 34 years before would have had their work cut out to cope with the brilliance of the 2005 All Blacks, marshalled by Crusaders' fly-half Dan Carter, who tore them to shreds as New Zealand coasted to a 3-0 series win. Woodward's original selection featured twenty English, eleven Irish, ten Welsh and three Scottish representatives, but three other injured

---

Opposite: Dan Carter spins out of Jonny Wilkinson's despairing tackle.

World Cup winners – Jonny Wilkinson, Mike Tindall and Phil Vickery – were also pencilled in. As it was, only Wilkinson made it to New Zealand and a third of the squad were over 30.

Wales had just won the Grand Slam under Mike Ruddock and as European champions were expected to supply the biggest proportion of the party, but Woodward put most of his initial faith in those he knew and trusted including flanker Richard Hill, just back from injury, and the rest of the 'Holy Trinity' of England's World Cup-winning back-row of Leicester's Neil Back and the Wasps icon Lawrence Dallaglio, although both had retired from international rugby. Dallaglio was to be injured in the first game and invalided home, a grievous blow.

The Welsh contingent included centre Gavin Henson who would prove to be a focal point of off-the-field news during the trip, but did not include his countryman and back-rower Ryan Jones, who eventually, as a replacement, would prove to be one of the few on-field successes of the trip.

There were no arguments, however, when Woodward unveiled Irish centre Brian O'Driscoll as his captain at a squad-naming press conference at Heathrow. Then aged 26, O'Driscoll had the respect of the rugby world, and was recognised as one of the leading midfielders on the planet, but his tour was destined to be short and not so sweet after he was injured during an incident in the First Test which would sour relations between the Lions and their hosts for the rest of their stay.

In keeping with the reputation he had earned with England, Woodward lavished money on his support staff. One masterstroke was to employ Ian McGeechan, the ultimate Lions coach, to head up the midweek side who were one of the triumphs of the time in New Zealand as they remained unbeaten. There were also jobs for Ireland's Eddie O'Sullivan and Wales' Gareth Jenkins as well as Woodward's former lieutenant with England, Andy Robinson.

As manager, the highly-respected Bill Beaumont, the former lock who toured New Zealand as a Lion in 1977 and captained the squad in South Africa three years later shortly after winning a Grand Slam as England's captain, was already in place. Beaumont was seen as a perfect buffer to the inevitable flak that would be flying in the New Zealand winter.

No one argued with the majority of Woodward's massive support team but there was one exception who would also prove to be one of the tour's central characters. Alastair Campbell, formerly Tony Blair's right-hand man when Blair was prime minister and an ex-political writer for The Mirror, *was put in charge of press relations and polarised opinion amongst the public and media at home and abroad just as he had done during his time at Downing Street.*

In another twist, Woodward's opposite number as coach of the All Blacks was Graham Henry, a former coach of the Welsh and the man who Woodward had openly criticised for his handling of the Lions in Australia four years previously.

Thus battle lines were drawn as the Lions headed to Cardiff for an unprecedented warm-up game against Argentina which has since been given Test status by the International Rugby Board. That match at the Millennium Stadium ended in a 25-25 draw but also ended in sighs of relief all round from the Lions' management as Wilkinson proved his fitness in his first international appearance since the 2003 World Cup final. And then it was off to New Zealand for the tourists with the words of Woodward – who claimed his party 'respect the All Blacks, but do not fear them' – ringing in their ears.

The first game, against the Bay of Plenty in Rotorua, was a triumph on the scoreboard as the Lions ran out 34-20 winners with the ever-combative Josh Lewsey scoring twice, but was a disaster for

Woodward as Dallaglio, who was having a massive impact on the match, was carried off after 25 minutes. Dallaglio, a great friend of the coach and seen as a potential lynchpin of the Test side, had had his tour wrecked by an ankle injury.

It all started to unravel from there on in. McGeechan's midweek side proudly battled their way to wins over Taranaki, Wellington, Southland, Manawatu and Auckland, all meaningful games, but the Test side were found wanting by their New Zealand counterparts.

The prohibitive costs of hotels and transport in New Zealand meant that many of the Lions' version of cricket's Barmy Army had to make do and mend by traversing the country in camper vans but that did nothing to dim the enthusiasm of the estimated 30,000 touring fans, some with tickets and some without, when the travelling circus arrived in Christchurch for the First Test match.

Henson was omitted from the team to play at Lancaster Park and was then pictured in conversation with Woodward in a photograph circulated to all the newspapers on Fleet Street. Henson claimed in a book published later that he was bemused by the whole episode, which to some observers had Campbell's fingerprints all over it, but worse was to come when the opening Test finally kicked off.

Woodward had gone to great pains to consult Maori elders and experts about how the tourists should respectfully face the Haka and came up with the conclusion that the youngest member of the Test side, Welsh scrum-half Dwayne Peel, should stand with O'Driscoll at the tip of an arrow-head formation. Although intended as a sign of respect, it appeared to rile the home team. One minute in, O'Driscoll was out of the tour after being on the wrong end of an alleged double spear tackle by New Zealand captain Tana Umaga and hooker Keven Mealamu and suffered a dislocated shoulder. The O'Driscoll incident overshadowed the All Blacks' 21-3 win which gave Henry first blood over his old adversary, but it went from bad to worse when Lions second-row Danny Grewcock was subsequently banned for biting and Richard Hill had his tour ended with a knee injury.

The fall-out went on long into the night in Christchurch with Richard Smith, the travelling QC with the Lions, putting their side of the story to Willie Venter the citing commissioner, but the cold facts were that the Lions were without a captain and 1-0 down in the series with two games to go. The 2005 tour party.

Gareth Thomas, the Welshman, was given the task of righting the ship in the wake of O'Driscoll's departure and he scored early in the Second Test in Wellington. It was a false dawn though as Carter produced a master class of fly-half play to take the series. The All Black No 10 ran through the full repertoire of his tricks as he scored two tries, four conversions and five penalties for a personal haul of 33 points in a 48-18 rout that left the tourists out on their feet. To rub salt into the wound for the Lions, Umaga also touched down, as did Richie McCaw and Sitiveni Sivivatu. The All Blacks were efficient, fast and deadly.

With only pride to play for as they limped to Eden Park for the final Test, the Lions drew hope from the fact that the magician Carter was injured. However, the New Zealand juggernaut was not about to let up against opponents who had been smashed from pillar to post in the Test series and they found an able deputy in Luke McAlister, who scored 13 points in a 38-19 win.

That was that. New Zealand were palpably the better team in almost every department; there was not one area of the game in which the Lions could seek refuge. The suspicion that the Lions lacked organisation grew with stories that they changed their lineout calls just before the First Test, and that no one really had any clear idea of the game plan. The tour was saved from disaster by the results of the midweek team, culminating in a win over Auckland just before the final Test.

Yet the players were not given the best opportunity to fulfil themselves; since they could no longer claim that they had enjoyed the festivities and the socialising and the sightseeing – all these were items from the past – then you had to feel sorry for the class of 2005 for all their aspirations had come to nothing.

JASON ROBINSON

I knew this tour would be extremely intense from the outset. Clive Woodward wanted to imprint the no-expense-spared model that had worked so well for England on the 2005 Lions. We had our own private jet to fly us around New Zealand; we had a

Eddie O'Sullivan, Sir Clive Woodward and Andy Robinson.

huge back-up staff to help support the players; and we even had Alastair Campbell, the former Labour spin doctor, as our head of media operations. We also had a huge playing squad to make sure that everyone was fresh and that there was back-up in every position on the field. The risk with this, of course, was that a good number of players would not be involved in the Tests and some would struggle for game-time on the tour at all.

MARTYN WILLIAMS (Wales)
Toured: 2001, 2005 & 2009

Clive Woodward's organisation was just incredible, there's no taking that away from him. We met up at the Vale of Glamorgan Hotel, which was our pre-tour base, and everything was just run like clockwork. We were all given these big red folders that were filled with tactical plays and so on, and they had our names embroidered on them; the team room, which was normally just a few tables and chairs when the Wales team were there, had plasma screen TVs, music all wired up and a podium with a microphone. All the chairs had been laid out with our names on them. And it was the same all week – every detail had been thought out and it was all run really efficiently.

I have to admit that I wasn't really into some of the team bonding stuff that was organised for us – we had to paint a big mural thing, which wasn't really my thing. The best thing we did actually, was totally impromptu. Before we played Argentina at the Millennium Stadium, me and a few of the other non-playing squad members – Dwayne Peel, Matt Dawson, Paul O'Connell, Brian O'Driscoll and Tom Shanklin – went for a night out in Cardiff and it was brilliant. Those are the kind of things that really bonds players together – blowing off some steam over a few beers, rather than painting a bit of a mural.

People have said that there were too many players selected for that tour, but I'm not sure about that. What I'm sure of is that there were too many back-room guys. It was just massive and the tour was run like a military campaign. There was no time off to bond all together – we were basically two teams on different tours – and that division was a real problem.

MICHAEL OWEN (Wales)
Toured: 2005

I was named captain for the Argentina match, with Jonny Wilkinson as my vice-captain, which was a huge honour – especially as we were playing in Cardiff. It was Jonny's first international since he'd kicked England to World Cup victory in 2003, so it was a massive moment for him as well. But as a team we didn't play at all well in that game – we just couldn't get going – there was no cohesion, our handling was poor and we got turned-over a lot in open play.

But Jonny kept us in it with six penalties and he set up Ollie Smith for our only try. It was a disappointing – and flat – start to the tour. And I was left feeling angry afterwards because at one point we had a penalty and I told Jonny to kick for goal; we were three points down, so I wanted to tie the scores, get the ball at the kick-off and look to work our way up field to try and win the game. I turned around and walked away and then when I looked back, Jonny was kicking for the corner – having been instructed to by the coaches. I felt totally undermined, and it was an indication of how Clive wanted to micromanage everything.

JONNY WILKINSON (England)
Toured: 2001 & 2005

The opening Test match against Argentina was a strange one. We had had hardly any time together, so it was almost like we were a Barbarians side, but with greater pressure to perform. It was a tough game and it eventually came down to me having to land a 40 metre kick out on the left to draw the game. Thankfully it went over, but it had been a shaky start.

GORDON BULLOCH

Simple things can make a huge difference on a tour – for example, the whole single rooms thing. The blueprint for the tour was England in 2003, and it's fine if that is what you have got used to – but a lot of guys from the other countries were maybe looking for a bit of support or a bit of banter, and being in a room by yourself is not really conducive to creating that atmosphere.

Lawrence Dallaglio is stretchered from the field after dislocating his ankle during the first mid-week game, against Bay of Plenty – ruling him out of the tour.

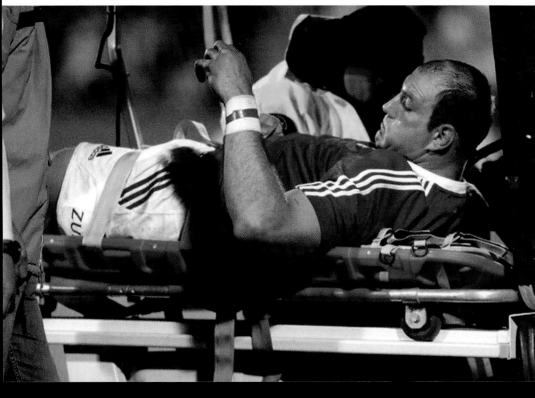

BEN KAY (England)
Toured: 2005

A Lions tour of eight weeks is a totally different coaching challenge to the four-year build-up to a World Cup. You have to draw a line and say you are not there to improve the player, but to see them more as a finished product, and be more pragmatic. I heard Johnno say at a dinner recently that the role of a coach on a Lions tour is more motivational than anything else, because you have less time to get the player prepared and attend to all the fine detail.

However, Clive was picked to coach the Lions because of the structure he had with England, so he should not take all the blame. The coaches can't take all the blame, because it's us who were out on the pitch. Too many players, myself included, were too quiet in team meetings, and we didn't tell them it was overcomplicated.

LAWRENCE DALLAGLIO

I dislocated my ankle playing against Bay of Plenty in Rotorua. It was the opening game of the tour and we had only played about 20 minutes when I went to help Brian O'Driscoll make a tackle – I slipped, my weight went one way, my foot the other and I tore my ankle out of the socket. I've never known pain like it.

When I was lying in the hospital waiting for some morphine, the doctor in charge asked me if he could have my Lions kit. Unbelievable.

I had a plate and five screws inserted into my ankle, but it meant that I wasn't able to fly home for a while. I stayed in the Hilton Hotel in Auckland, where the squad had been based when we first arrived. Simon Taylor was there too – he had been forced to quit the tour with a hamstring injury. Even though we didn't know each other very well, I called him to see if he wanted to go out for dinner. He agreed and I booked us a table at a local restaurant and ordered us a taxi. I called Simon to let him know and he told me that he'd changed his mind and didn't want to go out. So I went out on my own anyway – and apart from Bruce Twaddle, a brilliant Kiwi surgeon, I didn't see another soul for ten days.

SIMON TAYLOR (Scotland)
Toured: 2001 & 2005

Looking back, it is always easy to pick out, or invent, a concatenation of factors leading up to an injury but, ultimately, it boils down to misfortune and possibly having offended the gods at some point.

Unfortunately, being injured prevented me from really getting stuck into the tour and from feeling a proper part of the squad. In fact, I'm sure everyone will have formed the impression that I am generally a depressive, insular oddball.

They may have a point, but being injured makes you go a bit strange. You feel guilty that you aren't involved in the really painful stuff and you begin to question your purpose in life.

It's a real shame, because they were a genuinely nice group of people and it would have been great to have played a game or two, had the chance to prove myself, which is the only time you can really become integrated. I would have preferred to have played and failed miserably, had a terrible game, than not fire a shot. As it is, I'll die wondering.

MARTYN WILLIAMS

It was pretty evident early on that Woodward and the other coaches wanted to go with the tried and tested in the Test series – they wanted to try and replicate the 2003 England team with one or two other guys, like Drico and Paul O'Connell tagged in along with the English old guard. You can understand the thinking, the English team in 2003 and in the build-up years were absolutely brilliant – but this was two years later, the guys were two years older and the game had moved on.

GORDON BULLOCH

I think the basic structure was there in 2005, and if the Test side had performed to any extent it would have been regarded as a success. But it was almost the case that people didn't want to be in the Test side because they were getting crushed!

Of course everyone would take their chance if it came along and would believe that they could improve things – but the difference between the atmosphere in the midweek side in 2001 and in 2005 was like night and day. In 2005 we won all our games, and we got a Saturday night outing in Dunedin as well when the Test team were rested.

Geech and Gareth Jenkins were the midweek coaches and this really great atmosphere developed – whereas the Test side got too serious, and couldn't really step away from it and enjoy the tour. It kind of got to them, I think.

The midweek team – who were dubbed 'the Midweek Massive' – almost had our

Geordan Murphy dives in to score against Taranaki.

own tour. We didn't really mix enough as a party.

Matt Stevens was one of the guys who had a good tour, really enjoyed himself and was the life and soul of the party. But we lost a couple of influential guys early on (like O'Driscoll and Dallaglio) and we were gubbed in all three Tests – so it wasn't really much of an environment for a laugh and a joke.

In truth, it was so organised that there wasn't much scope for spontaneity and for characters to come to the fore. The Test side were just so focused on results.

BEN KAY

There was a more positive atmosphere in the midweek side than in the Saturday side. The midweek coaches made a big effort to be positive, there was less fear of the opposition, and more focus on how we would play, rather than how they would. But, remember, the midweek team is under less pressure.

SHANE BYRNE (Ireland)
Toured: 2005

I couldn't say being selected for the Lions was all my dreams come true because I never dreamed that big. The Lions never crossed my radar. I never said, 'Wouldn't it be great to be a Lion,' because it was something I never thought would happen. It was a very strange tour. I went a couple of weeks without seeing Mal O'Kelly who was on the same tour I was; we were like ships passing in the night. He was away with one team and I was away with another. It was mad. There was a paranoia around the place. The splitting of the squad was an experiment but it was an experiment that failed. There was a Them and Us split. The first time the First Test side stood together was on that day of the First Test. We had no experience together.

BEN KAY

The team could have done with playing together more before the First Test – and Clive has come out and said so since. With the benefit of hindsight, if we had known each other better, we would have known how to put it right when it went wrong. We certainly weren't the best prepared touring side there's been. We should have spent more time on actually winning the ball, rather than on what we would do with it in phase play. We did not get enough time on the set piece, which was often bolted on to training sessions at the end. I know some of the props felt not enough time was spent on the scrum, and I would have liked more time on the lineout.

SIMON SHAW (England)
Toured: 1997, 2005 & 2009

New Zealand was a bit of a nightmare all-round. For me, it was frustrating because the midweek side went unbeaten. However, we didn't feature in the Test matches, and it never felt as if we were going to. It was like two separate tours which didn't marry together as Lions tours should.

If anything, we were over-planned. It was all pre-ordained who would play in every game, and that's a big mistake. Lions tours are about personalities who come out during a tour, and find great form. Pre-selecting is the worst way to go about things, and it gives the opposition a real advantage too. The Kiwis knew exactly what they would come up against, and by the time the Test series started they had the armoury in place to deal with it.

I arrived about a week into the tour as a replacement for Malcolm O'Kelly and my head was completely scrambled by the line-out calls for the match against the Maoris. Paul O'Connell was our line-out leader, and he didn't really understand them, and nor did any of the other forwards. I couldn't really get anyone to explain them to me.

If you are going to spend nine weeks touring and playing you've got to enjoy it, and if you get too technical or scientific the enjoyment tends to go. The most important thing on a Lions tour is that you have to get unity in a very short time, and over-analysis can sometimes get in the way. With international players, who are meant to be the *crème de la crème*, there has to be an expectation that they know what they're doing, and coaches have to trust that.

That means you get line-out leaders and callers to relay systems that they are comfortable with, rather than something imposed from the outside. In 2005 our line-out systems had probably been devised months before the tour by someone who'd never played. Our coaches were so concerned that New Zealand knew our calls that you needed a code-breaker to work them out. Even if New Zealand knew our calls, if you execute them well, it doesn't really matter. We got too bogged down in detail.

DONNCHA O'CALLAGHAN (Ireland)
Toured: 2005 & 2009

In the build-up to the First Test, members of the midweek team were refused entry to the video analysis room because we weren't in the match-day 22. What did they think we were going to do? Sell our secrets to the All Blacks? There was an element of paranoia around the place that was uncomfortable and that incident caused some bitterness among the midweek players. We probably felt like second-class citizens at times, even though they didn't treat us like that.

GORDON BULLOCH

A lot of the time the midweek squad and the Test team didn't train together.

The Midweek Massive had a really good core of guys and Geech kept it low key and calm. When you go on these trips, guys are full of information from their national team – tackle techniques, stats, lineout codes and all that kind of stuff – so you have got to keep it as simple as possible, and I think Geech managed to do that.

Meetings were kept to a minimum and time was made for a bit of fun like playing football as a warm-up to training – whereas the Test side was just so focused on results that they perhaps lost a wee bit of who they were as people, and as a player you've got to be enjoying yourself to play well.

IAN McGEECHAN

Clive was trying to get exactly the same things out of the group of people that every Lions coach has tried to do: a squad coming together, well supported, well prepared and with a clear direction to try and win a Test series. He had his own principles. I wouldn't have gone to New Zealand if I thought, 'This is wrong." I had a specific role: looking after the midweek team. And I was very comfortable about accepting that role. But I've always felt that the more time you can spend together, the better, because then you can have honest conversations with each other and players can also know that they have an honest chance of a Test place. Some of them will only get two games to take it in because that's all that's available before the First Test, but they should all be given that opportunity.

SHANE BYRNE

When they announced the squad for the First Test it was a dream come true only then to be told a few days beforehand that they were going to change the lineout calls. That was an absolute nightmare. Once that decision had been made we then had to go and come up with a set of lineout calls that were going to work. To get a set of lineout calls out of the blue and functioning in such a short space of time was hard. The Irish lads came up with a set and the English boys couldn't get their heads round them. It was a ludicrous situation but we had to embrace it wholeheartedly and go for it. Right into the day of the Test I know lads didn't know the lineouts. What I would describe as knowing them is being able to do it without thinking. It drove uncertainty. It was Andy Robinson who told us. He reckoned that the All Blacks had our lineout calls. I didn't

Gavin Henson stretches to score against Southland.

give a damn whether they did or whether they didn't. A good functioning lineout can act before they can react. You can call it before you get there. There are ways around it. Once we gathered our jaws off the floor and argued a little bit, saying we'd be mad to do this, I as the person who was running the lineout had to very quickly embrace it and push it.

Putting hoarding up around our training sessions, changing our lineout calls days before the First Test. They didn't do anything to stop New Zealand, they just undermined us. The set-up was paranoid. You had two full squads travelling independent of one another and it made it harder to get the spirit in the camp. As we know in rugby, when your back is against the wall it's things like spirit – things you can't coach – that help you get through a game. That's why Ian McGeechan started what was called the Midweek Massive, trying to get that team bonded. It was fantastically done but it didn't help the Test squad when the rails started to come off it. Within the coaching staff there was a Them and Us thing. I was very aware that there was conflict within the coaching structure because you had such large personalities, O'Sullivan and McGeechan and Robinson and Woodward. These guys, some of them, are polar opposites. You'd meet up with Eddie and his eyes would go to heaven.

GORDON BULLOCH

They were so paranoid about anybody finding out our plans that we had SAS guys patrolling the training grounds, and the back-up players didn't even know the lineout codes. When I was called into the squad for the Third Test I had to learn the codes on the morning of the match.

The Lions adopt a unique line-up in response to the All Blacks' Haka.

STEPHEN JONES (Wales)

Toured: 2005 & 2009

To finally get the nod and be told I was wearing the number 10 shirt for the Lions in the First Test was very humbling and daunting... But the Test was a major disappointment. We started badly and left ourselves a mountain to climb for the rest of the series.

BRIAN O'DRISCOLL

I have a scar on my shoulder that reminds me of the First Test every time I put a shirt on. You can't get away from the fact that it happened, but I don't live it every day. Bad things happen throughout your career and your personal life and you have to be able to shelve things and move on to the next level.

No, it wasn't deliberate. I think it was very, very reckless and careless, but not deliberate. I spoke to Tana (Umaga), but not to Keven (Mealamu), but that's not because I'm holding a grudge against him, it's just because I haven't had an opportunity for chit-chat. I've spoken to Tana and I'm sure he stands by his view that it wasn't deliberate and I take him at his word. The law of spear tackles has changed as a result of that. If that happened in this day and age you wouldn't be on the end of a week or two ban, you might be looking at something a bit more substantial, but unfortunately I had to be the guinea pig for that. At least some good has come out of that situation. Red cards became more prevalent in that situation and rightly so because it's about protecting players on the field. It was the first time I felt vulnerable on a rugby pitch. I wasn't in control of myself.

As I was thrown down, the only thing in my mind was to somehow break my fall. Much better to break my hand or my arm than my neck. I stretched out with my right arm just in time and hit the ground with a thud. The pain was instantaneous.

Just minutes into the First Test, Brian O'Driscoll is injured out of the series.

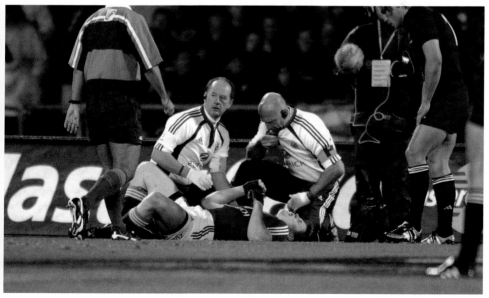

Something had to give and it was my right shoulder, which had sheared away and, as I now know, dislocated. I tried to shout out to Andrew Cole (touch judge), who I could still sense standing by the ruck, but I had no voice at all – either I had been winded or the shock had numbed me for a minute, I felt like a drowning man, I wanted to shout for help but no one could hear me.

SHANE BYRNE

If Brian was on the pitch you would have hoped he'd have had a galvanising effect because all it would have taken was something for us to get behind, something to happen, a big hit or a good run, anything. You'd have thought Brian could have done that, could have been that person. We're not talking about winning the game but we could have changed the manner of the defeat, rather than it being such a low. We had already lost Lawrence Dallaglio and Richard Hill and Hill to me is one of the greatest players who ever played the game. He had more effect on a team than any other single player I've ever seen. It was a disgrace the way the Drico thing was dealt with by the authorities and it just added to the paranoia and suspicion. It started to snowball from there.

RICHARD HILL

I was tracking across field as the All Blacks attacked wide, and then they cut back infield and I checked to align with them. My studs caught on the turf and my leg, from my knee to my ankle, was at a 45 degree angle below me. Ali Williams, their second-row, had the ball and was running at me, so I made the tackle and threw everything into it. I was happy with the tackle, it was just a meeting of forces. Unfortunately, my left leg wasn't in a perfect position and got caught underneath the two of us and I had to take all of his weight. I can still remember the crunching noise as my knee went. The pain was terrible. And my world just collapsed.

I'd fought extremely hard to make the tour and make myself available. I was feeling

The heavens open during the First Test – conditions that the hosts adapted to with greater effect than the Lions.

confident that it was all sorted but nothing could have prepared me for the position I got myself in.

I knew on that tour that I was never going to play in 2009 so it was just all about trying to rehabilitate the knee to get myself back on to a rugby pitch. I'm not saying I rehabilitated properly or fully but I certainly got back on to the pitch, which was my desire, and I was able to retire somewhat on my own terms, rather than the end coming out there on the pitch in Christchurch. But it was a sad end to my Lions career, nevertheless.

GORDON BULLOCH

At that level you need someone who can create something from nothing because defences are so well-organised and tight. We lost Brian O'Driscoll at the start of the First Test, and he was the one guy we had who could unlock a defence and could bring others with him.

The selectors picked a lot of guys who had performed for England in the World Cup but hadn't really reached that level since then. Dallaglio was injured early on, Hill was never fit and Back was a shadow of his former self – and when Ryan Jones was flown out, he just turned up in Otago and played and you could see the freshness he brought. Apart from that, nobody really shone and I think that was the problem – we had nobody who was really at the top of their game, whereas you could take your pick with the All Blacks – Dan Carter, Richie McCaw, Tana Umaga, the list goes on – you can't pick one of those guys ahead of the others. They had been waiting for the Lions for 12 years and they were ready. We just didn't have the players.

Dan Carter, who was imperious during the first two Tests, launches an attack.

MARTYN WILLIAMS

The Kiwis were just too good for us. I felt that even in the provincial games, and in the Test series they just hammered that home. They were miles ahead of us in the way they played the game, their tactics, their running angles, everything.

SHANE BYRNE

I'll be remembered for the First Test and the lineout being a complete disaster which was an integral part of what went wrong. All facets of the lineout disintegrated.

Doubts gnaw away at you. Things you thought were the most basic imaginable you'd call them and it didn't work and you'd say, 'Jesus, that was my banker ball.' It was a horrible scenario. An impossible situation to be in. Rugby has such unbelievable highs but then on the final whistle such unbelievable lows. I mean, catastrophic lows that you cannot possibly share with anybody else. Adding to the burden wasn't just the fact that I played in the game but the fact that I was part of the reason why it fell apart.

BEN KAY

When we changed our lineout calls in the week of the First Test, rather than working smoothly, it put an element of doubt into our minds. At the lineout all you need is a split second of hesitation, and you lose your fluidity. It is lethal, because if someone hesitates, the whole chain breaks down. It's made worse if the opposition pick off a couple of throws early on, and get into the hooker's head. To change the calls completely in a week is very difficult, and by the time of the Test series, with four inputs from four different countries, we had a massive number of them. We switched to Shane Byrne calling them because I felt that my calling was affecting his throwing-in, because it was going through his mind whether it was the right call. But, I would have preferred to have called them, definitely.

JONNY WILKINSON

The gulf between the teams was so great that even though we lost 21-3, we should have lost by even more. It was a huge loss when Brian went off. I played inside-centre, with Stephen Jones at stand-off; he's a great player, but we'd only tried the combination out for part of the game against Wellington and in training – not that it really mattered. We basically spent the whole game defending.

BEN KAY

It was definitely a mistake to have taken Alastair Campbell with us. I'm not critical about him personally, but the New Zealand, and British, perception of why we needed a spin doctor had a negative effect. I think he got the whole thing wrong – from the way they dealt with Gavin Henson, to the ridiculous speech he made to us in the changing room after the First Test – and a number of my team-mates agreed with me. I thought the content was wrong; he made comparisons with the Bosnian War, and SAS involvement in it, which had no place in sport. He was going on about people laying their bodies on the line, and suggesting we had not. We may not have played well, but no one could question our commitment. And we were the guys out there doing it; I may have felt differently if someone like Johnno, who had been there and done it all, had said something like that, but not a guy who had never come close to playing rugby to any high standard.

DONNCHA O'CALLAGHAN
Alastair Campbell decided to erect a 'war-wall' in the team room, where he pinned every bit of anti-Lions coverage from the local press that he could find – and he filled it up in about two days. That was tough for younger fellas coming into it. I'll be honest, it was hard for me. You're going down the road and they're abusing you – 'You're no Lions, you're more like pussycats'. And the lady in the shop thinks she's doing her bit by abusing you, as much as Richie McCaw does by poaching the ball.

STEPHEN JONES
Clive didn't do much wrong at the time. He was criticised for taking too many staff, players and of course, Alastair Campbell, but I always thought we just weren't good enough to win that series. I actually got on very well with Alastair, he was a fascinating bloke to talk to and a good man.

I don't think that Jonny Wilkinson and I got the best out of each other when we played together at 10 and 12. We had different approaches to the game. I had just won a Grand Slam with Wales and wanted to attack and play from anywhere, while Jonny had won a World Cup with England by playing mistake-free rugby and to the strengths of a great pack. There is no right or wrong way, it was just a disappointment that we didn't click on the pitch. Mind you, I don't think it really mattered because we were playing one of the great All Black sides.

JONNY WILKINSON
Going into the Second Test, I didn't feel confident about winning – for the first time in my career. The whole team was so disjointed, we didn't have any structure – or at least, not one that we stuck to – and we didn't have any chemistry either. When things go badly on the rugby field, that's what you fall back on to try and get yourself back in the game – the structure of your plays, trying to get an element of control from which to build, or fighting for your lives with your mates and reacting instinctively with one another to create chances. But with neither in place, we were on a hiding to nothing – and the All Blacks were just on fire.

I had to leave the pitch with concussion and a stinger that went all down my left arm. It was so bad that I couldn't move my arm during the week without it hurting, and I had to watch the Third Test from the stands.

GORDON BULLOCH
The final midweek game came between the Second and Third Test and we headed off on our own up to Auckland for it. For the midweek team to finish with a victory

against Auckland, which made us unbeaten on the tour, was some achievement.

The Auckland game was by far our toughest on the trip, as they had a side packed with Super 12 players, and it says a lot for our spirit that we managed another win.

IAN McGEECHAN

It was a real team performance against Auckland – everybody gave everything. It would have been easy to come off tour or think it didn't matter, but that performance shows how much it meant to the players to be Lions.

MATT DAWSON

It was fantastic for the Midweek Massive to finish the tour unbeaten. Sitting in the changing room afterwards, the boys were acknowledging it was a big win.

We had focused really hard on this game since selection at the weekend. This was our Test match.

A great team spirit had built up within the whole Lions squad and, as we saw with the celebrations in the changing room after the game, the whole tour party was chuffed to bits that we went undefeated.

The focus of a Lions tour has got to be success in the Tests. But to have won every midweek game and to have done that in New Zealand, where rugby is a religion and every game is so intense, is an immense achievement that the coaching staff and all the players should be proud of.

GORDON BULLOCH

Straight after we played Auckland on the Tuesday before the Third Test, they sent the midweek side down to Queenstown for a night out. Our tour was over and we all had a few beers and enjoyed ourselves.

Leon MacDonald carves through the Lions' defence with Richie McCaw in close support.

Then we came back up to Auckland and Jason White suggested we go for a few beers on the Friday night before the Test, but for some reason I decided to have a quiet night in – and that proved to be a great call because the next morning I got a knock at my hotel room door and James Robson, the tour doctor, was standing there. He told me to go down and see Clive in the team room because Steve Thompson had some sort of fever.

When I walked into the room Clive looked me up and down, and said, 'Are you alright?' Meaning, 'Have you had too much to drink these last few days?' He'd be thinking that he should maybe have asked Andy Titterrell, who is a teetotaller.

I said, 'Yup, I'm fine,' and tried not to breathe on him. And that was me into the Test squad. If I had been out until 4 a.m. I would have had to tell him to go for the teetotaller, and that would have been devastating.

BEN KAY

The 'Power of Four' hype wasn't hugely to our benefit. There's a danger of becoming too media obsessed – but you can't lock yourself away, or you get turned on by the media. Clive has admitted that if he had his time again, he wouldn't be as nice to the New Zealanders as he was. He said in a team meeting between the Second and Third Tests, 'Sod being nice,' – but by then the series was over.

DONNCHA O'CALLAGHAN

Gareth Thomas took over as captain for the Second Test. The Welsh lads really respected him but I found nothing inspirational in what he had to say. His speech before the Third Test was poor. It struck the wrong tone. New Zealand had crushed us in two Tests and we should

Jonny Wilkinson, playing in the centre, lines up a kick.

have been bursting ourselves to burst them. Instead he went on about 'doing our best'. Then he said something that really stuck in my throat: 'I know we all want to get out of here...' We were preparing for a Test match. That thought shouldn't have been entertained for a second. Anybody who thought that should have kept it to themselves. Thomas was captain of a Lions team against the All Blacks. It should have been one of the greatest days of his career. The only thing on our minds should have been winning and salvaging some pride for the jersey. Instead some fellas were feeling sorry for themselves and only thinking of the plane home.

SHANE BYRNE

I came on during the Second Test, having lost the starting shirt to Steve Thompson, and the lineout went excellently for me, and then I was selected to start the Third Test and, lineout-wise, what they did to us in the First we did to them in the Third, but that was never written about.

I still struggle with the realisation that 2005 will always be 'that' tour, you'll always have been involved in 'that' Test. That is a pretty hard thing to live with. Then again, you step back and look at it with a sensible head and you realise you are a Lion. Tens of thousands of players would like to have been where you were and maybe as the years go by that will be the dominant emotion. Looking back now, it was like death by a thousand cuts. It was an experiment, but one that failed. A Lions tour is not a time to be experimenting. It's too important.

JASON ROBINSON

New Zealand is the toughest place in the world to win a Test series – but no one was more disappointed than the players that the series was lost in the way it was.

GORDON BULLOCH

Playing for the Lions is incredibly special. I only played ten minutes of the First Test in Australia in 2001, but I was still a part of it – and there are not many Scotsmen of my generation able to say they have won a Test match as a Lion.

Captaining the Lions three times on the 2005 tour and going undefeated is another great honour. Things like that I will look back on with a lot of pride in the years to come. For many players, it was hard being selected for the midweek side time and time again. Many of these guys are used to being first picks for their clubs and their countries, and I think it says a lot for them that we didn't have any cases of guys 'going off tour'.

It proved what great coaches we had in Ian McGeechan, Gareth Jenkins, Mike Ford and Craig White. They created a side from nothing and brought a real attitude to it. They drilled into us the attitude that, once you take the field in that famous jersey, you need to show it the respect it deserves and perform to your very best, whether you're playing a Test match or a midweek game.

MARTIN CORRY

When you look back at 2001, that was a massive high for me, but 2005 was a big disappointment. To go over there and be uncompetitive was frustrating. When you get on the biggest stage you want to play your best rugby and the Lions fell well short. That was disappointing but, as an organisation, I think they've learned a hell of a lot from that.

PAUL O'CONNELL (Ireland)
Toured: 2005 & 2009

Clive tried something different by taking a lot of players and coaching staff. On paper it was probably a good idea because it's such an attritional game now. But the trade-off is you don't get to gel as a team because there are so many players. We didn't gel as well as we would have liked. Gelling is the most important thing to the success of the team. When you look back at some of the players who have worn the British & Irish Lions jerseys down through the years they are great players. In 2005 we didn't live up to that. A lot of things went against us on the tour, but at the same time I don't think that we did the tradition proud.

Sir Clive Woodward congratulations Graham Henry on his series victory.

CHAPTER TWENTY-EIGHT

OLD SCHOOL VALUES
2009
SOUTH AFRICA

IT IS *in many ways a strange thing that the popularity of the Lions amongst players and followers of rugby is as high as ever, despite the overwhelming number of desperate disappointments that have been suffered. Perhaps this says good things about the resilience in the spirits of British and Irish rugby people.*

The scale of disappointment may be a personal matter which can only be judged in the individual heart and mind. But it is still somewhat doubtful if any Lions team has been as devastated, or as shockingly treated by fate, as the 2009 party during the Second Test on a warm day in Pretoria – an occasion which must arguably also rank as one of the most massive and awe-inspiring, not only in Lions history but in sport anywhere, for some time.

The Lions, needing a win to rescue the series, had turned in one of their greatest performances, and shut South Africa, the world champions, completely out of the game. The Springboks had escaped censure after a disgraceful gouging incident by their flanker Schalk Burger led only to a yellow card; then the Lions were hit by what amounted to a double-double whammy, losing both their dominant props and both their illustrious centres within a few devastating minutes.

They held the lead into the last seconds until a moment of madness by Ronan O'Gara gave away the winning penalty to the Springboks. To say that the Lions were thunderstruck afterwards is a gross understatement, and there are players who to this day struggle to cope with the defeat. There are also Lions supporters having the same problem – on that day in Pretoria, there was the astonishing sight of a whole side of the grand old stadium at Loftus Versfeld packed and boiling in a sea of red.

If the final result of the series, 2-1 to the world champions, did not entirely suggest that British & Irish rugby was in the best of health, then the existence, and the concept of the Lions, was clearly still of quite stunning importance. And not least to South Africa itself, where the economy was boosted in remarkable numbers by the spending power of tens of thousands of British and Irish of all social classes and persuasions who poured into the country to follow their heroes.

In the aftermath, history will recognise the pride that was restored in the Lions jersey despite the 2-1 series loss. The people of South Africa embraced the tourists and many highly experienced players – such as Phil Vickery and Lee Mears – still rate the trip as the best of their careers. The Lions abandoned the fruitless kick-chase game that was prevalent in the domestic leagues of Europe, played some classic attacking rugby and were agonisingly close to success.

When Ian McGeechan, the head coach for the fourth time, arrived at the Landmark Hotel in London's Marylebone in May 2008 the assembled gathering knew the future of the Lions was in safe hands. After

Opposite: Ugo Monye celebrates scoring the Lions' third try during the Third Test in Johannesburg.

the heart-breaking disappointment of 2001 in Australia under Graham Henry and the more drastic rever-sal in 2005 in New Zealand under Sir Clive Woodward it was only natural the Lions would turn to him.

Off the field things changed as well as the Lions went away from the claustrophobic model of the modern tour. McGeechan asked the players to become part of South Africa and to understand the country rather than be holed up in their hotel rooms playing video games – and they responded, even donating the fines from the players' tour court to local charities.

There were coaching clinics for local children in impoverished townships where the players were greeted as heroes and, wonder of wonders, the Lions actually got out and about and saw a few of the local sights. In the build-up to the First Test match the Scotsman ensured the players ate where the fans ate so they could see the magnitude of the occasion coming up.

He also ensured there were no cliques – something which had dogged previous tours – by making the team room the hub of all activities and making separate players responsible for things such as discipline, music, golf days and outings. It was back to an old-school-type of tour and it was all the better for it.

The choice of manager was as sound as the coach he chose – with Gerald Davies, the urbane former Wales winger and a two-time Lion put in place. Davies loves the whole concept of the Lions and although he admitted winning was important on trips like this, he said it was not the only thing. He promised the players the experience of a lifetime. And they got it.

McGeechan's backroom staff contained the guts of the Welsh coaching team with Warren Gatland, Shaun Edwards, Neil Jenkins and Rob Howley all travelling along with English scrum coach Graham Rowntree.

McGeechan's captain was Paul O'Connell, the great Munster warrior, one of the few players who came out of the 2005 tour with his reputation intact and who had turned into one of the best locks in the world. It was a choice based on the same principles as that of Martin Johnson in 1997: a big man to loom large at the coin toss and to cast a dominant figure on the field.

The initial party for the ten-match tour comprised 37 players, a significant reduction from four years previously, and the balance between the Celtic nations and the English, which had been lopsided in New Zealand was redressed. Leinster, who had won the Heineken Cup that year, were represented by the likes of Brian O'Driscoll, Luke Fitzgerald, Rob Kearney and Jamie Heaslip, who along with Munster men such as O'Connell, Ronan O'Gara, David Wallace, Keith Earls and Donncha O'Callaghan gave the Irish a powerful presence in the squad.

The Welsh contingent included the massive trainee doctor and centre Jamie Roberts, who was to be the Lions' man of the series, as well as, amongst others, Gethin Jenkins, Matthew Rees and Adam Jones, who would form an all-Welsh front-row in the Second Test. England flanker Tom Croft was considered unlucky to miss out on selection but by the time of the first match against South Africa in Durban he would be embedded in the Test side thanks to Alan Quinlan's pre-tour suspension for foul play and his outstanding form in the early matches.

Croft improved immeasurably after a plea from McGeechan to get more involved in the game than he did with England or Leicester. A brilliant athlete and lineout forward, Croft often missed phases of play but on this trip the coach told him to roll up his sleeves and graft as well as doing the fancy stuff out wide and he did – to spectacular effect.

McGeechan also abandoned the principle of having a separate coaching team for the midweek side thus encouraging players that everyone was in the running for a Test place from the word go and that *he had no preconceived ideas of what his best XV would look like.*

But the Scot was hamstrung with injuries before the Lions had even left Pennyhill Park, their base near Bagshot, a luxury hotel that England use for national training. Irish hooker Jerry Flannery went lame, Welsh winger Leigh Halfpenny was struggling and centre Tom Shanklin and scrum-half Tomás O'Leary were other casualties.

Yet there was also the eternal question of the Lions place in the game at home. The players arrived immediately after major end of season games. Northampton would not even allow Euan Murray, their prop, to attend an administration session. Everything appertaining to proper preparation for a great rugby team had to be curtailed, short-circuited. It was a crying shame.

The list of injuries would, as ever, grow longer during a brutal tour and by the end of the trip James Robson, the Scottish doctor on his fifth Lions trip, would be questioning in a major media conference how long players' bodies could stand up to the extreme demands of modern rugby.

McGeechan was also restricted by a fixture list that he had had no input in putting together, as the itinerary had been formalised before his appointment. Before the Second Test, for example, the Lions were forced to fly up to altitude without much time to get acclimatised, but typically they just got on with it. While they were playing at sea level in Cape Town, and flying up to altitude only 48 hours before the game, the Springboks had long been checked in to their Pretoria hotel.

With the First Test looming the Lions were six from six with wins over the Royal XV, the Golden Lions, the Free State Cheetahs, the Sharks, Western Province and the Southern Kings in the bag and McGeechan's idea of his Test team was forming. Perhaps the only drawback was that the top Springboks were kept out of the provincial games, diminishing them as occasions. That was sad.

The Western Province clash and the match with the Cheetahs were close-run things resulting in three and two-point wins respectively and by the time the Lions arrived in Durban for the First Test the massed ranks of red-shirted fans were there to greet them. Croft had forced his way into the side and would score two tries in a game that ultimately ended in a 26-21 defeat for the Lions who at one point were 26-7 down before battling back.

The major talking point occurred at the scrum where Phil Vickery, the Lions tight-head, struggled against Tendai 'The Beast' Mtawarira. McGeechan still maintains that the penalties that went

The 2009 tour party.

against Vickery could just as easily have gone the other way. Yet although the Springboks took a big lead, once driving through the Lions pack as if it was made of paper, the Lions came roaring back, dominated most of the second half, and could have won.

The final midweek match, against the Emerging Springboks at Newlands, ended in a 13-13 draw and then all roads led to Pretoria for one of the most astonishing Test matches ever played, and in which Simon Shaw, the giant lock finally making the Test team on his third Lions tour, achieved the admittedly unwanted distinction of giving arguably the greatest individual performance in a losing cause in Lions history.

With fullback Lee Byrne joining the ever-expanding casualty list, Ireland's Rob Kearney came in at fullback, the front-row was rejigged and the remarkable Shaw was given his start. O'Driscoll set the tone with a big hit on massive second-row Victor Matfield then controversy struck when the South African flanker Schalk Burger, in his 50th cap, appeared to gouge Luke Fitzgerald, the Lions winger. Burger got an eight-week ban and there were also two weeks off for home lock Bakkies Botha for a charge on Adam Jones that dislocated the prop's shoulder. No one could explain why a gouging should only be a yellow card.

Going into the final quarter the Lions were 19-8 in front until the unthinkable happened. Gethin Jenkins and Adam Jones, clearly on top in the scrum, were both injured within seconds of each other, O'Driscoll and Roberts both went off, with the Irishman reeling about like a drunk after a clash of heads. Suddenly, key Springboks like Fourie du Preez, the scrum-half, and Pierre Spies, the No 8, were seen in a game from which they had been entirely shut out.

Bryan Habana and Jaque Fourie scored for the 'Boks and gave them a three point lead. Somehow, the Lions rallied with a penalty from Stephen Jones to make it 25-25. But then O'Gara made his calamitous error. He kicked ahead but lunged into du Preez as the scrum-half leapt to gather the ball in the air. This gave Springbok stand-off Morné Steyn a penalty from halfway to erase 12 years of hurt that had built up since the 1997 series. Steyn kicked an ice-cool goal in the last second and the tourists were left numb.

With the full support of the coaching team, many of the party went to lick their wounds on safari, with a few drinks to ease the pain, whilst the coaches tried to pick up the pieces of a battered group of players. There were plenty of enforced changes for the final Test which was held at Ellis Park, the traditional stronghold of Springbok rugby and the Lions were up against it to salvage anything from the series at a venue where South Africa rarely lose.

But it was now that the expertise of McGeechan and his deputies and the spirit of O'Connell and his team shone through. Shaw delivered another huge performance, a rejuvenated Shane Williams scored two tries, one beautifully created by Riki Flutey (who created his own piece of history by becoming the first man to appear both for and against the Lions on a tour, having faced the 2005 team in New Zealand playing for Wellington), and there was a sensational breakaway try from Ugo Monye.

Vickery took his revenge on The Beast up front, taking total control as the Lions recorded a 28-9 win – equalling the biggest winning margin by the Lions against South Africa and their first Test win for eight years. In truth, the South Africans were never in it even though they desperately wanted to chalk up a clean sweep in the series. It was an epic Lions day, even if it threw their disappointment over losing the series into even sharper relief.

It was the last time many of the players would wear the Lions shirt, as Gatland had told them in the dressing room before the match, but they had done their bit to restore pride in the jersey and ensured that the players who were to wear it in Australia in 2013 have a legacy to defend, and embellish.

In the aftermath of the tour, debate once again centred on the position of the Lions in the sporting scenery in Britain and Ireland. Preparation and recovery time is now so vitally important, and if the Lions are as important to as many people as all the evidence suggests, then why is there so little stomach to alter the domestic season in order to accommodate their needs?

History has proved that it is a herculean task to win in the major southern hemisphere nations. But with an arm tied behind your back, it becomes almost impossible.

PAUL O'CONNELL

I came home one night and found five missed calls on my phone. There had been a guy on an English number trying to sell me shares over the last few weeks, so I was avoiding his call.

Then I saw the number again on the Tuesday morning. The voice on the other end said he was Ian McGeechan but I still wasn't sure because we've got people at the club like Brian Carney and Frankie Sheahan who are always making crank calls.

This time I thought the accent was too good. Once I was sure, we had a chat and, straight out, he asked me to be captain and I said I'd be delighted to do it.

The results secured by Willie-John McBride and those fellas back in 1971 and 1974 has made all those players legends. The same can be said about the guys in '89 and '97. That was the goal that we all set ourselves – to join them in the history books.

A Lions tour of South Africa is the ultimate, the pinnacle for any player from the Four Home Nations. I wanted to make sure we do justice to the Lions jersey; I don't

Tour captain, Paul O'Connell.

think we did that in 2005. It was essential that we lived up to the tradition and history of the Lions. A lot of things went against us in 2005 but we did not do the tradition justice. That was a big motivation for me and for a lot of us who were on that tour. We saw 2009 as a big opportunity to put that right.

IAN McGEECHAN

When the management board asked me to have one more crack at being Lions coach, I told them, 'There are certain principles I think we have to work to. If you don't agree with them, please don't appoint me because I am not going to change my values.'

Those values meant improving the future by using the best of the past. Things like players sharing rooms, hanging out together, travelling together, really getting to know each other. It did not mean staying in one big centre in the country, flying in and out and never coming into contact with the country or its people.

I also wanted the players to understand the rugby – with one coaching team, one medical team and one strong management team that set an example to the players. In every way it was a blueprint put together from all my tours and all my experiences, good and bad.

LEE MEARS (England)
Toured: 2009

The squad announcement was a weird experience. I was in the club bar at Bath with a few of the boys and a couple of the management waiting for it to be announced on TV.

In true Gerald style, he went through the squad backwards from 15, 14 and I was thinking 'Oh God'. Then I thought, 'At least two is before one,' but then he did all the props! I think I was the second to last name to be read out so it was pretty nerve-wracking.

You never know if your name will be read out. I've been in similar situations quite a few times. Sometimes you're picked, sometimes you're disappointed. It was amazing just to see my name up there. Everything Gerald did in the build-up was just fantastic.

It dawns on you that, if you have a good Six Nations, you could be a British & Irish Lion, something no one can ever take away from you.

Ian McGeechan and Paul O'Connell did an amazing job at Pennyhill Park. Paul stood up in front of the boys and said, 'This is a different tour to normal. It's harder than an international tour, but we've got the best players here and you can't just shut yourself off and hide away. You've got to come out and be open and friendly. If you do, you'll have a better time for it.' That's what we all tried to do.

It probably took a couple of weeks to get to know everyone properly but it was really interesting to see how friendly everyone was. Everyone bought into the camaraderie side of things and it was a fantastic tour. We bonded over a beer or out for dinner. Paulie O'Connell said early on, 'I won't refuse a beer with anyone. If you want to come and be social, come and be social.' That's pretty much how it went. We all went out for food as often as possible. A few of us went to watch the golf at Wentworth and we went to the races – all the things that boys love doing. That bonding carried on on tour.

MIKE PHILLIPS (Wales)
Toured: 2009

I tore medial and anterior cruciate ligaments playing for the Ospreys a year or so earlier and I went through some very low moments – dark times when I didn't think my knee would ever come back right, times when I thought I'd never be the same player. If you get dropped, you only have yourself to blame, but when you're injured it's so frustrating because you can't do anything about it. You just don't know what's going to happen. It was my first injury as well so I wasn't sure how to cope with things.

But I kept my focus on recovering and coming back as the number one scrum-half for Wales. So it was huge for me when I did that. I played well and things were topped off even more when I was selected for the Lions. It was amazing.

UGO MONYE (England)
Toured: 2009

You go into the Six Nations with a thought at the back of your mind which says, 'If you play well here, you might be in with a shout.' Fortunately, I was able to give a good account of myself and then it became a realistic target. I knew I was in the mix somewhere but no more than that.

I couldn't bring myself to watch the squad selection on TV so I stood outside. I've never been so nervous and I've never experienced a more anxious wait in my life. Then I heard the lads shout out my name and I just screamed with delight.

I watched the last Lions tour of South Africa as a 14-year-old schoolboy. It was beyond my wildest dreams to be part of the tour in 2009. I felt so drained emotionally after the announcement that when it came to training, I'd used up so much nervous energy that I felt exhausted. It was the proudest moment of my life. I phoned my mum straight away and she was so happy, shouting down the phone. Then I called my dad. We didn't say anything for a while and then we both laughed in sheer delight.

PAUL O'CONNELL

I must say from a players' point of view and getting to know guys and the whole Lions experience, I feel I can finally relate to the guys from the '70s who talk about the Lions being the ultimate thing. You read a lot of guys from the modern era talk about their Lions experiences from 1993 to 2005 and they were really, really tough slogs that fellas didn't enjoy very much – with the exception of '97, of course. And I can see that, definitely. You're miles from home, you're with a bunch of guys who, no matter how sound they are, they're still fellas you don't know very well and it can be a strange place to find yourself at times.

But this tour was quite old-school in that we actually went out quite a bit at the start of it. The big challenge of tours in Australia and New Zealand is that all the games kick off at seven or eight at night because of TV. But because South Africa is more or less the same time zone as us, most of the games were three o'clock kick-offs. So we had all this time to spend with each other in the evenings after the games which was a big thing for us coming together. In the context of a Lions tour, that's massive because you've got to become a team some way. You've got to become team-mates and not just fellas wearing the same shirt.

PHIL VICKERY

Geech gets the best out of you because he trusts you to do the right things. Nobody went over the mark and everyone respected the rules, and it was nice and refreshing to be on a tour where people wanted the best for you.

The management told us just because we're the Lions we didn't have to be tee total. As long as we did our prep work they didn't have an issue with us going out for dinner or drinks. It was like, 'Christ, we're actually being treated like adults.'

STEPHEN JONES

Ian McGeechan made a point of trying to reclaim the Lions ethos and values, and that really struck a chord with all of us. The way the tour was structured and the attention to detail was just startling. The coaches all knew that they had to manage players who had come off the back of a long season and they did it really well. I felt it was the little things, like all the players sharing rooms, something that we didn't do in New Zealand, which had the biggest impact on the squad. It brought the squad together and it's fascinating how something like that could bring such a positive feeling to a Lions tour. It was these kind of things that made the 2009 Lions tour one of the most enjoyable experiences of my career.

SIMON SHAW

Geech had a massive impact on the 1997 tour. While the New Zealand tour in 2005 wasn't that successful in terms of the Test matches, the side that he looked after went unbeaten and that says a lot about him. That side probably enjoyed the tour more than the side that predominantly played on a Saturday. He was able to keep spirits high and to keep things positive. That's something he does very well and was at the core of what he brought to 2009.

JAMIE ROBERTS (Wales)
Toured: 2009

Geech is a pretty special bloke, he's down to earth, a lovely guy and he knows what he wants from players – commitment and effort. And that's what we gave.

MIKE BLAIR (Scotland)
Toured: 2009

There was a big farewell dinner at the Natural History Museum before we left. It finished about midnight and then we all headed back to Pennyhill Park, pretty tired. We were scheduled to have a day out sailing, which was a couple of hours' drive away, and doing various bits and pieces like that, so Leigh Halfpenny and I, who were sharing a room, piled back and started getting ready for bed, when we both got missed calls from a number neither of us recognised. We listened to the voice mail and it said that the activities and training the next day had been cancelled and that we were all to get down to the hotel bar immediately. Geech and Gerald had obviously discussed things and decided that the best thing for team-bonding was for us all to get together and have some beers. And it was excellent, an old-school attitude to things that created a great atmosphere with everyone just chatting and mingling and having a laugh over some drinks. They were obviously so conscious about the mistakes made in 2001 and 2005 and wanted to get back that old Lions feel to things. For all the team-bonding exercises that you can do, there are few – if any – that work as well as going out for some beers, relaxing and just enjoying one another's company.

Things like that were organised and handled so well on the tour and the coaches and backroom staff were all tremendous choices. Gerald Davies was magnificent; a true gentleman, in every sense of the word and such a legend. Chatting to him and hearing him talk about his rugby experiences, especially with the Lions, was just incredible – he was so knowledgeable, great fun and such a nice guy. He struck the chord as tour manager perfectly.

GERALD DAVIES

It is very important for those who have been Lions to be part of the administration, because they are passing on the inheritance from one generation to another and that is crucial. You have to understand deep down what it means to be a Lion. It is only a Lion who can truly understand what the experience is like.

Right at the start I stood up in front of the team, me from an amateur era, managing a totally professional team. Why should I do it? I was only an amateur. But what I told them was that I had come from an amateur era to join them in their professional era, but that being professional never simply meant being paid to play – it is a philosophy about giving your very best, using your talent to the maximum and being highly, highly competitive in all those things. I told them that there were players I knew in the amateur years who were as professional, and in a few cases more professional, than some people in the room. It was an attitude of mind.

There were a lot of things I wanted to bring from the past into the present, into this ultra-professional tour. Players sharing rooms, which is what we had always done; the need to be mixing with the supporters, not to be aloof; to touch the community in South Africa, not to tour in ignorance, not to divorce ourselves from the media.

And I told them that for one point in our lifetime, we would be together as one group. Some people might again go on a tour in the future, but that would be a different group. We needed to focus on doing it then, that day, not the next day, not tomorrow.

The managership is an odd post. He is part of a team but not part. The coaches are always in the room together. The medical people are always together. The media have their own team. The manager is not part of anything, just overseeing everything. He tries to set the tone.

LEE MEARS

Powelly (Andy Powell) was our main entertainment but there were so many characters. I had some great room-mates. I had Powelly, 'Bomb' [Adam Jones], Alun-Wyn Jones, and Brian O'Driscoll. Nathan Hines gets a special mention – we were little and large and we bonded really well.

MIKE BLAIR

Powelly was hilarious. He was the butt of a lot of jokes, but I think he quite liked it. He's the perfect guy to have on a tour like that – a great player and a great guy off the pitch. We always used to start training with a piggy in the middle game of football and Powelly was hilarious when he was in the middle one time. He was there for about five minutes – which is a pretty long time when you're doing something like that – and he was charging around, almost getting to the ball time and time again, but just missing it. Everyone was roaring him on, but eventually we could hardly breathe it was so funny. Eventually he got to the ball and just hoofed it out of the circle, shouting, 'Have it!' like Peter Kay in the John Smith's advert.

The tour was full of great characters like that – Wagga (Nathan Hines) is a great tourist; he has the ability to break the ice with anyone almost immediately and get on with them as if he's known them for years. I had some great room-mates, guys like Leigh Halfpenny, Tom Croft, Tommy Bowe, Donncha O'Callaghan – everyone I shared with was great. Donncha is one of the funniest guys I've ever met, he's a great guy and a great man to have on tour – the life and soul of the party on big nights out, even though he's tee total. I was hugely impressed with how he reacted to his dirt-tracker status as well; it was pretty evident early on that it looked like they were going to go with Alun-Wyn Jones and Paul O'Connell in the second-row for the First Test, but Donncha just worked his balls off all the time and was incredibly supportive to both of them. He typifies what makes the Lions so special.

TOM CROFT (England)

Toured: 2009

There were great characters on the tour. I had never met Donncha O'Callaghan before, but one day in Cape Town I returned to the room I was sharing with Tommy Bowe to find my bed missing.

Donncha told me that he had seen everything and one of the cleaners had nicked it. So I went up to the cleaner to ask why they had moved my bed, and it turned out that Donncha had dismantled it and put it down the fire escape.

STEPHEN JONES

Some real characters did emerge on the tour and usually had us in stitches. Ugo Monye, the England and Harlequins wing, was our travel guide and took it upon himself to always give a speech, detailing the history and facts and figures of every new place we had arrived in.

BRIAN O'DRISCOLL

We reverted to old-style touring, all training as one team instead of being split. It was a big difference to 2005 and even, in many ways, to 2001. You felt a real togetherness throughout the squad and we were all playing with smiles on our faces.

PAUL O'CONNELL

There was a big buzz within the squad. There were a lot fewer people than I was used to in 2005 and that was the best thing about it. Everyone was on the pitch at the same time, everyone was in the gym together and everyone fitted into the team room as one.

Clive tried something different which looked good on paper but we struggled. It was a tough tour because so many things were not in our favour. We had a very big squad and a very big coaching staff and, straight away, we failed to come together as a team.

First of all, you have got to be a team. You have got to want to play for each other, first and foremost. If you have bonds, you will always be willing to play for others in the team and that always makes a big difference.

MIKE BLAIR

The strength and conditioning guys, (Paul) 'Bobby' Stridgeon and Craig White, also played a big part with raising spirits and keeping everyone's morale high. They were hilarious, totally mental. They assigned Euan Murray the task of telling a daily joke on the bus to training – which was always terrible – they organised a Through the Keyhole video thing of people's rooms, had all sorts of weekly challenges and so on – really, really good guys. There was one video thing they did where they asked various members of the team and management a question, but then dubbed a different question over the final cut. So you had someone like Alun Wyn Jones being asked to describe a gorilla, which he did, but on the video they changed the question to: 'How would you describe Warren Gatland?' So, he's there saying, 'Silver hair, long wrinkly face, big nose, massive head, pretty grumpy, likes to lie around eating and sleeping all day…' It was hilarious.

ROSS FORD (Scotland)
Toured: 2009

He's called 'Bobby' after Adam Sandler's character in *The Water Boy*. He's the perfect kind of guy to have on tour. He has so much energy, he was always bouncing about the place causing mischief and keeping everyone going. There was never a dull moment when he was around.

MIKE BLAIR

Another really good guy was Rala (Paddy O'Reilly), the Irish kit guy. He's an absolute legend among the Irish players. They have a tradition in the Ireland squad of the players going to pick up their socks and shorts from Rala the night before a Test match and the players spend the evening coming in and out of his room, hanging around for quite a while getting his banter and chatting to the other guys, and they instigated that on the tour. He was such a nice guy. I remember one evening having a chat to him about sweets that we all liked and I said that I loved Skittles. The next day after training we headed over to the tables where all our recovery shakes and protein bars and things like that were laid out for us, and in my compartment he'd put a bag of Skittles. Little things like that can make such a difference when you're away for so many weeks on tour – you really felt well-looked after.

I was disappointed not to make it into the original squad selection, but was obviously delighted when I was called up after Tomás O'Leary was injured playing for Munster. I loved working with the coaches – I thought they were all tremendous, particularly Rob Howley and Shaun Edwards. It was interesting seeing Shaun's approach to defence. Everyone calls it a blitz defence, but as he says, it's not really a blitz – the players stand a little wider than in other defensive formations and go up straight – and just keep going, as opposed to pushing up and out, or up and in. By continuing to push on, you hold your line and close down the options out wide. Then the key is in the aggression and power of the hit. As a scrum-half, I'm used to a kind of sweeper role in defence, but Shaun likes to have his scrum-halves in the line; so I could see with the systems they had in mind and the style that they wanted to play in South Africa, why I maybe hadn't made the initial squad – they picked Mike Phillips, Tomás and Harry Ellis, all solid, robust players that could hold their own in the defensive line. What was really great, though, was the sense that once you were there you stood as good a chance as any to make the Test team. I had visions of coming in and making a big push towards the Test team. Things went really well in training at Pennyhill Park and they selected the team for the game against the Royal XV while we were still there – and I was in. At the time, I thought, 'Brilliant, what a great opportunity,' but it didn't really turn out as well as I'd hoped.

Playing in that game was obviously an early opportunity to catch the eye, but it was the first time we had really played together as a team and we were all a bit rusty.

RONAN O'GARA

The altitude we played at for that first game made me feel like an imbecile. The mind was telling me one thing and the body wouldn't get into the position to do it. I certainly underestimated the effects.

JOE WORSLEY (England)
Toured: 2009

The Royal XV match was my first game for four weeks and the altitude just made me feel like a zombie. Once your lungs are struggling, the rest of your game suffers. It was really, really tough.

MIKE BLAIR

With 13 minutes to go we were 12 points behind and you are thinking that you are going to be involved in the most disastrous start to a Lions tour ever. Then Lee Byrne sent an up-and-under out of defence and it bounced into his hands for a try, Ronan O'Gara kicked a penalty and Alun-Wyn Jones barged over from a driven lineout to put us ahead with five minutes to go.

In the last play of the match, Rog (O'Gara) touched down under the posts and we ended up winning by 12 points – but it had been touch-and-go for a long time.

There was a really small crowd and there was a racetrack around the pitch, so it was a pretty strange atmosphere for a Lions match. And I remember Martyn Williams saying at the end of the tour that the toughest match we had was that first one. But we got through it, and that was obviously the important thing so far as the tour was concerned.

SIMON SHAW

With Warren Gatland as your coach, if you play badly, he'll tell you. After that first game he told me in no uncertain terms I'd played crap.

I'd probably have given myself a C-minus and accepted that I hadn't played for five weeks. Warren was blunt but that's his way. But the flipside was that after I got on against the Sharks and played well, he said it was a remarkable turnaround. I like that honesty in a coach.

PAUL O'CONNELL

Geech and the others were always straight down the line. The coaches didn't tell the players anything that wasn't true and in that respect all places were up for grabs. Having a wise management like that was massive for us.

MIKE BLAIR

We were invited to a big party one evening at the British High Commissioner's house in

Mike Blair spins the ball away under pressure from the Royal XV's Jacques Lombaard.

Johannesburg and we were all in our number one suits. Brian O'Driscoll was out in the garden and there wasn't much lighting. He thought he was walking over some paving but it turned out to be the cover of a swimming pool and he ended up in the water – maybe not up to his neck but certainly past his ankles. He was obviously fined for that.

UGO MONYE

We played the Golden Lions in our second match on tour and they weren't perhaps the best opposition, but it was a great confidence booster to score 74 points and answer a lot of chat that was coming from the Springbok camp after the Royal XV game that we were in for a hiding. We really showed a ruthless edge. When you have guys like Stephen Jones who can put anyone through a hole, a fantastic footballer like Brian O'Driscoll and someone like Jamie Roberts who always gets over the advantage line, it's a great place to be a winger – there are so many opportunities for you to sniff around to take advantage.

PHIL VICKERY

I was asked to captain the side against Western Province. When you're asked to be captain you say, 'Fantastic.' Then, within two seconds, you think, 'Shit, this is quite a big deal.'

When you play for the Lions you're carrying the dreams and frustrations of millions of people. Sometimes you have to remember that there are a hell of a lot of people who are right behind you and want you to do well.

When you're in that environment it's a small bubble. You can get carried away and the most trivial little things become a real big problem. It's important to step outside it, realise what you're part of and enjoy it.

Lee Mears scores against the Natal Sharks.

I've captained England to a World Cup final, won a bundle of England caps and been asked to be captain of the Lions. That 2009 tour was the most unbelievable experience and I can honestly say it far surpassed anything I thought I'd reach.

SIMON SHAW

I came off the bench against the Sharks and then again against Western Province and it's always difficult to make an impression off the bench. While we all have ambitions, the main thing is to try and maintain the winning streak by playing for the team.

But we all knew that a huge performance could just as easily get us into the starting line-up with the Test team. Geech had a three-word sentence that he said to me: 'Remember Jeremy Davidson.' In '97 I thought I had done enough to get in the Test side, but then Jeremy played against the Emerging Springboks in the last midweek game before the First Test and played so well that he was selected to partner Johnno in the Test. He held that place for the series and I never got capped. So I know that selection is never decided until the last minute – you always have a chance to play. As it turned out, I missed out on selection for the First Test again, but I didn't give up. I knew that there were still other games to go and at that stage you had no idea how the Test squad would go in that first match of the series. So I just kept my head up and kept working.

There were a lot of parallels between 1997 and 2009 – the togetherness, the ability to grind out wins when not playing well and also to play some good-looking rugby at other times. The older I've got, the more I've come to appreciate that a Lions tour is more special than anything else.

Captain's words: Paul O'Connell gives a final changing-room pep talk.

RONAN O'GARA

The game against the Southern Kings was our last before the First Test, and it was brutal. There were more cheap shots in that one match than in the whole tour put together. The general consensus in the dressing room was shock over some of the things which went on.

Gordon D'Arcy took an awful cheap shot from an elbow when he was running wide. He was disgusted with De Wet Barry. James Hook got smashed and had to go off. There was a lot coming at us but we backed each other up 100 per cent. We weren't prepared to sit back and see one of our own side going through that.

Jaco van der Westhuyzen, their fly-half, was still being lippy at the end, saying, 'You're going to get smashed in the Tests.' I didn't think there was any need for stuff like that. I had it out with him and we then made our peace.

There's no doubt they were more interested in the man than the ball, but we stuck in. It wasn't pretty but it was another win and we were six out of six on the tour, which was a big thing going into the Test series.

MIKE BLAIR

It was a pretty horrible old game. I'd knackered my ankle in training a week or so earlier, but was asked to play that game and to try and make it through the whole 80 minutes. The management wanted to keep Mike Phillips and Harry Ellis fit for the First Test, so I knew that unless I was badly injured, I was going to play the whole game. With the stuff that was going on off the ball, I was just happy to make it through unscathed – and I'm sure the management were pleased I did too because it meant that Mike and Harry weren't exposed to potentially being taken out deliberately before the Tests. A lot of other boys were less fortunate, and James Hook was poleaxed early on and had to be helped off, which was a shame because he is class and I'd been looking forward to playing with him.

Andy Powell leads the celebrations after the Lions scraped past the Free State Cheetahs.

LEE MEARS

Putting on the shirt for the first time brings a bit of pressure but also lots of excitement. But it's the same even in training when you look around and see all the boys that you're surrounded by get that buzz.

I thought I had a reasonable tour and was in with a chance of a Test place but everyone's so good at that level that you don't know if you're going to get the nod. When Geech read out the team and you turn the page over and there it is, I was just thinking, 'Here we go – this is everything I've ever dreamed of.'

BRIAN O'DRISCOLL

The competition throughout the squad was intense. There were some great players who didn't get into the starting Test XV. Not only did that drive up the intensity of our training and the way we played, but it kept those who were starting completely on their toes. When people get the jersey, they know they don't own it. They know they are only borrowing it.

UGO MONYE

Twelve months before the First Test, I was on the bench for the England Saxons against the USA in Chicago. It was some journey to go from that to starting a Test match for the British & Irish Lions.

On paper, everything was against us – we were playing the world champions in their backyard, and they were a hugely experienced and physical team – but we all felt that we were part of a fantastic squad, with real speed and a big power game available to us.

The pack prepares for engagement during the brutal encounter against the Southern Kings.

TOM CROFT

We were given our First Test shirt by Willie-John McBride and he gave us a talk at the hotel before we got on the bus. Half the boys were on the verge of breaking down. He explained what the shirt represented and spoke of the history of the Lions.

I still find it bizarre discussing that tour. Before I went I didn't realise it was such a big thing. It was almost as if the fact that I was involved meant that it couldn't be important. But in South Africa it was humbling to see how the Lions fans reacted whenever we drove past in the bus.

JAMIE ROBERTS

When I got picked for the tour it was certainly a life-changing moment. I was one of the inexperienced guys out there but halfway through, I found myself in the Test team.

It was nerve-wracking before the First Test, and doubts are always on the edge of your thoughts. The Lions is a unique and special team. Not many people get the chance to pull on a Lions jersey and you are just desperate to give a good account of yourself. You have to remember, and keep telling yourself, 'You have been picked because you are good enough to be there.' I was the youngest player in the Test team but I was with a good bunch of guys that I had grown with throughout the tour. You have to trust yourself, trust those guys around you, and then prepare yourself to go out to do battle for one another.

Running out for the First Test match was incredible. There is nothing else like it as a player. It is like running out in the Coliseum as a gladiator. You expect it to be a sea of green. But it was full of people in red following us.

IAN McGEECHAN

Unless you've been in a Lions Test before, nothing prepares you for it. You are in for something you have never experienced before.

PHIL VICKERY

I've never known a Test match start so fast or so furiously. After 15 minutes, we were all absolutely hanging. There were guys calling for the ball to be kicked out so we could get a breather. It was incredible.

Then the problems with the scrum started. To be honest, I still don't know to this day exactly what the problem was. The Beast got under me every time, squatting low and forcing me up – which is illegal, by the way – but there was nothing I could do to counter him and Bryce Lawrence, the referee, did nothing about it. He just gave penalty after penalty away against me.

I was eventually subbed off to chants of, 'Beast, Beast, Beast!' from the home crowd. It was the most humiliating experience of my career.

GERALD DAVIES

We were steamrollered in the first half of the match. Going into the second half the Springboks made this long, long drive and scored with seeming ease. But from that moment on, the game went completely our way, and we were steamrollering them. Carwyn James felt after the Second Test in 1971, when we lost, that maybe we did have the measure of them, and I had some feelings like that in Durban.

JAMIE ROBERTS

It was incredibly frustrating. We had a couple of great try-scoring opportunities. Jean de Villiers made a superb try-saving tackle on Ugo Monye, then Monyé Steyn tapped the ball out of Ugo's hands when he was about to touch down a second time. A couple of opportunities really went begging. The controversy of the scrum has been well documented and we certainly felt we were in the game, so it was hugely frustrating. But that game was the best buzz I've ever had in rugby – running out in Durban to a sea of red. It was the stuff of dreams.

UGO MONYE

You look back on a series like that and you see all the fine margins that changed each game – the red card that should have been shown to Schalk Burger at the start of the Second Test, the problems we had in the scrum in the First Test, the injuries to key players – and then you have things that you were personally responsible for, like the two tries that I nearly scored in the First Test, and I can't escape the truth of how crucial those two moments were because we lost the First Test by five points. Tries are so invaluable and opportunities to score them so few and far between that when the opportunities do arrive you have to take them.

My initial impression, for the first one, was that I had scored. I celebrated and ran back to the halfway line, not thinking it would be referred to the television match official. When he took a while to decide I began to have some doubts. Eventually it was concluded that Jean de Villiers had managed to get under the ball and stop me

The Lions line up before the First Test, with a sea of red in the stands behind them.

from grounding it. I'm not sure you will ever see a tackle like that again. I was six inches from the ground at the time and God knows how he got his hand under the ball. Sometimes you have to sit back and applaud great defence.

The worst was the second one where I had the ball knocked out of my hands. If I had my time again, it would have been a simple case of tucking it under my left arm and diving over. At the time I didn't think that was necessary otherwise I'd have transferred it to my left and looked to fend off with the right, but I didn't think Morné Steyn was in a position to make the tackle. But hats off to him, that was fantastic defence as well. I stepped off my left to get past the full back and I was getting ready to get the ball down. I didn't see Steyn coming across but you've got to credit him. He attacked the ball and knocked it out of my hand.

While the first Test was the proudest moment of my life, I was absolutely gutted at the end, not just because we lost but because I probably contributed towards it. That's what sport at this level does to you. It takes you to the highest peak and brings you down to the darkest troughs, all in a few days.

LEE MEARS

It was a tough old arena. We probably played against South Africa at their height. Being selected was definitely the highlight of my career – it would just have been nice to have won.

But that's sport: the what ifs. The margins are so fine. I've got so many good memories but, unfortunately, we didn't get over the final hurdle.

PAUL O'CONNELL

I think in the end we just ran out of time in that First Test. We started slow and got

Tom Croft dives over for his second try of the series.

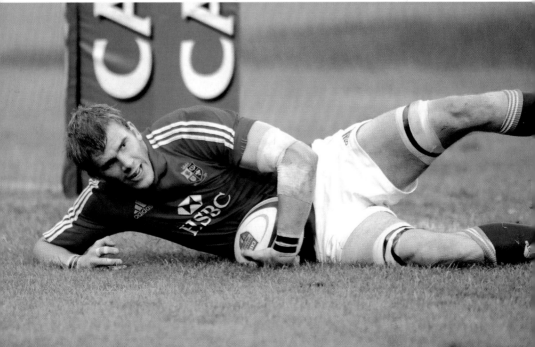

better and better, but when the ref gives that many penalties against you, you don't really stand a chance. It was just penalty after penalty after penalty. Undoubtedly some were our fault but it was a killer for us.

BRIAN O'DRISCOLL

With four minutes to go we still had everything to play for. We were in the ascendancy, had ball and they were panicking a bit. So the overriding feeling was huge disappointment at a missed opportunity.

We scored three tries against the world champions and looked like we were in full control by the end. There were a lot of missed opportunities in that game, but I really felt that if we had just a few more minutes we could have done it. But that's sport.

SIMON SHAW

I'm a bit of a pessimist when it comes to selection and always think the worst is going to happen. I suppose it is so that if anything good happens it is a bonus and I get excited. But before the First Test the way Gats (Warren Gatland) was going in training I thought I had a good chance of being an impact replacement, and when I was left out completely I was absolutely gutted. It was even worse being in the stand during the game and seeing the Lions scrum and driving maul go backwards and thinking, 'That's my bread-and-butter, I should be out there.' There was the added frustration in Durban of thinking that if it had gone on another five minutes we would have scored again.

Mike Phillips celebrates his try in the Durban Test.

For the Second Test it was back to pessimism again because I thought they wouldn't change much – but they did. Once I knew I was in the starting line-up I had a very strange three or four days. I got nervous, which is something that had never happened to me before in 19 years of playing. I couldn't sleep. I thought to myself that it was because of the weight of expectation on me and Adam Jones, the incomers in the pack, to fix things. So, if I'd been picked to fix things, I came to the conclusion that I better go out there and do it.

It had taken a lot of hard work to get to that point. The tour didn't really start that well for me and I then began to think I might go back empty handed again in terms of a Test cap. Over the years I've learnt you've just got to keep plugging away and keep trying. Then, hopefully, someone will see something positive in you and give you a chance. I think it's just self-belief. Your friends and your family will keep telling you that you're the best but, at the end of the day, you have to believe it yourself. I just kept trying to believe it and then it finally happened.

PAUL O'CONNELL

Shawsy's passion for the Lions jersey is tremendous. There's not a lot of talk from him on the pitch but he gets the job done and he couldn't have done it better than in the Second and Third Tests. I hope I'm going as well when I'm 35.

IAN McGEECHAN

We said to the players we would pick on form and we did that. We thought we'd got the right combinations and we weren't far off. Yes, there were some things in the scrum that the referee picked up on, unfortunately. It made it difficult in that first half

Jamie Roberts thunders through the Springbok's defence.

in the First Test, but they were redressed and it was just about analysing and tweaking and I felt we had a good balance.

GERALD DAVIES

We went into the Second Test and it was an incredible, incredible occasion, and crikey, did we play. The game was ours. Then we made a few errors, and there were lots of injuries. Towards the end we were level. I said to Andy Irvine beside me that after all the hurly-burly, I might even settle for a draw – we would then go to the last Test with everything to play for. Then they got the final penalty. That was a rollercoaster… tough game… great game.

IAN McGEECHAN

In the first half, we played the rugby for which I have always searched. We were playing the best international side in the world and taking them apart. It was superb. South Africa knew they were lucky to be anywhere near us at half-time and lucky to have 15 men on the field after Schalk Burger gouged Luke Fitzgerald. But we were still 19-8 in the lead going into the final quarter.

Then Gethin Jenkins and Adam Jones were hurt in the same move, we lost both centres, Jamie Roberts and Brian O'Driscoll, to injury and a Jaque Fourie try was given although the question remained over whether he had a foot in touch. But we will never know because none of the television cameras provided a definitive answer.

At 25-22, Stephen Jones struck a late and courageous goal from distance but then Ronan O'Gara ran into Fourie du Preez and the referee awarded a penalty. Morné Steyn kicked the goal and the whistle was blown. It was a horrible moment, the lowest I have felt.

PAUL O'CONNELL

It was very disappointing the way the game panned out. We had a lot of injuries and I suppose they told. It was tough, but we just didn't play enough in the second half. We were all over them when we played in the first half.

I thought we had done enough to get the draw and keep the series alive. Before we went on tour I knew we could do it – but we needed to do it for 80 minutes. We did it for the second 40 in the First Test and the first 40 in the Second. The commitment was incredible, but in the end it came down to the finest margins – and we were on the wrong side of them. It was a tough finish, but it had been tough all the way through – right from the kick-off and then a few minutes later that whole thing with Schalk Burger gouging Luke Fitz.

LUKE FITZGERALD (Ireland)
Toured: 2009

It was a proper gouging. I kind of panicked because I had blurred vision in that eye for about 10 minutes afterwards, and it put me off. But look, those things happen. You could say it changed the series in that he should have been sent off and the series would probably have been 1-1 but I'm not bitter about it.

He was probably a bit more friendly to me than I was to him when I met him after, but there were a few things going on. We had just lost a series we know we could have won and I had made a mistake for a try. Plus, I had to miss a safari tour I was dying to go on to go to this disciplinary hearing two hours out of my way, and to talk about something that wasn't going to change the way the series had gone, so I wasn't in good form. He had a big smiley head on him having been out celebrating, so I was probably thinking, 'Arsehole,' at the time but if I met Schalk now I'd shake his hand and say, 'How's it going?' There's no issue.

MIKE PHILLIPS

It should have been a straight red card. Luke had to pull Burger's hands off his eyes. That's not sport, that's not the way we play, that's not a gentlemanly thing to do, it's disgusting. It should have been a red card, simple as that – and it cost us the game. You can't go doing things like that or throwing punches off the ball. That was all they seemed to do – there were lots of punches off the ball all through the game.

Unfortunately, you've just got to leave it in the referee's hands and if he doesn't see how bad something is, like the gouging, the guy who did it gets away with it. It was a clear thing and the referee is paid to do a job. We're paid to play and entertain, not to ref. But there should have been no other thought than to give a red card.

Then to make it all worse, Peter de Villiers came out after the match and said he didn't think it even deserved a yellow card and that stuff like that is all part of the game. That was a ridiculous thing for the head coach of the Springboks to say.

IAN McGEECHAN

I was very disappointed that he said that. I cannot see that ever being part of the game. It certainly won't be part of a game I want to be associated with. I could never condone actions like that. I would hate to see that sort of thing happen again. It should automatically be a red card.

BRIAN O'DRISCOLL

When I first heard Peter de Villiers' comments, I wondered how someone could get away with something like that. Irrespective of any apology, I find it an absolute disgrace that a coach of a national team can make comments as he did about gouging being part of the game. Someone made a really good point to me that youngsters watching an interview like that, questioning whether they should play rugby or soccer, that's their decision made right there.

To hear a national coach saying, in any shape or form, that gouging is acceptable in the modern-day game is despicable. I find it mind-boggling that you can have a national team coach saying something like that. It brought the game into disrepute.

JAMIE ROBERTS

The Second Test was the most brutal Test match I have played in. Schalk Burger should have been sent off. I ended up in the hospital with four others. My wrist was done, Melonhead [Gethin Jenkins] had his face smashed up, Adam Jones had done his shoulder, Brian O'Driscoll was in no man's land and Tommy Bowe injured his leg. The hospital was a sombre scene afterwards and I always remember seeing Gethin Jenkins lying there with his face in a state. The boys were chatting away but it wasn't a good place to be.

TOM CROFT

That Second Test was the most physical I have played, one of the biggest games I have played. At the end of it I was absolutely battered.

SIMON SHAW

After we kicked off they received and drove it 10 metres into our half before winning a penalty. I remember Bakkies Botha shouting to me, 'I thought you were meant to be here to stop this!' The rest of the game is a complete blur. I remember carrying the ball once, but that's it. I didn't know what the fuss was about – and I've never watched it since, so I still don't know.

During the game I try not to get too emotionally caught up in refereeing decisions – like the Schalk Burger gouging incident – you cannot change a ref's mind, so I get on with it. Seeing TV replays of the incident afterwards it was pretty clear. I remember them scoring in the corner through Jaque Fourie, but I wasn't really aware of the score at the time. I was just head down and playing, not really aware of the impact.

RONAN O'GARA

I got knocked out [by Pierre Spies] and I tried to get back into the defensive line and missed a tackle. I was aware of Shaun Edwards in my ear going, 'Are you badly hurt? Get back off the ground.' That's exactly what I was trying to do. I wasn't really badly hurt. I was knocked out and didn't really know what I was doing. I can't recall the incident. I was knocked out. I just remember trying to throw myself at Jaque Fourie and I couldn't see him properly, you know. So I missed him and he scored.

Under the posts I kind of had a little time to get myself together. But that decision [to keep the ball in play when the

The decisive moment: Rona O'Gara chases his up-and-under and takes out Fourie du Preez.

scores were level at the end] doesn't cost me a second thought because I'd do the exact same tomorrow. People ask me, 'Would you not kick it out?' but it never entered my head to kick the ball out. I couldn't see what a draw would do for anyone. The way I look at it you want the win. I know a draw is better than a defeat, but it didn't enter my head to go for touch. I kick a contestable garryowen and maybe we'd score the other end of the pitch if we could get ourselves back in possession and look to score a try, get a penalty or drop a goal. That's the way my mind works anyway. Obviously now people will remember me for those incidents in the Second Test. What frustrated me was with Paul as captain, it was a massive opportunity in both our careers and I felt we left the Test series behind. I find that hard to take.

PAUL O'CONNELL

Rog was in pieces after the game, as you can imagine. There wasn't much we could say to him, except that we'd all been there and experienced similar tough times. The truth is we shouldn't have got ourselves in that position to lose at the death in any case. We should have played more rugby in the second half. It was another opportunity lost. It was very disappointing to concede a late try we should never have conceded and then the penalty at the end was heartbreaking.

We had a lot of injuries and that told. We lost Brian O'Driscoll, the linchpin of

Simon Shaw carries strongly into the Springbok defence.

the team. We were all over them when we did play in the first half. That was the way I knew we could play on this tour. But we had to play like that for 80 minutes.

STEPHEN JONES

What happened at the end was a prime example of how brutal and ruthless professional sport, let alone professional rugby, can be. Ronan, who had been the Grand Slam hero of Ireland a few months earlier with his last-ditch drop-goal, became the so-called pantomime villain of the contest… He tackled Fourie du Preez in the air and the 'Boks were awarded a penalty. I knew they would convert it.

RONAN O'GARA

I wish I could change the way it finished. It was grim alright but there is nothing I can do about it now.

SIMON SHAW

You couldn't have asked for more from anyone. The way we went about it, approached it, you wouldn't change a thing. Leaving it all out there is the best way, and that's what we did. Then you can't argue with anything. It could have gone either way, just like Jerry Guscott's drop-goal in 1997.

IAN McGEECHAN

To look around the changing room and see such a lot of sadness is something I shan't forget. It was as low as I have felt in a very long time because I knew how much it meant to the players. I told them I was very proud of them, and that they didn't deserve to be 2-0 down in the series. They put in a fantastic effort and it was a tremendous performance.

We had a couple of chances but needed a bit of composure to put them away. We could have been almost out of sight by half-time but in the second half we sometimes didn't make the best decisions to keep the pattern we wanted, which caused problems.

JAMIE ROBERTS

It was easily the worst I have ever felt in the changing rooms after a match. But you learn from those defeats. Someone always has to lose but to lose a game of that magnitude and after performing so well was soul destroying.

SIMON SHAW

It was devastating to lose, especially in that fashion. There is no doubt the injuries disrupted the second half performance. We hoped to keep a better tempo and a bit of continuity, but unfortunately, for one reason or another, we didn't and the injuries were part of that. Even if we'd drawn and taken it to the last game it would have been some comfort. Geech said we should be proud of ourselves but it was a bleak atmosphere in that changing room – we'd just lost the series that we had come to win and worked so hard to do.

I'd have rather been taken off at half-time for playing poorly than won man of the match and lost. I would rather have won that game and played badly – but that's how it goes.

I watched Steyn's kick all the way. It went straight down the middle. I thought at the time that we might have had a chance to kick-off and go for another penalty but we didn't. That's the way it goes. When it's all-or-nothing and you lose by such a narrow margin, and then you realise that you will never be able to contribute to a winning Lions series, it is really gut-wrenching. I gave it my best but I know that in the years to come we'll all look back at that series and always wonder about what might have been.

IAN McGEECHAN

We abandoned the policy of recovery with a bottle of water and a health drink and went back in time with a fair amount of alcohol. But we drank together, we stayed together, we slept it off and then we found that defeat was out of our systems.

We took three days off and then the players came back in on the Wednesday and had three superb days of training.

Ellis Park was an epic finale and we reached another Lions height with that 28-9 victory. But it was important to remember who had won the series.

PHIL VICKERY

The Third Test was a fantastic day. We won the match and I felt that I made some amends for my performance in the First Test. When we won a penalty at the first scrum, it was a huge, huge moment.

JAMIE ROBERTS

It was a great feeling to see the boys win the Third Test. It was tough because I was

The Lions' front-row put in a dominating performance in the Third Test.

not involved but we had all become such good mates on the tour. To see them win in Johannesburg we were all so happy. There were tears of joy for everyone. Seeing guys like Stephen Jones, Shawsy and Martyn Williams, none of whom will play for the Lions again, win a Test match was great; that was the most special thing for me.

SHANE WILLIAMS (Wales)
Toured: 2005 & 2009

It was a massive game for me. I knew eyes were on me because there were a lot of doubters out there and I knew it was my last Lions game, so I would have to perform.

I wasn't going out there to dazzle but to work. I got involved as much as I could, played first receiver, second receiver and nine when I had to. I could see when I got my hands on the ball that the Springboks were looking for me to do something and when I was offloading to other players, that gave me as much satisfaction. We were a tight-knit family on and off the field from the start. We worked hard from day one and we felt we deserved something out of the tour – and to score two tries in my last ever match for the lions and to a win a Test match was fantastic.

UGO MONYE

I thought I was going to pull my hamstring when I ran in that intercept try! And then after I scored, I thought I was going to break down and cry.

We didn't deserve what we got the way the Second Test finished, but it finally came right in the Third Test, which was hugely satisfying.

IAN McGEECHAN

It was a massive win. The players were superb. The dressing room after the Second Test was one I never wanted to be in. To come and play like that in the Third Test showed that they were an outstanding group of players. I was worried that we might go into our shells but we didn't do that and we scored some great tries.

To finish off the way we did give us satisfaction but it was secondary satisfaction because we went to win the Test series and we didn't manage that.

SHANE WILLIAMS

We proved the Lions have a massive future. I've never been on such a good tour and it's the toughest rugby you're ever going to play. Playing for the Lions is the pinnacle of my career and it is something that should continue for ever.

JAMIE ROBERTS

It was the ultimate challenge – the British & Irish Lions touring South Africa, a real rugby-mad country. To go there and win a series is a huge ask. We didn't grasp it and missed out by fine margins but that's top international rugby.

MIKE BLAIR

About half an hour after the Third Test was over, I was one of four or five of the dirt-trackers that were pulled aside and asked to come through to do a Q&A at the HSBC corporate hospitality event. There were 300-odd people in there and we sat up on a stage, with Gavin Hastings compering. I was sitting between Lee Mears and Donncha O'Callahan and we'd had a few beers by this time having watched the game and then been celebrating with the team in the changing room. Gav eventually asked a sort of general question about the experience of South Africa and how we'd enjoyed ourselves. There was a bit of a pause as no one stood forward to answer, and then Donncha took the microphone and said, 'Well, that's a very good question, Gavin, and it's probably not one that any of the players feel qualified to answer, so I think we should maybe ask Ian McGeechan about it,' and he turned the microphone towards me. I'd been sharing a room with Donncha that week and we'd been doing impressions of various people on the tour and he'd loved my one of Geech. Now, normally, you would sort of laugh that kind of thing off and not do it, but we'd had a few fairly swift beers and the atmosphere was pretty euphoric, so I went for it. I'm not quite sure if the audience really had any idea what on earth I was doing at first, but they got into it pretty soon and it was well received. Donncha and Lee were pissing themselves about it, at any rate.

LEE MEARS

I've stayed quite good friends with a few of the boys. I still speak to Gethin Jenkins a fair bit, plus Jamie Heaslip and Paul O'Connell. The whole experience was amazing. I had a wonderful time.

MIKE BLAIR

Like any guy who has ever been a dirt-tracker and not made the Test squad, I felt like I'd failed to play to my potential on the tour. I was hugely disappointed not to make the original tour squad. I felt that I was definitely one of the best three scrum-halves in Britain and Ireland at the time, and so also felt that once I made it on tour, that I was good enough to make the Test team. But it wasn't to be; these things happen – and I know that every midweek player who has ever toured with the Lions but failed to make the Test team will have felt the same as me. But the 2009 tour was still one of the most incredible experiences of my life.

I grew up with the mystique of the Lions firmly imprinted on my mind. As a rugby player, that's your pinnacle. I remember watching the 1989 tour with my dad and just loving it – remembering how great it was, as a young Scottish kid, to see Gavin Hastings scoring that crucial try in the Second Test, then my jaw dropping at the beauty of Jerry Guscott's try, before going through the roof when Ieuan Evans scored the winner in the Third Test.

I was hooked after that and as the years passed I followed the '93 tour closely and then got swept up in the whirlwind of '97. I was playing for my school first XV and at that stage all your dreams of playing international rugby gradually become more focused as you play with increasing seriousness; *Living With Lions* had a profound impact on me – and it cemented the Lions' jersey as the Holy Grail in the sport. I was disappointed not to tour in 2005 – but then, I was disappointed to be sitting on the bench for Scotland throughout

2004 and 2005, so I knew I never stood a chance of going – so to make it on tour in 2009 was an incredible moment… and to be handed that jersey for the first time, with my name on it… well, that was something else altogether. I'm a bit obsessive about the history of the game, so to be holding a number 9 Lions jersey… all I could think about were the players who had worn it before. Utter legends, from Haydn Tanner and Dickie Jeeps to guys like Roy Laidlaw, Robert Jones, Gary Armstrong, Matt Dawson, Rob Howley, and, of course, the greatest of them all – Gareth Edwards. And I'm sitting there in the company of guys like Geech and Gerald Davies. Amazing, incredible… an experience that no words can come close to describing. Those six weeks will stay with me forever. Did I play to the best of my ability? No. Does that hurt? More than you can imagine. But does that take away from my pride in realising my childhood dream? No. Nothing will ever take that away.

PAUL O'CONNELL

I hope people didn't misconstrue our lap of honour after the Third Test. We were under no illusions that we had lost the series, but a lot of people had paid a lot of money to go out follow us, and their support was just incredible, so we wanted to thank them.

The guys are very conscious of the Lions ethos and wanted to do it proud. The First Test we could have won, the Second we should have won… we were eager that people's memory of the Lions wouldn't be upset by a poor performance in the Third Test, knowing we were beaten and throwing in the towel.

It was a tough week mentally for everyone. We just had to dig deep. Some guys produced some serious form and produced some great scores. We were determined to put in a performance for each other, the fans and the jersey. We managed to finish the tour with a Test win, so the next time the jersey is worn, it has that history and momentum attached to it. That's our legacy.

PHIL VICKERY

It was a great tour, one which I certainly won't forget in a hurry. I'm very, very proud of the guys. Ultimately, we lost the series but we'd taken home a huge amount of pride. I just hope and pray that Lions tours will always go ahead. That tour was very special for me, being with that group of guys, that group of coaches, the backroom staff and everyone else. It was just absolutely fantastic and a real privilege to be a part of it.

GERALD DAVIES

People are asking what will happen to the Lions now, where will the Lions go? They are as big as ever, probably even bigger. There is massively keen interest from Argentina, Japan, and other places keen to have the Lions.

But we cannot expand under the current system because all we have is a ten-week window every four years. We would love to incorporate new countries because everyone believes the Lions is a great thing for the game. Though perhaps one of the great things about it is that it does only happen every four years.

To be a Lion in 1968 and 1971, and especially to be manager of the 2009 Lions, was a great privilege and one of the highlights of my career. We had great rugby players and good people, which you need when you are living in each other's pockets and for ten weeks. You need that if you are to develop the togetherness which is the feature of the Lions.

What we must do in the future is take that and make it even better. The Lions spirit is the quintessence of rugby and the quintessence of great sport.

IAN McGEECHAN

The Lions changed me. When I came home after the 1974 tour, Judy, my wife, said that I came back with a new confidence and a belief in what I had been involved in, and my part in it. You look back on those experiences and you realise that they were exceptional, and incredible. They change the way you see rugby and the way you live. They give you a completely different perspective on life.

Those were the memories that stayed with me when I coached the Lions, because I wanted the players to have that kind of life-changing and positive experience, just as I had. It is so rewarding when you hear great men such as Phil Vickery and Brian O'Driscoll talking about the Lions experience after 2009 – they both said that now they understand what being a Lion is, they understand its uniqueness. If you can get the chemistry right, that group of players, brought together for the first and only time, can do something that they will never repeat.

Look at Brian O'Driscoll and Jamie Roberts on that tour. It gave them the chance to play as the best centre partnership in world rugby in three Test matches, and

Rob Kearney leads a counter-attack during the Second Test.

because of their quality together and the quality of the people around them, they had an experience that was incredibly special. We were disappointing in the first half of the First Test in 2009, but even in that 40 minutes we made eight line breaks.

Dick Milliken and I were the centre partnership in 1974 and our friendship has never wavered – I was at his house recently to visit. Sometimes you don't have to say anything to a fellow Lion, there is just a look. Many of my Lions feelings spring from the Third Test in 1974 in Port Elizabeth. We had to win it to take the series and the first 38 minutes at the start of the match was the toughest thing I have ever been involved in.

Dick and I were so under the cosh with these big men running at us time and time again that we never even had time to speak to each other. But we didn't have to. We just looked at each other and got on with it, we had to find a way to exist in those long minutes, with the big men coming at us in waves, until the course of the match changed.

The Lions chemistry, the communal feeling, springs from respect. Even if you are battling against each other for different countries at international level, you have an inbuilt respect for the people who do it, in whatever jersey. The challenge for the Lions is that you are bringing the best of the best together, and the best from another team is coming to play alongside you. Then you are both going to challenge each other in a different way, this time internally. It is that new level of competition that you must come to terms with.

The chemistry can be elusive, and its importance is something I grew to appreciate more and more. Selection is so important, which is why some of the least happy tours were those chosen by committee, such as in 1993. Selection of the Lions is the art of

Ugo Monye and Phil Vickery embrace after the Third Test victory.

acknowledging the differences in people as well as their similarities. You have to pick complimentary qualities. You look for players who don't have an ego, and for players who will come with an open mind. You have to be prepared to give whatever you have got, however you came by it, whatever journey you took. You lay it out on the table.

If you have this open and honest approach and the characters come through, it will all come together. The chemistry is also important in the management. In my early tours as coach, there were only two people. Dick Best and I coached in 1993 and are still the best of friends. I would still walk across half the country to talk to Jim Telfer. I still enjoy their company and hopefully they still occasionally enjoy mine.

And if you talk about the need for open minds, then those with the most open minds have to be the coaches. They have to put a Test team together based on what is happening in front of them, not based on what has happened historically. People say that you have to get your Test team together in the first week and give them every opportunity to play together. But personally I think that goes against everything that the Lions challenge represents.

Every tour has been special, win or lose. My vote as the greatest Lions marginally goes to 1974, for the unbeaten tour in a fierce environment. But 1997 was the highlight of my involvement as a coach because we won the series but also because of some of the rugby that we played; the South Africans expected us to be pretty cautious and we blew that expectation apart.

Yet in a strange way, despite the 2-1 defeat in the series, 2009 gives me an incredible amount of satisfaction as well. We played really intense Test match rugby and the quality in Riki Flutey and Shane Williams cut the Springbok's defence to ribbons in the Third Test.

those matches was way above anything that we had been playing in our own internationals at home. If you watch it all again and take in that physicality, intensity and the quality of involvement that the players put in, and you can start to appreciate it properly.

Obviously that Second Test in Pretoria, lost so agonisingly, is the one people still talk about. People ask me whether I feel frustration that all the coaching work we did during the tour and in the run-up to that Test match was, essentially, invalidated – because the result seemed to be decided on ill luck and circumstance. Well frankly, I think that about many matches!

In Pretoria, though we never said it publicly, the injuries we had to both props and both centres quite clearly affected the result. All the momentum that we had, all the things that we got right to build on as the game progressed suddenly evaporated because of the injuries and the whole match became a different ball game. Suddenly we were managing the situation rather than trying to dictate the tactics as the game evolved. It was a bitter disappointment, but I am proud of many of the things that we achieved.

People talk about extending the Lions to other venues, but realistically we are going to have to concentrate on beating the three old enemies. The Lions and the World Cup are the first things that go on the fixture list of world rugby when the IRB are planning it.

Quite right. It was a worry when the game went professional as to whether the jersey would lose its value but the 2009 players talked about it in such a very powerful

Ian McGeechan congratulates Paul O'Connell after the final whistle.

way that the impact and appeal is probably bigger than ever. Commercially we have become one of the biggest teams in the world, we have one of the best supported team in the world, and we have nothing that so rigorously challenges the players. They are still desperate to wear the jersey. The season prior to the 2013 tour to Australia will show that clearly. If there is one thing that is easy when you are coaching the Lions, it is motivation. The chosen want to be part of that tradition and the history that goes with the jersey. They are holding that jersey for a few moments in time, and they are adding to it. Then they are passing it on, they are part of it without ever owning it.

My great worry is that there are administrators around in the game who've never been closely involved with the Lions who completely underrate its impact, not just on players but on supporters and on the whole game. This means that the players, pretty much starting from scratch, now only have seven incredibly short weeks to win a Lions series. When I played for the Lions, we were away for what seemed like half a lifetime; our wives back at home had to write to a PO Box number to stay in touch. We had four months to develop our game, our playing style and our friendships, and we had time between the Tests to recover.

Could we not find a way of spacing things out, so that players are no longer coming to the Lions just after leaving the field of a major domestic final? We must appreciate, totally, what is of importance to the players and we have to work together to plan it. If we can prepare teams properly for a World Cup and all that that entails, surely we can find an extra week's preparation for the Lions?

And whichever country the Lions are visiting, they have to come to the party, they have to go out of their way to give the Lions their best opportunity. They have to come to it with the same open mind as the Lions – not making the itinerary deliberately awkward, not switching the tour from altitude to sea level and back, not putting deliberate obstacles in the way. It is the peak for them too, and for their players, to play against the Lions.

At the moment, there is a huge future for the Lions, the excitement is rising as usual. But if the Test series stopped being competitive, there is no future. The game at home and in the visited countries has to take great care. Upwards of 30,000 people are going out to Australia in 2013 to watch the Test matches and they need to know that the Lions are playing on a level playing field and they have an equal chance of succeeding.

This book shows how strong the link is with the first touring teams, how similar such tours are, and how different. How remarkable are the legends and the standard of play on both sides. The Lions are an awesome story. Those who do not give a priority to the Lions should be harshly judged. They are standing in the away of the most magical experience that sport has to offer. It can changes the lives of everyone who takes part. Long may they roar.